Happy reading,

Marsha Newman

Joseph

and

Emma:

A Love Story

Volume I

Wellspring Publishing & Distributing
P.O. Box 1113
Sandy, Utah 84091

First Printing August 2001
Second Printing January 2003
Third Printing April 2005
ISBN 1-884312-25-X
VOLUME 1

Printed in Korea

Joseph and Emma:

A Love Story

Volume I

by Marsha Newman and Buddy Youngreen

Acknowledgements

No one person, or even two, is ever entirely responsible for a work like this with such an incredibly wide scope. We consider it an honor and a calling to treat such sacred material as the personal relationship between the Prophet Joseph and his elect lady, Emma Hale Smith. Therefore, first among our sincere acknowledgements must, respectfully, be Joseph and Emma Smith for the exemplary lives they led and the incredible legacy they left to us, the generations who look back with awe upon their accomplishments.

In our own lives, there have been many who have provided information, consultation, encouragement, and inspiration. We would like to thank Gene Newman, our publisher and consultant for his faith in the project and the investment of time and heart, as well as finances. Thanks also go to Larry Porter for background information on early church history, to Scott Fullmer, Russell Jorgensen, K. Laura Sommer, and Barbara Miller for editing assistance and consultation.

Special thanks to Randy Osburn, to Merle and Janet Reitinger, and to Nola Sims for making possible a writing retreat on-site in Nauvoo.

Finally, we appreciate all the wonderful authors who have researched and written excellent historical books on the Smith family, the events, and the times. Many fine literary works have contributed essential material for the writing of this historical novel, *Joseph and Emma: A Love Story,* and are listed in our references. Thank you all for helping to make our work possible.

Foreword

"Mormon literature," as Editor, Neal E. Lambert, so aptly described it in the Winter 1974 *BYU Studies* edition, contains ". . . significant writing, both imaginative and critical, by and about the Latter-day Saints." He stated further ". . . wherever the author's imagination has come into play, wherever he has begun to use the tools of the imaginative writer to shape and form an image of the Mormons, there we have a situation that is of literary interest."

Prompted by spiritual assurance of interest in our work of love, we offer this item of Mormon literature to LDS and non-LDS readers at large, *Joseph and Emma: A Love Story*, in two volumes. It focuses on Joseph Smith, Jr. (1805-1844) and his wife, Emma Hale Smith (1804-1879).

This work is categorized an historical novel and is offered in the "presentational" style of an artist, rather than the "representational" style of an historian. It has been crafted from the factual chronology, geography, and theology regarding singular events in the life and times of the Mormon prophet and his elect lady.

We hope they will become for our readers, living, vital human beings, for unlike other historical novels, the leading characters are actual people, living documentable occurrences with other real individuals, in nineteenth-century America. Literary license has been taken to cement all the elements of the story together. Still, it is hoped this work will be understood as depicting epic reality rather than idyllic fiction.

Marsha Newman   Buddy Youngreen

The Prophet

The Prophet arrives,
Veiled in the cloak of future thought,
'Mid people hid in ancient garb
Who could not see the gift he brought.
He is a stranger to this life,
Stranger to those who praise or blame,
For he upholds the Torch of Truth,
Although devoured by the Flame.

Kahlil Gibran

Chapter One

The River Stranger

He was too poor to possess a horse of his own. This fine bay mare would have cost a year's wages. Joseph absentmindedly stroked her mane. Her dark flesh was smooth and damp under his hand, and her swelling sides lent warmth to his own body this crisp, clear fall day. He wouldn't be poor always; of this he was certain with the surety that comes with youth and high spirits. His father was a farmer, struggling to scrape together the finances that would purchase the land he worked. Joseph had never known any other life than constant labor, but another world lay in store for him, though he but dimly sensed his fate.

At nineteen years of age he didn't look the part of a scoundrel, but in a short time, half the people who knew Joseph Smith, Jr. considered him so, while others who knew him intimately regarded him as a latter-day prophet. An unlikely prophet, he wore a scrap of a hat on his fair head, and bare ankles and wrists appeared where he had outgrown pants and shirt. Congenial and cheerful of countenance, he traveled with friends wherever he went, for he never met a stranger. This cool October day, late in 1825, Joseph Jr. and his father, Joseph Sr., were winding through dense, quivering forests, heading south from their home near Palmyra in Manchester County, New York to

1

Pennsylvania. They stopped beside the blue expanse of Lake Cayuga, one of the Finger Lakes in Ontario county. The Indians believed when the sun rose for the first time upon this land, the Great Spirit saw it and thought it so beautiful that he laid his hands upon the ground to bless it. When his hands were moved, the hollows left by his fingers filled with water. Thus were born the shimmering blue Finger Lakes.

It was about one hundred and twenty-five miles from Palmyra, New York to Harmony, Pennsylvania — a wilderness so dense that little could be seen from the well-worn trail except the looming mountains speckled with flaming reds and golds of autumn. The two men traveled light, carrying only the biscuits and fruit that wife and mother, Lucy Smith, had tucked into their knapsacks. They had taken the coach as far as Colesville, stopping two nights along the way. Occasional farm houses popped up around a bend in the road, a welcome sign of civilization, laboriously hewn from the virgin forest. A few miles from the Pennsylvania border they borrowed horses from friend and employer, Josiah Stowell, for the rest of the journey. Their destination, Harmony, lay just beyond the next bend of the river road.

Conversation had waned in the cool afternoon, and Joseph kept a watchful eye on his sleepy father dozing in the rocking saddle. The son was deep in thought, too deep to take pleasure at length in the vivid piles of leaves skirting the trees beside the winding, bubbling ribbon of water. Steep ridges and hills rose on both sides of the Susquehanna River, part of the vast Appalachian range profusely covered with trees of every color: bronze, salmon, burgundy, yellow, and green.

Joseph was en route to a new work assignment, having been pressed into an agreement with Mr. Stowell to look for ancient treasure. A Spanish silver mine! How was he to find such a thing? Stowell was convinced that Joseph could discern its location since he had already found other precious metals. But they were different. They were not really his. They belonged to an ancient Indian tribe. However, rumor had gotten around about golden plates, and Joseph was watched, and often followed when he went out at night, his neighbors hoping that he would unknowingly lead them to the gold. When he did not, rumors multiplied and transformed him into the wily scoundrel some of the townsfolk came to consider him. Now, the closer he got to the meeting place with Mr. Stowell, the more his spirits sank. He was no mystic. He had no special powers in himself to seek a treasure. The only discernment of which he was capable belonged to the spiritual realm. Even the quietude of the afternoon seemed to reflect his own unusually solemn mood.

A sudden burst of shouts, rustling leaves, and mocking laughter roused Joseph from his reflections. A flash of purple between the russet leaves of saplings lining the river bank caught his curiosity. He sat up in the saddle and leaned toward the river bank on his left. There it was again, a swish of purple, then a glint of sun from the rippling water. This was followed by gruff protests and light laughter.

"Hey, I never hit you in the neck with my chestnuts!"

"Only because you are not very accurate, Reuben. There's no virtue in bad eyesight." The retort came from a tall, willowy young woman. Her dark eyes were flashing as she cautiously peered at her brother from behind a thinning curtain of yellow hickory leaves.

"If you think you are hidden from me, Emma, you are mistaken. I'm simply too much of a gentleman to pelt you back. I'm loading the canoe with my chestnuts and onions. You'd best come along unless you want to walk back home."

Carefully, the girl slipped around a tree and into full view of Joseph. He put one hand on his mount's neck to keep the horse quiet. He watched from across the meandering stream. Hickory and maple trees spread tremulous limbs over the river, casting shadows and shade in the late afternoon sun. The tangle of vines and bare limbs obscured his presence from the brother and sister playing in the crisp, autumn sunlight. The girl called Emma had barely shown herself when a young man rushed upon her from behind, clasped her slender waist in his arms, and lifted her off her feet.

"I've got her, Reuben! She's mine. Now we can throw her in!"

"Isaac Ward, put me down. You're supposed to protect me. Mama said so. War-r-d." Her voice was light and breathless as she pleaded with his better side. "There'll be no biscuits for you tonight," she threatened.

"I'll eat cake," he laughed.

"You won't eat at all. You'll do the wash if my dress gets muddy."

Isaac Ward rubbed his bristling chin against the softness of her cheek. "Say you're sorry," he commanded.

"I'm sorry . . . to be a better shot than either one of you!"

"Nope. Won't do. Say you're sorry you are so cruel to your brothers."

"I'm sorry I'm so loving to my brothers." Her low voice cracked with barely contained laughter.

"Say you're sorry you're going to be thrown into the river."

"I'm sorry! I'm sorry!"

Reuben had a bucket full of spiny chestnuts. He stood dangerously close to the edge of the swirling water.

"Please be kind, Reuben," the young woman pleaded. "The good book says to forgive. Seventy times seven you are supposed to forgive, and I have only hit you twice. All right, all right, three times, but one just grazed your sleeve."

Joseph watched the play and smiled silently. Tall as she was, her brothers were both several inches taller than she, and well-muscled from daily labor on the land. All three siblings had rich, brunette hair and deep-set, dark eyes. Although at her brothers' mercy, the young woman struggled to remain in control of the situation. Joseph grinned. It was the first time today he had smiled. It felt good. It was also the first time in a week he had seen a pretty, vivacious face. He found himself wishing he were the one holding the squirming, kicking girl. He had no doubt the playful brothers would take only a mild revenge. There was too much fun in the moment for bad feelings. The lavender skirt danced about as she kept up a staccato beat with her feet. Isaac Ward, stronger by far, scooped her up and strode along the bank. Amid much protest, he unceremoniously dumped her in the canoe, got in, and handed her the oar.

"You can paddle us home, Em, and I expect doughnuts as well as your biscuits for dinner."

Reuben, six years younger than his sister, proudly asserted himself, "And, I like that special honey-ham gravy. That might be enough penance."

She took the oar and settled herself in the wobbly canoe. Then she turned, grasped Reuben by the shirt collar and pulled him through knee-deep water into the boat, quickly planting an apologetic kiss on his cheek.

"Cooked just to your liking," she conceded.

With several quick strokes, the canoe was in the middle of the river. Late afternoon sunshine cut through the branches and laid warm fingers of light on her back. Her dress pulled tight across her shoulders while strands of dark hair escaped the perennial bun and streamed behind her. Her cheeks were flushed from the struggle and exertion.

Joseph's smile widened into an appreciative grin as he shifted in his saddle. The mare began to shuffle, a raccoon scuttled from behind a log, and with a snort of Joseph's mount, Emma's head snapped about. Dark brown eyes, rich as the damp Pennsylvania earth, went straight to his hiding place, and she drew in her breath at the wide grin of a stranger. Through the dark profusion of shadows, his blue eyes reflected lights, and she was momentarily mesmerized by them. Their eyes met and held, as the canoe glided smoothly with the current, heading westward through Harmony to her home. Self-conscious and flustered by his frank stare, she was first to look away.

Joseph chuckled as he guided his horse back to the trail and urged him into a trot to catch up with his father. Immediately, he spotted a frame house built on a small bluff beside the river. The canoe was just putting ashore at a well-worn footpath. There, on that path, were gathered a band of men, Josiah Stowell among them. This then was his destination. Joseph grinned. The afternoon had suddenly changed from somber and uninteresting to a day charged with possibilities.

"Mr. Smith Sr. and Mr. Smith Jr., let me introduce you to Isaac Hale, Esquire." Josiah Stowell enjoyed ceremony. Short and rotund, he resembled a plump, Bantam rooster. His florid complexion and spikes of hair completed the image. He was in his glory at the moment. He was the one who had engineered this contract, found the Smiths and the three other men to work the plan, and was now about to put together this strange alliance. A lost, Spanish conquistador's, silver mine was said to be hidden in the hillside across the river on William Hale's property. Stowell had obtained an actual map from the red-haired, husband-hungry Widow Harper. He knew Isaac was suspicious and somewhat disgruntled that his lazy, ne'er-do-well, distant cousin was about to come into a tidy fortune.

Isaac Hale, at fifty-five, was solid as a rock. Six feet tall, almost barrel-chested, he was a massive figure. His hair was a little grizzled, and his leathery skin betrayed his middle age, but hunting and constant labor kept him fit. Black eyebrows lowered over small, hard, dark eyes that were as direct as a Mohican arrow. Isaac would never have entered into such a contract for treasure digging, except for the excitement generated by the cock-sure attitude of William. But William had no money with which to pay the workers. While Isaac was by no means rich, he had means and was in an excellent position to contribute room and board for the five workers.

"Pleased to make your acquaintance." Joseph Sr. put out a rough hand. Isaac murmured something and abruptly struck hands, then quickly shoved his hand back in his jacket.

Joseph Jr. merely nodded respectfully to the older man, acknowledging Isaac Hale's position of seniority. Then he nodded briefly to the three other men. They were obviously farmers as he was. Shirt sleeves too short, pants baggy and worn, boots muddy, they all reflected the constant need for money that plagued most of the rural population. Life was a continual struggle to wrest a living from the land, to bring in a better wheat crop than last year, to purchase more land. Men died young in 1825. They died, crushed by falling trees, from snake bites, from pneumonia, scarlet fever, whooping cough, infections, appendicitis, typhoid, and from the relentless, hard work. And their women died young, too, adding childbirth to that list of afflictions.

The Smiths were here for the same reason the others were; they needed the money. The Smith farm had another mortgage payment due, and father and son hoped to make enough money here to completely pay it off. Joseph Jr. remained apprehensive, but his father had gotten excited about the potential of the hidden silver mine. After all, a woman named Odle, using a peep stone, had actually seen a vision of treasure on William Hale's farm. The Smiths had known others who saw things with special stones. A neighbor, Sally Chase, had used a peep stone; it was not uncommon in the Christian community of the day.

Smith looked at his son and a flush of pride warmed him. This boy was special. Never mind that his shirt was a faded blue, and his pants were the dark gray which had at one time been black. They were rough cloth and patched more than once. Tall as his father at six feet two inches, Joseph Jr. had worked like a man ever since he was a boy, working alongside older brothers to clear thirty acres of heavily timbered land in Fayette, New York. They had chopped trees, pulled out roots, put in crops, and worked the land for their family farm. Consequently, at nineteen, Joseph was strong as an oak, with a fist like a hammer and broad shoulders thick with well-honed muscle. More than that, he was devoted to his family. Something special radiated from Joseph, a clear conscience and cheerful nature that was constantly evident in the undeviating gaze of his blue eyes. Fair, light brown hair glinted with bronze highlights and fell across his forehead when he removed his cap, softening the angular bone structure of his face. Only his lips betrayed his tender, even vulnerable nature, for they were soft and full. Though congenial by nature, fun loving and outgoing, he had a deeply spiritual side that had already manifested itself. Joseph was favored with insight into the scriptures, his face often luminous with pure, bright light when speaking of God.

Right now, Joseph Sr. dearly hoped that his son's spiritual ability would discern for them where to dig so they might soon uncover the ancient silver mine. After all, Joseph had obliged and delighted neighbors many times finding water for a new well. If he could find water under the ground, he could find silver. If they did, the Smiths would share in the profits. With this money, the farm mortgage could be retired, and the Smith family would own the land they had lovingly worked and developed for eight years.

Stoically, Isaac Hale put his signature on the paper contract. One by one the men all signed it. Then Josiah Stowell broke the solemnity with a hearty slap on Joseph's strong young back.

"There! It's done! Next year at this time we'll all be rich men."

"I hope you're right." The words echoed around the small circle of men. Isaac's inflection was more somber than the rest, but he rose to the occasion and played the gracious host.

"Gentlemen, there's dinner a-plenty on my table at home. Let's fill our bellies and hope for a prosperous dig tomorrow."

The Hale home was a simple, gray clapboard, two-story house set in a small clearing about two hundred yards from the water. There were several outbuildings for livestock, which marked it as a prosperous farmhouse. The forest was thinner there, just a single row of trees lined the playful, twisting river, and a little clearing exposed a charming view of the water from the door of the Hale home. As the other homes in the small community of Harmony, it was built of hand-hewn wood. It was tight, with clay stuffed into the chinks to keep out the elements, and roomy enough to accommodate ten people. Elizabeth and the girls kept it neat and tidy inside. When the older children had married and moved away, Elizabeth Hale had been industrious enough to propose boarding the occasional travelers who came their way. Tonight she would have to board five extra men. Reuben and Isaac Ward would simply have to share a bed. That would leave one bedroom free; another two beds could be made up on the floor by the kitchen stove.

"I think they are here," Elizabeth warned softly. "Are your biscuits ready, Emma?"

"Yes, and the ham and gravy also." Emma pulled out the heavy wooden covering for the brick oven, slipped in a long-handled, paddle-like implement and deftly extracted a large, heavy pan overblown with the fluffy, white biscuits for which she was well known. She glanced over her shoulder for Reuben, but he hadn't come in yet from the shed. She smiled, remembering the afternoon. Such a punishment! she thought. Biscuits, doughnuts, and ham gravy; I hope God is so lenient with all of us.

The shuffling on the porch told her that her father was home. She set the pan on the backboard by the stove and went to greet Isaac. She was special to him, and he always had a hug for her when he came in from the day's work.

"Emma," Isaac's husky voice deepened. He almost smiled as he clasped his burly arms around her slender figure. "Mother," he called out, "see here, we've got five more for dinner, and they will be staying with us a spell."

With a cheek buried against her father's shoulder, Emma's eyes scanned the guests. To her surprise and discomfort, she found herself perplexed once again by the spell-binding gaze of the blue-eyed, river stranger. His light auburn hair was slightly tousled by the wind, and his skin was lightly tanned from the autumn sun. My, he was bold, staring at her like that. His eyes were remarkably clear, a light blue ringed by a darker indigo rim, and they seemed filled with natural good humor. Most unnerving was his apparent capacity to look right into a person. Automatically, Emma reached up to smooth her own hair, and then downward to the skirt of her dress. I wonder if my frock is dirty, she thought. I wonder if he'll mention this afternoon. Mother won't like all that tom foolery. At that thought Emma made her own gaze more purposeful as she returned his stare. Politely, he removed his cap and nodded to her.

"You're very kind, Mrs. Hale," the elder Smith said to Elizabeth. "Your keeping room smells as fine as my wife's back home."

"Well, it's a woman's room. We spend nearly our whole day here, baking and cooking to keep our men happy," Elizabeth noted, somewhat proudly.

Chairs scraped and bumped as the men gathered to the table already laden with steaming food. There goes Reuben's honey ham, Emma thought as she glanced at the circle of men eyeing her cooking.

"Let us give thanks," Isaac gruffly ordered.

Emma and Elizabeth stopped in their work, heads were bowed, and Isaac offered his usual terse prayer. "We thank the good Lord for this food and for our many blessings. Amen."

"Mrs. Hale, on behalf of myself and son, thank you for such a fine meal. Our name is Smith. Real easy to remember. And since we only have one first name between us, you'll probably find it especially easy. I am Joseph and so is my son."

Elizabeth Hale had stopped beside Mr. Smith's chair. She smiled an acknowledgment to the older man and then gazed into the eyes of young Joseph. For just a moment her matronly heart became a little flustered. The young man stood politely as he was introduced, reached out to take her hand, and a smile wreathed his young face. Elizabeth brightened visibly at this special attention, glanced into his eyes, then looked at Emma as though she were silently pleading for help. Emma, herself, was still a bit flustered by his frank look and memories of the afternoon, but remained composed and focused her attention on the doughnuts she was shaping.

"Where do you come from, Mr. Smith?" Elizabeth asked the young man.

Joseph's voice was soft and deep. "We hail from upstate New York, ma'am," and he smiled slightly at his little word play. "We have a farm near Palmyra in Manchester County, some thirty acres, and we'd like to buy more land. That's mainly why we are here."

Josiah Stowell broke in. "You'll buy a lot more property than thirty acres if our little business venture is successful. And you are the one we are counting on, Joseph."

Emma glanced covertly at young Smith. Her mother's sharp eyes caught the slight movement, and she called to her daughter. "Emma, is there more gravy? Bring Mr. Smith the bowl, will you. This is my daughter, Emma, gentlemen. She is the best cook of the family." Clearly Elizabeth's real introduction was for the young Mr. Smith, though she included the other guests as well.

Isaac scowled as Joseph Jr. stood again, this time for his daughter. The boy was turning Elizabeth into a perfect ninny. Hale's dislike for Joseph Jr. was almost instantaneous. He was too polite, too handsome, and it was plain to see he was nothing more than a plowboy. Why, his pants and sleeves scarcely covered his ankles and wrists. The scrap he used as a hat was embarrassing. This boy had obviously never rubbed two coins together, and Elizabeth was almost simpering over him. Isaac watched Emma. At least his daughter was more circumspect than his wife. Emma barely acknowledged the young man while he stood beaming down at her.

Emma was five-feet seven inches tall, too tall for a girl. Perhaps that had some bearing on why she was still unmarried at twenty-one. Scared 'em off, she did, Isaac thought, with her height, those unflinching dark eyes, and her keen, well-educated mind. She was above involvement with the Harmony farmers, much less this plowboy from Palmyra.

"Pleased to make your acquaintance, Mr. Smith. Will you have some more honey...uh, I mean gravy? Actually, it's . . . it's honey-ham gravy." Surely he had the longest lashes she had ever seen on a man. She could scarcely think straight while he smiled like that. He is quite impertinent, she thought.

"Certainly. I'd love to, but I thought you might want to save some for your brothers." Joseph's face was the very picture of innocence, but his eyes twinkled wickedly for a moment.

"I, uh . . . well, of course. But please, help yourself. I can . . . uh, I can make more for them. Have some, Mr. Smith," she finished lamely.

"If you insist. I'm certain it must be a special treat, probably their favorite."

Emma brushed past the tall stranger and busied herself with the doughnuts. After a few moments, when she heard his chair grate as he sat down, she allowed herself a glance over her shoulder. He was still watching her, and the severe look she gave him would have wounded most men. She didn't hear the rest of the dinner conversation. As soon as the doughnuts were placed and rising, Emma slipped from the kitchen and hurried upstairs to her bedroom. She was sure her cheeks were pink and her clothing all askew. Why hadn't she changed from her lavender frock? Only one clean dress hung in her closet. She was saving it for Wednesday night's church meeting. Now she removed it from the wooden hanger and laid it on the bed.

"Whatever are you doing?" her sister spoke from the corner rocking chair.

Emma started, gasped a little, and turned to her younger sister, Tryal. "I forgot you were here. Are you better? You are supposed to stay in bed until tomorrow at least."

"I'm much better, and I'm tired of staying in bed. I can't stand it any more. I had to get up and at least rock awhile."

Emma went to her and bent over, brushing the hair from her sister's forehead. "You do look better. Not so white. Is your breathing better?"

"Almost perfect. There's no more wheezing. Are you sleeping here with me tonight?"

"Tonight and all the other nights until our boarders are gone."

"Do we know how long that will be?"

"No." Emma began unbuttoning her lavender dress. "I hope it isn't long."

"Why? Have you met them? Are they nice? Do you like them?"

"For goodness sake, Tryal, I don't even know them. I suppose they are as nice as they should be. They seem polite, but they are strangers. They make me nervous."

Her sister was curious. "They do? I didn't think anyone made you nervous. You are always in perfect control."

"Yes, and I still am. I don't know. I guess I'm just uncomfortable with so many strangers staying here. It crowds us up."

"I hope I won't keep you awake with my coughing tonight," Tryal apologized.

"Don't worry." Emma was into her good, navy-blue dress so nicely starched, it's dainty white collar setting off her graceful, long neck. "Do up those back buttons, will you, please?"

"You look fine, Emma, but why are you changing now? The evening is half over."

Emma blushed and turned away to the smokey looking glass atop her bureau. "The other frock was a little damp, and I feel as though I have flour all over me after making those doughnuts." She

13

turned suddenly to her sister. "Tryal, have you had any dinner? I completely forgot to make you a plate." Emma was genuinely horrified at her forgetfulness.

"I'll eat whatever is left. Just save me one of your doughnuts; you know they are my favorite." Tryal continued to scrutinize her sister. "Emma, is there someone special down there?"

"Of course not."

"You were saving that dress for Wednesday."

"So, I shall wear another!" Emma swished out of the tiny bedroom, composed herself at the top of the stairs, then started sedately down to present her "river stranger" with a much more dignified young woman than he had seen in the canoe.

Joined by William Hale and Josiah Stowell, Isaac and his five boarders stood on the mounded hillside sloping gently away from the bank of the river. The eye rose naturally to the steep hillsides across the water. They were richly clothed in the evergreen of pine. The morning was chill. It had been a mild October when they left home. Now November had arrived, the tail end of autumn. Soon the snow would fly. Perhaps this was the wrong time to begin the project, but Josiah could not wait. Greed superseded reason. Joseph had with him a special stone which he used to find many hidden things. Now he fingered its cool, hard surface. He was somehow reluctant to use the seer stone for this venture. It seemed to Joseph a gift from God, and he used it to help others. Certainly he had never meant to use it for greed. He suspected that God would not reveal anything that smacked of greed through the special stone.

"Well, Joe, does your peep stone tell you where we start digging?" Josiah asked, anxious to get on with the business of becoming rich.

"No, not really. I'm not sure it will work."

"Why not?" William demanded.

"I generally use this with prayer, and I feel strange asking God to help me find riches. He said that we should not lay up store for ourselves with gold and silver, but riches in heaven where moths do not come and corrupt."

"Fine, we'll split your share," a short, dark man from Colesville laughed.

Joseph Sr. spoke softly. "Do you have any impressions at all, son? Have you walked the hillside and tried to discern the earth beneath?"

"I have. I even have some impressions, but I'm not sure it is what you all want. Perhaps this was once a sacred place . . . I'm not certain. But silver? I have no idea."

Josiah put his hand on the young man's arm. "Then follow a hunch, Joseph. I know you can do it. It is important to me and to your family. There's nothing dishonorable in finding a hidden fortune. Money can do much good in this world if a man uses it right. If it is meant to be, God will bless us."

"That is correct," Joseph acknowledged. Then he looked about. The hill was heavily wooded with flaming sugar maples and bronzed chestnut trees. The sun overhead warmed the back of his neck as he bent and touched the land. He always had a holy feeling about the earth. Some faint voice from the depths of it seemed to whisper to him. Some spirit communed with his own. They say Indians have such feelings, Joseph thought. I almost feel that to dig here is intruding upon the earth . . . but that is what we are here to do.

Kneeling in the rustling leaves, he carefully took out a small stone and placed it in the bottom of his cap. Bringing the cap close to his face to exclude the light, he gazed intently for several minutes while the men shuffled impatiently waiting for his word. All was dark. Though concentrating carefully, he received no sensation at all. Still, he persisted in focusing all his mental, spiritual forces to detect any small impression that would direct them. After several minutes, Joseph absently fingered a crust of dirt, then finally stood and spoke hesitantly. "If I were to guess, I'd say we should dig yonder." He pointed to the west side of the hill. "Mind you, I'm not guaranteeing anything, but I reckon it to be about the likeliest place to start."

"Well, that's it then! Anything one finds, we all find!" Josiah grabbed a shovel and started off at a quick pace. "Tell me when to stop, Smith."

The men stopped about two hundred yards around the northwest side of the hill, in a small clearing out of sight of the river, but warmed by the sun. They dug their shovels in with enthusiasm. For an hour there was no conversation, only the scraping and thumping of shovels and dirt. Soon Joseph shucked his wool jacket and worked in short sleeves. He was a young man of considerable strength, powerful shoulders and forearms, wrists made of steel, and the hands that wrapped about the shovel handle were work-hardened. He set the work pace. When the others began to slack, chatting, spitting, and leaning on their shovels, he made the dirt fly faster. Side by side, they worked, cutting a yawning hole in the green grassy slope.

When Joseph was younger he had sometimes gone with a few boyhood pals looking for Indian artifacts in the mounded hills of upstate New York. Many valuable relics had been found by farmers plowing their land, and it was a common pastime of boys to hunt for supposed "Indian treasure." The plan was they would all share and share alike whatever they might find. They had never been successful in finding relics. But it didn't matter to Joseph. He had other dreams.

Often he would spend hours sitting on a log, staring up through the branches of a tree at the splintered sunlight. Joseph, like his Biblical namesake, was a dreamer. His mother, Lucy, said he was the most religious of her eleven children, though he rarely went to church. He couldn't seem to agree with what her Presbyterian minister said. He would debate with all preachers and had made some enemies for his efforts. Because he was a dreamer and a visionary, the Reverend Lane said Joseph was bound for damnation. Deacon Jessup said he was a trouble maker, and he'd see him in hell before he'd welcome him into his church. Joseph grinned amicably and replied that if he were ever in hell, he'd stop by and say hello.

The men were not discouraged at midday, when all they had dug up was dirt. And they were not discouraged at supper time, when the sun was setting. It was only the first day, after all. By the end of the week, some of the men were tiring of the search, but Josiah was greatly encouraged by the few authentic relics uncovered. Besides several fine Indian arrowheads, strange pottery fragments were found, as well as a few metal coins of uncertain origin. Stowell insisted that they must be European, although the markings on them were all but obscured with rust and age. Josiah was most triumphant when on the sixth day Joseph Sr. uncovered a large chunk of metal which they all agreed must be a belt buckle. But of money or chests of silver, they found nothing.

Before the middle of November, the group of would-be rich men tired of working their hopes up, only to find everything under the sun but treasure. One morning Isaac announced that he was going hunting. If they wanted to waste the remaining good days of fall with money-digging they could go ahead, but he wanted winter meat. Isaac's fame as a skilled hunter extended about the countryside, for many of his neighbors had been grateful recipients of his bounty. The day after he left, the men whom William had hired did not report for work. When Josiah sent to inquire about them, William said his man had a lame back and could not dig, but he certainly encouraged the rest of them not to give up. Josiah Stowell was a patient man; he was not about to give up. Rome was not built in a day, and somewhere under this covering of dirt lay a hidden treasure that God meant for them.

Joseph did not complain of his employment. It was no more taxing than felling trees and clearing land for the family farm. He was only sorry that he had not found Mr. Stowell's fortune for him. He tried. He really tried to fathom the bowels of the earth and discover where the riches lay. Perhaps his mind was clouded with other thoughts, persistent thoughts of a dark-haired, olive-complexioned, young woman.

Seeing Emma Hale was his reward at the weary end of every day. With all his muscles taut and tired, he would walk up the path to the Hale home, go to the back door between the kitchen and the wood shed. Hat in hand he would softly say, "Miss Hale," and she would turn toward him, her trim waist encircled with apron strings, her lips and cheeks red from working by the warm brick oven. Her soft contralto voice was his balm in Gilead.

"Are you finished for the day?" Usually forthright, Emma had acquired the habit with Mr. Smith of looking elsewhere when she spoke, at the hearth, at the oven, the table, the floor, anyplace but into his eyes. His clear blue eyes were too arresting for her. He seemed to see into her heart, to hear its quickening pace, and to know the rush of feeling that flooded over her.

"Yes, we are finished. I fear your father is sorely disappointed. He has given up the project. But Mr. Stowell is not dissatisfied yet. He is determined that we go on until snow flies."

"Your bath water is ready, Mr. Smith. Right there." She indicated a large kettle filled with steaming water. Joseph stepped into the keeping room, reached past her, his shoulder brushing hers, grasped the heated kettle and carefully lifted it off the heavy metal hook in the hearth. Emma pressed against the dry sink to give him room.

"A man sure needs a hot bath at the end of the day. Thank you, Miss Hale." He paused just inches away from her inscrutable, polite face. There was a serene quality, steadying and comforting, in the presence of Emma Hale that filled an empty spot in his heart. There still clung to her a warm, vanilla scent from baking, and dark wisps of hair brushed the olive skin of her neck. Joseph was fairly swallowed up in the enchantment of her bewitching brown eyes.

"Would you . . . be going . . . to the Wednesday night prayer meeting at my uncle Nathaniel Lewis's home?" Her voice was barely above a whisper, and her eyes still didn't quite meet his. He was too near; it would be brazen.

"Am I invited?"

"Of course. All good Christians are invited." She moved over to the table, then looked up fully into his gaze. "You are a Christian aren't you, Mr. Smith?"

"I certainly am. If anyone loves Jesus Christ, I do! But, you should know, I'm not a Methodist, and I've been asked to not attend their congregation at home."

Those large doe-like eyes blinked in alarm. "You were? What on earth for?"

"I disagreed with the minister."

"Over what? Why would you be barred from meeting?"

"Over the character of God. He said that God has no body, no hand, no foot, no face, that the Almighty is only spirit. Why, that's practically what the heathens believe. God does have a body. He's a man in form, just like my father — just like me — and Jesus looks as much like his sire as I do mine."

He was a fool for saying too much. He could have kicked himself to New York and back. Emma Hale was orthodox Methodist. Her family members were all Methodist, and her uncle was the local minister. Her lovely eyes had become almost black and hard as coal. She backed away from him ever so little.

"Well, I didn't know you were a theologian. Have you had training for the ministry, sir?"

He shook his head.

"So your opinions are the speculations of an apostate."

The challenge hung between them. His gaze was unswerving, his voice firmly insistent though he spoke softly. "Not speculation. I have seen Him."

She gasped. Her hand went to her heart, and she searched his eyes for a lie. But she did not find any trace of falsehood. She found instead a piercing gaze that locked with her own and dared her to believe.

"That's blasphemy!"

"That's truth! If you dare believe it, someday I'll tell you all you want to know about God and his son, Jesus Christ."

Joseph's countenance had taken on a white radiance. His eyes bore witness to the sincerity of his words, and she became more shaken than she had ever been. Emma Hale was not a silly young girl, easily taken in by a fine-looking stranger. She was staunchly religious and fiercely dedicated to Methodism. Now this young man, younger than she, poor as a church mouse, obviously uneducated, was asserting that her family's religion was wrong, and he claimed the impossible — to have seen God. Really, it was too much. How could anyone be so arrogant and so ridiculous? Did he really expect her to believe him? She looked away, then turned her shoulder and busied herself with a dish towel.

"Thank you for the water, Miss Hale." Joseph studied her back for a moment, then pushed open the kitchen door, carried the hot kettle to the shed, and poured it into the larger tub. He pumped another several splashes of cold water directly into a tub. Ah, well, she could believe him or not. It was up to her. Joseph grinned suddenly with just a hint of mischief. That Wednesday prayer meeting might be fun!

"Well, that was about as satisfying a meeting as I've been to," Elizabeth spoke between a sigh and a yawn, and pulled her cloak tighter as the chilly night air encircled the little group.

Joseph Smith Jr. smiled up at the sky full of stars. Emma fastened her top button and asked, "You find that funny, Mr. Smith?"

"Not at all," he now looked directly at the young woman by his side. "I completely agree with your mother, and the best part of the meeting was at the start when you played and sang. 'Blest Be the Tie That Binds' is one of my mother's favorite songs. You are a very accomplished young lady, Emma. You play, you sing, you cook, you teach school, you dress fashionably, and you paddle a canoe. You even excel in throwing chestnuts. Is there anything you don't do?"

"I don't walk home with impertinent strangers. I walk with gentlemen or I walk alone." She quickened her step to catch up to where Elizabeth, Reuben, and Tryal were talking.

Overtaking Emma, Joseph reached out for her arm. "Whoa. Whoa, there. You take offense at compliments? Emma, you surprise me. Are you embarrassed by that little tom foolery down by the river?"

"Embarrassed that a stranger should spy on me."

"Well, don't worry. I promise not to be a stranger long. Anyway, that's not what is really bothering you. You're still upset over what I said today. You imagine me to be an irreligious, uncouth rascal, don't you?"

"Sir, I hardly imagine you at all. You're not my every waking thought, you know."

"Truly, Emma? You are mine."

She was glad the darkness hid the flash of pink that suddenly lit her cheeks. "I'm sure your thoughts are more taken with the treasure that brought you here."

"I have found a greater treasure here than silver or gold." She tried to turn away, but he whispered, "I have found you. You are the treasure I came for."

"Stop, Mr. Smith. You are much too direct for me. You are a stranger. You have no right declaring feelings for me. At any rate, I can't listen to a man who has apostatized from God's church."

"Good. I don't blame you. If it were truly God's church, I would want you to feel that way."

"And you think it is not? Please tell me which church you do profess then?"

From her tone, he thought she would be grateful if he would only name any church that was respectable. Joseph knew she would be disappointed in him. "None," he replied and tightened his grasp on her arm as she began to pull away. "None on this earth. Christ's true church is not on the earth at this time. Just think, Emma, there is no actual authority. Methodism doesn't claim authority from God. Only the Catholics do, and Protestantism broke away from them centuries ago. Where is the direct authority from Christ to act in his name? Has Jesus laid hands on your uncle Nathaniel's head as he did Peter's? Were any of your pastors ordained as Aaron was by Moses, with real authority? No. They teach God's word as best they are able, with their own interpretations of the Bible. But they are wandering sheep, with no shepherd to lead or speak to them. I didn't hear your uncle Nathaniel say, 'Jesus spoke to me in the field yesterday and interpreted the scriptures for me.' If he had said that, I would have listened to every word he spoke. But God has not spoken to him. Your uncle does not profess to talk or listen to God. Why should I follow him? I would follow a prophet, but not just any man without authority from God. I can do better than that."

"You are unreasonable. The prophets of the Bible are all we need. It is up to us to try to interpret their words. There are no more prophets today. People simply don't talk to God in the field and ask Him questions."

"Why not?" Joseph asked simply

"It's disrespectful, that's why."

"David didn't think so. Noah, Moses, Jacob, Abraham, Elijah, even Saul, Jonathan, Hezekiah . . . these men spoke to God. If you really know God, why not talk to Him? And why not face to face? The scriptures tell us we can."

Emma was caught. She was mesmerized by the light reflecting from Joseph's face. Was it starlight that shone in his eyes? He was serious. He really believed God would personally communicate with him. So did she, but not exactly like he did. Joseph's perfect faith was overpowering — and frightening. She shivered.

She whispered. "Have you truly seen Him, then, face to face?"

He held both her hands tightly against his threadbare coat. "Oh Emma," he breathed, "I have. I have!"

She could feel the thundering in his chest from the force of his emotion. He went on.

"Mine is not a dead Christ, but a living Christ, a beautiful Savior, as bright as the noonday sun. And he came to me one splendid, spring morning five years ago. I was just a boy, young but deeply disturbed over the conflicting claims of your church and all the others. I become obsessed with knowing the truth. I listened; I studied; I contemplated. I begged to know which church to join so that I could properly worship God. Properly, not just conveniently. What did He want me to do? That was my only concern. So one morning before the others were aware, I went out into the woods to pray. It's beautiful there, Emma. You'd love it. Sugar maple and hickory trees twenty-five feet high, and just the singing of the breeze through the tree limbs. No one else was around. I knelt down and began to ask God to tell me what to do. I wanted to do right, and I had to know what that was."

Now Joseph began to tremble. His sight was fixed beyond her, beyond the little river road. Out past eternity, Emma thought. "But I had only knelt for a moment when the bright morning sunlight seemed to change to darkness. Some dark, evil power overcame me entirely. I couldn't pray. I couldn't speak. I seemed to be sinking into an awful pit of blackness from which there was no escape. Surely I would be utterly destroyed. I actually thought I might die."

Joseph paused in his story. Emma gazed enrapt into his face. He shivered as he stared beyond her out into the darkness. After a moment he sighed and continued.

"But, summoning all my strength, I cried out to God to deliver me out of the power of this enemy, and at the very moment when I was ready to sink into despair, the darkness fled, and the evil spirit left me. There above my head appeared a pillar of light, shining even brighter than the morning sun, and it descended gradually, almost gracefully, until it encompassed the little grove of trees where I lay and finally, me."

Joseph's voice had gained power and now he rushed on. His grip on her hands was like a band of iron. Skepticism vanished, and a thrill of excitement ran through Emma. Certainly this was no ordinary nineteen-year-old youth.

"I saw two Personages in that pillar, so bright and so glorious it is impossible to describe them, and they were standing above me in the air. One spoke to me. He pointed to the other one and said, 'This is My Beloved Son. Hear Him!' Tears sprang to my eyes. My heart was full and overflowing. They were the most splendid beings you or I, or anyone, could possibly imagine — brilliantly white, pure as sunlight on the snow. And their faces . . . well, only heaven can endow so much magnificence. When I gathered my senses, I asked them which of all the sects was right, which I should join. I was answered that I should join none of them, for they were all wrong. The very living Christ made the charge, 'They draw near to me with their lips, but their hearts are far from me; they teach for doctrines the commandments of men, having a form of godliness, but they deny the power thereof.' His words, His voice, His will, from these I have taken my command ever since, and earth nor hell can make me say any differently."

Joseph was silent. He seemed to have come to the end of his story. Emma stood still, watching him. Her family had walked ahead. The dirt path that lead through Harmony was deserted except for the two young people about to make an eternal resolve. All was quiet but for the whisper of an errant breeze stirring up dead leaves. The ring around the moon spoke of snow soon to arrive.

She had been holding her breath, studying his face. Then an unfamiliar sensation, as though a basin of warm water were spilled over her head, trickling down her face, washing over her breast, warming her through and through — some unspeakable joy and love and faith took her completely in its power.

"I believe you," she whispered, trembling as she stood grasping his hands. "Joseph Smith, I actually believe you." All her breath rushed out at once. She forgot herself and leaned against him for support, while the warmth flooding through her seemed to take away all her strength. A powerful right arm encircled her slender back. She felt him draw a deep and ragged breath, and suddenly remembering where she was, she pulled away. When she looked into his face, those mesmerizing eyes were wet with tears.

"Thank you," he whispered brokenly, his lips pressed against the hands he still held captive.

"Emma, I want to speak with you." Isaac Hale pushed open the door to his daughters' bedroom just before dawn. Tryal and Emma both sat straight up in bed, then Tryal fell backward into the pillow when she realized it was her sister who was summoned. She pulled the covers over her head as Emma swung her feet to the cold floor boards.

"Coming, Papa." Hurriedly she pulled on her petticoat and work-day dress. She plunged her washcloth into the icy water basin and gingerly wiped her face and neck. Smoothing her hair as she made her way downstairs, she looked curiously at her father who was sitting in front of the cast-iron stove, warming his hands before the small open door.

Before she could ask what he wanted, or why he had called her before any of the others were up, Isaac waded in, "Your brothers have told me that Smith fellow has been unusually friendly towards you. Is that so?"

"Mr. Smith and I have been talking about religion," she replied calmly. "Is that what you mean?"

"You know that's not what I mean. If your talks were just about religion, I wouldn't object. Although I notice you don't talk religion with any of the boys around here."

"None of them talks religion with me." Emma was as completely composed as her father was agitated.

"Joseph Smith is not worthy to tie your shoelaces, much less take up your time in idle conversation. I can't imagine a girl with your good taste and training caring to even converse with him, much less be seen walking about with him. From now on, I forbid it."

Emma was not rattled. She sat still, calmly watching her father's face, which at the moment was blotchy pink with anger and emotion.

"All right, Father."

All the air seemed to go out of him. He looked at her with surprise and then settled back into his chair, more comfortable now. "You're not set on him then."

She smiled softly. "No, I'm not set on anyone. You know that. I've never thought I'd like any home more than my own with you and Mother, and I've never found a man I revered more than my father. You know your word is law to me. If you don't wish me to speak to Mr. Smith again, I won't."

Her father sighed in relief. "Good. Now that they've abandoned their money-digging until spring, he won't be staying here anymore. His father has already gone home. Wish he had taken his son with him, but I hear the lad is staying over at Josiah's place." Isaac scowled again. "Can't understand why Stowell believes in that boy and his magic stone. He couldn't find the treasure. The only power he seems to have is over people. Just see that he doesn't go working his magic on you. Of course, I don't mean you shouldn't be civil. After all, he hasn't exactly done anything to warrant ill treatment."

"No, he hasn't," she agreed. "And he has been to church with us several times, both to the Wednesday night prayer meeting and to church on the Sabbath. I believe he is quite religious at heart."

Hale frowned. "He doesn't seem to believe anything your uncle Nathaniel says, even though Lewis has been a preacher for years. That Smith boy has his own mind about everything."

Now Emma smiled and patted his arm. "Just like you, Papa. I remember a time when you didn't believe anything the preachers said either. In fact, you wouldn't even go to church with Mother."

He chuckled. "So, you've got me there. Yes, I was a reprobate — probably still am. It was you, Emma, that got me going to church like I should, you and that prayer you said back when you were just a tiny thing. It was right out by the river there that Sunday morning when you all were ready for church, and I lit out on my horse to go hunting. Well, shoot, we needed the meat, didn't we? But there you were, in the woods beside the river, kneeling like a little angel, praying for your father. I 'most fell off my horse, I was so affected hearing you pray for me, and me not deserving it one bit. Guess I'll have a hard time letting any young fellow carry off my girl."

"You don't have to worry. Mr. Smith and I are more interested in the nature of God than in each other. I believe he means well, and I do find him quite intelligent, if uneducated."

"I might have known Reuben was excited about nothing. I sort of figured you might be trying to set Smith straight. There aren't many boys or men who can beat you in a discussion of religion. So, is the plowboy thinking of living with Stowell all through the winter?"

"So he said. Mr. Stowell has only two daughters and no help on his farm. He says Mr. Smith is powerful and fit to cut timber, repair fences, and clear land."

"If he's so fine at it, why doesn't he get his own land to work and follow a respectable vocation like farming instead of hunting for buried treasure."

Emma wisely refrained from reminding him that he had also entered into the money-digging contract. "I suppose it is because Mr. Stowell pays him well for his work. Also, he wants an education and means to go to school while he lives in Colesville this winter."

"Huh," Hale cleared his throat and managed to sound disparaging to boot. "Well, let him steer clear of Harmony."

"Shall I turn him away if he happens by?" Emma asked innocently. She watched her father's face to see if he had calmed sufficiently.

"Certainly not. That's not Christian. You don't have to turn him away. Just don't encourage him."

"Well, I absolutely won't talk to him — no, not one word — if you oppose it."

"Be reasonable, daughter. Be civil to the man. Just don't be taken in by a handsome face."

She laughed and pulled at his face whiskers. "Now Papa, I already have been. Your old face is the dearest of all to me. Joseph Smith is still just a boy, not twenty years old. What would this 'old maid of Harmony' want with a boy?"

Hale smiled at his daughter, but secretly felt a little guilty. He knew that some had called her that, an "old maid," and Isaac wondered if he might be the cause. He was a hard man, strict, often stern, and protective of Emma, the light of his life. Between his gruff nature and her aloof disposition, the two of them had managed to scare off every suitor. He had always told himself that she wanted it that way, but now he wondered. After all, a girl had to marry one day and start a family of her own.

"Well, Emma, at twenty-one you're not too old yet . . . ."

"Twenty-one and a half," she interjected calmly.

". . . and you're still as pretty as a picture. Mark my words, there'll be someone for you, someone special for you, as befitting your upbringing. That Palmyra plowboy is too common for you."

"You and Mother taught me never to look down on a person because of his station in life. Honesty is more important than wealth, a good heart than a fine face, and good character a better dowry than a hundred acres. So, I'll be just as civil to Mr. Smith as would do honor to the Hale name." And Emma kept her word.

Joseph walked from Stowell's place in Colesville, New York, across the state line to Harmony, Pennsylvania on Saturday. The fifteen mile walk seemed more like two, for he had visions of Emma to keep him company as he walked. He brought with him a cedar log for her mother's fire. The first snow of the season was tripping along before him, dancing in his face, and swirling about the dirt path like dervishes. At last he caught sight of Emma out under the shed, getting wood for the fire. He quickly strode up the embankment from which the Hale home presided over the feckless, winding river. Courteously he took the wood from her and went down on one knee beside the wood pile, placing log after log on the stack to carry in.

A mischievous smile washed over his face. "Well, here I am, down on one knee before a most beautiful young woman who has captured my heart. Some would say that this was the time to ask for your hand." Then as she began to protest, he finished, "However, since you still seem doubtful about me, and your father has become downright hostile, maybe I'd better just content myself with being your beast of burden. Lay some more of that wood along the top of the load. I brought a cedar log to sweeten your fire. Your mother mentioned once that she liked the odor. There, this should keep you for a while, anyway."

He looked up into the troubled gaze of a pensive young woman, but went right on, "Emma, I've missed you and your wonderful doughnuts."

"Right there," she anticipated his question and shoved open the door to the kitchen, gesturing toward the wood bin beside the fireplace. "Put the wood right there. That is perfect, Mr. Smith. You're very kind to help. You're a ways from Mr. Stowell's farm, aren't you?"

"A ways," he acknowledged nodding.

"I'll. . . just . . . I'd best . . . umm . . . I'll let Mother know you've come."

He held her arm fast as she sought to turn away. "I didn't come for your mother. I thought we might go walking."

Hastily she started, "There's work to do and I . . . ." She made the mistake of allowing herself to look into his eyes. Those flashing eyes were pleading now, begging her to be true to what was happening between them. "I promised Father . . . ."

"You promised him what?"

"That I would not . . . that I would be . . . civil. I said I would be civil to you, and certainly going on a walk is, well, very civil, isn't it? Besides, I do need to gather the last few leaves of mint from beside the river." She couldn't help herself. His smile was positively engaging, and her heart was racing. What on earth was wrong with her? It happened every time she was in his presence. And, in truth, Father was right; he was simply a common farmer from New York. Still, she reached for a small bucket for the mint. "Just a moment while I get my bonnet and cape. Have the snow flurries stopped?"

"Somewhat. But hurry, before they start in earnest again."

Emma reached for her cloak hanging beside the front door. She called up the stairs to her mother and sister. They were working at the spinning wheel, processing the wool to be woven into sweaters and coats for Christmas gifts. "Mother, I'm just going out to collect the last few herbs. I'll not be long. The biscuits are raising."

Before any protest could stop her, she grabbed Joseph's hand, and they slipped from the warm, fragrant kitchen into the chilly outdoors. Great, feathery flakes of snow drifted lazily from the gray clouds overhead. The forest had grown silent with the anticipation of a cool, quiet blanket to come. Only the muted sounds of the stream below disturbed the silence. She wrapped the cloak tightly about her and allowed herself a side-long look at the young man beside her. His broad shoulders were scarcely contained in the brown wool coat, and his head was bare. Wayward snowflakes settled and melted swiftly on his brown hair. He met her gaze thoughtfully, and Emma felt an intense desire to brush the snow from his hair. She disciplined herself and looked away to the rapidly descending ground. They shuffled down the incline toward the river. The river's fringe of trees seemed thin now. The maples and poplars were barren in late November, their leaves stripped and blown by the wind. No hiding among the trees now. Brown, dry leaves, inches deep, crackled and protested under their feet.

"Your Father is afraid of me," Joseph mused.

"Not afraid, really."

"Yes, afraid is the right word. He's afraid I'll take you away from him."

"You couldn't, of course. No one can 'take' me away. I adore my Father. He's a wonderful man. I've never met his equal."

"Is that why you haven't married? Deep down do you want to marry someone like your father? You can't, you know. It would be a disaster. You're too much alike. Your mother gets on well with him because she is gentle and accommodating."

"And I'm not?" Emma's eyebrows were raised.

"You are as strong-willed as he is, honorable as he is, straight as an arrow and resilient as these poplar trees. You bend with the wind and seasons, but you remain well-rooted and steadfast. These are admirable qualities, Emma, but what exactly are you are rooted in?"

"Why, in my family, in my religion, in my God." Her answer was quick and certain.

He started to answer, then fell silent, staring at the river. It had risen somewhat with the rains they had. The surface still seemed quiet and slow, but the current underneath was strong. Emma tossed a twig into the river, and it was quickly sucked under, carried swiftly away from their sight.

"Perhaps some day I will feel rooted as you are," Joseph mused. "Right now I see myself much like this river, running, flowing, seeking a larger body. And I think my life will be like this also, some parts deep and smooth and satisfying, some parts rapid, dangerous even. I've seen a little of the rapids already. People are not very tolerant of others who are different, who think differently. I think my life will never be comfortable and secure like the one you have known. If you want a man like your father, you don't want me. I am nothing like Isaac Hale. I can't believe in all the traditions that bind your small community together. There is more to life than we know. I am a discoverer. I will never stop asking until I find the answers. And there is far more to life than meat and bread, or a warm bed and a well-plowed field."

"What is it you want, Joseph?" This was strange talk from a suitor. It concerned her. She would be more pleased if he could be content with a well-plowed field and a warm bed. Those things she knew. There were strange, enigmatic depths in this man who was well on the way to claiming her heart.

"I want to understand God, to think with His thoughts, to see with His vision, to see myself as He knows me, to know all that He knows. It's a hunger that drives me, Emma. It pushes me when I walk. It swings the axe when I'm felling. It wakens me in the middle of the night. It rides my shoulders and penetrates my soul. It is my constant companion. I feel it is possible to live in the world of angels and spirits. I've been there a few times. The veil is very thin, and the hunger to live in that world won't leave."

He turned to her. "You are one thing that makes me want to stay in this world. None of the angels I have seen are as beautiful as you."

Her heart seemed to be melting. "Joseph, Joseph," she spoke his name softly, tasting it, puzzling over its sweetness and the quickening of her soul. "And there are no men I have known who speak as you do. I hardly know what to make of you."

A sudden smile banished all serious thoughts. "A husband!" he exclaimed. "Make a husband of me, Emma Hale, for I do intend to ask your father for your hand in marriage. Not now. I know he wouldn't give his consent yet. This winter I shall be working, saving money, going to school, making myself worthy of you. I won't be a pauper when I ask for you."

She shook her head. "I don't think he will ever agree. It would take too much for him to accept you."

"I am not worried about him, only you. If you love me, we can overcome anything. Tell me if there is a chance, even a small chance, that you could love me and agree one day to be my wife."

Emma was in a quandary. Her promises to her father weighed on her mind. Even now she was breaking his trust by sitting with Joseph and allowing herself to feel as she did. Isaac's face, flushed red with anger, seemed to appear before her eyes. She stood up.

"I can't talk with you about this. It's a betrayal of my father's confidence in me."

She turned away from him and looked at the sky. Dark mists obscured the mountains and trees. Gray clouds were gathering lower now. Snow was falling faster. Her cloak was almost covered. A storm seemed to be brewing. Any longer out here and she would certainly be caught in it. Her wide, brown eyes glinted with a determined light as she gathered up her bucket full of mint leaves and a few stray onions she had dug. "It's too soon, Mr. Smith, too soon. I have known you barely a month, and you indulge your impetuous nature by talking of love to me. I'm going home."

This prize was not easily won, Joseph could tell. He resolved then and there to wait until she wanted him as he wanted her before he spoke to her again of marriage. He would wait, but he would not be idle. He would prove himself to Emma and to her father, and by the time he turned twenty-one, he would be her husband.

Chapter Two

Discord in Harmony

oseph woke to fluffy mounds of snow piled up softly against the window. Indeed, only a small spot as big as his fist was still clear enough to see out. Among the fields and farms of South Bainbridge, Josiah Stowell's property stood out, even in comparison with resort properties. It was well cared for, almost groomed, and it ran alongside the picturesque Susquehanna River. Newly fallen snow gave a ghostly aspect to this early February morning. The air hung thick with large white flakes that seemed suspended in time. Daylight was still an hour and a half away. Joseph rolled over beneath the handmade quilts that conquered even this wintery February cold. One last, luxurious stretch and he would get about the day. Instantly, his thoughts went flying across the miles from South Bainbridge to Harmony. Emma was probably stretching beneath her quilts this morning too. He warmed at the thought. Did she dream of him as he did of her? He smiled, knowing she would never admit it! Still, he was making progress, though Isaac Hale was fiercely jealous of him. Joseph couldn't blame the man for thinking that no one was good enough for his daughter. She was certainly a prize, and Joseph was determined that he would be worthy of her.

He had gone to work and board with Josiah Stowell after his father returned home to the comforts and companionship of his family. It was a difficult choice. Joseph had never spent more than a few days away from his home. He knew Christmas would be especially hard to endure without the beloved faces of his parents, his brothers and sisters. The Smith family had a special closeness. They had already shared persecution for their unique religious convictions. Grandfather Asael Smith had had many visions which he told to his posterity with regularity, impressing them with one firm belief — that God could and would answer their prayers. So the Smiths built their family tradition of studying the scriptures and discussing them over meals. Joseph Sr. had also had dreams of a highly spiritual nature, and Lucy Mack Smith seemed possessed of a sixth sense about people and events. Their oldest surviving son, Alvin, had once seemed most promising of all the Smith children. His was a pure nature, spiritual and Christ-like, and young Joseph had adored his brother. But Alvin was too good for this life, as Lucy often said to comfort them all. Illness and, finally, death had taken him while still a young man, and the household grieved over him ever after.

The Smith family was a hardworking family; indeed, it took all their collective efforts to make mortgage payments on their farm. Joseph Sr. was a cooper, skilled at making barrels, and successful at raising wheat. The sugar maples on their land were unequaled in giving their sweet sap for maple syrup. In this effort the whole family contributed, winning prizes at the county fair for the best and the most maple syrup produced. Lucy's hand-painted, oil-cloth table coverings won awards also and added to the family's diversified income. Unfortunately none of their enterprises were lucrative enough to amass much of a fortune. The last one-thousand-dollar payment was coming due on their farm, and the time was nearing when that obligation had to be met.

Joseph stood musing before the frosty window and summoned the face of his older brother Hyrum to mind. Joseph's closest friend on earth — kind, loyal Hyrum, the peacemaker of the family — and

Sophronia, serious and diligent, Samuel and young Don Carlos —
they would all be meeting around his mother's table. Over biscuits and
gravy they would greet the day with a prayer of faith. No doubt they
would pray for him. That mental assurance gave Joseph the impetus
he needed to throw off his reverie, jerk on his work pants, throw his
shirt over his head and hastily dive into his woolen coat.

Even indoors, Joseph could see his breath in the frosty morning
air. The small room where he slept at the rear of the home was
unheated, but then so were they all except Mr. and Mrs. Stowell's
room. They had a little stove in their chamber that kept off the worst
of the chill. At this early hour the parlor fire would be out and the
kitchen still dark. The only place to go for warmth was the barn where
he could lean against Bossy's side and collect the milk for the day. It
was not altogether unpleasant staying with the Stowells. There was
plenty to eat, plenty of work to keep him busy earning money, and
several fine horses which he exercised frequently. After his daily chores,
he walked half a mile to school. Held in another farmhouse down the
lane, this school served children as young as six and pupils as old as
Joseph. Emma's brothers had laughed and asked if he wasn't ashamed
to go to school with children. Joseph was not embarrassed. He liked
the children as much as the learning.

Joseph Sr. had once been a schoolteacher himself, and had seen
to it that all his children could read and write, but clearing and settling
virgin land had taken most of their time and effort. Joseph had never
progressed much beyond the elementary stage of reading. Now he was
reading on, making the acquaintance of the great English poets and
the framers of the American constitution. His admiration for those
men knew no bounds. Jefferson, Franklin, Adams were brilliant men.
Joseph felt his mind expanding as he meditated on their ideas
expressed so articulately. It felt good. Always a young man of action,
he was also a man of principle. The truth made sense; it tasted good. It
wore well, like an old coat. A certain burning in the bosom infallibly
told him when he had hit upon a sound principle, and he tested it in

every conceivable circumstance until he had fully incorporated it into his thought process. Knowledge was a good thing. He was sure God endowed man with sufficient intelligence to make a civilized world and to comprehend even things beyond the veil.

Joseph's small stash of money was growing, even considering that he set aside a portion of it to contribute to his family fund used to meet the mortgage. Soon he could ask for Emma's hand without shame.

One day he had gone riding to Harmony, taking wool to Nathaniel Lewis, goods which had been purchased from Josiah. He had stopped to pay his respects to Mrs. Hale. . . and of course, her daughter Emma. He found Isaac butchering a freshly killed deer.

"Mr. Hale, I'd like to be of help if you'll let me. I can see I have a lot to learn about wild game."

"Yup," the older man responded without enthusiasm. Isaac's shirt sleeves were rolled up to his elbow, and he was covered from his chin to his knees with a grimy sheet which was strapped to his considerable bulk around the chest and above the hips. Joseph watched the knife trim the fat and the connective tissue from the meat of the animal. Isaac was fast and efficient. Following the older man's instructions, Joseph began to salt the meat and layer it in the barrel. Before long, Joseph's hands were numb from the damp meat and salt, and small spots of blood sprinkled his clothing.

"Do you suppose this is anything like being 'spotted by the sins of the world'?" Joseph asked wryly.

Isaac chuckled in spite of himself. "Could be. D'ye think your shirt will ever be made 'as white as snow?' Not every man has the stomach for this. Somehow I didn't think you would."

"You don't know me, Mr. Hale. If a thing has to be done, I will do it. I'm not afraid of hard work."

"But you lack sense, boy. Money-diggin' and peepstone gazin' ain't the way to make a living. Get a piece of God's good earth and be a farmer. Settle down! Put these foolish games out of your head. A fine family and a fine farm, that's all it takes to really make a man happy in this life."

"Well, I'm willing to try. Mr. Stowell pays me to work on his farm, and now Joseph Knight of Bainbridge hires me occasionally to cut timber and work on his place. I expect to have enough money for a small place within the year."

Isaac squinted in his direction. He growled, "Sounds like you're wanting to settle down. Ain't looking for a wife, are you?"

Joseph pursed his lips and carefully answered, "Yes, sir, I am."

"Got somebody in mind?"

"I have."

"Wouldn't be my daughter would it?"

"I expect it would, sir."

Isaac slammed his knife down on the work bench. Turning to Joseph, he stared directly into his eyes and commanded, "Look somewhere else. I'll not have Emma married to any money-diggin' plowboy from Palmyra!"

Joseph did not flinch. Calmly he responded, "If I had been successful in finding our Spanish treasure, would you feel the same way?"

A slow, fiery red spread across the older man's face. "Why, you young whelp! I signed that contract before I knew they intended to use peepstones and soothsayers. Stowell may believe you have special powers, but I'll never be taken in. Emma deserves far more than you could ever provide."

Joseph wiped his hands on a rag. "I love your daughter, sir. I hope with time you will see that there is more to me than being a plowboy. I have talents that you know nothing of. God has a purpose for me. He has set His hand over me, and with His help, I can do anything. Emma could do worse than marry me, and I'll not give up unless she tells me herself she won't have me. I'm sorry if that upsets you. Good day, sir."

For all his words of confidence, Joseph left dejected. It had been a week since he had seen Emma, and it would likely be longer. Isaac

Hale had made it very clear that he didn't welcome Joseph at his home. But he was in the minority. Young Smith found himself invited to community work parties and many good Sunday dinners. Among his newly found friends, Joseph Knight Sr. took a personal interest in Joseph, finally inviting him to lodge with the Knight family and work at the family saw mill. The Knight home was in Colesville, a good five miles closer to Emma. Joseph was tempted to move, but he had to complete his obligation to Stowell. Many evenings Joseph took dinner with the Knights and spent hours sitting with the family around the parlor fire, which eventually led to his talking freely of his spiritual experiences.

It was hard to doubt Joseph when his face began to shine with a white light. Joseph had learned the hard way to be careful about sharing confidences. Anxious to share the word of God with concerned neighbors, his family had quickly found that Joseph's visions were distorted by others and viewed with suspicion. Suspicion was natural enough. After all, he was just the long-legged Smith boy to the people of Palmyra. Skepticism soon changed to outright persecution. It had been fairly acute at times in Manchester. So, carefully he chose a few friends in this new location, namely the Knights and the Stowells, and gradually began to share more and more of his experiences.

This snowy evening Joseph was invited to speak after dinner at the Knight home. He had decided to confide the story of Moroni and the gold plates to them. It was an unusual story, he knew. If it hadn't happened to him, he knew he would doubt the probability of an angel appearing to a boy and revealing the secrets of heaven. All he could do was tell his story, bear testimony that it was true, and trust the spirit of God to convince his listeners.

Tonight he would be in the company of friends, as likely to believe him as any people on earth. Mother Knight was plump and pink of cheek, and as kind of heart as she was expert in cooking. She fussed over Joseph nearly as much as his own mother did, and Father

Knight seemed almost next of kin. It felt good to be so warmly received. It nearly made up for being so far away from his own family.

Joseph cleared the drifts of snow from before the shed doors and from Josiah's front door. Using a large board obtained from Knight's sawmill where he had been working just yesterday, Joseph broke a path from the back door to the barn, then laid down straw so the little path would not be so slippery. He saw to the animals, fed the cows, threw hay to the horses, slopped the pigs, and spent an exhilarating few minutes chasing the largest piglet.

"You'll be bacon yet," he threatened when thoroughly out-maneuvered by the swine.

By the time chores were done, smoke was threading its way from the chimney of the Stowell home. Joseph went in for breakfast, carefully stomping off the snow from his boots at the back door.

It was nearly noon, and Joseph was just clearing the snowfall from the salt licks for the livestock when he heard the musical clip-clopping of a horse's hooves and the light jingling of a harness bell. A sleigh came gliding over the frozen Colesville road and into the clearing around Josiah's farmhouse. A familiar figure stood up in the sleigh.

Wading through the snow drifts, Joseph reached the sleigh in a rush, almost throwing himself into the vehicle with exuberance. Emma's dark eyes were dancing, her cheeks pink with the deep chill of mid-February. She was bundled up in a rich, dark fur cloak, with a matching muff for her hands and a hood that all but obscured her face. Joseph pushed her hood back and beamed as he observed the neat dark curls and the exhilarated smile of the woman he loved.

"You're here! I can't believe you're here! You came alone? Won't your father be angry? What about your promise to him? No, don't answer that. I'm just glad you're here. Do you know how I have suffered knowing you are only twenty-five miles away, seemingly a hundred? Emma, my dearest, kindest, loveliest Emma." He reached into the sleigh, clasped her in his arms, and lifted her from the sleigh. A lurch, then a sudden movement of the horses, and the couple found themselves tumbling in a billowy blanket. Emma's dark fur was dusted in white, and Joseph was completely coated, eyebrows, hair and all. They sat up, breathless from their tumble.

"Mr. Smith, you are quite incorrigible," Emma laughed and tossed a loose clump of snow onto Joseph's already encrusted collar. "You did that on purpose."

"I did not!"

"Of course you did. It's just like you to take me off guard like that."

"So you don't think I'm a gentleman, is that it?"

"I have never accused you of that."

"Thank goodness there's something. Emma, my love, you . . ."

"Shh," she warned him with a finger to his lips. "You mustn't call me that. You mustn't speak of love at all, or I won't come again. I am here on business. Yes, business," she rushed on as he started to protest. "Mama needs wool from Mrs. Stowell. She is collecting wool from all our neighbors because a family arrived in Harmony day before yesterday completely destitute. They were nearly frozen to death and barely arrived before last night's storm. We'll be making blankets, coats and clothing of all kinds. They came down from Massachusetts, said the weather there was killing the cattle, and they wanted to get further south. Anyway, I'm to travel about and ask the neighbors for wool and any other help they are inclined to give."

"I don't believe it. I won't believe that's the only reason you came. Why not send Reuben or Isaac Ward?"

"They're needed at home."

"And you're not?" He pushed her backward into the deep, fluffy snow. "Tell me no fibs, young lady. You came to see me. That's why you didn't bring your snoopy brothers. The truth, I'll have the truth, or else."

"Or else what?" she laughed.

"Or else I'll kidnap you and run away with you to the ends of the earth."

"Where would that be? Missouri?" Emma's eyes were dark, shimmering pools as he bent over her. Playful as a puppy, Joseph dropped soft spots of snow onto her forehead, her cheeks, her pink lips.

"If you were my wife, I would kiss those spots of snow and the warmth of my love would melt them beneath my lips."

"Joseph," she whispered a warning.

"What?" he dared her.

"Let me up now. Immediately, I say. Someone will see us."

"They'll just think you were careless and had an accident and I, being the perfect *gentleman*, am assisting you out of this incredibly difficult snow bank." He easily picked her up, set her on her feet and then instantly collapsed again, pulling her back into the snow. The mare was snorting and edging sideways, wary of this strange behavior from the love-struck humans.

"You're acting like a child. Now stop this," Emma commanded in her most assertive tone. "If you want me to be able to visit again, you must be circumspect!"

"All right, my little Miss Schoolmarm, what is 'circumspect?'"

"Proper, Mr. Smith. You must be proper with me."

"Never. I love you."

"You're an exasperating man."

"I'm a cold and lonely man, and I missed you at Christmas. I tried to see you, but your father wouldn't let me. Did you get the stockings? I knitted them for you. Mrs. Stowell helped me at first, then I did it all alone. She also taught me to crochet. I'll be making you handkerchiefs next. See how domesticated I've become?"

"Just how domesticated are you? I hear reports that you are seen walking about with Mr. Stowell's daughters." Emma's pink lips pursed almost petulantly.

Joseph's heart leaped. *She cares,* he thought, *she really cares.* "The Misses Stowells sometimes need an escort to church on these snowy days. That's all, I promise."

"For a man who doesn't go to church, that's very charitable of you." She was still haughty.

"Can't you be just as charitable? Take pity on me and say you'll marry me, Emma."

She struggled to her feet, shaking her fur cloak like a dainty mother bear. "Not without my father's permission. You must convince him. I have loved him and respected him all my life, while you, Mr. Smith, are a stranger and a newcomer to my love."

"Ah, so you do love me."

She started to shake her head, but he raced on. "That's the implication and you know it. A 'stranger' at first, a 'newcomer' perhaps, but a settler just the same. I am here to stay."

"You have to convince Papa. I'll never marry without his permission."

Joseph changed the subject. "How long can you stay?"

"Just a bit, really. I have other friends to visit, and I'll be staying the night at my aunt's home."

"And where might this auntie live?"

"In Colesville, near the Presbyterian church."

"Wonderful. I have an invitation to speak at Joseph Knight's home. His place is right next to the river in Colesville. His entire family will be there, and we will be discussing religion. Say you'll join me there, Emma."

"Would I not be intruding?"

"Not at all. I know Mr. Knight well, and his family would be delighted to receive you."

"I'm not sure . . . ."

"I have something special to share with the group tonight. You must hear it." Joseph's light auburn hair was fluttering with the slight breeze. The blue of his eyes seemed to match the clear skies.

Surely he is too young for me, Emma thought. "Joseph Smith, you are certainly the most unusual person I have ever met. Yes, you may call on me at my aunt's home, if you're quite sure I won't be imposing on Mr. and Mrs. Knight."

He shook his head 'no' to the idea that she might be an imposition, even as he reached for the horse's bridle to steady the animal. Emma cut off his protestations, querying him, "What is this 'something special' you'll be discussing?"

"You'll find out soon enough," Joseph responded over his shoulder as he urged the horse forward.

Joseph Knight's home was more spacious than the typical farmhouse. That night his sitting room held fifteen people, most of whom were Knight's family and a few neighbors who were interested in the young man from Palmyra. Joseph was nervous. He had hoped to speak to only the most receptive of his friends. With Emma there he was most anxious to have the evening go well.

Joseph Knight stood before the small black stove. His substantial bulk was neatly encompassed by his Sunday-best clothing, and his usually sallow complexion was flushed with his sense of excitement. "Friends, I'm glad you came. The good book says 'where one or two are met in my name, there will my spirit be also.' We should have a good portion of it. There's more of the spirit here than some Sunday meetings I've been to. 'Course, young Joe Smith sitting there is the cause of it. More than likely you folks have all heard of this man's visions. Some of you believe them, and some of you don't. Tonight you're going to hear these experiences from his own mouth. Then decide whether he is telling the truth. After all, you can't judge a man on hearsay."

Knight settled himself down in his oversized chair and arranged his hands across the girth of his stomach. Joseph Smith stood and moved to the side of the stove. It was warm, mighty warm. He longed to loosen his cravat, but knew he should not. This small group was made up chiefly of persons much older than himself; he had to summon all his poise if he was to appear credible in their eyes. And then there was Emma. His eyes flickered lightly over her lovely, oval face.

She too was enrapt, watching him expectantly. He knew that she and her family had heard rumors of his angelic visitations, and that the quickest way to eliminate distortions was with the truth.

"Mr. Knight has been my friend and benefactor for some time." The older man pursed his lips, nodded his head, then began to study the floor boards intently, striving to accept the compliment graciously. Joseph continued, "He is anxious for me to share my sacred experiences with you, his family and his friends. He has always believed in me. I especially appreciate that. Not everyone does."

He then began in earnest to relate in much the same words the story he told Emma. He stood up a callow youth, nervous and naive. But he soon transformed before their eyes. Already tall, Joseph seemed to grow four inches. He stood with his legs somewhat apart, his shoulders squared, as though settling in to accommodate a heavy weight. The recitation about the power of the dark forces held his audience spellbound, but his description of the Father and the Son simply took their breath away. No one moved; no muscle twitched, no shoe scraped the floor. Indeed, the room was so quiet Emma could have heard a feather fall. His face, normally all angles and planes, was flooded with an inner light which gave it an ethereal look all its own, holding his audience captive during an ensuing narrative of angels.

"On the night of September twenty-first, I had spent sometime in prayer and supplication to Almighty God. While calling upon my Father in Heaven, a bright light began to illuminate my chamber, until the room was lighter than at noonday, and immediately from within that light, a personage — a heavenly personage — appeared at my bedside, standing in the air as his feet never touched the floor.

"He had on a loose robe of most exquisite whiteness. It was a whiteness beyond anything earthly I had ever seen." Here Joseph began to tremble, his entire body reliving the incredible visitation. No looking off into the heavens, his piercing blue eyes delved deep into the hearts of his audience, demanding that they see his vision as he saw it.

"His hands and arms were bare a little above the wrists; also, his feet and ankles were naked. His head and neck were also bare. His whole person was glorious beyond description. His countenance truly like lightning, and when I first looked upon him, I was afraid; but the fear soon left me as he called me by name.

"He said he was a messenger sent from God, and that his name was Moroni; that God had a work for me to do — a mighty work — and that there should be both good and evil spoken of me among all people."

Emma was acutely aware of the good and evil he mentioned. Her own father insisted that there was nothing good about Joseph Smith, and now her brothers had started berating him. But these people — and she glanced quickly at the faces around the room — these sober, hardworking neighbors were responding to his incredible tale with complete accord. To be a skeptic while Joseph emanated this unusual light was almost impossible. She wished Isaac could see him like this. Surely then he would cease his unreasonable antagonism. How could such a young man so enthralled with heavenly matters be the rascal her father made of him? Her mind and heart rejected the idea completely.

Joseph went on with his story, engrossed in the memory and almost unaware of his current surroundings. "The angelic messenger said there was a record written upon gold plates, giving an account of the former inhabitants of this continent. They were his own people, and he said that the fullness of the everlasting Gospel was contained in their ancient record. Also, that the Urim and Thummim spoken of in the Old Testament was deposited with the plates. It was the possession and use of these stones that constituted seership in olden times, and God had prepared them for the very purpose of translating this record.

"Again, he told me that when I got those plates of which he had spoken, I should not show them nor the Urim and Thummim to any person, only to those to whom I should be commanded to show them; if I did I should be destroyed. While he was conversing with me about the plates, a vision opened to my mind and I could see the place where the plates were deposited so clearly and distinctly that I knew the place immediately when I visited it.

"After he delivered his message to me, the light in the room begin to gather immediately around his person, and it continued until the room was again left dark, except just around him. Then, instantly, I saw something like a conduit open right up into heaven, and he ascended until he entirely disappeared, and I was left alone to ponder on the things that had been told me."

The energy that seemed to almost consume the young visionary began to ebb. Somewhat as though he had reached out into eternity with a large net and swept his spirit back into the confines of mortality, he came slowly down from a high celestial plane. Gently putting back on the human character, Joseph became again a simple plowboy from Palmyra.

He appeared to be finished, and stood looking into Mr. Knight's pleased and satisfied smile.

"Joseph, did you really experience all this? Can it be true that God still speaks from heaven?" his benefactor inquired.

"Yes, sir. I experienced all this and more; three times that night the angel appeared and rehearsed his message to me, occupying the whole of the evening and once during broad daylight the next morning. It left me as weak as water. I was of no help at all to my father that day. Conversing with heavenly beings requires just about all one's strength."

And that did seem to be the case. To all appearances Joseph was quite exhausted in merely retelling the experience. Emma studied him soberly, trying to discern any part of his tale that might be fabrication and, at the same time, attempting to sort through the feelings that consumed her. He might have been dreaming, but not lying. It would be impossible for even an accomplished actor to speak with the special power that radiated from Joseph. Her father might say he simply sought notoriety, but the kind of attention he most frequently got was not flattering; it was derisive. No, he was not polished; he was not learned. He was very poor as to worldly things but, oh, how rich in spirit she was only just beginning to know!

Newel Knight, the oldest son of Joseph and Polly, broke the astounded silence which had fallen on the group. "Mr. Smith, have you actually got these . . .these golden plates then?"

"No sir. Not at this time. I have seen them though. For the past three years on September twenty-second I have visited the spot where they are hidden, but have never been able to obtain them . . . I have had some repenting to do of my levity, tomfoolery, and occasional temper. But I have been striving to rectify my faults. My brother tells me I need a wife," Joseph began to smile, "as they are most helpful in bringing faults to one's attention. And the last time I conversed with the angel, he told me next time I must bring someone with me, the right person."

Now his good nature was returning, and he couldn't restrain a meaningful look at Emma with a teasing smile which brought tell-tale pink to her cheeks. She tried to look severe. He had no right to imply any such personal thing in company of distant neighbors. Papa would be livid if it got back to him.

Polly Knight hoisted her corpulent self from the chair with a wheeze and a grunt, and announced in her high, thin voice. "Well, I haven't seen an angel. Don't expect I ever will, but if I should, I imagine he wouldn't shine any brighter than young Joseph here tonight. Just tell me one thing. What about wings? You never described the angel's wings."

Joseph broke into a wide grin. "Why, Mrs. Knight, I believe you're looking forward to wings yourself one day. Therefore, I'm right sorry to tell you that angels don't have wings. Angels are just like us, made in the image of God, only more glorified."

Her expression of delightful anticipation dissolved and left her three plump chins trembling with disappointment. "Well, anyway," she recovered her manners as hostess, "there's hot cider in the kitchen for all."

The group began to come to life, buzzing between themselves. Newel Knight came forward from his seat in the corner and engaged Joseph in lively conversation about this visionary experience. Newel was darkhaired, clean shaven, and exceedingly neat in his appearance. He was slender and his clothes were of good quality. Capable and successful in his own right, tonight he was a student at the feet of a younger, more humble youth. Before long, Joseph was surrounded by the men in the room, while the ladies visited around the table in the keeping room.

Emma tried to keep her opinions to herself. Never one to gossip anyway, she did not want tales carried to her family. If word got back that she had attended this meeting, she knew Isaac would take her to task. Through the open doorway she could see Joseph earnestly responding to questions. He had acquired new breeches, fawn gray, and a starched white shirt which amply covered his wrists. He was becoming more polished, though eager answers still betrayed his youth. Many older men that her father favored could certainly offer her more comforts — but the fire of life, only Joseph Smith the visionary had lit that in her! She acknowledged to herself the great danger she was in, the danger of falling in love with this extraordinary young man.

Chapter Three

Meeting the Angel

et's see him walk on water!" Reuben Hale had assumed the derisive attitude of his father toward Joseph. "He talks to angels; he talks to God. Let's see if he can walk on water." He stood on the shallow shoals of the Susquehanna. The river was low this July. Spring rains had been scarce, and the river had dropped until, in places, it barely bubbled over the rocks.

Emma sat with Joseph on the other side of the river. Both Isaac and Elizabeth were gone to South Bainbridge to visit an elderly aunt. Her time with Joseph had been limited during the winter, and though she tried to discipline her heart as her father wanted her to do, she found excuses to be with him. She told herself they were not courting. She was simply helping him with his education. Today she was snapping beans into an apron, trying to appear industrious. He had abandoned all pretense and lay with his hat over his face while the hot sun made a lazy slug of him. Emma knew he was not asleep. He had only just been humming and quoting Shakespeare to her. During the previous winter of reading the writings of Thomas Jefferson, Joseph had turned to Shakespeare, more particularly to his love sonnets, and to please Emma had memorized bits of them.

She wished he were asleep. Her brothers had taken to teasing them and deriding Joseph unmercifully. Now he sat up, his hat still low over his brow. With one hand he pushed back the brim and squinted at his tormentors across the river. After a moment he grinned and turned to her.

"Shall I show them?"

"What?" she demanded.

"My walk-on-the-water trick."

"Can you do it?" Emma had come to appreciate Joseph's many unusual abilities. Then she caught herself. "Of course, you can't. People can't walk on water, not even you, Joseph."

"I can. Really. Want me to show you?" He stood up. "Reuben, he hollered, "want to see me walk on water? You don't believe it, do you? Meet me down stream," he pointed to the bend in the river. "If I can't do it, you can throw me in. If I can, I'm gonna tan your hide for disturbing my nap. Come on."

Emma started to get up. He motioned her down. "You stay," Joseph commanded. "This won't take long, and you can see me perfectly from here." Emma twisted around, watching him and wondering what on earth he was up to.

About fifty yards downstream an old board had wedged itself between the rocks. Normally well-covered and hidden when the water was deep, Joseph had noted it was barely submerged in this dry July. Reuben and Isaac Ward were whooping on the other side, calling challenges to him, exulting over the prospect of throwing Joe Smith into the river. Joseph knew quite well that they could not see the board from their side of the river. Enough water flowed over the top to prevent that. Unless you knew it was there, it was quite invisible from the bank. He almost chuckled aloud with the enjoyment of his little prank.

"You'd better pray, Joe," Ward called out. He was a thinner, unwrinkled version of his father, right down to his stiff walk. And he seemed to feel it his duty to act for his father in heckling his sister's suitor.

52

Smith yelled back, "Oh, I am. I'm praying all the time, Ward. You'd better pray too; you and Reuben are soon gonna be visiting the fish in their own element. Get down on your knees, Reuben. Maybe I'll have mercy on you." Emma could hear the laughter in Joseph's voice. How does he put up with them, she wondered. Her brothers were obnoxious in the extreme to Joseph, and with absolutely no cause. He was unfailingly good-natured with them as with everyone.

She could see him walking carefully along the bank, studying the water's flow. She guessed he would find a shallow part and walk on the rocks. But no, he stopped at a deeper place. He stopped and dropped to one knee. He extended his hat up toward the sky. In a loud voice he called, "Oh Lord, give me the power to walk across this river and confound those two scoffers on the other side."

Reuben and Ward broke into peals of laughter, slapped each other's back and dared Joseph to show them. In a twinkling he arose and stepped into the bubbling water. His hat still in his hand, he looked as though he were walking a tight rope, and to the young men on the far side he seemed to truly fulfill his promise. The laughter stopped; the two boys stood with open mouths, incredulous. Ole Joe Smith was walking on the water! Maybe he really did see angels! Pa should see this. On he came, carefully, with the water flowing smoothly over his feet. In a moment they looked at each other, surprise, and then fear, awash in their faces. He was almost across! He'd be on them in a moment. Out in the middle of the river, Joseph began removing his shirt. He was broad-shouldered, his arms tanned with working outdoors all summer. He rolled up his shirt and tossed it behind him to the bank.

"He's just faking, Reuben. He's walking on rocks," Isaac Ward scoffed.

"You walking on rocks, Smith?" Reuben called out, the laughter gone now.

"Nope. Not on rocks, my friend. Water'd be bubbly if I was."

They looked at each other again. How did he do that? Water seemed to be too deep there for him to be on rocks. He was almost across. They took off through the clearing.

Joseph jumped to the bank and laughed at their backs as they sprinted for the bluff. "Come on back, boys. Don't you want to go for a swim? Water's fine today." He walked back upstream until he was across from Emma. "Well, what do you think? Is that going to help or hurt my reputation?"

"Oh, nothing can help your reputation with those that don't like you."

"What about with you?" he called.

"I'd like to see you walk across the water here, right here," she teased.

"All right then. Here I come." He strode purposefully out into the water and instantly was up to his waist in a deep hole. Under he went, splashing in the coolness, stroking the dark depths, and emerging dripping and laughing as he staggered up to the shallow part again. In a moment he was upon her, swinging her up into his arms.

"Joseph," she squealed, "what are you doing? Put me down."

"Where? Exactly where, my lady fair? See, I'm a poet too. If I put you down right here, you'll be in a foot of water." He shifted her weight enough to threaten her and listen to her protests, then he waded out toward the deeper part. "If I set you down here – my, oh my, but you might become a water nymph such as those old poets wrote of." He made a movement as if to drop her. She clung ever tighter and hid her face against his shoulder.

"Joseph! Joseph, please!"

"Wouldn't you like a pleasant swim in the water?"

"I have my good dress on."

"Marry me, Emma," his voice was serious.

She was startled at the change. She stopped struggling, and gazed into startling, cobalt blue eyes, that had changed in a split second from laughing to intensely serious. Those eyes seemed now to consume every detail about her face and stopped with tender longing at her lips. Self-consciously she moistened them, her heart thumping against his bare chest. Her hand went up as though to shield herself from him, but when she touched his face, her fingertips came to life and began their own exploration of features she adored each night in her dark and lonely hours. She touched his eyebrows, traced the brow line down to his cheek, crossed the smooth valley of his cheek and followed the straight line of his nose downward, to the curve of his lips. It was shameless of her, she knew. Why should she dwell on the curvature of his lips, she who never noticed the physical appearance of men? Emma had always been more moved by a man's mind than his looks. But now she was positively taken, entranced, captivated by Joseph's person. Her cheeks grew pink with the realization that she was behaving like a wanton, and she could hardly bring herself to care. If Papa saw her now . . . well, she'd have to marry him, that's all.

Joseph well knew he was taking liberties with Miss Emma Hale. How dared he? Not another man in Harmony would take her in his arms as Joseph did. She was a lady and well-nigh untouchable. Joseph lost himself in the incredible joy of holding her in his arms, her warmth surging into him, her fingers playing over his face like a summer wind. No turning away this time; the dark depths of her eyes did not evade him now. He pierced the flimsy barricade of propriety, and gazed into the passionate truth of her love. When he saw it finally and without doubt, the fact of her love, which she had always managed to shield from him, he lost all sense of what was proper and what was not. Strength surged through him, head to toe. His arms tightened around her, and he found himself tasting those beautiful, sweet lips. Nor did she protest. She was perfectly still in his arms; their first kiss lingering like twilight of a summer day, soft, tender, filled with gentle wonder.

After a few breathless moments their lips separated, but after one desperate, longing look of love, they kissed again, this time with a sense of fervor that took them both by surprise. After a moment, when the intensity left them trembling, Emma drew back.

"Joseph," she whispered a warning, beginning to push against his chest.

"I love you," he stated simply. And then, before serious conversation could ruin the moment, Joseph stepped into the deep pocket of water, and they both sank beneath the coolness.

She broke the surface protesting indignantly. He tugged her back down. Bobbing down the stream, she found her footing and pushed herself away from him. While she floundered toward the shallow water, he pulled her back into his arms. Her long dress soaked and streaming water, she eluded him, struggling toward the bank. He let her go a few steps, and with a taunting laugh, he easily pulled her back into the swirling water. Emma dared not cry too loudly. She knew it could bring her brothers running back or even her parents. Isaac was gone to South Bainbridge today, but she never knew when he would be back.

"Stop, this moment!" she commanded with all the force she could muster.

"Only if you promise to be my wife."

"Why should I marry such an impossible man?"

"Because you're madly in love with me, as I am with you."

"You're the one who's mad."

"No!" he challenged, standing knee deep in water and pulling her back into his arms. "It's true and you know it! Don't put me away from you now, Emma."

"I won't," she submitted easily. "Do with me what you will. Drown me in the depths of the water, if you so please. Take me to the farthest ends of the earth. I love you, Joseph. And you are the first and the only. I have never loved, truly loved, before. You have taken possession of all my senses, my thoughts, my dreams."

Ah, surrender — it was sweet! Joseph smiled. He beamed. Then he threw back his head and laughed out loud. A moment later, he pressed her against his chest, his hands caressing her dripping hair and smoothing her soggy dress across her shoulders and back. "Oh, Emma! Oh, Emma," was all he could say while they both stood smiling at each other, glistening in the hot July sunshine.

"Do you think Papa will say yes?" Emma was careful to keep her voice calm.

"To Mr. Smith? When Lucifer's tail freezes! You must know your father took an instant dislike to the young man," her mother responded adamantly.

It was Tuesday, and Elizabeth was mending, rocking and darning. "Isaac doesn't hold with visions and angels. Oh, I know, I know. Don't sputter at me like that. He's never heard it straight from Mr. Smith's mouth, I know that. But t'wouldn't make no difference. Isaac considers it all lies." She held up her hand to silence her indignant daughter. "And you taking his part won't help either. Your Pa would rather see you an old maid than married to Joseph Smith."

"Well, I almost am. Mama, I'm twenty-two, not exactly a young frivolous thing. Mr. Smith is the only man I have ever even considered. Frankly speaking, the men around Harmony are dull, ignorant, and about as visionary as their dinner plates. Now if there were some-one like Uncle Nathaniel or Papa, but there isn't. Alva is probably the best man in the township, and he's my brother. Besides Mama, I don't think Joseph's visions are lies."

Elizabeth paused in her mending, looking up and squinting at her daughter through the afternoon shadows. Emma was kneading dough. "You don't actually think he saw the Lord, do you, Emma?"

There was silence. How many times had she asked herself that question? How could she possibly believe it? Could the dead come back to life? That was just about as probable. Still, when Joseph spoke of his spiritual visions and convictions, something came over him. She smiled unwittingly. Something of light, of strength, some strange intensity lent power to his expression and fervor to his words. "I guess I do," she admitted quietly, and started pinching off bits of dough, rolling them quickly and lining a baking pan with them.

"Well!" Her mother was shocked. Her mending was in her lap. She looked about the room like one lost in a fog. "I declare! Emma, how could you?"

"You would believe him too, mother, if you had seen him and heard him as I have."

"You are in love with him, then." It was a statement of recognition as well amazement.

"I am."

"You'd as well ask for a slice of the moon from your father. He'll not give his permission to marry that young man." Elizabeth smoothed back her hair, then resumed her mending of Reuben's shirt as though it were a great burden.

Emma finished shaping the biscuits, wiped her hands on her apron, and went and knelt before her mother's chair. "Speak to him for me, mother. Try to soften his heart. Joseph is a good man. He's gentle with me, funny, good-tempered, hard-working, God-fearing. He prays with me. He prays for me. He loves me."

"Emma, your head is turned by a handsome face."

"It is not, mother. How can you say that? I have never been affected by looks, only by character . . ."

Isaac's deep voice shattered their intimate conversation, "Which Mr. Smith appears to have little of. Character is built by consistency, hard work, daily prayer, good deeds. Joseph Smith spends his time day-dreaming about angels and silver mines and getting rich quick. I don't hold with any of that. Men of good character aren't called up before the magistrate on charges of fraud and glass-looking. Why are you two wasting your time talking about a ne'er-do-well like Smith?"

Emma purposely kept her voice calm, refusing to allow a heated argument about Joseph. "Even a good man can be falsely charged. We both know that. Josiah Stowell's nephew brought the digging charge, a nephew who thought his uncle deluded and deceived. Joseph never tried to deceive anyone. He was always skeptical of the venture. He was the one who persuaded Mr. Stowell to stop digging. Even the judge could see through those charges. Mr. Smith was promptly acquitted."

"The charge was being a disorderly person and an imposter."

"I know, and it was dismissed. He is hardly disorderly. He is a hard worker and employed by both Mr. Stowell and Mr. Knight. As far as being an imposter — well, Joseph has never pretended to be anything than what he is . . ."

"A plowboy," Isaac interrupted. "With the gift of getting into trouble. You seem to know quite a bit about Joe Smith. Didn't we agree that you would not keep company with him?" Isaac's gaze was unusually stern with his favorite daughter.

"Occasionally he stops by," Elizabeth answered for Emma to avoid a confrontation. "He's very thoughtful, Isaac. He always brings me things from Martha Stowell, or bulbs he dug up in the woods. That's where I got the onions for your stew on Friday."

"I don't want his onions, and I don't want him around. Last week Reuben told me that Smith thinks he can walk on water. He even threw off his coat and challenged the boys to fight him."

Emma laughed. It was a delighted, refreshing bubble of remembrance. "He was playing with the boys, Papa. There was an old board under the water. It was all in good humor."

"Reuben didn't laugh," Isaac grumbled darkly.

"Well, Mr. Smith has a grand sense of fun, and so do you when you're not acting like an old bear." Emma kissed her father's cheek.

Isaac combed his beard with his fingers. Talk of Joseph Smith had ruined his day. "Why doesn't the boy go home? He doesn't come from our parts. Let him go back to New York where he belongs."

"Let's see, now Papa, how far was it that you and Mama traveled to get here? Almost everyone in Harmony comes from someplace else."

"Doesn't matter. I wish he'd never come. He's set this town in a flurry since he got here. Half the people believe his stories and half believe he's crazy — talkin' with ghosts, digging for money."

"And hired to do that digging by some very respectable citizens so they wouldn't get their own hands dirty." Emma spoke softly but pointedly. "You wouldn't mind if Mr. Smith had found that Spanish mine, would you? It would make us all rich."

"No, it wouldn't; it would make us all lazy! That's what it would do. Besides, I sold my interest in it. Fool thing to do anyway, get mixed up with digging for silver."

"Well, don't get all flustered about him. Mrs. Knight told me that he is going back to Palmyra in September. His brother is getting married."

"That's fine. Hope it doesn't give him any ideas."

Elizabeth relaxed as the tension dissipated. "Surely he won't come all the way back to Harmony. Mr. Stowell has pretty well given up on that old Spanish mine. Mr. Smith hasn't really any business here to bring him back."

Emma turned away from her parents. She didn't want them to see her face. The same thought had occurred to her. Was there reason enough for Joseph to come back? Would he simply elect to stay at home and find a wife there? He would certainly not be lacking for candidates. Strong, tall, and handsome as he was, surely there were girls there, younger girls, Emma thought ruefully, who would not object to a proposal of marriage. Her cheeks burned pink with carefully held emotion. In her mind she saw him standing beside his bridegroom brother, and she imagined the small gathering of friends around them, friends with daughters who smiled and giggled and whispered of young Mr. Joseph Smith. Unfamiliar anger rose up, hot and fervid. Her hazel eyes glinted, and she threw down her towel on the sideboard, grabbed a bucket, and slammed the door behind her. "Going down to the river," was all she could manage to say.

Joseph left on a hot day in September. This time he didn't travel on foot. Joseph Knight loaned him a horse, a big bay gelding. It had been a frustrating summer. Once Emma had acknowledged that she loved him, he had assumed that she would quickly capitulate and agree to marry him at all costs. Isaac remained firmly opposed to their union, but for Joseph, that had ceased to be an obstacle. They would simply elope. But Emma was just as stubborn as her father. She had made him a promise once that she would not "court" with Joseph. One impassioned kiss was all that Joseph had to give him hope that she actually did love him. Emma seemed determined to keep her promise, however difficult, to her father, and all their meetings had resumed an innocuous character. It was this contradictory relationship that finally wore on Joseph's resolve. When he received a letter from his mother telling him of Hyrum's impending marriage to Jerusha Barten, his loneliness overtook him.

So, Hyrum was getting married. And high time, too. He was older than Joseph, taller, and some said better looking. If he'd been born into money, the world would have been his toy. His good nature was just as appealing as his looks. He was a natural peacemaker, bending over backward to be fair to neighbors and friends. Joseph tried not to be jealous of Jerusha. Now she would hold first place in his brother's heart, and he, Joseph, would be more alone than ever before.

The night before he left, he rode a moonlit path into Harmony to see Emma one last time. The heat of the day had faded with the breath of the evening breeze. All around him the trees whispered, the night birds called, and the moon followed every clip-clop as he made his way to Emma's darkened house. He tied his horse down by the river so as not to disturb the Hale animals. In the bright moonlight he climbed the embankment to the frame house on the bluff. He had left a small white pebble in the lap of the oak tree where three limbs converged. He knew she would know what it meant. "Meet me" was the understood message. What it didn't say was all the other things in his heart, "I'm desperate for your love," "Marry me this instant," "If I go away, will you long for me as I do for you?"

Joseph had not yet reached the barn when the shadows moved, and Emma came running toward him. Her hair, normally tidy and pinned into a bun, was flying around her shoulders, tumbling in heavy locks down the front of her dress. He braced himself to catch her impetuous assault, but she stopped short, just inches from him. He reached out to take her in his arms, but she moved back.

"Emma," her name had become delicious to him. "Emma, come with me."

"I can't."

"Just tell me if you want to, at least."

"I want to."

"If you wanted it as much as I do, we'd have eloped a long time ago."

"If you knew it would kill your father, would you run away to marry someone he despises?"

Joseph shook his head. "What have I done to make him hate me so?"

"You dared to come here, an outsider, and win his daughter's heart. Joseph, I'm afraid we can never marry. I would completely lose my family."

"That is what the scriptures advocate, leave your mother and your father and become one flesh. That is what it says. Become one flesh with me, Emma. If you don't marry me, I promise you will not marry at all. You will stay Isaac's daughter until you are old and gray of hair, and you will weep at night, knowing that there was a man who loved you once, more than life itself."

Tears began to shine on her cheeks. He had never seen Emma in tears before. She was always composed, in command of herself and her circumstances. His heart seemed to melt within him, but still he gave no quarter. "Other women will have children, their own home, husbands who adore them. But you will have only memories and the knowledge that you completely ruined two lives, yours and mine, for it is utterly impossible that I should ever in my lifetime love another as I love you."

"Stop!" she begged him.

"You know it is true. Are you going to sacrifice us both to your father's jealousy?"

"Please stop," she cried.

"Emma. Darling Emma, come away with me to Palmyra. We'll marry at the same time as Hyrum and Jerusha. My family will adore you as I do. Isaac will finally give in when he realizes that you are gone. He'll see how miserable he has made us. It will all work out in the end. When he sees what a wonderful husband I am to you, he'll accept me."

"Joseph," she cried, turning her back on him, "you must stop now. I can't stand this."

"Because you love me? Because you want to marry me as much as I want you to?"

"Yes! Yes! I do. Of course I do, but I can't, not like that, not behind my father's back."

There was silence for a moment, then Joseph's voice came out of the darkness, quiet and defeated. "I know you're right. Marriage should be a happy time." Tenderly, he put his arms around her, pressed his cheek against her heavy, dark hair, and breathed in the warm scent of her. "It's best that I leave. I go tomorrow. Will you miss me, or will you forget?"

A sob escaped her, and she shivered in the mild evening air. His breath was warm on her neck. Her whole body seemed to be on fire, and she suffered almost unbearably with the effort of denying him. "Will you ever come back?"

It occurred to Joseph then that this stubborn, beautiful, highly-principled woman thought that she might truly lose him for good. He could let her believe that. Perhaps it would sway her if she thought he might not return. Perhaps she would go with him. He could say no. He should say no. It would be his best argument and perhaps put an end to their suffering.

"Your Shakespeare says, 'we love that well which we must leave ere long.' I can't bear to leave you, Emma. Only heaven can call me away." He could not bring himself to take advantage of her fear.

She stiffened and turned toward him. Her dark eyes were brimming with tears. Her face was troubled. "What do you mean?"

"Hyrum's wedding is only a part of my reasons for returning home. I have an appointment with the angel. I have met him at Cumorah every year on September twenty-second for the last three years. It is one call I cannot refuse. Perhaps this time I will be allowed to take the record. Each time I have hoped to be worthy to receive it, but each time I have failed. Time is growing short. I feel that the opportunity will soon pass me by if I am not prepared to grasp it. Perhaps I'll come to you triumphant this time, and you'll see that I'm not the ignorant "plowboy" your father thinks I am. Strange, the angel has admonished me over many things, but never has he reproved me for being a plowboy. Ignorance is a state of the spirit more than the mind. Between heaven and the Hales, I'm receiving an enviable education."

"Joseph," she whispered his name so endearingly as to stir his heart. "I've never thought of you as ignorant. Your mind and soul leave me quite breathless. No one compares to you."

Her arms twined about his neck, their breath mingled, then their lips touched. An explosion erupted inside Joseph, and he crushed her to him. He grasped a handful of thick, shiny hair, groaned and buried his face in it, then rubbed it across his cheek and mouth savoring the fragrance and the silky touch.

"Oh, Joseph, my love, my love," she barely breathed. "You are tearing me apart."

"I love you, Emma, and by the angels in heaven, I'll have you one day for my own. If God holds me in any favor at all, if I may ask any blessing of Him, I'll ask for Emma as my prize for eternity."

Back in the shadows of the trees, Joseph's horse shook his head and whinnied. A sudden rustling of grass and leaves startled the couple. They stepped apart, attention turned toward the river. The rustling ceased, shallow water was calmly bubbling over the rocks, and moonlight danced on the banks. The sultry night air hung heavy and quiet across the little meadow. But the magic moment was broken. Joseph took her slender hand, raised it to his lips, for one last tender kiss, and with dearly won composure, bade her farewell.

"You won my heart from the first moment I saw you by the river. A man cannot live without a heart. I'll be back, sweet Emma. Be ready for me."

Just before the silver dawn, Joseph came riding into the outskirts of Palmyra Township. He had been on the road for nearly four days, the big bay gelding carrying him steadily to an appointment he couldn't miss, not even for Emma. But with home just around the bend, Joseph wasn't thinking about the angel, though he was riding the trail at the base of Cumorah Hill. Unconsciously he was urging his mount to a fast canter; he was almost home. His family would be rising, doing chores, eating breakfast, and he would soon be with them!

The sky was flooded with white, dawn light when he jumped off the horse, tied it up outside, and vaulted the steps onto the back porch of the Smith home. The door was unlocked. He knew it would be. Samuel and Don Carlos would already be about their chores. Joseph held back just a moment, just long enough to relish the sight of his mother as she bent over the hearth where the smells of breakfast grabbed at his stomach. Then he was upon her, hugging her from behind, grabbing the ladle and flinging it onto the table so he could swing her around.

"Joseph!" she exclaimed. "Joseph, you're home! You're home. I've been counting the days. Here, what are you doing? You'll turn over the kettle," she laughed with reciprocal excitement at her son.

They were whirling around at the end of the table, all the while holding each other tightly in a bear hug. When they finally stopped to catch breath, Lucy pushed back a little from her son and noted the bright, clear countenance she loved so dearly.

"I knew you'd come by the twenty-second, but I dared not hope for anything sooner. Did you bring . . . anyone with you?"

"Anyone? Let's see, Mother, who could that 'anyone' be? Perhaps you mean the angel? No, well then, Mr. Stowell or Mr. Knight? No? Could it be you were hoping I'd bring a wife? As in Emma Hale, the legendary Emma? I wish I had. I tried. But she is devoted to her family as I am to mine, and so far, we haven't gotten their approval."

This was incomprehensible to Lucy. She savored the very sight of this boy, this big boy, who stood grinning before her, his kisses still damp on her cheek. Lucy was a short, small boned woman, proud as a mother hen continually watchful over her many chicks. This particular chick had been out of the nest too long. Look at him, thin, almost gaunt, rumpled, hungry, and utterly irrepressible. What was wrong with the Hales that they couldn't tell a good boy when they saw one? How could they not accept him? She shook her head and squeezed him tightly once more.

"Pa and the boys will be in shortly for breakfast. Sophronia and Kate are upstairs tidying up the beds. You look like you've been riding all night." Lucy turned back to stirring the mush.

"I have," Joseph affirmed before taking the stairs two at a time. "I'll bring these two lazies down for breakfast," he called over his shoulder. Bursting into the bedroom where his two sisters were bent making the bed, he swept them both up in his arms.

"My girls!" he declared with satisfaction. "You're still my girls aren't you? No suitor on the sidelines threatening to take you away from us? Better not. He'll have to pass muster with me first."

Sophronia and Katherine had encircled the long lost one in their arms and pressed their faces against his chest, snuggling into the brother who teased and loved and inspired them. Joseph! Joseph with his sweet ways, his meditations and revelations, his countless tales of ancient people and the angels who visited him and told him such stories. There was no other like him. He was like a young eagle, spiraling to heights the rest of them could not quite comprehend, coming back reluctantly to earth and stretching to describe the glorious worlds he knew beyond their own. And he had been gone too long. A brilliant beam of dawn streamed through the window, heralding, it seemed to them, the return of one whose personal light they had come to depend on.

"Come, Katherine, those aren't tears, are they? Where's my kiss? Sophronia, I've missed you, especially your preserves. Pennsylvania doesn't make the likes of your preserves!" Joseph squeezed his older sister, pleased to see her blush. "I brought you something special, sis. It's downstairs in my saddlebags."

Sophronia generally quiet and reserved could never be so with Joseph. Now her pleasure at seeing him again transfused life into her sober nature. Almost as tall as her brother, she gave an impatient jump and grasped his arm to drag him down the stairs. Katherine, younger by three years and shorter by several inches, stood on tiptoe to kiss her brother's forehead.

"There's your kiss, Joseph. Where's your bride?"

"Ah Katie, I've needed you to plead my cause. She won't have me. At least, not yet." At Katherine's astounded look, he twirled her around. "She doesn't love me as you do. But I'm working on it. I have to convince her father that I'm not a scoundrel — a mighty difficult thing to do when I'm charged and brought before a magistrate for glass looking."

"But that's not a crime!" she protested. "Lots of people do it, not so well as you though. Did you tell her about the angel?"

"Yep."

"Well, didn't she believe you?"

"I think she did. But she's honor bound to obey her father."

"Didn't he believe you?"

"Didn't tell him. With Isaac, well . . . it would be like casting pearls before swine."

Sophronia tugged at him again. "Speaking of swine," she enticed him, "mother has sliced ham for breakfast."

But before Joseph could make it down the stairs, little five-year-old Lucy, sleepy head as she was right now, came fairly flying into his arms. "Oh, our Joseph is home," she squealed in a high- pitched voice.

"Lucy, you're growing up! How'd you get so tall? You were barely walking well when I left."

"No sir. I was four. Now I'm just five. That's how I got tall. I growed."

"Grew," Sophronia corrected.

"Uh huh, and I still am growing. When I'm all done, I'll say `grew'," Lucy agreed to disagree with her older sister on such an important point.

"Well, you're getting prettier too. How do you account for that."

The little girl grinned with importance at her older brother. "Just comes when you're five," she asserted.

Joseph laughed and carried her the rest of the way downstairs, into the keeping room. Breakfast was laid on the table, eggs, ham, biscuits, milk and cream.

"I'm not sure I ought to get married. Look at all these sweethearts I'll have to leave if I do." Joseph looked about him, satisfied to be home at last, surrounded by love.

"Whose getting married?" a deep voice demanded. "I thought I was the only one." Joseph turned, right into the iron grasp of his older brother, Hyrum.

"Are we going to have a double ceremony?" Hyrum beamed as he and Joseph locked in a hearty embrace. Next to his parents, Hyrum's was the dearest face on the earth. There was a special bond of affection between the brothers. Joseph's was the more reflective nature, given to dreams, and intense feeling, Hyrum's the more steady, loyal, and gentle.

They stood with hands on each other's shoulders. They had shared so much — fishing at the mill pond, chopping wood together, milking cows before dawn when both wanted to be asleep, but neither would leave the other to do it alone. It had been a year of loneliness for Joseph and a year of loss for Hyrum.

Joseph swallowed down a lump in his throat and spoke unsteadily, "You're a better man than I am, Hyrum, you've got your woman. I still can't persuade mine."

"Ah, well, she just doesn't know you yet. She'll come along, I expect. How long can you stay?"

"When's the wedding?"

"We've decided on November. Want to wait till all the harvesting is done and the house is ready."

"Then that's how long I'll stay." The creak of a door announced another arrival. "Pa!" Joseph exclaimed and stepped around Hyrum for an enthusiastic embrace by his father, and following hard on Joseph Sr.'s heels were more brothers — William, Sam, and Don Carlos. The Smith men crowded up a room. They were all tall men, heavily muscled from working the land, and they were devoted to each other.

"Joseph! We saw your horse. I expected you'd be coming home soon for your meeting with the angel."

"Yes, but not just that. I've missed you all so much, I doubt if I could have stayed away any longer anyway. I have much to tell you."

"Then tell it over breakfast," Lucy took charge. "Come, let us pray and then eat. Your breakfast is hot right now."

Over breakfast Joseph recited his experience in March being called before the court in South Bainbridge. "Worst of all, it was an embarrassment before Emma's family. The whole town was talking about it. You would have thought I had been found guilty. Josiah felt terrible about the whole thing and positively denied that I had ever tried to cheat him out of money or deceive him in any way. I've worked for him, and worked hard these last ten months; he knows that. It was just a means of harassing me. But it tells me there is more to come. The angel told me my name would be had for good and evil, and I'm sure he is right. I never meant to cause such a stir. I like people. I wish they would all like me. They don't have to believe me, just treat me civilly."

Joseph Sr. watched his son intently. It was true. Young Joseph was a friend to everyone, and would offer his help to any passer-by. Before all this hubbub about religion, the boy was popular enough in the town. Now he was met with either sneers or smirks. "Joseph, you'd best try to keep quiet about the angel and the gold plates. I don't think we've seen the worst yet."

Joseph nodded soberly. "Well, so far, the angel hasn't found me fit to be trusted with the plates. Maybe I'm just not good enough. I wish I had more education. I feel almost stupid in his presence."

Mother Lucy had been removing plates from the table and stopped to put a hand protectively on her son's shoulder. "Don't ever think you're stupid. God himself has chosen you. He doesn't make mistakes. Your secular education may be lacking. Heaven knows we've seen that you children had the basics, but we haven't had the means to send you for higher learning. But, don't you worry, you'll get your higher learning from the angel, and he'll teach you what God wants you to know. All the fancy learning of man is secondary to that."

Lucy was right, the angel was ready to teach him. Joseph left the house just before midnight on September twenty-first, too anxious about his appointment on Cumorah to sleep well. The sky was black, and the night sticky with stars. He turned south and headed across the fields toward the phantom hill that rose up in ghostly splendor in the moonlight. Higher than other small risings in the area, Cumorah was largely clear and grassy, decorated but sparsely with trees, except on the western edge and southern base where a sizeable thicket stood. As a boy he had played there many times. All the children in Palmyra played on the hill. From the top one could see for many miles around. All was quiet as he walked. No breezed fluttered; no birds sang. There was only the soft sound of his shoes in the dust of the road.

Meeting the angel every year was like sticking your arm into a flame. Angel Moroni was a stern taskmaster, terrible and beautiful at the same time. He was the guardian of the plates, a charge given to him by his father, Mormon, centuries ago. These thin metal plates contained the history of his people over a thousand year period. Mormon had condensed that history from many other records, written it succinctly and protected it with his life. The golden record had been hidden in the earth for protection during the final battle between Moroni's people and another, more savage tribe. He had entrusted them to his son, and Moroni was still fulfilling his charge, for these golden plates had a great purpose. They held a second testimony of the Savior, Jesus Christ, written down and preserved so as to come forth as a warning in the last days to the people of the earth.

Long before Joseph began climbing the west side of the hill, his heart was pounding, every nerve was tingling, his body felt as though it were on fire. In the darkness he nearly lost his way, then he stopped and marked his position by the trees. There, over where the three trees grew tallest, just where the earth jutted up and the stone crowned the grassy knoll — that was the spot. Shadows laced the ground in the little clearing. Joseph glanced about him nervously. Had he been followed? Despite his advice of caution to his family, word had gotten around Palmyra about his heavenly visitations. Most people shrugged it off, but there were a few malicious youths who liked to torment him and wouldn't be above following him to the hill. He drew a deep breath, held very still, and listened for any suspicious noise — sticks snapping, birds calling, heavy breathing. No, there was nothing, only the silence of a cool September night and his own heart like a hammer in his chest.

Next to the cresting stone, Joseph threw himself down on the ground, kneeling and praying and waiting. His mind seemed to have wings and flew across the starry skies to the very edge of the universe. Where art Thou? his soul cried out. Father, my Father, where art thou? I am here as thou has called me, he pleaded silently. The darkness still prevailed quietly around him, and Joseph persisted in tugging at the celestial sleeve, begging for an audience. Presently a conviction of his own unworthiness overcame him, and his pleading gave way to heart-wrenching sobs. His mind went back over the frivolities of the past year. Had he sullied the high and holy calling from God with his light mindedness, his use of the seer stone to gain money, by talking too much about his heavenly visions? Would he be cast away as totally unfit to serve God? Hot tears washed down his cheeks, erupting from a great fountain of humility within.

Only after a total emptying of pride did the tears begin to subside and profound stillness come over Joseph. Feeling like little more than a limp rag, he sat back on his heels with his head bowed, scarcely breathing as the calm deepened into a wealth of silence found only in the quiet recesses of eternity. Just as he felt as though he were sinking into the arms of death, a shaft of moonlight began to quiver and to brighten as it cut through the tree limbs. He waited patiently. He knew what was coming. He knew *who* was coming. Moroni's form became visible, filling the shaft of light until the column of moonlight seemed a glowing, vibrant, pillar of fire, and Joseph fell backward on the earth. The angel was a man of might, not a filmy spirit with wings and a harp. Beneath his luminous, white robes he was broad-chested, muscular, and solid. He stood over the stony earth, and he pointed a finger at Joseph.

"Behold, thou art Joseph! Hast thou forgotten? Hast thou put aside the things of God for the things of man?"

Joseph struggled to his knees before his heavenly tutor. "I have not forgotten," he whispered. "I have been weak."

"Weak? Thou canst not be weak! God has called thee! Joseph, thou shalt be the head of this dispensation of time, even the last days of the earth. His word shall come forth through thee. His church shall be established through thee. His priesthood shall be restored through thee. Know who thou art, and be not led away by things of this world."

Joseph trembled with the vibration of the angel's voice chastising him. He could scarcely look at Moroni's face. It was terrible as lightning, and his eyes burned with a zealot's fire. In times past, when the angel had visited Joseph, patient instruction had taken place, even visions of a people long dead — Moroni's people and their awful destruction. Each encounter with this being of light had left Joseph drained and exhausted. Now he felt as though his body and soul hovered on the verge of complete destruction.

"What must I do?" Joseph's voice was a croak.

"Finish quickly thy mortal pursuits and be about thy Heavenly Father's business. I cannot give thee the plates until thou canst devote thy time to protect them and to translate them. The plates will draw unto thee all the evil of the world. Wicked men will attempt to take them from thee, and thou must be prepared. Nevertheless, God will protect thee and the plates. Take no thought for thy bread and meat. It shall be provided as needed. And let no thought of earthly wealth nor gain enter into thy heart again. These gold plates are only for the instruction of man in the ways of God."

"Shall I take them today?" Joseph asked, though he already knew the answer.

The angel's voice boomed like thunder, "No! It is not time. Thou art not yet prepared. If thou comest next year to this spot and bringest the right person with thee, thy mind and soul being dedicated and pure before God, thou mayst receive the record then. If thou shouldst fail, thou shalt lose all. The time is growing short. God's kingdom must be established."

Joseph was confused. Moroni had mentioned once before that he must bring the "right" person, and Joseph had thought it might be Alvin, his oldest, most spiritual brother. But Alvin had died. Who must it be?

"How shall I know this 'right' person?" he asked.

The angel almost smiled. The rugged features of his face softened, and he regarded the boy prophet almost affectionately. "Thou shalt know when the time comes. Do not fear, Joseph, God is with thee. Put thy life in order so thou canst serve well."

With that parting admonition, Moroni seemed to gather all particles of light to himself until his form quivered with intensity. Then in an instant, the light was gone, the sky appeared over Joseph's head with pink and lavender hues. Dawn was breaking, and he was exhausted. It felt good just to lie back on the ground and let the morning light tickle his face with fingers of warmth. More than ever Joseph's entire body was afire, as though a million ants rushed through his veins. His countenance was white and drained of color as he lay recovering from the angel's chastisement. With all his soul he determined that it would not happen again. Not for all the silver in Stowell's lost mine would he put his eternal salvation at risk. And if he were to get his life in order, he simply must have a wife, and soon.

Chapter Four

The Right Person

Joseph set out for Pennsylvania at daybreak Friday, November third, the day after Hyrum's wedding. As happy as he had been for Hyrum and Jerusha, his winsome new sister-in-law, Joseph's spirit was restless, pulling him relentlessly away from the festivities. It was welcome relief to turn the horse's head toward Harmony and know that with every stride he drew closer to his beautiful Emma. Joseph passed the hill Cumorah, and whereas once he might have been whistling as he urged his horse southward, now he spent the time in solemn reflection on what was to come.

Anxious about Emma's state of mind, he drove his mount perhaps harder than he ought, stopping only for brief respites beside a pond or stream, and occasionally at carriage way-stations. He rode straight to Joseph Knight's farm where he had been invited to stay. He arrived at mid-day. He was tired and dusty, but his first concern was dark-haired, dark-eyed Emma Hale.

"Have you heard anything from her?" he queried Father Knight.

The older gentleman shook his head. "Nope. But then I don't get to Harmony too often in the fall. Too busy with winter preparations. My boy, Joseph, took a young lady to a Methodist social last month and said Miss Hale was there with her parents and her younger sister. Isaac Hale provided all the meat for the feast. His daughter,

Emma, provided the music. She has a mighty fine way with a song, and she's the only pianist in the area. The Methodists ought to feel lucky to have her. You still set on her?" He peered at Joseph from beneath thick, graying eyebrows.

"Yes, sir, I am. I'd like to take your carriage and call on her today, if I could."

Father Knight chuckled. "If you can get around old man Hale. 'Peers to me he doesn't favor you coming around much."

"You're right about that. Why does he dislike me so?"

"Folks never like someone who tells them they're wrong about their religion. A man's religion is the most important thing next to his family and his farm. Hale figures you're just a mite young to be judging all the Christian churches as wrong."

"But you listened. You believe me."

Knight rubbed his beard and eyed Joseph thoughtfully. "True, but I'm not the stubborn old coot that Hale is, and I don't have a young daughter you are wanting to marry and carry off. I'm afraid you'll have a lot more people like Isaac Hale than Joseph Knight if you keep insisting that our churches are wrong."

"They'll have to believe me when I get the golden plates and translate the book."

"Nope. They won't have to believe any of it. Folks that don't want to believe can find a thousand reasons not to."

"But it will be proof."

"We'll see," Knight grunted skeptically. "Anyway, hitch up that sorrel mare over in the barn. She's my best buggy horse. Should we expect you back for dinner?"

"Don't wait for me, sir. I'm not sure exactly how long it will take to see Emma alone!"

"Well, if we're not up when you get back, just roust me out, or there's a blanket in the barn if you'd rather."

Joseph grasped his older friend by the shoulders and thanked him fervently before hurrying off to the horse stall. Emma! Emma!

Emma was waiting! At least he hoped so. A fleeting shadow crossed Joseph's mind. Hale would marry her off to someone else if he could. No, Emma would never allow herself to be pressed into a loveless marriage, not even for her father. Hastily Joseph found the bit and traces and fitted up the mare to the carriage. In a few minutes he was off, his rig bouncing jauntily down the road toward Harmony. Around the bend in the river he drew up the mare, tied her to a limb, then took clean clothing from his saddle bags at the bottom of the buggy and strode down toward the river to bathe. He would be spruced up for his lady.

The water was so cold it was numbing. In a few shallow places there was a thin pane of ice near the bank. But Joseph had washed in many a cold stream, and this morning he hardly noticed the chill. He stripped off his shirt and quickly splashed the clear, cool liquid over his neck and sinewy shoulders, scrubbing longest under his arms and about the lean waist where his belt rubbed. His skin was pink and tingling when he finished. Then he braced himself on the river bank and plunged his head into the icy water. "Hoo!" he snorted and puffed a few times, while he lathered, then rinsed, his hair.

Soon the clean shirt his mother, Lucy, had provided was jerked on over his damp hair, and tucked into his pants. He pulled out a comb and went to work on his appearance. His razor completed the preparations as he scraped off the three days growth of beard. Truth to tell, there wasn't a lot to scrape. Fair-haired as he was at twenty years of age, his beard was hardly a problem, but today he must look his best. After a two-and-a-half months' separation, Emma deserved a clean-shaven man to woo her.

The mare stood waiting patiently. Before long, Joseph jumped back into the carriage and had the old mare trotting down the river road to Harmony. The sun was shining like shimmering ribbon through bare limbs of the trees. The fields were still frosted white from last night's dew. Crisp, cool air invigorated the would-be, young lover, and Joseph began whistling, and eventually singing, in a high baritone, "Lou, Lou, skip to my Lou, my darling."

He pulled the buggy over, tied it off the road under a tree just north of the Hale home. Smoke billowed from the chimney. He could almost smell the biscuits and gravy Emma was serving for dinner. Joseph stared at the family homestead, and was lost in deep thought as to how to circumvent Isaac Hale. Was there anything he could say or do at this point to reconcile himself to Emma's father? He could try to be a farmer. His ancestors were, and he expected to have a farm and a home himself. Perhaps if he bought a little piece of land from Knight or Stowell, Emma's father might look more favorably on him. Instantly came the memory of the angel's warning — he must not be concerned with things of the earth. True . . . but he must have a wife. He must have Emma! He could hardly rest, nor think of any other thing, as long as he was separated from her. She was woven into his heart and thoughts until she was inseparable from his very sinews and bones.

"I do not ask for anything else of you," he pled with God. "I stand ready to do your work, to suffer all manner of persecution if need be. Only give me the desire of my heart, a wife, my Emma for a wife. If I have her, I can bear all else." Then he bargained, "And I can be a better servant to you."

After what seemed like an interminable time, the back door of the house opened and Isaac Ward came out with Reuben. Tryal stepped out and tossed a dish-pan of water out onto the grass. Still no Emma. An hour passed. The family bustled about the place, but Emma was not to be seen. Disappointment crept over Joseph like a black fog. Could she be away? Could Isaac have sent her away to prevent any further contact between them? No, Joseph couldn't believe she would go. But then, she might have wondered if he was ever coming back. Two-and-a-half months is a long time. Finally, in a dark and somber mood, Joseph made his way to the large hickory tree where he and Emma had left messages for each other. Carefully he chose a white rock from the ground to put in the hollow space of the tree. From that she would know he was back and wanted to see her. But when he reached in to leave his rock, there was a scrap of paper weighed down with a brown river stone. He snatched it up and scanned the dear familiar handwriting, so precise and proper.

"I pray you come soon," it said, "for I am ill and dearly in need of a blessing. Your Emma."

It was all Joseph needed to make up his mind. Isaac or no Isaac, he would see Emma. She needed him; she had prayed for him to come! Joseph left the mare and buggy tied securely. He broke into a run and covered the ground quickly. Passing the smoke house, he strode to the farmhouse doorway and knocked loudly. Tryal answered.

"How long has she been ill?" Joseph asked without even a proper greeting.

"Em has been in bed for a week with bilious colic."

Joseph's heart fell to his shoes. His brother Alvin died of that very illness. "I must see her," he urged the young sister.

Tryal looked about nervously. "Mother and Father have gone into town. I don't think it would be advisable . . . ."

"It would be quite advisable. Tell her I am here, Tryal! And get her ready. I'm going to give her a blessing. Go on," he commanded as the girl hesitated.

One more worried glance from her gray eyes and Emma's youngest sister scampered up the stairs. She barely had time to blurt out that Mr. Smith was downstairs and to tuck the covers about her sister, when Joseph took the steps two at a time and filled the doorway of the tiny bedroom chamber. Emma had pushed herself up a bit against the pillow. No time to fuss with her hair. Before any vain preparations could ease her sick appearance, Joseph was on his knees beside her bed. The fever had left her weak and susceptible to chills, so Emma had remained in bed thinking that surely tomorrow she could be back on her feet again. All through the long days and nights, burning up with a fever and refusing even chicken broth, she had prayed for Joseph to return. Just the sight of him would make her better. His hand on her forehead would banish the burning headache that tormented her. But the days had passed, interminably long, and she had almost given up the hope that he would return at all. Now he was here.

Tears sprang in Emma's eyes and splashed down her cheek in huge droplets. "You're here! You came back," she said simply.

"Of course. Didn't you know I would?"

"How I hoped."

"It was a long time. I know. I was with you every day in my mind, but I had to wait out Hyrum's wedding. Now it is finally time for me to be with you. I rode straight here in two days. Emma, I hate myself knowing that you have been ill, and I haven't been here to help you. Emma, darling . . ." then he choked up, grasped her hand and brought it to his lips.

Tryal looked on all this in amazement. Emma had managed to hide the extent of her feelings even from her curious sister. The girl stood in the corner, a slightly disapproving look on her face. This was not proper behavior from a gentleman caller, and this caller did not have her father's sanction. They would all get in real trouble if Isaac should reappear. Joseph also realized that possibility, but swept it aside. Emma needed him now. Nothing else mattered. Besides, her father could hardly disapprove of him more than he already did.

Emma's skin, always creamy, was abnormally white since her illness. Her dark eyes and eyebrows seemed enormous against the pallid complexion. Her long hair, normally so tidy and curled, hung down over her nightdress in two heavy, dark streams. Joseph laid his cheek against her hand while he composed himself. Her other hand crept across the covers and made its way to his bowed head. When he felt her touch, his heart leapt up to his throat. After a moment he took both hands in his and covered her fingertips and palm with his kisses. Tryal blushed and looked away from the scene.

"Bless me," Emma whispered.

"Gladly. A prayerful blessing from my heart," Joseph's responded ardently.

Then he began his most unusual way of talking with his Heavenly Father, as if they were face to face. No officious words, no repetitive phrases; Joseph spoke as a child to an attentive parent, pleading her cause as one righteous and pure in heart. He begged for her recovery as one dear and precious to him above all others. His voice broke as he prayed, and Tryal opened one eye, peeking at this passionate young suitor. The girl didn't know love could be so intense. Her own brothers and their wives were much more guarded in expressing deep feelings. She knew this couple had forgotten about her, so caught up were they in their love. Tryal felt a twinge of jealousy, but quickly put it away from her. Emma deserved a man who loved her profoundly as Joseph did. When he pronounced "Amen," Tryal slipped quietly toward the doorway.

"I'll go watch for Mother and Father," she whispered, leaving them to their privacy. She hoped her father would take a good long time at the flour mill in town.

Joseph pulled a chair up next to Emma's bedside and told her all about his trip home to Palmyra, not skipping the angel's chastisement or his own unworthiness as the Lord's servant. Emma lay quiet and content against the pillow, watching his expressive face. His eyes were a constant window to his heart. At times they twinkled and shone as he talked of his family; other times they seemed to flash with pain and anguish. After two long months of separation, it was a feast to lie quietly and bask in his robust, fervent spirit. Life without Joseph seemed dull. Every hour had dragged. Every day was wasted time. Only his passionate spirit breathed life into her commonplace existence.

"I came back to marry you, Emma. That's my only reason for being here. We must decide when. I know, you've been ill. I won't press you now. But soon, when you are better, you must tell your father. If he could be made to see into our hearts, surely he would give in. After all, I know he wants you to be happy."

"He doesn't think I could be happy with you."

"What do you think?"

"I think I couldn't be happy without you. You have spoiled me for ordinary love, Joseph. Now only the sublime will do." She could still smile, if only faintly.

"You be my guide. I want to talk to your father. He simply must give his approval. Tell me when to return and how to reach his heart."

She shook her head. "Please wait a while longer. I'll talk with him first, then I'll leave a note for you."

"It can't take long. I don't have long. I must go back and help my family. There is one more payment to make on the farm. We've worked that land for ten years, we have to make it ours."

"Before Christmas we'll ask for Father's blessing."

"All right, before Christmas." Joseph could see she was tiring. Her movements were labored, her eyelids drooping. He must let her rest. "I'll check every day for your note or a white stone to tell me we can meet." She smiled weakly, amused at his vitality.

He stood beside her bed. In the dim light he towered over her, still clinging to her hand as though willing her to shake off the illness. Her body was weak from her long bout with stomach pains and little nourishment, but her spirit responded to his enthusiasm. Like no one else, Joseph could raise her spirit to greater heights than she had thought possible. Tomorrow she would put off this illness and prepare herself to talk to her parents. Perhaps by Christmas she would at last be a married woman. The thought sent a small shiver throughout her frame and a blush to her cheek. Finally, Joseph said goodbye to the most beautiful patient he had ever seen.

But Isaac was not easily approachable. As soon as Emma began to mend, he left on a trip south, trading animal skins for other goods, needles, cloth, sugar, tea, shoes. Emma and Joseph met almost every day. Her mother, Elizabeth, discreetly closed her eyes and wished for Isaac to return and take the matter in hand. For her part, she had no quarrel with young Smith, though she had hoped for someone steadier and more financially set. Her daughter would not have an easy row to hoe with this young man. Still, she had never seen Emma so vibrant. The pale skin gave way to a rosy glow, and her shining eyes were an unmistakable sign of love.

Isaac Hale was not interested in the rosy light of love. "No!" was the emphatic answer when he returned and Emma asked if Joseph could take Sunday dinner with them. "No!" was the still more emphatic answer when she told him that both she and Joseph wished to speak with him. Finally, three days before Christmas she rode in a sleigh with her father traveling to a neighboring farm when Joseph intercepted them on the road.

"Young man, you are in the way," Isaac asserted.

"Sir, I am sorry to cause you any inconvenience. However, I am happy to have encountered you both. I have long wished to discuss a personal matter with you."

"I have no 'personal' relationship with you at all and do not desire to discuss anything. Now, kindly move aside, we have business elsewhere."

Joseph's mount did not budge. He would not be put off again. With great persistence, he continued to press for his heart's desire. "Respectfully, sir, I wished to speak with you about your daughter, Emma."

"There is nothing to speak of. I shall never give my permission to a union with such as you."

"We would settle right here in Harmony, Mr. Hale, for I know how dear she is to you."

"That's kind of you," Isaac scoffed.

"And I am saving money for a farm of my own. I assure you I am not the ne'er-do-well you think me."

"I try hard *not* to think of you at all. Move aside, boy."

Emma's lips were compressed into a thin line. Her eyes were full of despair. Joseph could scarcely look at her for her discomfort was evident.

"Look at your daughter, sir. We have made her completely miserable by this discussion in public. Speak with me privately, I beg you."

"Never! I have no desire to speak with you at all." Isaac clucked to his horse and the carriage jolted forward. Joseph's mount moved back. "And I will never give in!"

"And I, sir, never give up!" Joseph caught the older man's eye and held it as the sleigh moved past. The Hales left him without a backward glance.

There was silence between Isaac and Emma as they continued their sleigh ride. He was too angry to speak, and she too careful. Isaac was tying up the horse at their destination when he finally spoke to his daughter.

"Your association with this man has had exactly the effect I feared, disharmony in our home and disrespect from an otherwise devoted daughter. I am disappointed in you, Emma."

She spoke quietly, as was her custom. "We know two different men, Father. I understand your objections to the Mr. Smith you know, but you have no perception of that man I admire and believe in. Were you to give yourself an opportunity to know him, I think you would respect him."

Isaac stared at his daughter in exasperation. "Exactly what is there to admire?"

"He talks with God."

Isaac snorted in disbelief. Emma continued unperturbed, "In a different way than you or I do. And he is trying very hard to live consistent with his beliefs."

"So are we all!"

"No . . . not all . . . you have never believed in persecuting a man for his religion, but you are doing so with Joseph Smith."

"I am protecting my child."

"Father," she put her hand on his arm, "I do not need protection."

"You certainly need something . . . perhaps I should send you to visit your older sister in Windsor. You would meet good families up there, and lots of visitors from good families come in the summer to enjoy the country and the river. I should have taken care to expose you to quality suitors a long time ago. You have no one with whom to compare that 'plowboy'."

She sighed, "You are too late."

"Don't tell me you mean to marry him!"

"I do esteem him very highly. He is a man of principle and complete dedication. And I am sorry that you do not trust my judgment in this, as you have always praised it so highly in other matters."

"It is not your judgment I fear, but that fickle thing women call love, thinking it to be some kind of cure-all."

She looked back as she entered the door to their home. "Men should be grateful for that fickle thing, otherwise how could we live with them?" Then she was inside, and the door closed between them.

Christmas passed quietly. There was no word from Joseph, no note in the tree. January buried Harmony under a thick blanket of snow. The Hales could scarcely break a path to the barn to tend their animals, and a path they cleared one day would disappear the next with a new snowfall. After a week of being shut in, Sunday dawned clear and sunny. The family made preparations for Sunday meeting; Emma made plans to visit her sister in Windsor. Isaac reluctantly gave his consent. She could take the sleigh. It was a short ride to the Colesville-South Bainbridge area.

"You'll go straight to your sister's?" Isaac questioned.

"That is my intention. I have only clothing enough for a few days so I shall be back by the end of the week."

"I could ride with you."

"Yes, you could. Come, if you want, but it isn't necessary. I shall be quite all right."

Isaac was decidedly uneasy, but deferred to Emma's well-known competency. The morning was crisp and sunny, and the horse and sleigh made good time as the runners slid over the snow-packed road. Next to boating down the river in summer, this was actually the best way to travel. Even heavy loads slipped along easily on the snow. She was soon within a few miles of her sister's place, but suddenly the sunlight had gone out of Emma's day. She hadn't seen Joseph in weeks, and was rather hoping that fate would throw them together if she could once escape her father's vigilance. Now she was feeling quite morose. She had come straight here, almost to Elizabeth's, keeping the promise to her father, and she was miserable. She was lost in melancholy thoughts when a dark horse and a dark-haired rider came trotting toward her. They were about to pass when Emma recognized young Joseph Knight, Jr. He removed his cap and nodded to her. She could not resist.

"Mr. Knight, how very nice to meet you on the road."

"Are you on an errand?" the young man inquired.

"No, not this time. I started out to visit my sister in Windsor. However . . . I . . . well, I have decided to travel first to Mrs. Stowell's in South Bainbridge and purchase some wool for a winter coat. I expect I shall be there most of the afternoon." She paused, hardly knowing if she should be so bold. "Perhaps you and Mr. Smith might enjoy a ride together and a visit there."

Joseph Knight, Jr. was determined not to smile at her obvious suggestion. Gravely he answered, "I'll be sure to mention it to Mr. Smith when I see him next. I'm quite sure he will fit his plans to your convenience. Good-day, Miss Hale."

The fifteen miles sleigh ride to South Bainbridge went flying by along with Emma's thoughts. After all, she had been intending to make Ward a new winter coat. He had outgrown his old one. Mrs. Stowell had the finest wool in the area, and already spun, ready to be woven. She could visit with the Stowells, and Joseph, if he came, and then go back to her sister's place. She simply had to know if he had given up his quest for her hand in marriage. She could hardly blame him; her father had been very emphatic.

The breeze had summoned a pink blush to her cheeks and the tip of her nose. Her bonnet was securely tied under her chin, protecting those dark, bouncy curls from the elements. She was bundled up in the dark rich fur of her cloak and muff, her face alight now with pleasurable thoughts of Joseph. She stopped the horse and stood up in the sleigh. She stood looking down on the river, only a few hundred yards away. It was almost hidden in places by snow drifts that reared fluffy heads along the banks. She was ready to climb out, when two muscular hands grasped her waist and turned her. She looked down into the clear, electrifying blue eyes which always produced those little chills chasing up and down her back.

"Joseph, you're here!"

"Exactly. And so are you." They stood still, simply smiling at one another. The sun seemed to stand still overhead, and as far as she could see, the world about her sparkled like diamonds.

"I just saw Mr. Knight . . . the young one . . . and suggested that you might visit me at the Stowell's. How did you . . . why are you . . . I mean, that is, how lucky you are already here."

"Not luck. I had a notion you might come here today."

"Did you? And how did you get such a notion, since I've not heard from you in almost a month." Emma didn't often play the coquette, but now she could not help herself.

He easily lifted her down and held her close, talking softly in her ear, "A still, small voice that whispers to me, like I whisper to you. I prayed you here. Since I can't come to you, the only way is for you to come to me."

Emma tried to maintain her composure. "I'm on a visit to my sister, Elizabeth in Windsor. I came on up here for some wool. Isaac Ward needs a new winter coat."

His gaze was absolutely fatal; it could stop her heart in a split second. "Uh huh, a new winter coat. I understand. What about me and my needs. I need something more important than a winter coat. I need a wife. I need you, Emma."

Emma Hale blushed. It had been on her mind for months. In fact, she could scarcely think of anything else, though she managed to hide it always from her family and even from Joseph. How much longer could she go on waiting for her father's approval? He had made it clear he would never give it. Now, in the circle of Joseph's arms, a warm flush was spreading through her body, making her weak. It disturbed Emma, this physical response whenever Joseph was near, for she wished to always be in command of herself. But oh, her heart was wayward. He was going to kiss her, she knew. And she also knew that she would not stop him.

But he did not kiss her, even though he felt her resolve softening. He held her, tenderly but firmly, scrutinizing her face like a hungry man, lingering at the gentle line of her lips. Memories of last summer at the river made her shiver and look away. Joseph sighed, then reluctantly, he tugged at her arm.

"Let's go inside. Mrs. Stowell has a fire. It'll warm you through and through. And I'll see how long I can detain you from your sister."

No sooner was Emma divested of her bonnet and cloak, than Joseph took her hands and held them before the fire, alternately rubbing them and kissing them. The small front room was easily heated by the warm hearth, and the couple was quite comfortable. Josiah Stowell joined them briefly, apparently interested in Joseph's courtship. The tips of his tidy mustache were fairly twitching.

"This young man has been telling me for days that you would come. Of course, I pay strict attention to whatever he tells me. He seems to have a more perfect knowledge than I do. I wouldn't have guessed you'd drive all the way up here for some wool. Jacobsens in Harmony have wool, haven't they, Miss Hale."

"Yes, they do, but," Emma added quickly, "not so fine as yours, and not spun and ready to be made up quickly. Besides, I was wanting a little outing after being snowed in last week."

"I see. Well, Joseph, looks like you were wrong. You prayed for a wife. Looks like you'd better keep on praying." Josiah's small, bright eyes sparkled.

"Maybe or maybe not. Perhaps together we could convince her." Emma had tried to pull her hands away when Josiah walked into the room. Joseph wouldn't let her, and still held them tightly, though she was blushing furiously by now.

"Joseph, you don't need my recommendation," Josiah protested. "God is your reference. If you are righteous enough to keep company with angels, I'd say you are good enough for me, or anyone else. Emma, I've known your family for years. I've always thought your father a man of sound judgment. But I believe in this case he is mistaken. This young man is the hardest worker I've ever seen. He is honest to a fault, and polite even under adverse circumstances. If he won't make a good husband, I don't know a man who could."

Emma's eyes had turned to flint now, and her back was ram-rod straight. "I thank you for your assessment, sir. But a man's character is his own best endorsement." She turned a stern look on Joseph and resolutely withdrew her hand from his. She would not be pressured into marriage. She moved across the room and seated herself on a settee a few feet from the hearth. It was pleasantly warm there, and she felt herself able to think more clearly away from Joseph.

"Perfectly right!" Josiah agreed quickly. "A woman of insight, Joseph. I think she is the person the angel spoke of. Well, I'll leave you young people to carry on your discussion. I just want you to know, Miss Hale, that I will do anything I can to help if you should decide to . . . well, to make my friend here a happy man. I have a horse and cutter for transportation, a room for your lodging, all the comforts of home. Good day, good day," he waved at them as he backed out of the room and closed the door.

"What exactly did the angel say?" Emma asked automatically as the door closed.

Joseph had seated himself before the fire on a small, sheepskin rug. He was quite serious now and seemed to be remembering. Actually he was deeply concerned about offending his heavenly mentor if he used their communication for a light-minded purpose. He gazed into the fire; he stared at his folded hands. Once he glanced at Emma, then he sighed and looked again into the quavering flames of the fire.

"You'll think I am making something up to persuade you against your will."

Her voice was cool. "Are you?"

"No!" He sounded perturbed. "I wouldn't do that."

"Then tell me about the angel!"

It was several minutes before he began. In the silence Emma made another assessment of this man she had come to love and her father had come to hate. Joseph Smith would, no doubt, always be at the crux of such divergence of opinion. Either he told the truth or he didn't. Was he a man of God, or the worst kind of impostor? Emma had always trusted her own judgment above all. This time she had to be sure.

"I must be the most blessed and the most cursed man on earth," he said finally, seemingly pre-occupied by the fire. He picked up a poker and jostled the coals. "God expects me to be perfect, or at least be far better than I am. He will allow me no mortal follies, no casual sins, no earthly concerns. I have been chastised for caring more about the necessities of life than for His heavenly purpose for me. Yet I must eat, I must work, and somehow I must put aside the foolishness of youth before I get the golden plates. I failed to obtain them last September because of my . . . shortcomings. The angel told me I might receive them next time, if I brought 'the right person.' Do I know who that person might be? My brother, my father? I don't think so; I could have brought them a dozen times. The angel knows that. It is someone else, someone more important to the work. I think it must be my wife. For whatever lies ahead, a man cannot face the uncertainty of life alone. He needs . . . I need . . . a helpmeet, a companion, a wife. You, Emma, *I need you!*"

He waited while that information sank into Emma's consciousness. His face was turned away from her as he contemplated the red embers and the tongues of fire. She could see only the back of his auburn hair, glinting with gold and red highlights, and the wide, muscle-rounded shoulders stretching hard and solid beneath the broadcloth of his jacket. She had never seen him so well-dressed. Joseph was wearing a tan, cotton cravat today, tied beneath his chin and tucked into a vest. He was obviously prepared to meet someone important. Her heartbeat quickened, and her resentment began to slip away. He was dressed up for her. A smile came to her lips. An instant longing took her to stand beside him, to touch those strong shoulders, to look into the face that sent her soul soaring.

Abandoning her last reserve, Emma rose and moved to Joseph. He looked up, as she stood beside him. Her skirt was deep purple, full and wide, and her waist slender as a flower's stalk. Her face was framed by dark curls and highlighted with dark slashes of eyebrows, regal and imperious over long lashes and brown eyes. She was queenly and unapproachable . . . but she came to him. She sank to her knees beside him on the soft rug, tipped her head to the angle of his, put her hands to his face, and drank deeply of the depths of his eyes.

"Joseph," she whispered softly, "you want a wife. I want a husband. In the eyes of God is there anything wrong with that?"

"Nothing." He held his breath. Did he dare hope?

"Only one thing stands in our way: my father's blessing. And that obstacle cannot be overcome. I have been wrestling with the question of whether the prize is worth the price, for if I marry you, I must give up my family, the dearest people on earth to me. This is a high, a very high, price to pay." Her eyes began to swim in unshed tears. "Help me," she pleaded.

He moved only inches, but his lips brushed hers as he vowed, "I will give you a family that will be dearer to you than anything else on earth. Babies, children, sons, daughters, and grandchildren, born of our flesh and blood, an eternal bond between us. I am grateful to your parents for all they have done to make you who you are — a polished diamond in a field of stone — and I feel less than worthy, actually, to claim the very best, the finest of women, for my own. But I will give you love enough to bring heaven down to earth. And if we try very hard, I believe we can coax your family to share our bit of heaven. You need not give them up forever.

"Emma, darling, you mean more to me than anyone on earth. You are the choice of my heart, soul of my soul, the only woman I shall ever want."

Then his arms took her in, his lips were softly insistent, and with a shudder she answered his kiss. In that instant, Emma knew but one sensation, the absolute, unspeakable joy of loving Joseph. Fire leaped as though from the hearth, searing her lips until she could hardly breathe. She was crushed against him, her softness against the lean, hard line of his chest and hip. She knew it was scandalous.

With a whisper, she capitulated. "We'd best be married, Mr. Smith. No man has ever held me like this. Still, I am not ashamed, for you are also the choice of my heart. There is no other I have ever wanted as a husband, and no other who could fulfill my dreams . . . just you."

"Today," he stated simply.

He felt her startled response, but held her securely and reaffirmed, "This very evening. We have waited too long as it is. Nothing is to be gained by waiting longer. Your father will merely find ways to keep us apart. We must be married today."

Emma's long fingers touched his shoulder, then his cravat. When they crept up to his lips, his full, soft lips, she repeated, "Today." Then her lips followed her fingertips and her heart was roaring in her ears, "Today! Today!"

Joseph's spirit practically burst the bands of the flesh. He felt himself tingling with fiery exultation as he held his precious, his darling Emma. Passion, surely he had heard that term before, but never really understood the word. Now he knew passion as he dared not imagine it. It was a burning within, the stirring of forces that threatened to consume him. It was beyond the flesh, it was a longing of the soul to be inseparably united with this rare beauty, a pure desire to luxuriate in the spirit and mind of this most extraordinary woman.

They sat transfixed before the fire, wrapped in the arms of love and contemplating a lifetime together. Once the decision was made, their happiness was almost an obstacle to the very deed. Neither could bear to break the spell. Emma's face was so beautiful that Joseph couldn't bring himself to think of anything else. And Emma was so captivated by Joseph's intensity that she was afraid to trust herself to behave properly. Her heart given at last to him, she was practically his puppet, moving at the bend of his finger, savoring his sweet words.

It was two hours before they could bear to allow others into their magic circle long enough to drive the sleigh to Judge Tarbull's home in South Bainbridge. Josiah Stowell, beaming ear to ear, and his sisters, Rhoda and Miriam, accompanied them to the judge's and witnessed their union. They took those singular vows before the judge, his wife, and the Stowells; common vows for such an uncommon union, the school teacher and the plowboy, the prophet and the lady, united and pledged to each other in a profound bond of spiritual communion and passionate resolve.

The remainder of their day passed like sequences of a dream. The young couple had eyes only for each other. There was supper with the Stowells, a visit from the Knights, another hour visiting with friends before the fire in the front room of Josiah Stowell's home, and then, at last, their precious moments of inexpressible joy. It was a bonding of love beyond life, beyond death and far beyond what their midnight whispers could communicate. They were husband and wife, nothing else mattered. Their lot was cast with each other, for better or worse, for richer and poorer, in sickness and in health, and only death could part them. He had come into her life and taken possession of her. She held nothing back from him. Indeed, he would not allow it. He looked into the depths of her heart and demanded all. With anyone else, Emma always closed a part of herself away. With Joseph Smith, she gave her whole being, unreservedly, freely, amazed at the fulfillment his love gave her.

The two young lovers lay between cool, crisp sheets, content in having overcome opposition, and with full faith that the future held happiness if they could be together. They knew nothing of the dark forces that were fanning other kinds of flames through which they must pass, a veritable volcano with built-up pressure which would eventually erupt, settling ashes across the entire earth. That night they dreamed, but not of conflict nor persecution, for the heavens had decreed peace for them this one perfect night, the lull before the storm.

Chapter Five

The Golden Bible

"W ho-o-a! Who-o-a! Whoa now, Bessie." Joseph stroked the cow's warm hide to settle her down for milking. She stopped shuffling, and Joseph set the pail underneath her udder. Squir-rt squir-r-t, white, frothy milk began to sing against the tin as he worked with a slow rhythm to relieve the cow of her full bag in time for the family breakfast. He rested his cheek against her warm flank and thought how good it was to be home. There was spring plowing to be done, and he was needed. Ten years on the land, nerve-splitting labor, and it came to this: one final payment and the farm would at last be theirs. For his parents' sake, Joseph knew they had to succeed. Joseph Sr. had had too many reversals in his life — being cheated while he always honored his debts, and toiling through capricious weather and crop losses. This land was important to the Smiths, their small part of the world. A man needed a place to call his own, a home for his wife and children. Joseph pondered this basic necessity. When the Smith farm was secured, he would set about obtaining a home for his own wife and family. Emma fit in well with his brothers and sisters and never complained, but she was not a girl; she was a woman and deserved a home of her own.

"You let me sleep," Emma's soft voice startled him from his reverie. "You were supposed to wake me so I could come with you and help."

"But you looked so content, soft and beautiful and sleeping soundly. Could a man shake the dew from a rose? You are my Emma-rose. I want to savor you just as you are."

"And you are a romantic, Mr. Smith. Wives are to be helpmeets for their husbands. I can't shirk my duty." She bent over him, resting her cheek against his forehead. "Besides, I want to be with you, whatever time we have. You're gone so much, and we're almost never alone. I cherish this time with you in the morning."

"Are you lonely?" he asked, knowing how difficult it had been for her to leave her family and come to New York. After their elopement, Josiah Stowell had driven them in his wagon to the Smith home in Manchester, Ontario County, just outside Palmyra. Emma came with only two dresses and none of her personal effects. After a week, she had posted a letter to Harmony requesting that her father send the personal belongings she had left. She had no idea if he would respond. They were still waiting to hear. Meanwhile, she had stitched a new dress and underclothing. She missed her books most of all, especially her own copy of the Bible.

Loneliness was a luxury which Emma would not allow herself. She had weighed possible consequences for a year before marrying Joseph, and she would not permit her happiness with him to be shadowed by anything so paltry as loneliness.

"Not when you're near. I would have been truly lonely if you had given up on me there in Harmony. That loneliness I couldn't bear. I scarcely survived your absence last fall."

He had finished milking Bessie, dried his hands, and Emma tugged him toward the barn door. "Come out for a moment," she urged. He slid back the heavy door, and they stood together in the opening, facing the eastern sky, where the sun was simmering in a rosy heaven. It seemed caught in the tangle of newly budding limbs, almost dancing in the early morning mist.

Joseph spoke quietly, "Every morning God gives us this immeasurable gift, the rising sun. We often take it so much for granted, too busy to notice, but He continues to give. So much beauty around us, and we see only the work and the worry."

"Not you. I've never known a man who appreciated nature's beauty as you do."

"Because I know the giver." A chill ran through her. Her husband's face was as radiant as the sunrise. His arm tightened about her shoulders as he added, "And He is far more glorious than any of His creations."

This spiritual awareness was ultimately the deciding factor in Emma's decision to marry. Joseph was an unlikely choice for a woman of her polish and accomplishment. She thought back to that first night when he sat at her mother's dinner table. His sleeves were too short; his pant legs barely covered his ankles; his homespun clothing was worn and dusty from his travels. No, he had none of the usual trappings of success about him. She knew her father's derisive reference to him as a "plowboy" was probably justified. Besides, he was younger than she. An older man would be already established, with a home he could offer a wife. Joseph was poor. Possibly he always would be. Certainly his family had little to offer in the way of worldly goods. If she and Joseph were to acquire even the bare necessities of life, it would be by their own hard work. Emma was not afraid of work.

All those considerations had been carefully weighed and balanced. There had been other men in Emma's life whom she could have married. She had not been seriously attracted to any of them. They had all seemed dull, dull of mind and spirit, uninterested in anything except hunting and farming. Education alone did not make for a keen intellect. Joseph, for all his lack of schooling, had the most inquiring, lively, challenging mind she had ever encountered. It was that which had first sparked her interest, then her admiration, and now, her devoted love. He brought excitement into her rather ordinary life. By nature Emma was a private, quiet, reflective person, given to spiritual devotion and duty. With Joseph came laughter, vigorous life, and speculations on eternal questions. He brought her out of her respectable shell and taught her to enjoy the world, to give of her inner self to others, to love profoundly, even wildly at times, and to receive love in return. He was emotional and constantly tugging at her heartstrings. She had seen him weep out of joy or tenderness. He was everyone's friend. Most people became friends as soon as he struck hands with them. He was a visionary, engrossed sometimes for hours in meditation, and emerging with unshakable confidence in his spiritual perceptions. Living with Joseph was a mountaintop experience, and Emma's soul had been yearning to breathe that fresh, clear air.

"Are you happy, Emma?" he persisted. "I would take you back to Pennsylvania, if I thought you were unhappy."

She smiled at this earnest, if impractical, statement. Of course it was impossible to return. Where would they go? Not to her father's farm. They would not be treated nearly so well there as here. Mother Smith was as warm and friendly as her Joseph. She chatted generously as they went about their daily work, keeping up a running commentary on her neighbors, on her various children and their virtues, and on the Smith history with all its twists and turns of fate. Emma already found it easy to call Joseph Sr. "father," and felt as though she knew Alvin, the elder brother who had died at age twenty-five. She was sure she would have liked this gentle, thoughtful individual. Hyrum, Joseph's older brother, now twenty-six, was apparently much like him, exhibiting the utmost devotion to his family, though he had recently married and moved a few hundred yards away into the old, family log cabin. Alvin had insisted on building the new, two-story, frame house for his parents and had nearly accomplished it when he died suddenly of internal problems.

Sophronia and her much younger sister, Katherine, were almost direct opposites of their effusive mother. Quiet — but not timid nor as serious-minded as Emma herself was — constant, steady and industrious, these new sisters were exactly the type of women Emma would have personally chosen as her best friends. Their large, deep-set eyes had been inherited from their mother. Sophronia had light brown hair tucked into a tidy bun. She was the more delicate of the two eldest, due perhaps to a childhood illness which had nearly cost her life. In recent weeks, Emma had noticed a decided blush of pink about her cheeks when young Calvin Stoddard happened to stop by the Smith home after a day of planting. Sophronia had just turned twenty-four and was still unmarried. Emma knew what that was like, and she hoped for Sophronia's sake that the budding romance would blossom soon.

Katherine was younger than her sister by ten years. Almost fourteen, she was tall, strong, and very capable. She had dark penetrating eyes, and her quick, decisive mind was firm in her beliefs. Her most cherished belief at this time was in the divine inspiration of her brother Joseph. He was her hero, her model of manhood, and she would do anything to please him.

Little Lucy, at five years old, was still full of the exuberance of youth and continually brought a freshness and a smile with her as she skipped in and out of their daily chores. Her mother was a little more lenient with the last child than she had been with the older children. They included Samuel, age nineteen, who was unusually quiet and dutiful, William, who at sixteen could lick the world, and eleven-year-old Don Carlos, so beautiful as a child that even strangers would comment. Not that young Lucy was exactly spoiled, but definitely more free of spirit, and more free to come and go as her whims directed her. Lucy was the comfort of her father's heart. This was an accepted fact in the Smith family.

"Am I happy?" Emma put her head on his shoulder. "Joseph, your family has taken me into its very heart. I have another mother now, a generous, warm woman who reminds me very much of her son, my husband. And I have new sisters and brothers, who try so hard to make me feel at home. I think they are pleased that I didn't keep you in Harmony. Yes, I'm happy. I never dreamed I could look forward with so much enthusiasm to each new day."

He was satisfied at last. His sunny blue eyes still thrilled her when he stood gazing into her soul as he did right now. Emma could hold nothing back from him. He saw it all, and he loved all that he saw there.

She was not like other women. There was nothing of coarseness about Emma, as there was in so many women of the frontier farming community. It was necessary in 1828 that a woman be strong, enduring, capable, and unafraid of work. Joseph could never have found a wife in the city who would endure the rigors of living off the land. However, as much as her strength, he admired the refinement and polish that Emma exuded as naturally as if she had been born to a genteel existence. She was a gem among pebbles. It was this uncommon quality that attracted Joseph to her. He looked down at her hand resting in his. It was a large hand for a woman's, large and capable, but not rough or calloused. It was the hand of a lady, and she carried herself with an awareness that she was, indeed, a gentlewoman. It would never matter to Emma whether she was rich or poor. In the direst circumstance, she would not be a beggar, for she was possessed of an innate gentility.

Deep down, Joseph suspected she was, as her father believed, too good for him, but he was also determined that it would not always be so. His formal education had stopped, but his capacity to learn was expanding. He was studying with a very special tutor, Moroni, of the ancient American civilization, who revealed in vision scenes from the past. Joseph could describe perfectly the attire, the government, the military, the social and spiritual life of Moroni's people, and he felt his self-confidence increasing with each revelatory experience. That he would outgrow this small township in New York was a fact he already anticipated. Just exactly what his role would be in God's plan was still veiled, but he knew great things were expected of him. Yes, he would be worthy of his calling, and his work would be significant one day. Joseph resolved that Emma would not regret her choice of husbands. He would be forever grateful that she had seen beyond the plowboy's guise and had faith in him. She would be his greatest asset, the polish his rough stone needed, the steady, unswerving hand that his fragmented life would require.

Somehow he sensed all this, though it seemed but a foreshadowing in time. All he really knew right now was simple joy in the love of this stately, beautiful young woman, whose dark brown eyes could turn his stomach upside down.

Isaac Hale pulled his bear-skin robe closer about his shoulders. The fire was dying, and the dank chill of night on the mountainside crept up his back. He had been hunting for three days and had strung up a buck in the branches of a towering oak tree. He had revived an old fire pit, one he had used many times before. To others, the mountains might be the wilderness, but to Isaac, they were his backyard. He knew every cave and hollow, every clearing and fallen log. He had hunted this land for twenty years. The fire crackled and spit for a while, long enough to cook the rabbit he had shot last. He hunched down in the dirt like an Indian, satisfied himself with the rich taste of seared rabbit meat, and refreshed himself with cool water from his flask. Evening twilight had quickly fled, camped as he was in the shadows of the Allegheny Mountains. The bear skin deflected even the coldest blast of frigid air, and the faint scent of it cleared the immediate area of other, smaller, curious animals. The forest night was peaceful to Isaac in a way that his warm, fragrant home was not, for here there was no human voice to demand his attention, only the wind humming high above in the tree tops and the night birds calling. He wanted no company, no polite conversation, and especially no more talk about Emma's betrayal.

The gnarled, old hunter dug into his shirt pocket, carefully bringing out a creased and much folded paper. It was his last letter from Emma. She wrote to request that he send her belongings. The letter had come barely a month after she had disappeared with Smith. His heart still hurt when he saw the neat, smooth handwriting that bespoke Emma's personality. He unfolded it meticulously, as he had many times, and pored over the few words. His face was a study in misery.

> Dearest Father,
> As you must know by now, I am married. I am well and happy. Joseph's parents have taken us in and treat me very kindly. I write to implore your forgiveness and ask you to soften your heart against my husband. It was my own decision. I was not forced.
> I would request that you send my personal belongings, with my Bible and rocking chair. I am most grateful and still your loving daughter,
> Emma Hale Smith

Isaac sat studying the limp, wrinkled paper, trying to see his daughter between the lines. Elizabeth could take it all in stride. "Send her things," the mother quickly concurred. "She'll certainly need them now that she is the wife of a poor man." Her daughter had stubbornly desired this husband, and her choice had shown them both a rebellious side. Well, she would learn fast enough of the burdens of a farmer's wife. Elizabeth repeated these platitudes with an admonishing wave of the hand. Her mind had already dealt with the reality of Emma's marriage, and she was resigned. It was not so with Isaac.

Initially he was angered when Emma eloped, since none of his other children had ever so flagrantly disobeyed him. His word had been law in his home, and even when they married, the force of his personality had kept his extended family in strict compliance with his will. Emma had her way of getting around him, of changing his mind on many things, of quietly going about her own business. He had given her the most latitude of all, not because he loved her more, but because he had trusted her good sense. Her steady, peaceable nature had been so soothing, he had been lulled into believing her incapable of capricious behavior. How wrong he had been. How blind! His woodsman's wary nature had been dull when it came to his most priceless possession. The wolf had been in the sheep's den, and he had not even heeded the warning signs.

Over and over Isaac mused on the phenomenon of Joe Smith with his faded shirt and ragged hat, walking into his, Isaac's, own home and stealing away his priceless pearl. In her absence, Emma's luster took on even greater beauty and worth. Just a brief, silent vision of her face would twist Isaac's heart. For the bereft father, the sun had gone out of the spring morning. She was gone, irretrievably lost, and to a common sort of man who could not possibly do her any good in this world or the next. Joe Smith had no prospects of success on earth except by trickery and evil design, pretending to "see" things with that peep stone of his! Pshaw! Isaac's mouth twisted in derision recalling the farce of hunting for silver with Smith's stone as guide. He sat before the glowing embers and shook his head, terribly amazed over his own culpability. Why had he not barred any meetings between the two? Why hadn't he chased Smith off, with a rifle if necessary? And then the darker vision of himself fixing the sights on the thieving devil. One slight squeeze of the trigger and . . . .

I'd rather have seen my Emma in her grave, the old man thought. I'd rather commit her soul into God's hands than see her with Smith. He turned her into a traitor, betraying my confidence. My daughter was no liar. He made her so. He taught her his evil ways. Oh God, where is my Emma, my angel, my beloved child! Can she really be happy? When will she see her terrible error? Could it be undone even now? I want that marriage annulled. People do get annulments. Of course, she would have to remain alone. Who would have her after this scandal? But she could live with us. She would always have a place with us. Isaac's thoughts continued to run. Emma would eventually come back. He just knew it. His heart would accept no other vision of the future.

The stars had shifted considerably in the blackened sky by the time Isaac rolled up tightly in the bear skin and drifted off to a restless sleep. The Pennsylvania mountains loomed like gigantic monuments of doom, ghostly dark and imposing overhead. He was a lonely man. No matter the neighbors, no matter the family left to comfort him, Isaac Hale had lost his beloved child, and he was inconsolable.

While Isaac remained in the mountains, haunted and unhappy, Joseph and Peter Ingersol drove an empty wagon one hundred and twenty-five miles to the Hale home. Elizabeth packed up Emma's belongings and sent them to her. Elizabeth was glad her husband was not home. There might have been violence. She patted the rocker as the wagon started off. "There," she said aloud as she waved goodbye, "she'll come back to us one day."

Joseph stood just inside the threshold of Lucy Harris' unsullied home, waiting for Martin, the proverbial hen-pecked husband. Joseph's head was bare. He held his scrap of a hat in his hand, and glanced with admiration about the polished, gleaming front room of this prosperous farmhouse. He had worked for Martin Harris since he was twelve years old, doing odd jobs, hard jobs. While Joseph was growing up, Martin often needed a young man with a strong back, and young Joseph would pitch in and give him his money's worth in labor. Harris was forty-four now, and having worked his own land of three hundred twenty acres all his life, found himself slowing down a little. He needed help more and more these days, despite Lucy's miserly insistence that they could still run the farm themselves.

Martin had married his first cousin. Lucy, a vivacious dark-haired woman who immediately took over the delicious task of shaping his life. Further, she felt a calling to direct the community affairs going on about her. She was vocal in the extreme, and backed by the affluence of their productive farm, she was sometimes respected, mostly feared, always flattered, and ofttimes hated in the burgeoning town of Palmyra, New York. The Erie Canal ran almost alongside the Harris farm. Shipping wheat, wool, maple syrup and other farm produce had become so easy since the canal opened that the Harris farm was one of the most lucrative in the area. They had four living children of their own, yet Martin had acquired a familial fondness for young Joseph, as well as genuine respect. Lucy had neither.

"Well, my gracious! Martin didn't tell me you'd be coming in the house after planting! Just stay put. I'll get your day's pay for you, but stay right there. I mopped the floors just this morning. Even Mr. Harris isn't allowed in my. . . rather, 'our' house in that condition."

"Mrs. Harris, ma'am, I didn't come for pay. I stopped by to relay a message from Martin. He's going to town and will be late for supper. He's out back, hitching up the wagon right now."

The near-sighted Lucy peered at him suspiciously. "Are you sure? He hasn't mentioned anything to me. Why's he going now?"

"Something about checking the barge for your cotton goods."

She stopped short. "Oh. That's right. I ordered two bolts of cloth, and they're taking much too long to arrive. People just can't keep on schedule these days. Well, then, tell Mr. Harris, I'll be waiting for him. Don't let him stay too long," her hard, shrill voice admonished.

Joseph smiled in good humor. "I won't. Why wouldn't he hurry home as fast as he could, Mrs. Harris? He's a devoted man."

Lucy muttered something to herself as she turned back to her spinning wheel. Joseph forgave himself the small, political lie and backed out of the door, bounded down the steps, and ran to close the barn door behind Martin's wagon already bumping down the lane.

The two men jolted along behind the mare in companionable silence, both observing with satisfaction the rolling hills of green crops and the two-story farmhouse disappearing behind them. Martin's bushy sideburns and graying beard were working and bobbing as he whistled a carefree little tune. His face was lightly creased with good-humor lines, his skin tanned from working outside in the sun. Martin had a reputation as an honest man, and his countenance reflected it. Today he glanced over at Joseph, reached behind him and pulled at his sack.

"Here's a partial bolt of oil cloth for your Ma," Martin said and winked with supreme good humor. The day's work was done, his wife was at home, and he could enjoy men's talk without her eternal chatter.

"Joseph, you're a fine young fellow. All you lack is a good start, a farm such as mine. If my son were like you, I'd be able to look at old age coming on with satisfaction, knowing he would keep up the place. That farm has been in the family for generations. Lucy and I inherited it together. Just seems like the good Lord don't keep a strict tally of blessings. There's your father with five strong, healthy sons and no secured property to leave them. And here I am working my big farm practically alone."

"I'm not sure farming is for me," Joseph mused. "I mean, I like it. I like the soil, growing things, the trading and bartering, and I don't have anything against hard work. I just wonder if I'm meant to be a farmer. From dawn to dusk, day after day, it is an all-consuming responsibility. There's so little time for reading, learning, or anything else."

Martin puckered his dry lips. "You have big dreams, boy. I guess I might, too, if I'd had the experiences with angels and such as you've had. If you don't farm, how are you gonna support your wife?"

Joseph stared off over the tree tops. "I honestly don't know, Martin. I'm just waiting for September, to see if the Lord will trust me with His holy record. I guess He means for me to do something with it, or He wouldn't have revealed it to me. I have dreams and have seen in vision a whole different people and way of living that once existed right here on this land. Why have I been given to know these things? I have seen ancient characters etched into thin golden leaves, or plates. It is all meaningless to me right now. I have scarcely enough education to read and write English."

"My guess is you're right," Martin mused. "Whatever you do with those golden plates, it will keep you too busy to farm. But you won't need to. You'll be rich. You said this golden record is ten inches thick. If . . . and I still say, 'if' it turns to be real gold, why that's enough to make you a wealthy man."

"It's not the metal that is valuable, Martin. It's the message. That's the real treasure. And besides, this treasure belongs to God, not to me or any other man. The angel has made that perfectly clear. When I thought once of profit for myself, he hid them from me."

The older man looked with amazement at the youth beside him in the buckboard. So much wealth almost right in his hands, and the boy prattled about ancient writing. Was he just the pretender other people thought he was? Martin shook his head. He couldn't reconcile that with the honest character he had known through the years.

"Well, boy, how's your wife getting on with the in-laws? And when are you gonna start a family? My missus has been curious as a cat. Asks me about it every time I see your folks."

Joseph, somewhat embarrassed, looked away. "I guess we'll have a family when the time is right. We are getting along just fine. Everyone likes Emma. She's a lady."

"Yup, guess that about says it." Martin's attention was diverted to the barges lining the banks of the recently completed Erie Canal, their lifeline to the world of commerce. He stood up in the buckboard.

"Hey, Wilson, I been waiting for a week on that harness," he called to a short, pot-bellied man who was just stepping off a heavily-ladened vessel. The long, flat barge was not designed for people, but for cargo, and this one sat low in the water, piled high with harnesses, furniture, boxes and boxes of ready made clothing, rifles, farming tools, and a livestock pen at one end. The noise at dockside was tremendous — cattle bawling, sheep bleating, barges creaking and groaning, and above all, the haggling and shouting of men over the high price of manufactured goods.

Joseph jumped down when the buckboard jolted to a final stop. "See you tomorrow, Martin. Thanks for the oilcloth. Ma will be grateful."

Harris waved absently. He was already engaged in the pleasurable business of getting the very best price he could on the fabric and tools his neighbor, Wilson, had purchased from the factories of New York City.

Just a block across the canal, Joseph continued striding along, heading for home, threading his way between groups of people chatting or negotiating. He was just past one small party, when he recognized a familiar, cultured voice.

"Mr. Banbury, this beautiful, hand-painted oilcloth, is certainly worth three bolts of your old navy blue fabric. But, then, you are the first I have spoken with. I'll take my chances with the other barge owners."

"Now, Missus Smith, I ain't in the market for no oilcloth. It's pretty enough. But tell me how much you're willing to pay for choice fabric like this."

Joseph stopped short, turned his back discreetly to the ongoing negotiation. A smile widened his lips as he listened to Emma haggling with the canal runner, consciously using her most refined tones.

"Your bolt has an uneven band of threads on this edge. Yet, its color is good, and the weave tight. Still, it is flawed, sir. Perhaps thirty-five cents."

"Thirty-five!" His hat slapped his knee. "Pardon me, ma'am, but that's . . .that's. . .purely insultin'! I can git fifty-five cents from any bargain-minded person in Palmyra."

"I regret that, sir. I'm sure you have other material of the exceptionally high quality that you deserve to sell at that high price. However, I am in the market for fabric of a more economical nature. Now, if you don't want to sell this bolt for a reasonable price, I shall look elsewhere. Good day."

The scruffy wharf-rat quickly jumped in front of her to block her departure. "Not so quick, missus. I can see you're a woman who knows her own mind. Well, I've got this 'un and another 'un too. It's a nice gray."

"Flaws?"

"A few. Can't hardly see 'em."

"Will they wash?"

"Pretty as you please."

"No fading?"

"Nope. It's Childman's factory. Just run a wrong thread or two, like this."

Joseph had moved to the doorway of a nearby storefront where he bent over, tying his shoelaces, listening in amusement to his wife barter with the hard-nosed barge owner. Well, he would never have an excuse to be poor so long as he was married to such a woman. In addition to her many other virtues, Emma would always get the best value for their money.

She was claiming her acquisition when Joseph straightened, turned, and with a wide, delighted smile proclaimed, "Why, Missus Smith, what a pleasure to observe the way you do business. May I help you with your booty?" Taking the two bolts of cloth easily under one arm, he took her other arm in his and escorted his wife down the uneven, clay streets of Palmyra. "A new dress is it?"

"For your mother and Sophronia. They are both patching their Sunday dresses."

"Ah, I see. And you, what about you?"

"I think there is enough material on the gray bolt for a vest, and the blue has so much, I should be able to get a skirt as well as Sophronia's dress."

Joseph listened for any tone of desire or envy. He watched her face for shadows of disappointment. There was nothing there to reproach him for their poverty. For a moment, a lump of tender pride choked him. "Never mind, Emma. It won't always be so. I may never be rich, but I swear I'll take care of you and at least provide you with a new dress occasionally."

"I'm not complaining," she responded mildly. Her hand closed briefly over his arm. "I am content, Joseph. I have enough of everything. God never promised excess."

"You are excess, my dear." His voice was low and intimate, meant only for her ears. "Just the sight and sound of you fills me with an excess of feeling that I can hardly contain.

"Joseph!" Her voice held a warning. "We are in public."

"I can compliment my wife in front of the whole world. Besides, who would blame me? Certainly not those who observed the splendid woman that married me."

Indeed, a few heads turned as the Smiths made their way to the edge of town. They were a tall couple — Joseph over six feet, and Emma stately slender, only a few inches shorter. He was fair, with a broad brow and dancing blue eyes, an imposing figure of a man, though dressed as a common farmhand. She was dark-haired, neatly coifed, with a mild, pleasant expression and warm olive skin. She enjoyed an outing into the commercial Palmyra with its crowded streets. After Harmony's quiet, rural personality, this was exciting. Emma rather enjoyed the challenge of business.

Before Joseph could ask his wife if she was up to walking the two miles home, a buckboard creaked, groaned, and bumped to a stop beside them. Hyrum jumped down.

"I see you got your cloth, Emma. Just lay it here on top of the barrel. And I see you picked up some scamp. I thought I was to be your escort. Oh well, if he'll act like a gentleman, I'll let him ride with us." Hyrum and Joseph embraced briefly, then helped Emma to the center place on the rough wagon seat.

"Two bolts of material for Mama's oilcloth? We'll send you to town to sell all our goods. The ladies will be in heaven when they get their hands on this."

"Did Martin pay you today, Joseph?" Hyrum inquired.

"Not until Saturday."

"Are we going to be able to make our commitment on the farm?"

"I think so. Money's coming in little by little. We've got another six months. God willing, it will be there by the time we need it."

"I hope so. Pa's worked too hard to lose that farm now."

"The Lord knows what is best for us in the long stretch. We shouldn't get our hearts set so much on things of the world."

Emma glanced from brother to brother on either side of her. Hyrum was perhaps the more polished, even, some might say, more handsome. But an inner power and confidence resided in Joseph. He was clearly dominant. His older brother looked to him on everything. He seemed to acknowledge Joseph's wisdom with no jealousy or resentment. Emma had ceased to be amazed that Joseph had assumed leadership of his family. Even Joseph Sr. deferred to him on most issues. Only William at sixteen seemed resentful of Joseph's privileged status. He often argued with his brother just for pleasure. Then, at other times, especially with outsiders, he would be Joseph's most loyal supporter.

Late spring evenings at the Smith home were much enjoyed. Days were longer now, and it was light until half past seven. The night air was languid and warm, so the family read the Bible out on the front porch, then sat gossiping and talking in the twilight. Emma was the hero of the day, having purchased an unheard of two bolts of cloth in exchange for Lucy's hand-painted oilcloth. Little Lucy sat close to Joseph and Emma, leaning against her sister-in-law.

"I think it's because Emma is so pretty," the little girl declared.

"I'm sure of it," Joseph agreed, smiling at his wife.

"Not a bit," Emma demurred. "It's because no one paints like your mother. Her oil cloths are popular all over the state."

"Where is Samuel tonight?" Father Smith asked.

"I think he is over at the debate society, listening to arguments about Southern slavery."

"Does he ever speak out?" his mother asked.

"Nope. Samuel isn't one for taking center stage. He likes to listen to the debaters, then make up his own mind."

"I notice you don't go anymore, Joseph." Mother Smith remarked over her needlework.

"I'm married now, Ma."

Without looking up, Emma remarked wryly, "A married man has all the controversy he can stand."

Joseph grinned and tightened his arm around her. "Yep, Emma keeps me on my toes, and I like it that way. Who wants to argue with some fool about politics or religion? My religion is all about me, right here on the front porch."

Sophronia looking out west all evening, now asked, "Are you getting anxious for September to come, Joseph?"

"'Anxious' is right. I'm praying every day and night to be worthy enough to receive the record. If not, my chance will be gone, and the angel will either hide up the plates again or give them to someone else."

"You'll get 'em, Joseph," little Lucy gazed up at her big brother. "No one is better than you."

"I don't think God would have shown them to you at all, son, if he hadn't meant for you to have them," said Joseph Sr. reassuringly.

"Why do you suppose our family was chosen for all this?" Sophronia pondered.

Mother Smith looked up in surprise. "Well, children," she admonished, "surely you know that you come from a long line of men who were valiant in testimony of the Lord, men who saw visions. Even the great religious philosopher, John Lathrop, was one of your forebears. God has been preparing our family for generations to receive this holy record. If it hadn't been Joseph, it would have been someone else from our family. It was destiny," she declared positively.

"Well, I think it will be exciting to actually have those golden plates in our home," Katherine mused. "I want to hear more stories about the ancient people who lived here. When Joseph translates them, we'll know all about their civilization. I wonder if they believed in Jesus, like we do. Were they wild, like Indians, or peaceful like us?"

"It depends on who you are talking to, Sis." Joseph commented. "If you're talking to the Indians, they probably think they are peace loving and we are warlike. Settlers haven't been any too kind to the red man, you know."

"Don't you think it will be exciting to translate those ancient writings?" Katherine persisted.

"Certainly. Especially since I can barely write a page of correct English myself. I'm sure Emma was sent to help me in whatever writing the Lord wants done."

He glanced fondly at his wife who was quietly embroidering a handkerchief for future sale. "The light is growing too dim for sewing," he gently took the cloth from her hands and laid it down. "Come, let's take a walk before dark."

So the small group broke up, Mother and Father Smith taking a turn about the grounds of their small farm, bolting doors and seeing that the animals were bedded down, Sophronia giving up with a sigh the vigil for her young Mr. Stoddard. Katherine took responsibility for getting little Lucy ready for bed.

In the deepening twilight, Joseph and Emma strolled along, sometimes stopping for a tender embrace, confident in the snug, dark covering of night for their sweet intimacy. It was a quiet, perfect evening. Stars glittered in the sky, moonlit shadows of trees spilled over the road, and impoverished or not, the couple felt richly in love.

"I wish it could always be so," Emma spoke longingly.

"Do you think it will not?"

"I sometimes have the feeling that a storm is about to break over our heads. Just the other day, Willard Chase asked if I had actually seen that golden record of yours, and his expression was one of pure avarice. If he thought I had it on my person, he would have torn me limb from limb."

"He better not touch you!" Joseph was vehement. "Neither he nor anyone else. People are greedy. They only think of the value of the gold. But they will never even see the golden plates. God doesn't intend to make them a circus sideshow."

"It will be difficult."

"Probably. At first."

"Are you nervous?"

"Yes. But God will help me. Why would He let me fail? He'll see that I get the job done. I just have to remember to stay in tune with the Spirit. And you will help me, too, won't you Emma?"

"I'll do everything I can, anything God wants me to do. I would welcome being your scribe."

"God has obviously provided me with 'the right person.' Tell me you're not sorry you married me."

"Silly," Emma murmured against his cheek. "I'll never be sorry. Life was terribly dull before you. No matter what happens, it will always be an adventure as long as I am with you."

Just how high the adventure Emma would not have guessed, until the night of September twenty-first. That afternoon, two visitors from the Colesville area came calling. Joseph Knight and Josiah Stowell rode into the Smith's side yard in Knight's fine buggy.

"Mrs. Smith," Josiah called out to Lucy, "it's a fine day I'll be wishing you!"

Mother Lucy and Katherine were hanging out the wash. A slight breeze chilled their hands as they handled the damp clothing. Lucy quickly dried her hands and went to welcome her guests. These two men had long been friends of the family, purchasing wheat and other grain, but she knew they were not here for that.

"Mr. Smith and Joseph are not home yet," Lucy volunteered. "They're working over at the Widow Duncan's. I'm expecting them back about supper time. Come in and set awhile. I can make you comfortable, with some cakes and buttermilk."

Joseph Knight had taken off his hat in her presence and murmured his appreciation. Josiah, always the more vocal of the two, waved a quick dismissal of the gracious offer. "You're kind, Mrs. Smith, too kind. But we can see you are engaged in your household chores, and we have business in town. You ladies go on about your business and so will we."

"Well, plan to come back and have supper with us," Lucy insisted. "We've been looking forward to your visit, especially my boy, Joseph."

"Only if it won't inconvenience you."

"Not at all," she peered with bright eyes from beneath her white cotton bonnet. "All the family will want to talk with you." She glanced quickly and furtively around, then stepped closer to the men. "Tomorrow is the day," Lucy spoke with excitement barely contained. "But then I 'spect you know that."

"Yes, ma'am, we do. That's precisely why we are here." Josiah was beaming with anticipation. "Maybe we can be of some help. But that is something the lad will have to tell us." He replaced his hat, climbed into the buggy beside Joseph Knight, and nodded a farewell. "We'll be back then to take supper with the family. Give our regards to the Mr. Smiths." Then they were on their way to Palmyra.

Supper that night was a noisy, talkative affair that went on until very late. No one noticed the food, what kind or how much. Even Emma's little cakes went unnoticed. The focus of the group was on weightier matters.

"Do we have a chest with a lock and key?" Joseph asked calmly, the only one of the group to seem unruffled.

His mother jumped up, nearly upsetting her plate. "Oh my, oh no! I meant to get that tool box of Alvin's from Hyrum last time I was over there, and I clean forgot it."

"Sit down, mother. There must be something. Pa, do you have any such chest?"

"No, don't believe I do. Used to have my own tool box, but I gave that to Abram Forsythe when his barn burned down." He rubbed his chin, musing. "First thing in the morning, we'll send Don Carlos over to Hyrum for his tool box."

"Can we see the plates before you lock them up?" Mr. Knight asked hesitantly.

Joseph shook his head. "Not unless the angel gives permission."

"Well, how is anybody gonna know they exist?" Stowell voiced the unspoken question on everyone's mind.

"Don't know. I guess you know enough or you wouldn't be here." Joseph finished his biscuit and syrup.

Lucy spoke with just the slightest reproving tone. "Mr. Stowell, Joseph doesn't lie. If he says they exist, they do."

Emma tried to change the subject, as the air charged with tension. "Mr. Knight, have you seen my father or mother by chance lately?"

Joseph Knight shook his head slightly, "Nope." But he was not sidetracked. "Joe," he suggested generously, "If there is anything we can do . . . anything at all . . . ."

"That's mighty kind, sir." Joseph looked first at Emma, then back to his house guests. "After all, I might have an eventful night." The tension in the room melted with his infectious smile.

"Just you be careful, Joseph" Lucy admonished. "I've seen some strange things lately."

"What strange things?" her husband's eyebrows went up.

"Gates unbarred that should have been latched. Footprints around the windows. I think people have been watching, that's what I think. And they are mighty bold."

"I'll be careful," her son promised and noticed that his wife's eyebrows had also gone up.

Samuel entered into the discussion. "Maybe I should lead our prowlers off in one direction while you go another," he proposed to Joseph. "That way, they'll follow me instead of you."

"They don't trouble me," Joseph was quite calm. "If God is with me, who can stand against me?"

"Well, I could 'stand' a little rest," Emma stood and began clearing the table. "Let's finish our work, ladies, and retire. It may be a long night."

The other women took their cue from Emma and began the cleaning up process, while the gentlemen rose and ambled out to the tiny parlor, feeling well fed and satisfied with the excitement of the adventure before them. When the keeping room was tidy and orderly again, the women joined the men for prayer, and one by one, they all went to their respective rooms for the night. On the way up the stairs, Joseph stopped with his hand on Emma's arm and held his finger to his lips. She stood stock still and silent. He hesitated for several minutes, then almost reluctantly resumed his climb.

"I thought I heard a horse whinny," he explained. "And it didn't sound like one of ours."

Emma responded, "Perhaps it was Mr. Knight's horse."

Joseph added, "And there were dogs barking during the prayer, down the road somewhere. I'd better check things," he said, quickly descending the steps and disappearing out the side door as Emma went up to their room.

As Joseph scouted the area around the farmhouse, he felt impressed to quietly hitch up Mr. Knight's horse and buggy. Hadn't Knight just said he was willing to do something to help. . . anything at all? The loan of this rig was just what was needed. Joseph stood by the buggy for a moment, listening for any foreign sound. There was nothing. Overhead a cool breeze stirred the tree tops. The stars seemed brighter. Was that one where Moroni lived, Joseph wondered of a winking, prominent star? He felt excitement and just a tinge of fear rising within. His body seemed to tingle with anticipation. He knew he couldn't sleep. Still, he went back in to Emma.

She was patiently waiting, having changed to a riding habit. The couple knelt beside their bed, and, holding hands, called upon the protection of their Heavenly Father. Joseph prayed with fervor, asking for forgiveness of his sins so that he could be worthy of receiving the sacred record. Emma wondered about the sins he mentioned. Did he mean the occasional practical joke he played on his brothers, or his light-minded, teasing conversations with her and others? Perhaps he didn't think he was sufficiently humble. He certainly knew he wasn't perfect. Whatever the sins, Emma did not know of them, but Joseph seemed very exercised, and prayed for cleansing of his soul. The boards were hard under Emma's knees, and when Joseph fell silent for several minutes still kneeling in silent prayer, she slipped from him into the comfort of the feather tick bed. Finally he raised his head and opened his eyes, staring almost vacantly at her.

Gently she called him back from his veiled world, "Come to bed, Joseph. God has heard your prayer. He knows your soul. What will be, will be."

His eyes focused on her face in the moonlit room, and he sighed. "You are blissfully practical, Emma. I need that. I am weary with waiting and wanting so long."

"Come," she whispered and turned back the covers. "Put your head on my heart. Rest while we can. Surely God will guide the events of this night."

Emma nodded off, but Joseph lay wrapped in memories of other nights, waiting for his angel, and grasping at impressions from another life, another time and place. Snatches of eternity came and went, intertwined with thoughts of an ancient people who had lived on the land before him. Voices whispered in his mind of prophets, temples, persecutions; voices he didn't know, but seemed somehow familiar. When his mind seemed bound tightly with the turmoil, he heard another voice. This one he knew.

"Joseph, my son. Trust in me and I shall give you peace."

It started at the crown of his head, spreading downward, bathing his body. Peace, yes! It was the gift of the quiet, precious voice that led him on. The message of his Savior was unmistakable. This peace would give him power over all adversity.

Just before midnight Joseph touched Emma's shoulder to awaken her, and they quickly rose, he finding his coat and she her cloak and bonnet. She sat on the edge of the bed, carefully tying her bonnet under her chin. Then quietly they started down the stairs and out the back door. Candlelight flickered on the parlor floor. Mother Lucy sat waiting and rocking. She whispered a farewell as they left.

Joseph went first, carefully. He slipped outside the door, stood very still, listening and watching for a moment, then reached inside and tugged Emma out. They covered the ground to the barn swiftly. Joseph Knight's bay gelding was still in the traces, hitched to the Knight buggy. Joseph helped Emma up, then led the horse-drawn rig out of the barn. Then, closing the door, he leapt up beside her. With a cluck to Old Thunder they were off, trotting down the dark road to the rounded hill where he would meet his destiny.

It was a clear moonlit night. The stars were unveiled as though all heaven watched this event. Emma clung tightly to Joseph's arm. Excitement was rising within her. Her sharp eyes swept the road constantly, along with the fields and bushes that lined it, but no unexpected movement startled either her or the horse. Joseph seemed intent on the dark hill looming up before them. Just on the western side of the base, he pulled the buggy off the road onto a grassy path that encircled the hill. Under cover of an overhanging tree, he reined the gelding in smartly. He stared up through the lacework pattern of tree limbs toward the top of the hill as if deep in thought. Then he nodded, a silent decision made, and carefully handed the reins to Emma.

"It's best that you wait for me. I'll return when I can. For now, just hold the horse quiet. You will be quite safe. Angels are round about, guarding and protecting us. Don't be afraid."

Emma's deep-set, dark eyes were wide with anticipation, but steady as always. "I'm not afraid," she assured him. "I'll spend my time in prayer for you. Don't worry about me."

Joseph kissed her quickly on the cheek, jumped out of the carriage, and was immediately lost from her view as he scrambled up the hillside. Emma pulled her cloak about her, adjusted her bonnet, and sat back in the shadows of the buggy. She closed her eyes to pray, but they would not stay closed. With exhilaration she gazed heavenward, expecting every moment to find the veil rent and to catch a glimpse of immortal beings. Soon her prayers turned to the future and their posterity. Beautiful children's faces floated through her mind, bright faces smiling and happy. She began to pray more fervently that she would be worthy of them and her husband. She felt her spirit being weighed in the balance.

After a time, Emma strained to catch the sound of Joseph's footsteps. Shadows intensified and seemed threatening. She now began to pray fervently for Joseph's return. Her earlier sense of foreboding came back triple fold and, with it, apprehension at every unfamiliar sound. Had something gone wrong? Still he did not come.

Joseph had hurried up the mountainside, more carelessly than he should have, hungering for his divine rendezvous. All the eternal forces which directed Joseph's life were coming together, engulfing his mind, and carrying him on the crest of a tidal wave. Heaven was waiting for him. Joseph had no sooner reached the hillside rock which covered the golden plates of Moroni than he sensed a battle of wills raging around him. The night had seemed translucent before, but now was blacker than black as it drew him into its depths. The breath was crushed from his chest; his body seemed heavy with an oppressive weight. He grasped his head and fell upon his face in the dirt, unnatural gravity pinning him to the ground. Agony wrenched a desperate cry from him, "O God, save me or I die!"

From the dark night which threatened him came a column of pure light. There was power in the light that spread over Joseph's head and dispelled the powers of evil which tormented him. On this unique occasion, Satan would have no sway.

Joseph shielded his eyes and looked up into the powerful light. Moroni's face was revealed in splendid radiance, and Joseph felt impelled to bow before his celestial tutor, but God's messenger would have none of it.

"Bow not to me, Joseph. Only God shall you worship. I came at His direction. Remove the stone lid and receive the ancient record."

Supercharged as he was with excitement, Joseph pried up the stone, rounded in the middle and forming the top of the stone box which held the golden plates shining with the angel's reflection. Hesitant, with schooled reverence for holy things, Joseph reached slowly into the box and withdrew "the voice from the dust." It was a history of Moroni's people. He had already tutored Joseph regarding their civilization and the prophets who had produced this record. The book was a stack of thin, golden sheets — hammered metal, almost as thin as foil. It was held together simply by three large rings on the side, and the individual metallic sheets made a rustling sound when Joseph fingered the edges. He was enthralled. For a moment he looked past the angel and everything else while he inspected the treasure with which he was finally being entrusted. Then, gazing further into the box, Joseph also drew forth something akin to old-fashioned eye glasses, inset with three-cornered crystal "seer stones." It was, as Moroni had previously informed him, what the Old Testament termed the Urim and Thummim. This curious device was to be his key in translating the strange, archaic writings on the plates. He held it up and gazed into the luminescent crystals. Then he peered into them. Moroni watched with some pleasure a young boy being groomed as a prophet.

"I can see nothing," Joseph said with disappointment.

"The time will come. Prepare yourself with fasting and with prayer. With a heart pure before God, you will see the translated words in the stones. Those words you must record, no more, no less."

"When shall I begin?"

"As soon as possible, but I warn you, attempts will be made to take these plates from you. You must protect them at all costs. Use every means to keep them safe. Allow no one to see them."

"Not even Emma?"

"No one, until God commands it. These are holy and sacred, not an object of curiosity."

". . . entrusted to me?" Joseph grew wary and a little doubtful of being capable of keeping them from all eyes, especially those of his family who could not wait to behold the amazing record of which he had told them so much.

"Yes, they are now yours for safekeeping until translation is completed. Then I shall receive them back. If you fail, you shall surely be cut off from God!"

Joseph was sitting back on his heels, looking up at the glorious man of light who spoke to him almost as an equal. Joseph felt anything but equal. He was experiencing feelings of trepidation and unworthiness. The "plowboy from Palmyra!" He had no education or earthly means that would mark a man of ability. Yet, as those thoughts fluttered through his mind, an amazing scene of his progenitors opened up to him, and he saw John Lathrop along with a great succession of noble spirits, men devoted to God, right down to himself. His bosom swelled with purpose. He would be that man God wanted for this time and place.

Joseph used his linen frock coat to wrap up the golden plates and Urim and Thummim into a bundle. He clasped it to his bosom. Replacing the stone that sealed the buried box, he turned and started down the hill. He had no idea how much time had passed, but a sense of danger now obsessed him, and he feared for his wife waiting below in the darkness.

Then suddenly before him, the carriage emerged unmoved, sheltered under the trees. His lady watched with anxious eyes for him. He fairly sprinted the last few yards to the buggy and collapsed with relief.

"You have it?" she whispered.

"Yes. This time I do! Emma, I am overcome." He gazed into her face, his eyes shining with amazement and gratitude. "I have waited years. Now people can't call me a liar. Here it is!" He held up his linen coat, still wrapped securely around the priceless treasure.

Almost hesitantly she asked, "May I . . . may I . . . see the plates?"

"Not now. They must remain covered. But you can feel them through my coat, and the translators also."

She reached out curiously to touch the objects wrapped in Joseph's coat, but scarcely had she done so than the forest came alive with harsh, crackling and the sounds of many feet scuffling.

Deep voices called out, "Smith, damn you, we'll take our share of that gold you found! It's ours as much as it is yours." Immediately, three burly, dark figures exploded from hiding places in the undergrowth.

Joseph sprang back away from the carriage and called to his wife, "Fly Emma. It's me they want. Take the carriage home." He smacked the horse's rump and she was off at a dead run.

When he slapped the horse, Old Thunder bolted, the carriage bouncing precariously over the rough, uneven ground. Emma jounced heavily on the bench, scarcely noticing the outraged cries of the men.

The carriage bounced and banged along the rutted road as the horse fairly flew over the ruts. The animal had been easily spooked all night, and now it was running headlong, not toward the Smith home, but exactly opposite. Joseph Knight's horse was heading for his home, dashing along the road south leading toward Pennsylvania.

It took Emma a good while to realize she was headed the wrong way. With wind in his face, an insecure hand on the reins, the animal seemed determined to gallop all the way to Colesville. But, after her first flush of fear, Emma calmed and gradually began to tighten the reins. A long, steady restraint began to have its effect, and eventually, the large bay responded by slowing to a walk, then puffing and blowing, he came to an uneasy halt. Carefully, Emma climbed out of the carriage and made her way alongside the horse.

"Easy, there," she cooed softly to the nervous creature. Her hand caressed the horse's hot, damp side, and she persisted in talking softly, stroking quietly, until she was at his head and had gained mastery. The horse still pawed the ground occasionally, but his head was down, seeming to hang in misery. She stood by quietly, letting him cool off. It was just coming daylight now. Ribbons of pink laced the dawning sky. Calm as she tried to be for the sake of the jittery animal, Emma was beset with emotions; fear for Joseph was uppermost, then concern for the Smith family. She and Joseph would be missed by now. What would everyone think?

She climbed back into the carriage and turned the rig around. She clucked softly, and Joseph Knight's horse began a slow, subdued pace back toward the Smith farmhouse.

Joseph struck out on foot through woods he knew like a rabbit knows his burrows. He zigzagged as he ran, leaping over fallen logs, branches and leaves tearing at his face, taking a circuitous route in hopes of losing his pursuers. But they came on, shouting obscenities as they ran, demanding the treasure, and calling him every vile name they could invent.

All the while the words kept running through his mind: this is just the beginning; this is just the beginning. Soon his heart was thumping savagely, and his breath was ragged, but his mind was clear, and he seemed to see through the jumble of vines and leaves and shadows as though they were transparent. His boyhood had been spent traversing these forests. Of course, so had the men who were now hotly chasing and calling him. They had been friends since childhood — friends of a sort. Many a warm summer's day they had all gone digging for gold or Indian treasure, and many artifacts had been found. Oh, nothing of great worth. Old man Robinson had found a brass pot and obtained a pretty price for it from a New York man. Most people believed there were curious artifacts buried in the nearby hillsides just waiting to make them rich, and digging was a favorite pastime of many local residents.

Joseph and his friends had agreed in their youth that they would share whatever treasure they found. He knew that now they would demand that he honor their childhood bargain. But this was something they could not share. In fact, he knew from Moroni's admonitions that he, himself, must not expect to profit from these golden plates which he now hugged against his chest. This was a treasure beyond price — a heavenly treasure! Others would not understand. The prospect of riches would overpower any sense of holy mission. That was one powerful reason he could not show them to others, even his benefactors and friends, Martin, the Knights, the Stowells, and no, not even his own family. The glitter of gold had driven many a man to unholy acts.

Joseph ran until he was breathless, dodging low branches in the dark, stumbling over logs, making far too much noise for someone trying to escape pursuit. At first, the three men made even more noise than he as they called angrily out for him to halt. Then, as that didn't work, they changed their tone and became conciliatory. He heard them in the distance calling, "Don't worry, Joe, we just want to see what you've got. We're all friends here, been friends a long time. Come back. Let's talk!"

Joseph just worked his way deeper and deeper into the woods. The golden record was like hot knives plunged into his chest. Sharp edges bit into his flesh, and his arms had turned to stone, frozen into a locked position protecting the treasure. His breath was coming now in short gasps, but he couldn't stop. Even though the voices had died off, he correctly supposed that the men were still pursuing him. And there were, at least, three of them. They could spread out, and when daylight came, track him easily. He had taken no care to cover his trail. He had to hide the plates. Even coming out of the woods closest to the house, they could see him and perhaps overtake him before he reached safety. Safety! What was that? His home would not be safe if they were determined to take the plates. Short of a musket, even he and his brothers could not hold off a horde of townsfolk.

Right now it would be best to hide the plates until the ruckus died down and he could recover them quietly. But where? Joseph began looking for a safe place. Nothing seemed likely. And he hadn't time to dig a hole for burying. He had stopped beside an old tree with its trunk partially dug out, when he heard a distinct rustling behind him. No animal would make such a sound. Joseph dropped to his belly. As he did, he spied a hollow log with its opening covered by bushes. Like a snake, he wiggled toward that log, stuffed the treasure into the depths of the old trunk, and then feet first, pushed his own body in afterward. Within minutes, the crunch of boots came closer, closer, until Sam Lawrence actually tripped over the log that held his quarry.

"Judas Priest!" he heard Sam swear as he fell heavily on one knee.

Then the other two griped, "Shut up! You make more noise than a bear."

"Aw, it don't matter no how. Smith's probably on the other side by now, or asleep in his bed. We ain't gonna find him, I tell you. We had him there for a minute, but that horse and buggy got in the way."

Willard Chase's voice grew harder. "You don't think he put that gold into his wife's buggy? Whyn't we foller her? Least one of us. He's probably just leading us around so she can git away with the treasure."

"You think he's really got something this time?" Joseph recognized the voice of George Proper.

"He sure as fire was a-holdin' onto something coming down that hill. I'll break every bone in his worthless body if I can just git my hands on him."

"Well, I think he put it in the buggy. I'm for going to Smith's place and demanding our share. Old man Smith'll hear us. He knows we had a pact. He'll be fair even if his son ain't."

"It's near 'bout light now. I say we've lost him. We'll find out if he's really got gold treasure, and we'll git our share one way or another. I'm going on home, boy." Sam had started off to his right, heading for the open fields.

Joseph became aware of his own heartbeat in the silence of the woods. The other two men seemed to stay put for a long time. If he should cough — if he should even breathe too loudly, they would hear him. Every nerve was on edge, stretched like a wire to its breaking point. Joseph lay at their very feet, partly concealed by the log and partly by the thick bushes, and they, in their frustration, cursed him for a dog. Suddenly, a high shrill sound scared him almost senseless. A magpie screeched his protest against the invaders, and Willard finally laughed and moved also in the direction Sam had taken.

"Reckon I will, too. Let's meet tomorrow night at your place. We'll see to Joe Smith and his precious treasure."

Joseph remained still, hardly breathing, as the sound of boots and rustling leaves diminished. Long after all noise had died away, he lay as still as death. Cramped and cold, he lay immobile in the darkness. Ants trickled through his mop of hair and down his shirt collar. Still he lay quietly, waiting for any brush of leaves that might signal a return of the men. But the woods were silent.

After what seemed an eternity, Joseph slowly stretched his neck like a turtle. He looked in every direction, blinking against the dirt and dust that clung to his eyebrows. No one else was there. Filtered light dimly streaked through the dense trees. It was morning. Emma would be worried sick. Joseph pried his body from the rough prison where he had been cramped for almost two hours. Once free, he peered down into the darkness of the log. Far down there he could make out the bundle. He gathered an armful of leaves and stuffed them as far into the log as his arm would reach. Joseph brushed off his pants and shirt, torn and dirty by this time, and kneeling down, offered a quick, but heartfelt, thanks to God and the guardian angel who watched over him. Then, leaving the precious golden plates hidden in a hollow log in the woods, he started for home.

Joseph Knight had awakened to the smell of Mother Smith's breakfast cooking. His toes were cold, sticking out of the blankets, but his belly was warm — and hungry! Shivering in the cool morning air, he reached for the water pitcher and doused his face with the cold liquid to thoroughly awaken himself. Brrrr. He shook his head, and droplets of water sprang from his beard and mustache. He dried his face and beard with the towel, wiped quickly about his neck and under his arms, then struggled into his pants and shirt.

Well, it was September 22! What had young Joseph done the night before? Knight had been hearing for two years about gold plates.

He had heard enough. Now he wanted to see them — if they existed as Joseph said they did!

He started down the stairs. There was Lucy sweeping out her kitchen in the early morning light. "Good morning, missus. Have you seen your son this morning?"

She shook her head no. She seemed to be lost in thought. He could see there was no conversation forthcoming from the usually talkative Lucy, so he started out the side door to the barn to make ready his horse and buggy. The interior of the barn was dim, but he could see that his rig was gone. What the devil? Knight turned and bustled back to the farmhouse.

"Missus Smith, Missus Smith," he called, poking his head into the parlor, then the keeping room where the table was already set for breakfast. "My rig is gone! My horse, my buggy, both gone. Where's Joseph?"

"Shh," Lucy Mack tried to quiet him down. "Mr. Knight, your rig is safe enough. I'm sure there's an easy answer. Everyone will be down soon. Just sit yourself right here, and I'll serve up some breakfast." Her manner was soothing, but he noticed that once or twice she glanced out the window, her expression fixed and set.

Joseph Knight still grumbled when Stowell descended the staircase, his nose guiding him to the aroma of hot breakfast. After greetings were exchanged and both men were served a heaping portion of eggs, ham and biscuits with gravy, Knight returned to his personal concerns.

"Well, that is mighty fine cooking, Missus Smith. But I'll be needing my horse and buggy. We are going in to Palmyra this morning."

"And you shall have it. Another helping of ham, Mr. Knight?"

He considered for a moment, then answered in the affirmative. "After all, we do have a long day of business." Several more minutes passed as the Smith children joined them and he finished up his third helping of breakfast.

"I can't wait any longer," Knight said, pushing back from the table. "I must start off even if Joseph isn't here. Are you ready to go with me, Josiah?" Knight inquired.

"Not until I've seen Joseph. I want to know if he got the plates."

"Well, I suppose he must have been disappointed again, or he'd be here, bearing them off like a treasure."

"Perhaps. Perhaps not." Stowell answered him tersely.

"Mr. Knight, my son, William, is probably down in the lower pasture rounding up your horse. If you would like to pay your respects to my husband, I'm sure your rig will be ready soon. Mr. Smith is out working in the fruit cellar." Lucy spoke through tight lips.

"All right, I shall take a minute to talk with Mr. Smith, but I hope my rig will be ready when I return." With that he pushed back from the table. He was gone out only a few minutes, when the front door opened, and Lucy and Josiah Stowell saw Joseph and Emma come in, quite out of breath, and hurry up the stairs. They looked at each other expectantly. Lucy strained to look up the staircase. Then she turned back beaming affirmatively at Josiah. His bushy eyebrows raised in question and she simply nodded.

Joseph stripped off his shirt and reached for Emma. They came together locked in a silent embrace for several minutes, she pressing her cheek against his shoulder, and he resting his chin on her head. He was weary. So very weary. She was conscious only of relief at having found him coming out of the woods and bringing him safely home.

"Will they be safe in the woods?" she wondered. A decaying tree seemed such an unlikely hiding place.

"Safe enough," replied Joseph. "The animals aren't going to bother them. Only greedy men are a threat, and who would think to look in an old hollow log? Besides, I need a locked chest to keep them in before I bring them home. Everyone is going to want to see them, and I can't let them. It's forbidden for now."

"That's going to be hard, Joseph."

"I know."

After a few minutes, he released his wife, wishing with all his might that he could simply throw himself in bed and go to sleep resting on her shoulder. But he had to do his duty and report to his parents and house guests on the happenings of the night. Emma put away her cloak and bonnet, straightened and repinned her hair. Joseph changed his clothing and washed his face. Together they went downstairs as if nothing of interest had happened during the night.

Lucy could scarcely contain herself as Joseph and Emma finished breakfast. Her lively eyes were fastened on her son. Emma ate quietly, looking down at her plate through most of the meal. Finally, Josiah started to ask about the plates, but Lucy stopped him with a hand on his sleeve.

"Let them eat, Mr. Stowell."

"Of course, of course."

Joseph was just finishing when the door opened. Father Smith and Joseph Knight came into the kitchen. They had located the missing horse and buggy on the west side of the farmhouse, and Knight was satisfied at last.

"Ah, here you are," Knight hailed Joseph. "Good. I see you've tied my rig out front for me. It's time I was headed into town, but I . . . we," as he indicated Josiah with a wave of the hand, "we're anxious to hear your report."

Joseph was uncharacteristically quiet for a moment, still gathering his thoughts.

"Well! What came of it, boy?" Knight prodded. "Out with it. Let's hear your tale!"

Joseph rose, a merry twinkle in his eye, and clapped a hand on Knight's shoulder. He glanced back at his family as he guided his friend into the parlor.

"Well, I'm disappointed," he started. "I'm greatly disappointed." He paused as he saw his friend's countenance fall. Then he couldn't conceal a smile and the twinkle in his eyes. "It's ten times better than I expected."

Knight looked up expectantly, cautiously. "Really?"

"Yes, really! Ten times at least."

"What? What is ten times better?" Knight became agitated and impatient with Joseph's teasing.

"Why the plates, of course."

"You got them, then?"

"Yes, and everything that came with them — the Urim and Thummim, and the golden breastplate."

The family had gathered by that time into the doorway and the parlor. All but Emma. She stayed seated at the table, her head resting in her hands. This was not fun to her. It was sobering and serious. Joseph could have been murdered for the gold plates last night, and she was almost thrown out of a run-away carriage.

"Yes, I got them. After four years of preparation, the angel delivered them up to my keeping."

"Where are they?" queried Lucy.

"I put them away for safe keeping. I need to lock them in a chest. These objects are not to be displayed like a common sideshow. They belong to God, and if they are to be kept safe, they must be kept secret. People will try to take them for the value of the gold alone. We'll have to be very careful. Sophronia, Samuel, William, Katharine, Don Carlos, and little Lucy, you mustn't tell your friends about this. I don't want the town to know, or we will have neighbors pounding on our door. Do you understand? They are not to be seen by anyone but me."

"We understand, Joseph," his father affirmed. "But can't your family see them?"

After a few seconds, Joseph slowly shook his head. "No. I was disobedient the first time, but I intend to be faithful now. I have been forbidden to show them to anyone."

William snorted and blurted out, "Then how do we know they are real?"

Joseph fixed him with a glance of his blue eyes. "Trust me, William."

Little Lucy tugged at his shirt, looking up into her brother's eyes with innocence. "I trust you, Joseph. And I will do what God wants me to do."

Joseph picked her up, swinging her easily into his arms. He kissed her forehead. "That's my girl. I want to do what God says, too. In fact, I'll only be able to have them if I do what He tells me." He turned back to William. "It is harder than you know, being the only one who can see them. But it has to be this way for now."

His mother said, "Joseph, if you need a case, you should go to Willard Chase. He makes cabinets, furniture and such. He can make you a small chest."

Joseph grimaced, remembering the hard edge in Willard's voice as he hunted Joseph in the woods.

Joseph Sr. mused, "How shall we pay him, Lucy? There isn't a cent in the house."

Josiah spoke up. "Joe, yesterday I overheard Sam Lawrence say he needed help repairing his barn."

Discreetly Joseph said, "Father, it's best I not stir Willard's imagination right now. God will provide what we need, when we need it. It's necessary that we recover the plates soon. They might be discovered where I hid them. But I need a box to put them in. It will have to be quite a sturdy box. The metal is quite heavy."

Joseph Sr. sat across the table from his son while Lucy put a glass of buttermilk in front of each man. Suddenly a smile broke the gloom that wreathed his face.

"Alvin's tool box! In all the excitement I plumb forgot about it. Hyrum has it now. I believe he'll be glad to lend it to you. I'll send Don Carlos across the fields to talk to him."

"Good, send him now," said Joseph. "While he fetches the box, I'll go for the plates." He drained the last swallow and stood up.

"Be careful, son."

"I am. I can't afford to be anything but careful. That's my life from now on."

Don Carlos was more than happy to escape his chore of pulling weeds. Now he had a really important assignment.

"Yes sir," the boy almost saluted when his father gave him the charge. He bolted from the doorway and was soon tearing across the field.

Hyrum was at home. In fact, he and Jerusha had company — Jerusha's sister. They were all just sitting down to eat when Don Carlos burst upon the scene. He was flushed and out of breath.

Hyrum, ever the gentleman, reproved his little brother mildly, "Excuse yourself, Carlos. We have guests today and were just about to say grace over Jerusha's fine meal."

"Excuse me." The boy was breathless and anxiously turned his cap about in his hands. "Hyrum, Joseph needs . . ." he followed quickly.

"It can wait until we say grace," his brother interrupted. With that the little party bowed their heads, and Hyrum offered a prayer on the food. Don Carlos fidgeted, standing first on one foot, then another. When grace was properly done, the boy began again.

"Hyrum, we need . . . "

"Would you like a plate?" Jerusha asked him.

"Thank you. Not. . . not this time. I'm here about other *plates*!"

Now he had caught his older brother's attention. Hyrum turned to him and put down his fork. "What does Joseph need?"

"He needs a box." Finally Don Carlos had blurted out his important message.

Still it didn't quite register with Hyrum. He stared blankly. "A box? What box? How big a box?"

"Alvin's tool b-b-box," the boy stammered in excitement. Hyrum stood up, beginning to sense something important. "It must be big enough to hold the . . . ." Don Carlos looked sideways at Jerusha and her sister, both of whom were staring at him, rather amazed at this interruption.

"The what?" Hyrum prompted.

"You know. Joseph's bringing something home!"

Light dawned on Hyrum's face. Joseph had been to the hill last night. He had been successful. Joseph had the record! The tall man exploded into action, jostling the table as he shoved his chair back and rushed into the bedroom. Kneeling beside the bed, he probed beneath it for the locked wooden chest which his deceased brother, Alvin, had made for architectural tools. He dragged it out, turned it upside down, and emptied it of his own things. Then he wiped it out with his handkerchief. Don Carlos was waiting impatiently at his side.

"Hurry, "the boy urged. "Joseph is bringing home the record and needs this chest to put it in."

"What? Are they not home now?"

"No, he had to hide them somewhere. We can't see them until God says so."

Hyrum paused before leaving his wife's breakfast party. "Is that so? I had hoped to see them myself. Well, come on Don Carlos, I'll go with you back home."

Jerusha appeared in the doorway. She glanced at the week old baby still sleeping soundly in the cradle despite the tumult. He could see she was disappointed.

"I'm sorry, dear," Hyrum reached for her hand. "Have a nice visit with your sister. Joseph needs this chest," and he followed Don Carlos out.

"Is it so important?" she asked, trying not to be petulant.

"Yes, I rather think it is."

"Is he given to flying off on tangents like this?" Jerusha's sister asked after the men rushed off.

"I'm still trying to understand men," Jerusha shook her head. "Usually *nothing* is more important than his breakfast."

The two eager brothers started off at a brisk pace across the field, while the women sat back down to their meal. A few yards down the road, Don Carlos broke into a run again, and Hyrum followed suit, his longer legs soon out-distancing his little brother. As he ran, excitement built up until he was fairly bursting to see his brother, Joseph, and hear his report from his own lips.

The woods were as quiet as a cathedral when Joseph came to the old hollow log. It was covered with smaller pieces of bark and a heavy branch which he had carefully placed over it. He had scattered leaves about the place so that not a trace of human footsteps could be seen. He didn't uncover anything right away. He sat instead on the thick part of the branch, his head down as if in deep thought. Actually he was listening for any foreign sound, any bird call, any rustle of dead leaves. There was nothing. So after several minutes, Joseph hoisted the heavy branch cover, moved it aside just a few feet and turned over the birch log. After cutting away some of the bark, he easily reached the treasure within. Enlarging the hole he had made, he reached inside, grasped the precious record still wrapped in his linen frock coat, and wrested it from its hiding place.

He re-wrapped the plates more securely. The thin, gold leaves rustled slightly, and an errant ray of sun pierced the branches high above. It touched the ancient record, and Joseph sat for a minute just marveling over the peculiar treasure in his possession. Then fierce determination moved him, and he secured the lustrous object, tucked it under his arm, and started from the woods.

At first, he thought to take the road. It would be faster going. He actually walked a few hundred yards in the hard rutted path, then decided he would be easy prey for any assailant. So he trekked back into the thicket. Picking out the straightest crooked way through the trees, he hurried on. Just as he was jumping over a fallen log, a dark figure stood up. Instinctively Joseph struck out with his free arm, knocking down a pistol and leaving his arm bruised and sore. He didn't recognize the assailant.

Fear spurred him on. Not fear for himself. He was afraid for the holy charge he had been given. He might be killed, but no one would touch the plates God had entrusted to him. A few hundred yards on, another man stepped out from behind a tree and blocked his way, diving for his legs. Joseph swerved and cried out. The smaller man looked up, and Joseph's hammer fist connected with his grisly chin. *Two down*, Joseph thought, and he was ready for another. The third attack came just as he was clearing the woods and sprinting toward the Smith farmhouse.

This time the assailant had soot smeared over his cheekbones and forehead. Still, something was familiar about him. He had a scar where the end of his eyebrow should have been. Joseph had seen him on the dock several times when he had gone with Martin. Joseph glimpsed a pistol being drawn from the man's belt. An arm was coming up. In a moment he would feel the shot in his shoulder. Reaction was instantaneous. He grasped the heavy bundle under his arm with both hands-and swung! The pistol flew! A cry of pain came from the taller, skinny man. Joseph swung again and connected, burying the plates in the man's midriff, who folded like a fan and dropped to his knees. Joseph felt a sharp pain travel up his arm, but didn't stop to wonder what it was. He was on the run, even while he heard a gagging sound behind him as his assailant hunched over on the ground, groaning from the blow.

Joseph threw himself down by the corner of the house, out of breath and speechless. Lucy peered out the door and then rushed to him when she saw his state of exhaustion. His father heard the commotion and left his pitchfork in the hay, hurrying to Joseph's side. He gasped out his story then asked for Hyrum.

"Has he brought the box?"

"He's inside with it. Have you got it?" Joseph Sr. asked, puzzled.

Joseph's elbow rested on his precious bundle. "Here," he said tersely.

"Where?"

A little impatiently Joseph replied, "Right here, father. In my frock coat." Straightening up, he insisted. "I need that chest now."

"Hyrum!" Lucy called, and her son thrust open the side door. Joseph jumped to his feet, stepped up on the porch, and embraced his brother. Hyrum clapped his brother's back several times, drew back and looked Joseph full in the face. Hyrum's eyes filled with moisture, and he embraced his brother again, too full of emotion to speak.

Emma had come downstairs and stood in the doorway watching this impassioned encounter. She knew of the special bond between Joseph and Hyrum, but had never seen it so clearly displayed. Everyone in the Smith family was close, but only Hyrum entered that unique place of trust and love, similar to hers, with Joseph.

"Tell me," Hyrum finally choked out. "Is it true?"

"Yes, I have them," Joseph spoke triumphantly. "The angel delivered them to me along with an ancient breastplate — I rather think it might have been his own — and the Urim and Thummim, interpreters spoken of in the Bible. It's an amazing instrument! With it I can see so much, almost anything I ask. I have the spectacles right in my pocket. The record is here in my frock coat." He patted his bundle possessively.

"When will we be able to see them, Joseph?" Hyrum's excitement was fairly tangible.

"The glasses you can inspect." He looked back over his shoulder, "The breastplate . . . I'm not sure. I need to ask. But you can touch it, even if it must be covered by a cloth."

"What of the plates?"

"Moroni said that only I am to see and handle them until they are translated. Then God may call other witnesses." He embraced Hyrum again. He tried to speak but his voice broke. He cleared it and said, "If permissible, you will be one of those witnesses." The men continued to hold each other, patting the other's back, until they recovered their emotions. Emma stood still by the door watching her husband. He was sweaty and disheveled, but happy.

"I brought the chest, Alvin's chest. It's in on the kitchen table."

"Good," Joseph responded. "Now I'll have a place for the plates. We are all going to have to watch and take care. They mustn't fall into the wrong hands. I was chased last night. Someone tried to take them from me. I finally had to hide them in the woods until I could safely retrieve them. I'm not sure you'd call my experience just now 'safe,' but I got them. Now the question is where else to hide them."

Hyrum was silent a moment. "You're in for trouble, Joseph. A lot of trouble," he wisely predicted.

"I know," his brother was equally solemn. "I'm almost sorry I dragged Emma and the rest of you into this."

His wife raised her eyebrows and fixed him with a look. "I have not been dragged into anything, and I'm not likely to ever be. I am here of my own free will. Wild horses could not tear me from your side. I shall see it all through with you."

140

Joseph hooked his arm over Hyrum's shoulder. They walked to Emma. He looked at each of them. "We will see it through together, for I could not bear the burden without both of you."

Joseph took his brother Alvin's toolbox, and carrying it under one arm, the plates under the other, he climbed the stairs to his bedroom. The Smith family waited below. William was impatient with the restlessness of a sixteen-year-old. Samuel, just three years Joseph's junior, his young face all bones and angles, sat in the corner quietly contemplating the strange position of his family. To have a golden treasure in their possession and yet be dirt poor just didn't make sense. Emma quietly went about dinner preparations. She knew her husband would bring the box down soon. She hoped there wouldn't be more trouble. She sensed a skeptical spirit about William, as he hovered there in the keeping room, leaning first on one chair, then another, annoying his sisters who were trying to be calm, despite the day's unusual events.

After a short time, they heard Joseph's footsteps coming down the stairs. He held the box out first to his father. Joseph Sr. hefted the familiar wooden chest his eldest son had made. It was heavy and it was locked. He stared at it as though his eyes could penetrate the wood. All at once tears welled up, and he looked up at his young namesake. Their eyes met and held as his son began to glow with an inner radiance. Then his father passed the box to Lucy. She simply burst into tears the moment she hefted it. Hyrum took the object reverently, smoothing the wooden top with his fingers as if to caress the precious object within. He would have passed it on to Sophronia, but William intervened and impulsively reached for it. He hefted it, feeling the weight. He jiggled it side to side. The objects inside barely moved. It seemed to be a perfect fit. He started to pass it on, disappointed in not being able to see what was within. Then something overcame him. His face flushed, and with a shamed look, he went to Joseph and embraced him, too choked up to speak. Samuel took the box next, held it, contemplated its weight and what was in it, then took it to the rest of the family who were seated at the table. Thus the golden plates came to the Smith family, unseen by their mortal eyes, but spiritually discerned.

Emma was the last to hold the box. She had no doubt what it contained. Her long fingers stroked the wood. A deep sigh of satisfaction tinged with some unknown sadness escaped her. Joseph heard it and thought she was just tired. But that sigh foreshadowed the coming storm.

After a time, Joseph held up his hand and said, "Father, I have to get you to put my thumb back in place. I think it is dislocated. It's been throbbing since I hit that last thief with the plates."

His thumb had swollen twice its size and was purple and blue. Emma started to jump up, but deferred to his father's attentions. She felt Joseph's pain shoot through her own body. Whatever he suffered, she suffered, and it would always be so.

Chapter Six

Pursuing the Plates

mma was tired, quite exhausted. She went upstairs, pleading a headache, and lay down to rest. In fact, Emma was with child. She had been feeling sick to her stomach every morning for a month, but hadn't yet told Joseph. At first she had thought she was just getting sick. She was always tired and often wanted to give in to the need to rest. Her body seemed to resist getting out of their warm bed, and the chilly boards of their bedroom offended her bare feet. One morning she had forced down a breakfast of hot cereal, then promptly ran outside and retched.

Sophronia had seen her sickness.

"Are you ill, Emma?"

"No, I don't think so, though my stomach has been queasy of late. Possibly a touch of the ague going around."

"No one here has it," her sister-in-law frowned. "Do you need more rest? I can do the wash today. Katherine will help me."

Her offer was tempting. Emma smoothed her hair, dried her mouth on her apron and sighed. "Why, thank you, Sophronia. You are a thoughtful sister, but I am all right. Actually, since my stomach cleared, I feel better. I'll just eat less."

Mother Smith was not fooled. When Sophronia told her about the incident, Lucy's bright eyes narrowed, her mouth pursed, and she predicted, "It's a baby, I'll warrant."

The women watched over Emma for the next several days. Each morning she looked pale. She hardly ate anything, and frequently wiped her brow as she leaned on a chair. Lucy finally asked her daughter-in-law, "Does Joseph know?"

"Know what, Mother Smith?"

"That you're expecting?"

Emma looked up from her stitchery in surprise. "You don't think I'm . . . ?"

"Sure as a rainstorm after a yellow moon."

Emma stared at her, dumbfounded.

"How many times have you lost your meal?"

"Four or five, "Emma admitted.

"Tired in the morning?"

"Yes, always."

"Queasy stomach?"

"Yes."

"How long?"

"About a month."

Lucy sat back, satisfied. "Well, I'd say you're about two months gone then."

"Two months?"

"Yep. My grandbaby'll be born about June, I reckon."

Emma sat staring down at her stitchery. Soon the needle began to move and a little smile curved her lips. In a few minutes the needle began to move even faster.

Lucy looked over at the stockings in Emma's lap and said, "We'd best be making you a baby quilt."

This time when Emma looked up, her eyes were shining. "Yes, and maybe a little dress from that material we bought last August." The two women sat there smiling at each other.

That night, Emma called Joseph outside after evening prayers. She wanted to be alone with her husband. It was a pale moon that lit their path as they ambled down the road.

"You've been awfully quiet lately," Joseph probed gently. He put his arm about his wife's shoulder and pulled her closer as they walked.

"I haven't been feeling well."

"I noticed you hardly eat anything. Is my Emma-rose getting sick?"

"Not exactly sick, but full." He couldn't see the curve of her lips in the shadows of her bonnet.

"Full! How can that be? There isn't a spare ounce of fat on you."

"I'll soon be plump enough."

"Sure, and I'll soon be president."

"My prophecy will be fulfilled sooner than yours."

"What?" Joseph peered into the face in the bonnet, then turned it up to the lucent moonlight. Emma's eyes were sparkling and she was all smiles.

"You are hiding something. What is it?" he probed.

"Take out your mystic spectacles, Mr. Smith." She was playing the coquette now. "They might reveal your wife's secret."

"I doubt it. Only Emma reveals her heart. Will you tell me for a kiss?"

She shook her head no.

"Two kisses? No? More? I can arrange more." And he kissed her tenderly, then passionately, until she became light-headed.

"Joseph," she started to warn him off. But he would not be denied. Now he held her captive, securely in his arms. "Joseph, wait. Please."

"What?" he challenged, "you don't like my kisses now? So soon regretful that you're a married woman?"

"No, that's not it. Something is coming between us."

"And that is?"

"My growing belly."

He drew back puzzled. Emma laughed and touched his full, rich lips with her fingertips. "It will expand at a marvelous rate, Joseph, for it carries our child."

He drew in his breath and held it as he stared at her in wonder. "Our child? Emma, is it true? You don't look like you're expecting. Are you sure? When will it come?"

"June," she answered gently.

"How do you feel? Shouldn't you be resting more? I can do your chores."

"Shh," she kissed his lips now to stop the flood of questions. "Just hold me and tell me you are as happy as I am."

Joseph's arms enfolded her to his chest, as they stood rocking slightly in the moonlight. "Ah," his breath escaped him in a contented sigh. "Yes, very happy. And eternally grateful for you. Your precious body will bring us children. My love, my sweet, sweet love! I can hardly wait to start our family."

He kissed her forehead, her cheeks, her neck and whispered, "I love you," with each tender caress.

Emma looked up into the starry night and smiled fondly. He was such a husband!

A week later, Emma sat on a low stool in the front parlor, almost buried under a pile of rags. Tattered fabric was concocted into a long, serpentine braid which wrapped around her lap and legs. The new rug she was making would be welcome on the cold floor of their bedroom this winter. Her reflections ran to her mother's home and the comforts she had left behind. She was lost in thoughts of her father and the estrangement between them. Joseph had gone to collect a few belongings she had requested, but Isaac had not even sent a note to enquire after her. She knew her father well enough to understand that his pride would not allow him to reach out to her. Still, she could dream of a warm, bear hug and the feeling of safety when he was near.

At precisely the moment she could almost feel the rough tickle of Issac's beard on her cheek, her father-in-law thrust back the door and called out for his wife. "Lucy! That Willard Chase and his meddling sister, Sally, won't rest until they find the golden plates! I just came from Lawrence's, and they had fifteen men all swarmin' around, fit to be tied that they weren't able to git those plates last time. Now they've called on that Chase girl with her peep stone. She says she can spy out those plates clear as day. How are we gonna protect 'em from the likes of her? I wish Joseph hadn't gone over to Macedon to dig that well."

Before he could finish, Emma was winding up the braid and stuffing it into the pillowcase where she kept her supplies. Lucy's hands were red up to her elbows. She had apples in a barrel of water, and she was washing them, preparing them for applesauce. "Sally Chase! What's she doing sticking her nose into our business? None of her affair, I say!"

"Emma, are the plates safe?" Joseph Sr. turned to her.

She went right on gathering up her rags. Her answer was terse. "I don't know."

"Has Joseph moved them?"

"I cannot tell."

"Well, Sally seems to think she knows where they are. How are we gonna help Joseph protect them? Lucy, I want my rifle."

"Father Smith, I can promise you Sally will not find them. No one will be allowed to take them. If we do our best, the powers of hell will not prevail. But Joseph must be warned. Do you have a horse I can ride to Macedon?"

Lucy was alarmed. "Macedon! You can't ride a horse that far. You're expecting!"

Joseph, Sr. took the pillow case from her arms. "Wait until William or Samuel comes home. They can go for Joseph. Lucy's right, you shouldn't be riding a horse. The jouncing is bad for you in your condition."

Emma was starting upstairs for a cloak. "We can't wait. We can't take the chance. Father Smith, remember that stray horse down in the pasture. Where is it?"

He called up the stairs after her. "But we don't even know if its well-broke. It's just got a green hickory withe for a bridle."

"It'll be fine. *I'll* be fine. I'm going for Joseph."

Lucy's anxious face appeared at her husband's shoulder. "Emma, no!"

Emma's face was almost lost in the hood of her cloak, but they could see the determined set of her lips as she swept down the stairs.

"Emma, you must think of your baby," Lucy admonished.

"We must think of God's work. What else can we do, stand in their way and bar the door? That won't keep them out. I have to get Joseph."

Lucy turned to appeal to her husband, but his face was resigned to the inevitable. "I'll bring the horse for you."

They walked out together, and Joseph, Sr. went down to the barn. A few moments later, he came back carrying a willow withe, or grass bridle that identified a stray horse. He hurried on down to the two rail fences just a few yards away. The stray was lazily munching the hay which Samuel had thrown in for him earlier in the day. Just a quick slip through the gate, and Father Smith slowed his pace as he quietly inched up to the horse's side. A hand on his neck, a gentle rub behind the ears, and he was passive, obviously well broken. He put his head down, making it easy to get the willow withe over his ears. Emma waited behind the fence while her father-in-law threw a blanket and a saddle on the horse and secured the straps.

It all took too long for Emma. She listened for any sound of people coming, but all was quiet. Joseph Sr. reluctantly gave her a leg up.

"It's not really a proper saddle for a lady," he said. "I should be going if anyone does."

"You must stay and protect the house in case they come for the plates." Emma brushed his objections away. "I'll get to Macedon as fast as possible." Then she was off, heading her mount to the road, and soon, all too soon, urging the animal to a full gallop.

Emma had been over the road to Macedon only once since coming to live with the Smiths. She and Joseph had gone riding one Sunday with Hyrum and Jerusha in a carriage. They had driven seventeen miles roundtrip to Macedon, talking and laughing, stopping once to picnic along the way. Now those miles seemed interminable. She passed one wagon with two young men very surprised to see a woman riding like a man, her cloak streaming out behind her, and her curls bouncing against her shoulder. She resisted the temptation to wave, laughing to herself at the astonished look on their faces as she swept by them.

The widow Wells had a small but efficient farm on the Macedon road. Emma almost missed the place before she caught a glimpse of a muscular arm upraised, and her husband pulling himself up, out of the well. She wheeled the horse into the yard and reined him up beside the back corner of the tiny log home.

"Emma! Why are you here?" Joseph's face reflected concern.

She glanced quickly around. The widow was nowhere to be seen. Joseph was alone, standing to one side of the well he had been digging. "There is danger! They're coming for the plates!"

Joseph steadied her horse. "Who? How do you know?"

"Your father overheard them. He was at Lawrence's and heard Willard Chase and his sister plotting with about fifteen men. They're very determined. Sally's green glass showed her where the plates are hidden. I had to come and get you. I didn't know what else to do."

"You did the right thing," Joseph assured her. "Still, the baby! You can't ride like that when you're with child. The plates are all right for now. But I'd best return with you. Wait for me. I'll talk to Widow Wells."

He knocked on the back door of the little house. A leathery face appeared at about his elbow height. He explained that his family had sent for him. He was needed at home, but would be back the next day. At first she complained. She had wanted that well finished in two days, and now he was taking off the rest of the day. He assured her that he would come early in the morning and the well would be done before he left. After awhile she seemed resigned, and he said goodbye. She stood in the doorway and watched the young man help his bride up on the horse. When she saw that he meant to ride behind her, she stepped outside and insisted that he take her horse from the barn.

Gratefully, Joseph went to saddle up a chestnut gelding, sleek and well-groomed. He was soon mounted and waved goodbye to Widow Wells, who called out after him, "I'll expect you and my horse back here by sun-up."

"Be here at dawn, Missus Wells."

The ride back home went more slowly than Emma's headlong flight to fetch him. Joseph was perfectly at peace and insisted that she ride more cautiously. They rode side by side through Palmyra, and there were few who noted their arrival.

When they reached the Smith farm, Joseph firmly escorted Emma upstairs and admonished her to rest.

"But Joseph, I'm all right. Really I am. I don't feel ill effects from the ride at all."

He would not budge. "You rest until dinner. After all, you are carrying my son."

She smiled up at him. "How do you know? Maybe it's a girl."

He put his hand on her abdomen, still flat. "I'd like that too. She would look just like you. Long dark curls and beautiful eyes."

She didn't argue anymore with him, but took his hand from her stomach and kissed the palm as he turned to go downstairs. Emma lay back against the pillow, more grateful than she would acknowledge, and soon fell fast asleep with no more thought about the safety of the plates. She had done all she could. Now it was up to Joseph and God.

The Smiths all knew they needed to concentrate on finding a place to conceal the plates. They finally resolved to bury the chest under one of the hearthstones. They pried one up, cleared away the dirt beneath and settled the box into the recess. It was dark outside. After the box was securely hidden, the stone was relaid carefully to prevent suspicion. They had scarcely finished this task when they saw torches dotting the field around their home. Within minutes, boots scuffed their porch and a determined fist hammered at their door.

Joseph Sr. answered, opening the door a tiny wedge. "Yes? What is it you want?"

A dozen bearded faces peered at him through the night. "Where's young Joe? We want to see that gold treasure he found."

Mr. Smith replied calmly, "You are mistaken, friend. We have nothing here of any earthly value."

The men surged forward, thrusting the door wide and Joseph Sr. backward into the room.

"That's a lie! We know he's got the gold. Joe! Young Joe! Might as well bring it out! We mean to see what you found. We'll help you cash it in. George here knows a man in New York City that buys Indian artifacts. He'll help you get the best price fer it."

Joseph stood up and faced the band of men. "Mr. Chase, I do not have anything to sell. God alone directs me. I quit your company of money diggers years ago."

"Was that before or after you found the treasure? What is it? Is it a kettle, like that feller from Canandaigua found?"

Sam Lawrence was at the back of the band. He called out, "Hey Joe, folks are saying you found gold plates. Real gold plates! I wanta see them, and I want you to share like we swore when we were kids."

"We aren't kids now," Joseph answered calmly. "And this isn't mine to share. It doesn't concern you and its not for public show. Even my family hasn't seen them."

"No? Well, this is the time! Where are they?" One of the men had grabbed Joseph by the shirt and shook him.

"See here, "Joseph Sr. started, "You can't break into my home this way. It's against the law. Let go of my son and get out of my house."

"Shut up, Smith. Your son is hiding a treasure that belongs to everybody here. Ain't this gold been hid for years right in our own land, on top of that hill? It don't belong to just Joe. It belongs to all of us."

"Not so," Joseph Sr. replied. "I didn't get a penny from anything the rest of you have found. You have nothing to do with anything my son finds. You have taunted him about his dreams and visions. You refuse to believe anything he says, and now you want to steal from him and God. Well, you will not, sir! Out, out of my house, immediately!"

His temper had flared and he began pushing men outside. But as voices rose, the effect was incendiary and the dozen men on the porch pushed back. Soon they had all spilled into the house and were ransacking every room, upstairs, downstairs, looking under beds, turning over chamber pots, pulling back bedding. Joseph Sr. started for the back room to get his rifle. Joseph restrained him.

"Pa, if you get out your gun, there will be worse violence. Think of our women. They are already frightened enough. Just stay calm. Let these devils look. They won't find the plates."

"Suppose they do."

"They won't," Joseph said positively, and he was right. They soon gave up the search, mumbling, grumbling and threatening to come back every night if need be. But for some reason, they didn't think to look beneath the hearthstone. They finally left amid threats on both sides. Joseph Sr. was highly incensed that his home had been violated. It infringed his rights as an American, and he promised to report the incident to authorities.

"We'll see who has the law on his side," he shouted after the disappearing band of men.

"Who are you gonna report it to?" Lucy chided as she pulled him back inside. "The constable's own brother was in that bunch of rowdies."

"The constable knows the law, and I mean to have him enforce it." Her husband was adamant.

But Emma and Joseph looked at each other over the heads of the rest of the family, and knew the truth. There would be no protection from the law.

Not a week later, while all the men were away from the house, Lucy answered a knock at the door to find a neighbor seeking to borrow some beans. She was no sooner in the house than six burly men pushed their way in after her. Lucy sat right down on a stool which was placed over her kitchen hearthstone.

"Well, that's a fine howdy-do, Missus. Make yourselves at home! I guess you think anything we have is yours!"

Her neighbor was apologetic. "I'm sorry, Missus Smith. I didn't want to do it, but my husband says your son stole some treasure."

"He never did! We have nothing of earthly value in this house. If we did, do you think we'd be living poor like this?"

The woman was clearly embarrassed. "No m'am, don't suppose you would."

Her husband and his friends were not deterred. They continued to search while the Smith women sat mending and weaving, not looking up, studiously not looking at the hearthstone. Lucy sat right there, talking and praying out loud, hoping to shame them into leaving.

"Dear God above, look down upon all us poor sinners,'" she intoned piously. "Keep us from trespassing." The men didn't pause. Her neighbor blushed. Lucy went right on. "Lord, show us the evils of filthy lucre. Help us remember that the love of money is the root of all wickedness." Her voice rose. "Help us love our neighbors, as you commanded." Now the poor neighbor woman, sorry to have opened Pandora's box, was thoroughly shamed and began urging her husband and his friends to leave.

Lucy went right on. Emma began to shake. She was still braiding her rug, and her hands trembled so badly she could scarcely twist the rags. Whether it was from fear or laughter, she couldn't tell. But her mother-in-law seemed determined to pray the rascals right out of the house. The Smith girls stuck to their tasks, amazed at the courage of their mother.

"Lord, forgive these men for frightening innocent women and tearing up our house. Soften their black hearts. Cause the remembrance of our Savior's love to teach them how to love their neighbors. Bless them not to persecute the poor or oppress the weak. Lord, bless us with your peace, that the things of this world will not entice us to wickedness."

Her voice had risen above the scuffling of boots and rummaging through barrels, cookware and such. They had begun to look surreptitiously at each other. A dark flush had appeared on a few faces. The search slowed down. The men began backing toward the door. A hat came off. A gruff voice mumbled an apology. Lucy went on praying, and before long, the last one closed the door and hurried away.

The younger girls erupted in relief, jumping up and rushing to their mother. Lucy gathered them in as a mother hen gathers her chicks. Emma put down her braid and sat back.

Lucy laughed out loud. "Why, sakes alive, you aren't scared are you? Did you see what effect prayer had on those ruffians? They're no match at all for an old woman's prayer. Look at Emma there. She's cool as a cucumber."

Emma shook her head in disbelief at what had happened. Then the shaking inside turned to laughter. Lucy had been magnificent. She had routed them all with a prayer! Then Emma's laughter turned to tears, and finally, she was just shaking.

Life became a constant guard-watch. Any sound of horses in the yard, any creak or crack of a branch breaking in the night and Joseph would wake. Lucy began complaining that she never got a good night's sleep. Little Lucy became afraid to go to bed, even though she slept with Katherine. William wanted to sleep with his rifle, but Joseph Sr. wouldn't let him. Samuel became very protective of Emma when Joseph was absent. At nineteen, he had studied his sister-in-law and admired her quiet strength. One day he would choose a wife, and she would be like Emma. He observed the little things she did to honor his brother, serving him at meal time, keeping his shirts clean and freshly ironed, mending his stockings with care, cleaning the mud off his boots, touching him lightly on the shoulder or neck as she went by. How beautiful are the ways of a woman in love, he thought, and he envied his brother for more than the treasure he kept locked in Alvin's tool box.

The hearthstone hiding place didn't work for long. One evening, Joseph announced they needed a different hiding place. He lifted the stone, took the wooden box and hid it in the cooper's shop across the road. A mob of prominent citizens came the next night as soon as dark fell. Carrying torches and stout walking sticks, they burst into the Smith home, roughly shoved the men aside, lifted Lucy, chair and all, and removed her from her place straddling the hearthstone. They pried up the stone to reveal just an empty cavity below.

One man called over his shoulder, "Tell Chase his sister's peep-stone is wrong! Ain't nothing here." He stood up and thrust his sneering face into Joseph's. "Where is it, Smith? I want that gold, and I mean to git it."

Joseph's blue eyes never flinched. He shook his head slowly. "You're wrong. There is nothing here for you."

"That's cause you hid it away for yerself. Give it up and we won't torch yer house."

Joseph was unruffled. "You don't want to do that. There is no treasure hidden here. We're poor farmers like yourselves. You know us. I've worked on your places. I've helped raise your barns, and returned your horses to you when they strayed. Now go back to your homes, to your land that I've helped you to clear. Go home to your only *real* treasure. Neighbors deserve better than this. Go home!"

A few of them were shamed, and some dispersed. Lucy and Emma stood in the middle of the front room, their arms encircling the girls, Lucy, Katherine and Sophronia. The men hadn't been able to look into Emma's questioning eyes or Lucy's blazing, blue ones. Joseph Sr. stood beside his son, shoulder to shoulder. The younger man could feel his father's tension, as he worked at soothing not only the mob but the Smith's inclination to fight back. The Savior's way was best — quiet, peaceful reasoning. Joseph's voice had almost a hypnotic effect on the mob, and finally the house was cleared of ruffians with no real damage done.

The cooper's shed, on the other hand, was almost torn apart. Many barrels were splintered. The floor was hacked apart in places. Flax was everywhere. Only after the mob had left and Joseph and his father examined the damage did they realize how bad it might have been.

William challenged Joseph. "Why didn't you let us fight back? I'd have liked to get my hands on one or two of those troublemakers."

Joseph was kneeling on the floor, gathering up the flax. "Fighting wasn't the answer. Think, William. Think how fast this shop would go up in flames if the violence had gotten out of hand."

Don Carlos knelt beside his big brother. "I'll help you, Joseph."

Samuel asked, "Where are the plates, Joe?"

"Safe enough, Sam. Under the floor over yonder. They gave up before they got to the right spot."

"How can Sally Chase use her peepstone to find out where we're hiding the plates?" Carlos asked.

"The adversary knows everything we do. And he has lots of people willing to listen. Sally just hears better than others. Whenever God uses a tool for good, you can bet Satan will try to duplicate it. Seer stones can be used for good or for evil. You've gotta be able to tell the difference."

Joseph was exhausted that night. Emma was already in bed when he sat at the edge, pulled off his boots and fell in beside her. She was almost asleep, but turned over and put her arm possessively over his chest. He buried his face in her hair and held her close, savoring the smell of cinnamon and apples that clung to her.

"How am I to start translating when the plates have to be hidden in a new place every day?"

"I truly don't know," Emma murmured.

"I know I'm supposed to do something more with this record than bury it in fifty different places. I need peace and quiet to work on it. I'm anxious to start. Emma, God has shown me the history of an ancient people. It's as fascinating as the Bible. There's even a prophet named Alma who teaches as powerfully as Isaiah. I *must* get started."

"Maybe the mobbing will stop when they see they can't get the plates."

He sighed and kissed her temples. "I hope so. These men are neighbors. I've worked for most of them. I've known some since I was ten years old. I can't believe they break into our home. I'm so afraid some hothead — maybe William — will start shooting, and someone will get killed."

"I have an idea. The Sabbath is in four days. Next Sunday afternoon let's go calling. We should visit these folks in their homes. We need to remind them that we are neighbors. When we talk to their women, maybe they will be able to calm the men down."

"It's worth a try, I guess."

"Surely the women will put a stop to all this."

"Well, they haven't yet."

They lay quietly together, enjoying the warmth and contentment of being together. Emma's presence was always soothing to Joseph, no matter how harried he might become. And Joseph was always reassuring to Emma. Surely nothing really bad could happen when he was near. He had magic in his voice and eyes that could calm a sudden storm. She tightened her arms around him possessively.

The next few days it rained, and the Smiths were left in comparative peace. Autumn was upon them. The trees had all turned vibrant colors of red and gold. Mornings were frosty. Lucy made pumpkin pies. William Stoddard came to call on Sophronia, and they sat up talking by the evening firelight until the scandalous hour of ten o'clock. Young Lucy and Katherine stayed up eavesdropping, then talking even later. Well after midnight, Mother Lucy came to their door and admonished them to stop talking. Soon only a few whispers and giggles were heard.

A week went by quietly. The Smiths were tempted to let down their guard. Maybe the worst was over. There was so much work to do, salting pork to store for the winter, digging potatoes and storing them in the cellar, mending woolen coats and socks for the men. They didn't have enough time to fret about mobs. Emma still had morning sickness occasionally. She was thin as a rail, and Lucy urged her to eat. Emma knew it was always done in concern and kindness, but it began to annoy her. She couldn't eat when she knew her stomach would reject it.

On the next Sabbath day, she and Joseph rose from their midday meal and borrowed the family wagon. They went visiting, calling at the homes of the men who had invaded the Smith house only a few days before. Joseph was warm and friendly as if nothing unkind had ever happened between them. These surprise visits left many shamefaced, staring at the floor, being nudged by wives as the Smiths continued on their way, visiting the next home. They went as far north as the Martin Harris place and paid their respects to "Aunt Dolly," as his gossipy wife Lucy was sometimes called. The rumors had made their way to her ear, and it was all they could do to escape with any secret still intact. She asked a million questions, and Joseph politely parried them all. When they tore themselves away, Mrs. Harris stood by the gate, calling after them that she would know the truth about the gold plates before anyone else or she wasn't a true daughter of the revolution.

They reached home just at twilight, satisfied that they had done what they could in stopping the mob activity that was terrorizing the family. Family prayer was held and everyone went to bed. Hearing whispers from his sisters, Joseph happened to pull back the curtain and glance outside. Far down the Canandaigua road he could see pinpoints of light bobbing, coming in his direction.

"Emma! They're coming! I must move the plates. Sally may have divined them correctly this time."

Emma sat straight up in bed, her eyes wide with fear. Joseph didn't take time to even jerk on his boots. Barefooted, he leaped down the stairs and ran across the road to the old cooper's shop. He didn't explain how he knew what he knew, but it was clear to him that the men would dig up the floor at the very spot where he had hidden the plates.

So he beat them to it. A few serious prys and the floorboards were up. Grabbing the locked box and hugging it to his chest, he cast about in his mind as to where to hide them. An impression kept welling up within him: give them to Sophronia! He ran back into the house. The girls were sitting up in bed. When he had gone rushing out, they knew something was wrong.

159

Katherine's eyes were big when Joseph dashed in, went down on one knee beside their bed and said, "Sophronia, Katherine, take the box! Hide it! Quick, they're coming."

"I don't know where to hide it! Don't give it to me."

"Yes. You've got to take it. Wherever you hide it, it will be right."

"How do you know? *I'm* not clever. *I* don't know where to hide it if you and Father don't."

He thrust the box into her arms and jumped back. "Just put it somewhere. God will make it right."

The girls looked at each other in consternation. Then Sophronia rose to the occasion. She jumped out of bed, pulled Katherine out and jerked back the mattress cover. "Help me, Katherine! We'll stick them under here, and then we'll get back in bed. They won't dare uncover us."

The deed was done in the nick of time. The girls had just climbed back into bed, pulled the covers up to their chins, and curled up around the peculiar lump in their mattress when ten men gathered around the house, pounding the outer wall and threatening to burn them out. Joseph and Emma braced themselves on the stairs as Joseph, Sr. reluctantly opened the door. Only the threat of fire could compel him to do so. Lucy, his wife, and little Lucy stood behind him. He opened it a crack. That was quickly widened as the mob leader thrust in a flaming torch and shoved. Joseph Sr. stepped back to avoid taking a brand in the face. Men poured into the room and began throwing Lucy's pots and kettles about. Her mending, her barrel contents — all were poured out on the floor. All the while, threats and demands of gold rang through the house. Joseph stood on the bottom step trying to calm the situation with reason and reassurance that there was nothing for them. The ringleader flung open the door to the girls' room. There was a shriek and Sophronia grabbed her covers, holding them close about her neck.

160

"Come on, men, them girls got nothin'," the leader hollered out. None of the family recognized him. He was not a neighbor. Of course, there were lots of strangers in the area lately with the Canal finished and all the commerce going down it. That was especially worrisome to Joseph. He had confidence he could reason with his neighbors, but strangers didn't have community conscience.

Two lanky men peered farther into the girls' sparsely furnished room. One of them spied a trunk at the foot of the bed and jerked it open, spilling linens all over the floor. But there was nothing more. Scowling at the two females cowering beneath the covers, they stomped out of the house and headed for the cooper shop. Other members of the mob were already there, upending barrels and demolishing the floor of the shop. Some were destroying everything they could get their hands on, when an amazing sound was heard.

Ten Indians on the warpath could not have bettered such a whoop! William had come home from a nearby friend's and found his house being ransacked. The boy came in wielding with both hands a "rascal beater" hickory staff four feet long and four inches thick. He was a whirling dervish, and he laid waste the unfortunate rascals in his path. Turning and slicing, whirling and chopping with his club, shouting at the top of his powerful voice, he knocked down four men within a minute and was turning his attention to the cooper shop outside. The invaders thought they had encountered a madman and began to run, some of them stumbling backward in an effort to get out from under his club. He twirled the club in the air around his head until the shop was also cleared, and then, followed by the other Smith menfolk, he pursued them out into the night air, whooping and hollering, threatening to break their heads.

When the mob was well routed and running down the road, William led his brothers back in the front door, his young face flushed, his hair standing on end, victory shining on his brow. Then the family all gathered around the fireplace. They faced William with stunned looks.

"Well?" he said expectantly.

There was silence. They were still too surprised to respond. Finally his mother spoke.

"And well done!" she said and nodded, her mouth pursed in determined approval.

Then everyone was talking at once, clapping him on the back, congratulating him. William was, unquestionably, the hero of the day.

The next day Emma sat at Lucy's desk and wrote a note to her father. She gave it to Don Carlos to post as he rode to town beside his father. How it would be received she did not know, but she swallowed her pride and fear of rejection. The letter simply said,

Dear Father,

May we come back to Harmony? We are beset with persecution on every side. The situation is intolerable.

Your loving daughter, Emma

Chapter Seven

Harmony, at Last

She would be home for Christmas. Emma pulled her bonnet tighter about her chin. The wind had picked up and whistled around the sleigh. Joseph and Alva Hale were in deep conversation about passages of the Bible. Joseph said little children didn't need baptism. Alva maintained that everyone needed it; it was a question of "original sin." At the moment, Emma was more concerned about the reception from Isaac when she should arrive with her husband. Upon receiving her letter, her father had immediately sent word to pack her belongings and be ready with the first good snowfall. He would send her brother in a sleigh to move her home.

She hoped her father would see the difference in Joseph in the months since they had left Harmony. Responsibility for the golden plates had added maturity and determination to his character. He spoke with more conviction and authority than ever before. He seemed to stand straighter and to look taller. She looked at his face in profile as he conversed with her brother. Joseph's face was leaner, stronger, more self confident than it had been two years ago when she had met him in her father's home. Alva, with his occasional attendance at his uncle's Methodist sermons, was no match for Joseph in a theological discussion. He grudgingly conceded the point that an innocent soul could not sin in ignorance of the law. Therefore, babies needed no baptism.

Emma took little part in the discussion. She had heard it all before. She had seen Joseph argue the point with Christian ministers far more knowledgeable than Alva. She had sat in the Smith family scripture circle and searched her own Bible for passages relating to original sin and baptism for children. She knew all the passages her husband would bring up. Still, in her own heart of hearts, she remained unconvinced. This, she did not tell Joseph. It would only bring on another effort of his to prove his point. Absolute proof for any theological point was hard to come by in the Bible. If you were skillful, you could argue almost anything. What she needed was a spiritual witness of the truth.

The day was fair. The sun was dazzling on the snowy fields as their cutter went skimming over the normally rutted roads. Through the clusters of trees on either side of the road, Emma caught glimpses of small deer bounding away and rabbits standing straight up, ears on the alert and noses working to decipher the strange smell of humans. Rabbits made her want to laugh. They looked like little deacons, ready to scamper off and tell the local clergy of the heated debate.

Isaac was right in waiting for a good snow pack to send for them. Travel by wagon or carriage over this road would have jolted her so badly. Almost four months along with the baby, Emma was not even showing, except for a barely perceptible thickening around her normally slender waist. The constant mob agitation had thoroughly unsettled her nerves. Normally she had nerves of steel, but then she had never been pregnant before or subjected to constant assaults on her privacy. Indeed, if it had happened in Isaac's home, she knew that someone would have been killed. And when bullets fly, who can predict what victim will fall? The last two days had seemed like heaven by comparison, just the three of them gliding so smoothly over the snow-packed road, the jingling of the horse's bridle. She silently thanked God once again for Martin Harris's generosity in giving them fifty dollars to help with their move and the translation. The only thing that could have gotten Joseph to go back and face Isaac was the promise of peace and quiet so he could translate the sacred record.

By late afternoon they were on the river road that meandered beside her beloved Susquehana. With every mile that flew away beneath the horse's hooves, Emma felt her excitement rising. The old, familiar sights sent a thrill of joy through her. The thought of her mother's full, apple-cheeked face, the smell of her kitchen, and her father's gruff embrace — it all choked her with unbearable anticipation. Finally, Emma put her hand on Joseph's arm and squeezed slightly.

He had come to know that meant to be quiet. She had had enough. Joseph looked at his wife and perceived for the first time how much this trip meant to her. She seemed to be all shining eyes, with her muffler about the lower part of her face. She was looking from side to side, up and down, trying to take in every little detail of the countryside she had sorely missed this last year. Those great brown eyes seemed brighter than usual, and Joseph caught the glint of unshed tears. He shifted on the seat and put his arm around his wife and squeezed her. He was immediately remorseful. He had been thoughtlessly chattering on in religious debate without giving a thought to her feelings. They would naturally be keen. She was coming home. Now he felt the shiver of emotion run through her. They had rounded the last bend. A mile farther on, just where the thicket of overhanging trees obscured the white ribbon of the road, the Hale home sat on a little knoll. He looked at his wife's face. She was trying hard to control her feelings, but there was no mistaking that radiant countenance.

Joseph was glad she was so happy. He was slightly less ecstatic. In fact, he wondered if Isaac realized that the husband was part of this deal. How do you greet a man from whom you have stolen a daughter? Joseph brushed back a tendril of hair and kissed Emma's cool forehead. Maybe her father would throw him out. But, no. Joseph knew his wife would not stay without him. No matter how much she loved her family, she loved him more. That was a humbling thought, for he knew how much he loved his own family. Why did it have to be this way? Why couldn't Emma's family just accept him? Was he such an unworthy husband? Yes, he was poor, but he wouldn't always be. Many men had become ministers with less understanding than he, and clergymen were well respected. A woman married to a minister might never be rich, but she would be provided for — if not by the members, by the Lord. Joseph was fully prepared to work as hard as necessary to care for his wife and coming child. He could hunt, build, or plow by day and translate by night. His arm tightened around Emma. She would never go wanting if he had breath in him.

And then the sleigh was off the road, the horse heading for the stable it knew well, and Emma was rising, standing beside him in the sleigh. Elizabeth came hurrying out of the house, drying her hands on her apron. Tryal leaped down the step and passed her mother in a headlong flight to embrace her sister. Isaac's bulk took up the whole doorway, his gray head just barely clearing the top. He showed no emotion, but his mouth worked strangely.

"Mother! Oh Mother," Emma cried in excitement.

Emma and her mother embraced fervently, after Tryal relinquished her. After a moment, Emma looked over their heads and her eyes locked with her father's. Isaac thought she had never looked so beautiful. His daughter's cheeks were pink with the cold and the excitement. Dark curls escaped her bonnet and blew lightly around her face with the afternoon breeze. His heart melted within him as he stepped down on the crunchy snow.

Silently, Isaac embraced his daughter. Words choked inside him. In an instant he forgave her all. Just the joy of having her back erased the bitterness that had consumed him. There never are adequate words for the prodigal. Love is the only language that matters. She was just a little thing in her father's arms. His big, beefy shoulders and thick arms simply enfolded her. For just a moment Emma was a child again, caught up in her father's bear hug at the end of one of his hunting trips, and Isaac was barely aware of his son, Alva, along with Joseph, the intruder, in the sleigh.

He had only a few moments to enjoy his wish come true — his daughter home again — when Joseph climbed out of the sleigh and stood facing him. Isaac's arm fell away from around Emma as he looked his son-in-law in the eye. Joseph's look was tender. He observed the depth of love between his wife and her father and it touched him. Isaac was resigned to reality. Emma had written "we," and he knew Joseph would be with her. The boy had been replaced by the man. This man had acquired some maturity. Good! Maybe Smith would stop having visions and start farming to provide for his family. Woodenly, Isaac stuck out his hand, and Joseph grasped it warmly. There was no apology in the younger man's direct gaze, but there was openness, and the gratitude which Isaac saw persuaded him to try to forgive and forget. Isaac shook hands more firmly than he had previously intended.

He nodded once and greeted his daughter's husband, "Mr. Smith."

Joseph responded immediately, "Mr. Hale. It's good of you to send for us."

Isaac nodded again. His voice grew steadier. "A cold trip?"

"Yes, but enjoyable, and more importantly, we're safe and sound."

"Go in by the stove. Warm yourselves. Alva and I will unhitch the horse and put away the cutter. Alva, your cow came down with udder fever. Had to shoot her a fortnight ago. Went ahead and butchered the meat for you. It's all in the shed."

Isaac patted Emma's shoulder as she and Joseph started toward the house, with Elizabeth going before. Elizabeth Hale breathed a sigh of relief. She hadn't dared discuss with Isaac how he would greet the couple. She had half-expected him to take his hunting rifle and be gone when Emma arrived. Tryal put away Emma's cloak, and Elizabeth looked more closely at her Christmas-gift daughter. Emma was blooming. Marriage was becoming to her. She looked healthy and happy, and when she glanced at her husband, her eyes took on a deeply contented warmth.

Joseph saw to his wife's comfort, excused himself, and went back out to the barn.

"No use unloading your things, Smith, we'll just have to move them to Jesse's old house. It's been empty for a spell. You might as well use it. There's thirteen acres of land goes with it. That way, you can farm and provide for your wife. When you're ready, you can buy it from us."

"I'd like that, sir. Can I be of some help?"

"No. We've seen to everything. I see you've brought the rocking chair."

"Yes."

"And a trunk."

"It has Emma's linens and dresses."

"Is that a cradle?"

Joseph's answer was measured. "It is."

"You got something to tell me?"

"That's Emma's privilege, sir."

Isaac was silent for a minute as he went on around the sleigh, examining the paltry belongings of his daughter and her husband. A grandchild! Emma's child. *She* was scarcely more than a child herself. Hadn't it been just a wink ago that he overheard her praying for him in that grove of trees? Now she was to give him a grandchild. Time passes so swiftly — too swiftly for grudges, he thought.

"What's in the barrel?" Isaac grasped the top and shook it.

Instinctively, Joseph knew he shouldn't show concern. There was a heavenly guard over the barrel of beans which secreted the golden plates. The keeper of the plates had been with them the whole way from Manchester. He would be forever on guard until the sacred record had been translated and safely returned to his keeping.

"It's just a barrel of beans my folks sent with us."

Alva, knowing what treasure the barrel held, started to speak, then shut his lips firmly. Isaac looked from his son back to Joseph. No one spoke, then he moved on. Joseph breathed a sigh of relief while Alva glanced around uneasily, but went back to work wiping down the horse.

After a few more minutes, the three of them started toward the smell of biscuits cooking that emanated from the Hale kitchen. Joseph looked back over his shoulder as they left the barn. He knew he was leaving the plates well guarded.

Elizabeth had supper all set. Emma was seated on her father's right, Elizabeth at the opposite table end, close to the brick oven. Tryal sat next to Joseph and noted the congenial spirit he brought to the evening meal. They were scarcely into the meal when Emma could hold her news no longer.

"Mama, I guess we had better start tying a new quilt."

"Oh, my! Didn't you come with bedding?"

"Oh, yes. We have enough bedding for Joseph and me. I'm talking about a smaller quilt."

Elizabeth looked a little puzzled. Then the light dawned and she boomed out, "A baby! You're with child. I knew it! I knew it. Your face is pink and fuller than it was. I told Tryal, 'something different about Emma.' Didn't I, Tryal? When is our grandbaby due?"

Now that her secret was out Emma was completely relaxed, obviously pleased with herself. She sat back in the chair beaming at her family. Of course, Alva already knew for there had been much talk about the baby in the Smith home, and she suspected that her father had guessed somehow, but her mother and sister were surprised. Emma felt secure for the first time in months. No mobs to threaten her or her husband. No more headlong horseback rides to fetch Joseph for protection. Now she could face childbirth knowing she would be under her mother's watchful care. She had dreamed of this.

"By my best count, I think some time in June."

"Well, yes," her mother said, all business now. "We had best start on that quilt, a christening dress, and some baby clothes. And you'd better be getting some rest, young lady. Spending three days in a sleigh in this weather! Land! It's a wonder you haven't caught your death! Will you have some more stew? There's plenty of onions and beef in the kettle. The meat'll help keep up your strength. Isaac, pass her those biscuits."

Emma was laughing. "Mama, I'm fine. I'm not starving, and I'm not sick. I feel perfectly fine, especially now that I'm here. I'm sure you won't let a single cold draft near me. I wanted to tell you our news in person. I hope you don't mind that I waited."

"Mind? Of course, I don't mind. What a marvelous Christmas present! A new grandchild, and you, a mother-to-be, at last."

"Yes, at last, Mama." Emma lifted her eyes to her husband. Joseph had pushed back in his chair and sat observing this happy exchange with pride. Their love had made her a mother, something she had wanted since she was a little girl.

The next day Joseph and Emma moved into Jesse's small frame house. It had three rooms — a good-sized front room with a beautiful maple floor, a kitchen, and a small bedroom next to the fireplace. At the top of the steep stairs which went up from the front entrance, the attic was partitioned off into a room with an eastern window.

Perfect for my translating, Joseph thought, as he looked through the snug little home. He went back downstairs to find Emma standing at the bedroom window looking out at the meandering river. It was just a hundred yards away. Snow covered its banks and piled up domes of sparkling powder on the rocks. Emma had the window ajar even though the December day was chilly. With the window open you could hear the gurgling water. She turned to him smiling and content.

"See. I told you it would be all right. Oh, Joseph, our own home at last. Isn't it wonderful? Look at the river! It's very special to me. I saw you for the first time hiding in the trees beside that river. You were spying on me!"

"I wasn't spying," he defended himself. "I was admiring. How could I help myself? You were charming. Yes, this is wonderful. I'll be glad when we can purchase it out right from your father."

"In the meantime, just be grateful that he has softened and even seems willing to help us."

"I am, dear, but I wonder how he'll react when I begin translating."

"Where will you work?"

"Upstairs. Come look. It's perfect up there. If I worked down here, I would always be interrupted. Up there I can work in peace." He took her hand and led her up the stairs.

"See, we'll put the little desk right here, and I'll hide my work with a hanging blanket, so if anyone does happen by, it will be shielded from view."

Emma was struggling to imagine the process. "Will you do the translation?"

Joseph considered, then shook his head. "I'm no good at writing. I misspell too much. I need a good scribe."

"My brother Reuben has a good hand, and he's a fair speller."

Joseph shook his head again. "I'm not comfortable with Reuben for a secretary. He's too much like your father. I'm afraid inspiration could not come." He rubbed his cheek against her sleek hair. "Besides, you're the only one I trust."

"Me!" She turned quickly to face him. "Oh Joseph. Could I? Could I really help? Have you asked the Lord if I should be a part of it?"

"Dearest, you *are* a part of it. You were the special person I was to take with me to the hill. Who else has the ability to comfort me and encourage me to do my best? I would not be half the man I am without you. This is an formidable task — to translate an ancient language that I know nothing of. I wake sometimes at night and lie there contemplating it. I know the Urim and Thummim will be the key to translating, but it also requires much from me. I must be entirely open to God's inspiration. I would be so lost in attempting this without you. You help me do my best. Emma, you shall be my scribe."

They stood locked in their embrace, they both knew it was right. Seconds later, when Reuben and Isaac knocked at their door, they broke apart reluctantly, leaving their little attic with keen anticipation.

It only took a short time to unload the wagon. It took longer for Emma to put out her pots and pans, place her braided rug on the floor, and sort through her linens. She was grateful to Lucy for sending three of her best woolen blankets for them and a large pillow ticked with goose down. Along the way, they had purchased a small desk. It had pigeon holes for pen and ink. It would be perfect for the attic. Elizabeth had contributed a bureau with deep drawers for holding their clothes. She had sent over a basin, pitcher and chamber pot. Tryal had sent a cross-stitch she had made for them. It was still on a hoop. Emma carefully placed it on the log wall opposite the table in the kitchen.

Isaac was helping Joseph load the salt pork into the cold storage shed outside. There was enough to keep them for months. Next came the barrel of beans. It took two of them to lift it off the sleigh.

"Never knew beans to be so heavy," Isaac growled.

Alva had told him the night before that Joseph and his father had hidden something in the beans to escape the notice of neighbors who still insisted that he had gold plates. Isaac had snorted in disgusted disbelief.

"Makes no sense! Him as poor as a church mouse, and holding a treasure of gold? Joe Smith ain't got no gold. My daughter is his only treasure."

Yet today he was prodding Joseph to see what he would reveal.

"Got anything besides beans in here?"

"Nothing to share with you, sir." Joseph always tried to be truthful.

"But there is something. What is it?"

"It's personal, Mr. Hale."

"I think I deserve to see what it is." And with that, before Joseph could issue a warning, Isaac started to wiggle his hand into the barrel. Joseph knew they were on dangerous ground. The heavenly instructions were clear: no one was to see the plates but him. Obedience was imperative. Four years of instruction at Cumorah had taught him to be decisive.

"I'm sorry, sir. This is personal property."

Isaac pulled back his hand and gestured toward the little frame house and the acreage. "So is this. And nobody can keep anything on my property that I'm not allowed to see. Understand, Smith?"

He was a man who was used to being obeyed. He stared into Joseph's eyes, waiting confidently for the boy to reveal what the barrel held.

Unflinchingly, Joseph stared him down. Quietly, firmly, the young man replied, "No, sir. I can't do that."

"Why?" Isaac demanded.

"I cannot cast pearls before swine."

Anger flared now in the older man. "You young whelp! You're a charlatan, Smith."

"No. The truth is that some things are not for unbelievers. Only those with the Spirit can discern things *of* the Spirit. Stand away, Mr. Hale."

Joseph's gaze was so steady, so absolutely sure of his declaration, that Isaac complied.

"Don't you go bringing tales of gold around here, young man. Harmony is a sensible community. We won't be hoodwinked. For my daughter's sake, I've given you a house to live in. Now get out and make an honest living for her. You're going to be a father. I won't see my daughter neglected. I'll turn you out first and care for her myself if you fail."

"Mr. Hale, I've never failed in anything. Do you think I would start now? I love your daughter as much, if not more, than you do. I would give my life to protect her."

"I'd give your life, too. Don't forget that."

"Believe me, I won't. And don't you forget, I don't need charity. I have money to pay for your 'hospitality.'"

"I don't want your money. Go to town. Buy flour with it. Buy sugar. You'll need it."

"God will always provide for us."

"Then let Him. I've provided just about all I'm going to."

In the days that followed, Joseph and Emma settled into a comfortable routine. Chores in the morning — chasing chickens around the yard, stealing their eggs, milking the cow, pitching the hay, digging for onions and potatoes, collecting herbs — then translating in the afternoon and evening. Joseph put the small desk upstairs next to the window, ran a clothesline between his chair and the desk and hung a blanket over it. Emma sat on one side with paper, a quill pen and a small jar of homemade ink which he made with lamp-black and glue. He alternately spoke and meditated on the other side of the blanket, all the while concealing the golden plates. He would gaze into the Urim and Thummim intently, contemplating the ancient markings on the plates. Often aware of a heavenly presence in the room, he knew Moroni was watching and quickening him as he opened his mind to inspiration.

At first, progress was slow. Joseph painstakingly developed a methodology. The words of translation would appear for him in the spectacles. He then dictated it to Emma, and she wrote down everything in neat, careful script. Soon, he began to find that small symbols which he had translated before would not reappear in the glasses, and he was expected to remember the previous translation. Some words he couldn't pronounce, he could only spell. Emma would write those down, and together they would decide on the correct pronunciation.

"Sariah" was one such word. He could spell it, but couldn't pronounce it.

Emma gave him the pronunciation."'Sa-rye-ah', she corrected him, "not 'Sa-ree-eye.' "

There was a short silence while Emma stared at the blanket as though she could see through it. Then he responded. "All right, Emma. 'Sa-rye-ah.' Thank you, dear."

Once while translating, Joseph stopped and pulled back the blanket. His face was ashen white. Emma looked up from the foolscap, her quill suspended in mid-air waiting for the next word. His brow was furrowed. His eyes held confusion.

"What is it," she asked in alarm. He rarely evidenced confusion.

"Does Jerusalem have a wall around it?"

"Why yes, Joseph. Everybody knows that!"

A look of relief washed over his face and he grinned foolishly at her like a little boy. "Thank goodness. I thought I was being deceived."

Closing the makeshift curtain, he went on translating a reference to the old city of Jerusalem. Emma became absolutely convinced that it would be impossible for even a learned man to fabricate such a work, much less the unlearned man she knew her husband to be. This knowledge made her even more proud of her husband.

Isaac would oftentimes see the little lamp glowing in the upstairs window of his daughter's home very late at night. What was she doing up so late? Working like a slave for that husband of hers, no doubt. When he asked her about it, she merely kissed his cheek and told him not to worry, they were studying the scriptures.

The rest of December passed quietly. Christmas was a time of rejoicing, and the Hales put aside animosities. Together they drove the sleigh to Lanesboro for a worship service at the Methodist church. It was cozy, squeezed side by side into the cutter, with warm bricks at their feet and Isaac's fur blankets tucked in around them. They arrived at the church laughing, with a better spirit between them than they had ever had.

Nathaniel Lewis, Emma's uncle and itinerant preacher, greeted them at the door.

"Well, well! Isaac Hale and family! Welcome to our service. And is this little Emma? Emma Hale?"

"Smith," she quickly corrected.

Nathaniel adjusted his spectacles on the broad bridge of his nose and peered at Joseph. "Oh," he said. "That's right. You're married. And back home again? For a visit or to stay?"

Joseph shook his new uncle's hand. "To stay," he answered positively. "We're anxious to hear some of your fine preaching."

"Are you? I hear you are a fair preacher yourself."

"I love the scriptures and love to discuss them. But we've come to hear your Christmas message today."

"Good. Good. Welcome. You are certainly welcome in my church."

Emma was grateful for the cordial reception. She squeezed her uncle's hand. "Today is Joseph's birthday, Uncle Nathaniel. Thank you for making us so welcome."

"Ah, just two days before the Savior's! Well, that's cause for celebration. Come on and sit up here in the front."

They walked forward to the front bench and sat down. Soon the little Methodist church was filled with neighbors and relatives. Familiar whiskers in the doorway caught Joseph's eye. The rest of the face appeared, and it belonged to Joseph Knight. He excused himself from Emma's side and went to grasp the burly arm of his friend.

"Mr. Knight, how good to see you here."

"Joseph, my boy! Didn't expect to see you back here again so soon."

"We came to Harmony for some peace and . . . well, 'harmony.' I couldn't translate at my parent's farm. The persecution was too great."

"So you are hard at it now?"

"Yes. We work every day."

"We?"

"My wife and myself."

"I see. And how are you feeding your family?"

"Mr. Harris gave us fifty dollars for God's work when we left. We must accomplish so much in our allotted time. We have a little one coming in June."

The Knight family had all gathered round and were congratulating him. Polly Knight pushed past her husband and went to Emma, welcoming her and asking about her health. The service that day consisted of reading and commenting on the Book of Luke, singing and praising God for the first Christmas. The Smiths and Hales parted from the Knights with an invitation to come and visit.

"Emma, you're tired," Joseph observed one afternoon, when he peered out at her from around the hanging blanket.

"Don't sound so accusing."

"I'm not accusing you. I'm accusing myself. I worry about you. I shouldn't put added responsibilities on you. You're expecting. You need more rest. All the housework, cooking, sewing, plus writing for hours. It's too much. I have to find another scribe."

"No! Joseph, no. I can do it. I *want* to do it."

He came around and knelt beside her chair. He took the quill pen from her hand, put it down and scooped her up from the chair. Then sitting, he cuddled her in his lap and held her head securely against his shoulder. He didn't argue with her. He had learned that his wife could be stubborn in her own sweet, quiet way. Tenderness and love won her over every time. He began to rock side to side. Soon his hand crept down to rest on her growing belly. Lately there had been no mistaking her condition, and since her dresses would no longer fit, there was the necessity of making new, more voluminous clothing. Emma was looking pale. She was tired more often, and though she didn't complain, he had noted her step was slower in climbing the stairs. His conscience convicted him. How thoughtless he was. The plates were precious, but *she* was his one priceless treasure.

The temptation to rest was too strong for her. Emma collapsed against his shoulder with relief. Then she gave herself up to the comfort of his rocking and caressing. Joseph could always silence her objections. He had the power. His love was the key. It was everything to her.

"Let my brother, Reuben, help us. He knows what we are doing."

"Do you think he could function discreetly? He's only sixteen. He might feel compelled to tell your father too much about the work."

"I think he would honor your wishes not to reveal anything. Just hearing you translate, word by word, like you do, never stopping, never going back to change anything — it's an amazing experience. It is perfectly obvious you are not *writing* a manuscript. No writer composes like that. And all the passages from Isaiah — you haven't a Bible to quote from. It must all be on the plates."

"It is. The Nephites seem to have valued the writings of the Jewish prophets. They also included some prophecies by Jeremiah and Ezekiel."

They sat for some time, Emma cuddled in Joseph's lap, considering the prospect of asking Reuben to help. It was now January. The snow was deep, and there was little to do around the farm. Emma's young brother had plenty of time on his hands. By the time they went to bed that night it was decided.

Joseph asked Reuben discreetly for his help, and after that Reuben came regularly to act as Joseph's scribe. At first he seemed almost embarrassed. Possibly he thought it was all a hoax — until he actually got involved. Then he began to look forward to the time spent writing out the sacred history. Emma was able to spend more time with household duties and resting. She finished stitching her new dress, and lined the baby cradle with cotton blankets for which she had also done the carding, spinning, and loom work. The blanket was soft and new, perfect for their baby.

She was still having nausea, not just in the morning, but after her evening meal as well. She had to take care not to cook anything with a strong odor. The smell of onions boiling would cause her queasiness. Consequently, Joseph's food was plain. He teased her about it, but declared he didn't mind. If they were to eat only bread, that was good enough for him. Indeed, bread and honey was a staple in their diet and one of the few things that didn't make her sick. Besides, flour was plentiful, and money was running out. Most of the money Martin had donated had gone for shoes, chickens, cotton, foolscap and kitchen supplies. They still had salt pork, thanks to her father, but now, feeding Reuben as well as themselves drew upon their little store of food until the situation became critical. It was mutually decided that Reuben return to his duties at home.

Joseph took Emma in the sleigh one day and drove to the Knights farm in Colesville where he had chopped wood. He could do it again. He needed money. Paper had run out, food was down to bare necessities, and he refused to ask Isaac for help, or allow Emma to ask. Knight was a true friend. He would help if he could.

The older man greeted them warmly.

"Mother, look here. Joseph and Emma Smith have come to see us. Set dinner plates for them. Come Joseph, look around at what I've done with the farm. That wheat storage shed is new. My boys built it last fall. Over here, I'm storing lumber for another barn. I've got so many hogs I need a pen. Thinking of building onto my house as well. My son, Newel, needs a place to stay while he's building his home."

Joseph could rejoice with his old friend. If anyone deserved good fortune, Joseph Knight did.

"Have you any work you could put me to this week? I'm out of supplies for translating and need to earn some money."

Knight stopped in his tour and turned to Joseph. "You're a good worker, Joseph, but I'm just not sure what there is for you right now. Come March, I think I'll be able to use you. Right now, we're kind of lazy, tanning hides, making glue. I even made Polly a chair for the front room. But farm work for you? It's too early."

They stomped the snow off their shoes at the front door and walked to the fireplace to warm their hands. Emma was seated, talking to Polly Knight and young Joseph Knight. They were asking questions about the translation, and she frankly told them about the process. Joseph could tell they thought it rather strange. He supposed it was, or at least, it must sound strange. But that was the way of it. He couldn't shout the translation from another room, and God had not yet given permission for anyone else to see the plates. Joseph studied his wife, sitting so straight and proud, even though it was getting hard for her as the baby increased in size. He was proud of his wife. Most folks would have been so curious they would have fallen to the temptation to look at or touch the priceless objects. Some would dwell on thoughts of their monetary value. Even he had done that once, and only once, on the side of Cumorah one night when the thought came to his mind that his family needed the money these plates might bring. Immediately the record was taken back, and the angel gave him a stinging rebuke. Joseph had fallen back onto the earth feeling as if he had been struck by lightning. That night he had learned something of obedience and purity of motive. It was indelibly embedded in his memory.

"It all sounds a little strange to me, Mrs. Smith," Polly spoke out. "How do your folks like such goings on?"

"My brother Reuben has been helping out with the translation. He knows it to be a holy work. He's been a valuable advocate with my father."

"I'm sure he has, and rightly so." Polly patted her hand.

180

After the light meal of ham, cheese, biscuits and buttermilk, the Knights retired to an upstairs bedroom to talk. Joseph and Emma sat in the parlor and heard snatches of the conversation.

"They need some money . . . there's no work . . . ."

". . . not rich, Joseph . . . own family needs . . . ."

". . . Lord's work."

". . . strange goings on . . . ."

". . . a few dollars."

"Joseph, let's go," Emma said softly. "We don't need charity."

"We haven't asked for charity. I can work, Emma."

"But he has no work for you now. We won't starve. There's plenty of fish and game, and we can get flour on credit."

"I know we won't starve, but I need more paper among other things."

She stood up, took her bonnet and cloak from the chair and began fastening the ties. He knew she would be leaving with or without him. So he also put on his hat and coat. As he pulled on his gloves, Joseph Knight hurried down the stairs.

"It's good of you to feed us and to catch us up on the news of old friends. Thank you." Joseph shook hands with the older man.

"You're not leaving already?"

"Emma is tired. Her condition is a little delicate right now."

"Joseph, I want to give you a little money for the translating."

"It's not necessary. I can manage."

"But I want to *give* it to you! What you're doing is the Lord's work. I know how you've struggled. And I know your story is true. I believe in your work. Let me help."

Joseph's blue, penetrating eyes returned his friend's heartfelt gaze. As long as he knew the help was not given grudgingly, he could accept it. "Thank you, my friend. God bless you."

Emma was waiting by the sleigh. Her face was pale, but, though fatigued, she stood regally. Joseph hastened to her side and helped her in, then tucked the blankets about her. They waved farewell, and the sleigh was off, skimming over the snowy roads toward home.

The work continued slowly, with Emma fighting sickness and fatigue while Joseph worked at odd jobs to bring in money. Tryal brought them apples from the fruit cellar once. Elizabeth gave them a jar of pecans. Fish appeared in buckets on their back doorstep. Isaac wouldn't talk about that. Alva brought them beef, which Emma stewed for days. She dropped in sticky biscuits that puffed up into delicious dumplings. As the weeks passed, her waist completely disappeared. Her eyes had dark circles beneath them.

Despite scanty provisions and the constant need for paper, it was a good time. They had privacy for the first time in their marriage. Love was freely expressed between them. Emma had no need to veil her adoration of her husband, and he was affectionate and tender with her. While she stirred the stew, Joseph would stand behind her, his arms encircling her and whisper to her of her beauty. At dinner, she would sometimes sit on his lap while he coaxed her to eat the few morsels she could hold down. In bed he would rub the length of her back, slowly, languorously. Emma knew her marriage was unusual. She watched other couples for signs of the tenderness she had come to expect from her husband. She came to the conclusion she was blessed among women.

Then one day in late February, Emma heard the clip-clop of horses and the whirr of carriage wheels. She looked out her window to see Martin Harris and Hyrum springing out of Martin's rig. A little cry of pleasure escaped her. Joseph crossed the room in three strides, and flung open the door.

"Hyrum! Martin! You came!" Joseph embraced both of them in turn, pounding his brother's back with glee.

"Yes! And without my Missus, too." Harris pulled out a large, red handkerchief, wiped his eyes and then his nose, chapped and reddened from the cold. Laughing eyes squinted at Joseph, and he chortled with satisfaction. "She had made up her mind to come with me.

That woman is harder to shake than a bull's tail. It's always 'Martin-this,' and 'Martin-that,' until I'm about ready to change my name. She thought she'd catch me before I could run off. But I fooled her! Danged if I didn't." He slapped his knee. "Went into Palmyra to fetch her worsted fabric for new curtains. Never went back. Sent her a note and came with what clothes I had on." He winked. "And the belongings Hyrum was keeping for me."

Joseph and Hyrum still stood gripping each other by the arm. It had been only a couple of months since they had said farewell back home, but it was too long. Their joy at being reunited was evident. They did not sit down for several minutes. They just stood face to face, sometimes an arm resting on the other one, sometimes just clapping each other on the back for the pure pleasure of being together. Emma watched this affectionate display with understanding. In actuality, she was almost as fond of Hyrum as Joseph was. Of all her husband's brothers, he was her favorite. He was the peacemaker of the Smith family, with a heart as tender as her own, and the demeanor of a minister. Joseph was the more athletic of the brothers. Where Hyrum was content with parlor talk, Joseph loved to be outside chopping, splitting, pulling sticks, wrestling or racing through the woods. She looked from one face to the other. Both countenances were pure and clear with strong foreheads and noses. Joseph's lips were a little fuller and his eyes more deep-set. Hyrum was a bit taller. As she made those mental comparisons, she knew that her destiny would be forever bound to these brothers.

Emma laughed at Martin's recitation. "You're most welcome here, Martin," Emma welcomed him. "Gentlemen, let me give you donuts for refreshment from your long trip. You can't refuse. It's my specialty. Joseph loves donuts for dinner."

"Give me your trunk," Joseph reached down beside the door and swung the small Morocco trunk, which Martin brought, up onto his shoulder. "I'll store it upstairs for you."

"So this is the place the golden plates are being translated! How's the work going?"

"Well! It's going very well. I have to stop and work from time to time, but the translating progresses steadily. There are many characters I now know by sight. Of course, I still rely on the spectacles for the entire translation. Good thing I married a school teacher. I didn't even know how to pronounce 'Sariah'. Emma had to help me."

Martin looked shrewdly at Emma's bulging waist. "Looks like you're gonna lose your scribe soon," his squinty eyes bright with humor.

"So it seems. Do you want the position? It doesn't pay much."

"Really? Do you think I could?" His demeanor had sobered immediately. "I'd be honored, my boy! Are you sure? But I'm just an old reprobate. The angel might object."

"Not if you are obedient," Joseph said. "One thing, before you start writing for me, I want to make a copy of some of those characters for you to take to Boston. There is an ancient language scholar I want to have look them over."

"But why?"

"Because that's what God requires. That's all I know."

"What can the scholar say? He doesn't know as much as you do." Martin was dubious.

"He can give a verification that they are authentic."

"That's good. We all know it, but others still don't believe. I'll help you, Joseph. I really want to help you. You know I stand ready to pay for publishing the book. Maybe this errand will convince my wife and family that this is a genuine translation from an ancient text. The Missus won't believe you or me, but once I have the word of an expert, she'll have to give some credence to it.'

"Martin," Hyrum said quietly, "your wife will never believe it no matter what you do."

Martin stamped his foot. "I know it, Hyrum. Dadgum, if anybody knows it, I do. But I've got to try. Besides, I might get enough

proof to shut up the mouths of skeptics. You see, more than a fortnight ago I had a unique experience. The Lord blessed me with an
assurance that this is His work which you are called to do."

Joseph regarded him seriously. "Martin, we need that verification."

Harris responded immediately. "I'll leave for Boston whenever
you say."

"Good," Joseph said with satisfaction.

Martin beamed, obviously pleased with his important assignment. Then he turned to Emma, delicately wiping his whiskers.
"These are the best donuts I've ever had, Mrs. Smith. Are there more
for you? They're an absolute tonic and you're looking a little peaked.
The little one taking its toll?"

"Oh, sometimes. I'm just a little tired today."

"Well, don't you worry. I'll take up your pen as soon as I get
back from New York."

Three days later, Martin and Hyrum left the Smith home after
many embraces and a lingering farewell, Martin carrying a copy of
seven lines of characters which Joseph had taken from the plates. It
would be two months before Martin returned.

Spring came gloriously to upper Pennsylvania. One day it was
still bitter cold, with ice on the puddles, and the next day yellow crocuses were showing. Joseph watched Emma walking down to the river
looking for pussy willow. There were sprouts of grass poking through
the rich, loamy dirt. The branches of the maple were nubby with
buds. Green leaves were not far behind. The sun was higher in the sky
than last week, and the air smelled fresh, like a burst of mints. Everything was growing, and so was Emma. He saw her absentmindedly
rub her rounded belly on the side and then lower where the pain was.
She did that quite often now. He had asked her about it, and she had
passed it off as nothing unusual. It wasn't a bad pain, she assured him,
more aching than sharp, but he was worried. He asked her mother
about it. Mrs. Hale couldn't remember such a pain with any of her

children. Remembering Mother Smith's firstborn child had been still-born, Joseph nervously watched over his wife. Emma was most private about her own well-being. She never complained, never chided him about their scanty supplies. Now that spring had arrived, he would be planting a large garden for them. Soon they would have all the vegetables and fruit they needed. His goal was to get the garden in before Martin came back and translating resumed on a greater scale.

Joseph put on his heavy shirt, wrenched his boots on, closed the back door behind him, and struck out for the shed. He found the rake leaning against the corner logs. Reaching down and wiping the dark prongs, he pushed out of the barn doorway with it, and headed toward the garden plot close to the river. It was grown over with dead weeds and cluttered with twigs, rocks and other debris. While Emma wandered the river path searching for mint, wild onions and such, Joseph worked up a sweat in the cool April air, raking, leveling and loosening the dirt. In a few hours, he had cleared a section fifty yards square, not nearly enough, but it was a good start for today.

He straightened up and leaning on his hoe, let out a trilling whistle, long and low as a bird's warble. He waited. She did not appear. So he whistled again, drawing out the melodious sound like a lovesick dove. Still, she did not appear. He stretched, rubbed his shoulder, propped his rake against a tree stump, and started for the river. He had just caught sight of her heading in his direction when he saw her stumble on the uneven ground and fall.

"Emma!" he shouted, breaking into a sprint.

He heard her cry of pain, and saw her face go white. Distraught, Joseph made a mad dash to where she lay on the ground panting with shooting pain in her side and knee.

"Oh Emma! You've fallen! Are you hurt? Is the baby all right? Don't talk! I've got you. You'll be all right. Put your arms around my neck. I'll carry you in. Shh, dearest. Shh. It's all right now. The baby'll be fine, just fine. Close your eyes. We're almost there."

He opened the door with one hand and pushed into the tiny bedroom. Carefully he laid his wife on the bed.

"Joseph, it's my knee."

"Here, let me see!" He pushed up her skirt and petticoat. Her right kneecap had already started to swell. "How painful is it? I think it is just a bad sprain. You'll be down a few days. I'm going to bandage it. It'll keep the swelling down."

He fished into her rag bag and drew out some strips she was saving for another rug. Deftly he wrapped the knee and drew the skirt back down, arranging it neatly around her.

Her face gradually lost its deathly white pallor, but her high, arched brow was still furrowed while the back of her hand pressed against her mouth, holding in moans of pain. Her abdomen had risen up hard and tight as though the child inside were standing at attention. Her breath was deep, almost a sigh or a moan. He couldn't tell which.

"Look at my belly," she groaned. "It's standing straight out. Roll me over on my side. The weight on my back is too much."

Joseph knew little about a woman's expectant condition, but he could certainly see that the baby was pushing hard inside his wife's stomach. He gently pulled her shoulder toward him, wedged his hand under her hip and lodged her securely on her side. Once Emma was on her side, she seemed more comfortable. Her moans turned into sighs. Her hand came down and rested on the pillow. She breathed deeply and tension seemed to melt away. Joseph knelt beside her and buried his head in the softness of her neck and shoulder. He stayed like that for a long time, praying for her safety and the well being of their child. Sweet, affectionate Emma! God had answered so many prayers, Joseph had full confidence that he would honor this one.

Emma was too weak to do much more than whisper his name. "Pray for me, Joseph. Pray for our baby. God will hear your prayer."

"God knows your name too, Emma. He knows your condition. Rest now, dearest. I will serve you. You stay in bed."

"Please go for my mother. It would make me feel better just to talk to her."

"I'll go if you promise not to move or try to get up."

"I promise."

He backed out of the room, then hastened from the house and hurried across the field to his mother-in-law's home. Elizabeth put down her spinning and scurried back the short distance to attend her daughter. Joseph sat in the front room listening to the efficient voice asking questions of Emma, clucking with concern at times, soothing at other times. He could hear the rustling of Emma's skirts, and caught the quiet words, "No blood." Eventually, Elizabeth came from her daughter's room, and sat wearily in a kitchen chair.

"I don't think she'll lose the baby. But I can't be sure. Her belly is soft and relaxed now. I don't believe labor is starting. Keep her down. That'll be a chore. She'll be wanting to be up and around when the pain goes away. Don't let her. I'll send over meals for a few days. Remember, keep her down."

"I will, Mother Hale. She sure scared me when she fell."

"What was she doing?"

"Collecting pussy willow and mint, mostly."

"What were you doing?"

"Raking out the garden. Getting ready to plow and plant tomorrow."

She nodded her approval. "Good. Well, I'll come back later and check on her. If she should start to bleed, come get me right away. That's the big danger now."

"Thanks. I'll see to it she doesn't get up."

Keeping Emma quiet was Joseph's main concern for over a week. When the pain left her side and her knee felt strong again, it took constant diligence to make her stay in bed. It almost caused an argument between them. Joseph knew he'd better follow his mother-in-law's advice, but his wife was determined to be about her work. She would quietly slip out of bed and creep to the doorway, making for the spinning wheel or bread bowl, and he would hear her, even while upstairs.

"Emma! You're not up are you?"

"Just a little. I thought I could do a few things."

His voice took on its note of authority. "Back to bed with you! You shouldn't be doing anything. Your mother will string me up if anything happens to you."

"I'm feeling fine, I tell you."

From the attic, a scowling Joseph poked his head from the doorway. "Back to bed!"

Emma was ecstatic when, in mid-April, Martin Harris arrived. Now Joseph could focus his attention on someone else. Besides, it was always a pleasure to see Martin. However, his buggy passenger was not such a favorite. Lucy Harris had commandeered her way into the carriage. Now she loudly demanded he help her down, and when he turned back to face Joseph, it was a very chagrined Martin who imposed his wife upon the Smiths.

When they were alone, Martin related his recent adventure. He had successfully sought out a Professor Charles Anthon in Boston who studied the characters that Joseph had copied from the golden plates. When the professor had asked to see the source of the characters, Martin told him it was forbidden. Anthon's response was a paraphrased verse from Isaiah, "I cannot read a sealed book." Since Martin recognized these words to be a fulfillment of prophecy, it quickened his resolve to continue in the work he was doing with Joseph. However, it failed to convince his wife. She insisted on accompanying her husband back to Harmony.

There was no more rest for Emma, nor for Joseph. He hid the plates in a different place every day because Lucy Harris was poking around, looking through all their trunks, desks, dressers, cupboards, under the bed, beneath the doorstep, through the hay — anywhere and everywhere she thought the plates might be hidden. Martin begged her to stop.

"Oh pooh! I'm just admiring the Smith's lovely home. Just lovely, Emma! Did you say your mother gave you all these linens? Any false bottom in this trunk? Looks like there could be. I'm amazed you have enough pots to fill such a large cupboard. What's in this box? I might as well tell you, I'm determined to see those famous golden plates of your husband's. I simply won't rest 'til I do."

And so it went for days. Emma became exhausted trying to remain courteous in the face of such unmitigated gall. One day, Mrs. Harris went outside, scouring the area for any likely hiding place. About two o'clock, Emma saw her hurrying up the path with her skirt pulled up, looking around about in every direction as she dashed inside.

"Are there many snakes in the area, Mrs. Smith?"

"Why no. I haven't seen one for months."

"Well, there's a big, black snake that reared its ugly head at me down by the ash pit. Scared me out of my wits, I do say. It actually hissed at me! You'd best be careful, living in such 'primitive' circumstances."

When she was discouraged with re-examining every inch of Joseph's home, she ventured to go inspect the Hale's. Dressed in her stiff, black silk dress, trussed up with ruffles and lace, she laid siege to the home.

Isaac was resting upstairs.

"Such a *lovely*, older home, Mrs. Hale! It reminds me of my first small house. Of course, we decided years ago to build a much larger one from brick. It's so much more permanent, don't you know. Look! How cunning! The dry sink is covered with colored candles. What's underneath? Why, what a large box. What's in it? You don't mind my asking do you? I'm just so interested in all these old-fashioned homes. They hold such charm for big city people like me."

Elizabeth was taken aback. She had never entertained a whirlwind before. She followed Mrs. Harris, straightening up behind her as the woman moved deftly through the keeping room, peering into nooks, opening doors, and keeping up a constant chatter. Why *wouldn't* she sit and be served tea like any normal visitor?

"Mrs. Hale — Elizabeth! May I call you Elizabeth? — We should be friends, don't you think? Elizabeth, I'm dying to know something. Have you seen the plates Joseph is translating? I understand your daughter has been working away her health. And your son Reuben, has helped too. They must have seen them. They must know where they are. Are they here, perhaps, on your property? Goodness knows, I've offered to pay Joseph and Emma if they would just let me inspect them. I can see they need the money. But *he* seems inclined to be stubborn. If I had a daughter married to such a man, I would simply insist that he use every possible means to provide for her. Just think about what one could do with *golden plates*. Now, I'm willing to pay to see them. I have my own money, you know."

"Your money be damned!" A deep, resonant voice bellowed from upstairs. Isaac had awakened.

Elizabeth stopped in her tracks. Lucy stopped and turned, her jaw dropped, her eyes popped. The word "well!" almost formed.

"Better yet, you and your money be gone! And don't let the door hit you going out!" Isaac deliberately showed his red, long john shirt with his considerable girth bulging over his pants.

"Well! I never . . .!" Lucy was astounded.

"No, and you're not ever likely to, either. If I can't see those plates, do you think he's likely to show them to you? Madam, you are on a fool's errand. Therefore, *you* must be a fool. And my patience for fools is growing short."

Isaac might entertain such thoughts himself about his son-in-law, but no one else had better blacken Joseph's reputation. He started down the stairs, and Lucy hitched up her skirt with one hand and lunged toward the door. Elizabeth stood stock still in the middle of the parlor, her eyebrows raised, her eyes wide in amazement and her bosom shaking with laughter. Isaac came scowling down the steps, and they could hear the woman's shrill voice calling, "Martin! Oh Martin!" as she retreated.

The Hales were not the last family to experience the living whirlwind. When she failed to discover the hiding place of the golden plates, Lucy Harris made it her objective to visit every farmhouse in Harmony, belittling Joseph to everyone she could.

"Oh yes, I've known Joe Smith. Known him since he was a lad. I could tell you a few things about that young man. He's received hundreds of dollars from my poor, unsuspecting husband. Says he has gold! Well, he does. My husband's. His family has always been poor as church mice. Either he's a liar, first rate, or he's as stingy as a miser not to share a penny with his family. Visions, peep stones, magical glasses, plates of gold! What a laugh! I ask you, does he look like a wealthy man who owns such treasures? Hardly! Joe Smith hasn't two pennies to rub together, and you'd best watch your own pennies, believe me. If he can't wrangle them out of you, he'll steal them outright."

For two weeks, Lucy Harris poisoned the citizenry of Harmony, while Joseph and Martin worked on the translation, little suspecting the damage she was doing. Neighbors began to avoid the Smiths. Finally, snatches of conversations were repeated to Emma. At last, Joseph talked to Martin.

"Martin, God means to use you, and I value your work as a scribe, but your wife is doing us considerable harm. I don't believe I have a single neighbor who hasn't been turned against me by her sharp tongue."

Martin was appalled. "We'll leave tomorrow whether she likes it or not. Joseph, what can I say? I didn't dream she'd behave like this, while she's living here in your own home. I thought she'd see the goodness in you."

"She chooses not to see. And those who choose not to see turn their souls over to the devil."

Martin was true to his word. The next day he packed his wife's things, bundled her up, nearly tied her down in the carriage and drove her away. When she had wrangled at him for three miles, he told her he would drive into the woods and leave her in a bear pit if she wasn't silent for the rest of the trip. She opened her mouth to protest, and he jerked the reins in the direction of the woods. She shut her mouth, not to open it again for the next three days, until they drove up to the front door of their large, red brick home outside of Palmyra.

"Martin, if you go back to Joseph Smith, I'll . . . I'll do something desperate!"

"I caution you, Madam, to exercise a little prudence. It is quite possible that no one would care!"

"You'll see! I'll sell your portion of the farm."

"No, you won't. I've got all the papers in the hands of my land agent with instructions that you are forbidden to do any business in my absence." And without so much as a goodby, he turned the carriage around and began the long trip back to Harmony.

Chapter Eight

The Darkest Days

The hour was late. Martin was stiff and sore. His neck, his shoulder, his wrist were all cramped and seemed to be on fire. He had been scratching with a quill pen and homemade ink since early morning, and it seemed that his hand was permanently frozen in a tight, stiff position. Still Joseph's voice droned on. He spoke, in slow measured tones. Often he would pause to interpret what he was being given through inspiration. He spelled out proper names so that Martin would not err. Some were familiar names of Old Testament vintage. Some were odd and different. Often Joseph did not know how to pronounce them, and they would figure out the pronunciation together. The first few weeks the task was exciting as a curious tale unfolded before their eyes. Now, however, the work had been in progress for several weeks, and Martin was fatigued with constant writing.

It had been the right time for him to come. Emma, who had written for Joseph earlier, was now in the last stages of pregnancy and quite unwell. She still continued to feel very nauseated, and had lost so much weight her face looked gaunt and hollow. Her movements were slow, and her lower back often hurt. She thought the baby would arrive sometime in June. She and Joseph were anticipating that arrival anxiously. She had sewn a little christening gown and cap. In the small trunk under her bed were several blankets she had made, carding the wool until it was white and beautiful, then spinning it into long, continuous, plump threads which she tightly wove into soft blankets for the little one.

Spring weather had been wet and cool. Emma was usually up before dawn and busy with the work of the day. Once her knee healed, she had insisted on taking over the planting, putting in peas and beans, squash, tomatoes, turnips and herbs. After she took over the responsibility of the garden, Joseph's attention turned to the translation completely. Still, when it came to planting the acreage across the road, he and Martin paused in their scholarly work and planted the corn and wheat. That work was much too heavy for Emma. As soon as the plowing and planting were done, they went back to the translation.

The story unfolded of a family rejecting the society of the day, leaving their comfortable world for religious conviction, striking out into the wilderness, trusting the direction of God, and establishing a different home in a new world. It was not unlike the sacrifices their great-grandfathers had made in settling North America, and it became a regular topic of discussion in the Smith home. Dinner and supper conversation always centered around the translation, the testimony of Christ it contained and about the time it would be published.

Martin had recently received a letter from his wife ordering him to return at once. Their crops needed to be put in, and she was dissatisfied with the field help she had hired. She also told him, in no uncertain terms, that if he had any notion of using their resources to print whatever it was Joseph Smith was pretending to translate, she would have him committed. She had already obtained the support of other members of the family in that regard. It was a mad project, and he had been mad himself to be so entirely duped by Smith.

Finally, Martin spoke to Joseph about it. "When the work is done, I will pay for the printing of it. The Lord put that in my heart long ago. But my wife is a problem. Joseph, I feel I need to take a short leave, borrow the manuscript, and take it home so all my family can see this marvelous work of the Lord."

"No," was Joseph's first instinctive response. At Martin's crest-fallen look, Joseph softened and reconsidered. "I understand, Martin. I'll go to the Lord and then we'll see."

Joseph's answer from the Lord was unmistakable. His prayer brought a clear voice to his mind. "Do not let this work out of your possession." Later that morning, as he and Harris resumed work on the project, he told him the Lord's command.

"All right, Joseph, but I'm not sure where we will get the money to print this manuscript."

"The Lord will provide. Let us go on with the work."

They plunged into transcribing words from the prophet Isaiah, writings from other metal plates which Lehi's family had taken with them into the wilderness. Added to them were comments from Nephi, the leader of this little band of emigrants. He had his own visions and stories of faith. He wrote of Jesus Christ who would come to Jerusalem six hundred years hence. He also recorded crossing the sea in a ship he had built, and then later, building a temple to his God. Martin and Joseph pondered all these things, envisioning this ancient society with amazing stories of faith.

A week after Martin's first request, he approached Joseph again. He had slept badly the night before. His mind had been disturbed by thoughts of printing the manuscript and wondering exactly how it could be accomplished in the face of Mrs. Harris' resistance.

"Joseph, will you go back to the Lord and ask again if I can show my wife and family the work?"

The young seer was doubtful. His former answer had been very plain. He started to refuse, but the look of anxiety on his friend's face softened him.

"Well, I'm not hopeful, but for your sake, I'll try again."

That day he took an afternoon turn about his little farm. Down by the water's edge he prayed again, and this time the sunlight seemed to darken. A feeling of dread came over him, and he seemed to understand, as though using the Urim and Thummim, "You must not let this work out of your possession." He knew Martin would be disappointed, and after all, he was indebted to his friend. This man had believed in him since he was a lad. He had already contributed generously to the cause. His faith and encouragement continued to sustain Joseph. It was very difficult to refuse Martin's request, seeming reasonable as it did.

Harris looked up from his dinner plate with anticipation when Joseph opened the door. At the slight shake of his head the older man's face fell. He wiped a hand over his brow, then stood up and said, "So, let's get back to the work."

But further work was spoiled for Joseph. The cloud of darkness that had come over him at the river persisted. He went out to the garden where Emma was bending over a hoe.

"Here, let me do that," he said. "You'll hurt your back again and be laid up."

"I'm just fine."

"You're too close to your time," he insisted and lifted the hoe from her hands.

"Are you done with translating today?"

"Yes. My mind is clouded. Besides, my wife persists in gardening, and I'm afraid she is going to do herself and the baby harm."

"Joseph! You know I'd never do anything to harm the baby."

"Well, what about all this garden work?"

Emma's usual mild temper flared under the heat of the afternoon sun and the unusual criticism from her husband. "Someone has to do the gardening. My husband hasn't the time."

"I have other work."

"Yes, but your work doesn't put food on the table."

The words stung. It was Isaac's criticism, and Joseph knew it was justified. That cut even more. He handed back the hoe, turned and left his pregnant wife wiping her brow and rubbing her back. He tromped down to the worn path behind the barn and, from there, to the river's edge. He didn't mind doing without things. He was well used to it. The Smith family had never had many worldly possessions, but they had always had enough to eat. He had never before asked anyone for charity. Martin had been quietly providing for their daily needs since he came, and that had played on Joseph's vanity. Practicality dictated that it was the only way to progress in the work. Now, with Emma's words still ringing in his ears, Joseph sat on a fallen tree and gave himself up to dark thoughts of wounded pride.

After a time he tried to pray, hoping to shake the darkness that had come over him. He found his mind blank. No words would come. That continued until he knelt down in the cool grass. He remained on his knees several minutes and still couldn't formulate words of a sincere prayer. He looked at the sunlit June day and thought how it now seemed so dull. At last he came to the realization that he had lost the Spirit. He knew what he must do and quickly started home.

Emma had gone in to start preparations for supper. He took her by the hand and led her back outside where they could be alone. His wife was stiff and unresponsive.

Joseph humbled himself. "Emma, please forgive me! I had no right to speak as I did. I've simply been too occupied to help you, and my conscience is bothering me. Sometimes my pride gets in the way of my love. I'm afraid today was one of those days. Martin has been begging me to allow him to show the manuscript to his family."

"No!" she exclaimed.

"That's what I said. But his wife is threatening to stand in the way of printing the work, and Martin is concerned."

"But to *take the manuscript!* After all our work, it's unthinkable!"

"I know, but tell that to Martin. Without him we haven't the funds to pay for publication. He is more than willing, but faces very stubborn opposition from his family."

"Oh, Joseph, don't let it out of your hands. There is so much at risk!"

"I know, I know. Just continue to be patient with me, please. I love you for your sacrifices, your faith in me. What would I do without my Emma-rose? Just promise you'll be careful. Let me do the gardening. I can get up earlier."

Emma laid her head on his shoulder. Tears came too easily since she became pregnant. Now that she was tired and hurting as well, she was far too susceptible to weeping. But her husband understood. She didn't have to be brave. She didn't have to be strong. He was strong enough for both of them.

The men got back to the work after supper, and Joseph's mind was cleared. He used the strange glasses to decipher the scripted marks on the metal leaves. After a moment the meaning appeared, and he began the translation again, symbol by symbol. When the lamp oil burned out, both men were tired and ready for bed.

As Joseph started down the stairs, Martin first said good night, then added, "What am I to do about my wife?"

Joseph knew the subject would not leave his friend's mind. "It's late, Martin. Let's consider it tomorrow."

But he put it off the next day and then the next. Then came the morning that Martin put down his quill. "Joseph, please inquire of the Lord again. Unless I show her evidence, the Missus will block my efforts to help. She has threatened to have me committed to an institution if I try to mortgage our farm, and that is what it will take to print this book. I simply don't know what to do. She has written that I must return and see to the farm work. I know she's right. The farm can't do without me. I can't stay much longer, and when I go, I need something that will convince her I'm not crazy."

Reluctantly, Joseph agreed to pray one more time. He put aside the glasses, put the gold plates in their box, and descended to the parlor below. He dreaded asking again. He had a heavy sense of heavenly disapproval. Realistically though, Emma was nearing delivery. This could be a good a time for them to take a break from the translation.

Joseph sought out a solitary place behind the small tool shed and bowed his head. The words of his petition came slowly. He knew he was importuning the Lord, and he feared the result. But no lightning struck, no thunder rolled. A short and direct reply came to his mind. "Do as you will, but remember, responsibility for the manuscript is yours."

There should have been a feeling of relief, but Joseph could feel nothing of the kind. His spirit groaned at the thought of turning the priceless manuscript over to anyone. Martin, on the other hand, was overjoyed. He grasped his young friend's shoulders and beamed his gratitude.

"Remember now, Martin, show the manuscript only as necessary to immediate family members, and return it to me here in two weeks. Do you promise?"

"I promise."

"This is our solemn covenant with the Lord."

"I promise, so help me God." Martin Harris raised his hand to heaven as though swearing on a Bible. He soon threw his things into a small trunk, hitched up his carriage and was gone by that afternoon. He carried the precious manuscript with him.

Joseph didn't have much time to worry about Martin and the manuscript. Emma went into labor that very afternoon. It was much more painful than she had thought it would be. The first pain swept over her as she stood stirring the stew pot. It started low in her back, wrapped around her lower belly and seemed to cut right through her. The baby rose up hard inside her womb. She rubbed her belly softly, hoping to relax the muscles, but the pain ran its course. Emma waited. Nothing else happened for a good while.

She had gone on scrubbing the floor when the next pain came. Joseph walked in from outside just as she was gasping and leaning on the bed post. He crossed the room in three strides.

"Emma!"

She looked up at him. Her beautiful, large brown eyes betrayed suffering, just as other females given the honor and the sacrifice of genesis. "Oh, my sweet Emma," he said, his voice full of compassion. "Is it time?"

"I think so. When this shooting pain is past, let's walk over to mother's."

"All right. Here, leave that. I'll scrub the floor. You lie down."

"If I lie down, I may not get back up." She felt a little gush and her thighs were damp. She left her husband and went to their room alone. Another sharp pain hit, and now there was no mistaking. Emma went back to Joseph. He was finishing the floor. She put her hand on his shoulder. "Let's go to mother's."

"Can you walk?"

The stabbing pain had subsided. She smiled determinedly down at him. "I'm fine. After all, women give birth all the time."

Yes, Joseph thought, and some don't survive it. That thought scared him. He could not stand losing Emma. He took her arm to steady her on the uneven ground as they strolled slowly toward her mother's home.

Just as they came to the Hales' back door, another pain struck Emma. Elizabeth opened the door and saw her daughter's white face. She knew immediately.

"It's your time! Just keep walking! It's good for the labor. Brings the baby faster." She picked up a small valise she kept under her bed. "Joseph will change the straw in the ticking. I want fresh straw and clean sheets. Let's go."

Elizabeth led them back toward their little home. Joseph felt excitement rising within him. Today they would have a baby. Maybe it would be a baby boy, a son. If so, they would name him Alvin, after his older brother whom he had idolized as a lad. Elizabeth went to work in the bedroom, pulled old straw out of the mattress and replaced with clean. Then she spread a tanned hide over the mattress, and over that she put clean sheets. She got a supply of clean rags ready and set a pan full of water over the fire.

Joseph walked with Emma around and around the yard. Then, as the pains grew closer, they walked the parlor. Finally, when her back felt as though it would break, she lay down. The pains were coming now every couple of minutes, and they were harder than she had ever expected. The shooting pain gripped her back until she thought her very bones would separate. Her belly rose up hard as a rock, as though the child within was standing straight up on her backbone. Emma moaned with each wave of pain. She had seen other women in childbirth when her mother was called to help deliver. She had pitied them in their agony, then rejoiced with them as the new little life came whimpering into existence. Now it was her turn, and she was determined to be braver than the others. But she found that courage was not the main concern of the day. Just delivering the child was as much as she could think about.

Joseph suffered every pain with her. It was harder for Emma to see him agonize than to work through it herself. At length she ordered him away from her bedside. "Go on, dear. It's better if you're not in here."

"No, I'll stay with you."

"You're not helping. You can't help. Just go outside! Here comes another pain. Go, Joseph, go!" Then her voice rose with the oncoming pain. "Mother! *Mother!*"

When night came on and Emma still had not delivered, Elizabeth ordered the nervous husband completely out of the house. "Go on over home. Go see Isaac. You two can have supper together. It could be a while yet."

So Joseph walked over to Isaac Hale's. His father-in-law was sitting at the table with a bowl of Elizabeth's good soup and a hunk of bread beside it.

"Come on in. Is Emma all right?"

"So far. I didn't think it would take this long."

"Sometimes longer. Sometimes not. First one's the hardest. Don't worry. How about a bowl of soup." Isaac had never been so cordial. Joseph was grateful.

"Thanks. I haven't eaten since morning."

The two men ate in companionable silence. Isaac was the more relaxed. He had gone through this experience many times. He had learned there were times when a man could not help his woman. For Joseph it was all new, and he was a very anxious husband. Finally, when he could stand it no longer, he said, "I'm going back. Emma's been laboring a long spell. Maybe we have a baby."

"All right. I'll go with you."

So they walked together, but as they came in the door, Elizabeth poked her head out from the open bedroom door. "Go for Sophie. This is taking too long. Emma's about worn out. Go right now. I need Sophie."

Joseph and Isaac fixed up a horse and wagon, and trotted off to Elizabeth's sister, Sophia Lewis, whose home was a few miles down the Colesville road. Joseph welcomed this chance to do something helpful. On arrival he jumped from the wagon and rapped on the door. When Sophia came with a sputtering candle, he told her that Elizabeth needed help. She put on her bonnet and shawl and came immediately.

Emma was weakening. She had been in labor ten hours. Her strength was nearly gone, and she cried with every pain. Joseph couldn't stand it. She was suffering so! He prayed for his wife and child, but every sound from the little bedroom startled him. Finally, he went outside to pace. Isaac sat rocking and whittling. He evidenced no particular concern. Only the notches he made on his stick with Emma's every cry of pain betrayed his anxiety.

Just before dawn, Emma collapsed into a near stupor. Elizabeth and Sophia loudly urged her to push. She could scarcely hear through the fog of pain that had settled over her mind. All she knew was the awful, gripping pain had ceased, and she felt a sensation in her pelvis that simply commanded her to bear down. When she tried, her strength gave out quickly, so Sophia gently pushed on her belly. A tingling sensation started at the base of her skull, moved up her face to her right eye lid. Emma felt it stiffen, but she was only dimly aware of it. With the little energy she still possessed she bore down, as Sophia encouraged. Her mother wiped her repeatedly with warm cloths to loosen her muscles and allow the baby passage.

"Here's the head. Another push, Sophia. Careful now; easy now. Shoulders are out. I've got it. Let the rest come."

Then came the pronouncement. "It's a boy. Emma, you've got a little boy."

Elizabeth wiped the baby's face and nose with warm water, clearing the tiny airways. She spatted his little bottom, but he didn't cry. She waited only a moment, turned him upside down, and smacked him a little harder. The damp, pink little body jerked, the chest expanded and a little kitten-like cry sounded in the bedroom.

In the kitchen, Isaac stood up. Joseph threw open the back door and rushed in. The two men stood stock still listening. Sophia stuck her head out from the bedroom and announced. "Mr. Smith, you have a son. Your wife is very low. Pray for them both."

Joseph and Isaac stared at each other as though thunderstruck. Joseph went back outside and threw himself on his knees. *O God, if Emma should die! How could I endure it?* Had he been thoughtful enough of his wife. Her wan face came to mind. The last few months she had lost her girlish energy. She had stubbornly stuck to her household duties and the gardening as well. Maybe he had brought all this on. He should have insisted that she rest more. The young father wrestled with his fear and guilt. No peace came as he prayed for his little family.

When he gave up and went back inside, Grandfather Isaac sat in the rocker with a new baby in his arms. His face was softer than usual, and he sat watching the little one intently. Presently he stood and held out Joseph's son.

Joseph received the precious bundle like a prize. His very own son! The baby stared back at him in the dim lamp light. He had fair, almost translucent, skin. Joseph could see tiny blue veins along the skull and down the head and neck. There was no crying. His breathing was shallow, but regular. Joseph thought he had never held anything so precious. Everything else paled in comparison. His son was a living soul. He was perfect.

Well, almost. When the new father unwrapped the child to examine every inch of him, he found the baby had been born with a deformed foot and leg. The sight of the tiny limb, distorted and shriveled, brought a stab of pain to his father.

"Look!" was all Joseph could say.

Isaac came to his side and commented soberly on the deformity. "It's a bad sign. He'll have trouble all his life. A man needs two good legs."

"Does Emma know?"

Isaac shook his head. Just then Elizabeth came out. She and Sophia had finished cleaning up, changing the sheets and making Emma comfortable.

"Joseph, I'll tell you straight out. I don't know about Emma. She lost a lot of blood. She doesn't answer when we speak to her. Her eyes are dull and don't focus when we pull back the lids. If she makes it through the night, she might live. She's in God's hands . . . ." Her voice cracked and she turned away.

Two lonely tears made their way down Isaac's face. His favorite child, like any other woman, was subject to the dangers of childbirth. Joseph carried the baby into the bedroom and sat down, cradling his young son and watching his wife who lay in an exhausted stupor. Her face was white. Joseph looked down at the baby, whose face had also turned ashen. The pink had left his skin, and the breathing was shallow. As Joseph studied his little one, a shudder passed through the tiny body. The child seemed to gasp for air. It was such a slight movement Joseph wondered if he had seen right. He watched. After a half hour, the baby's eyes fluttered open. He whimpered as another shudder ran through him. He seemed to be fighting for breath.

Fearfully, Joseph called out to his mother-in-law. Elizabeth came running.

"Watch," he said. They stood together, intently focused on the child. When the baby shuddered again and panted for breath, Elizabeth emitted a little cry. Immediately Joseph took the baby to Emma's bed. He grasped his wife's shoulder. She did not respond. Almighty God, he prayed silently, please don't take my wife and child! He shook Emma's shoulder gently once again calling her out of her dark world.

She seemed held in a dark, paralyzing fog, but could hear Joseph's voice, very far away. He was calling her. He needed her. Joseph. Joseph! Joseph! Where are you? She opened her eyes, and he was kneeling at her side with something in his hands. Was it her baby? He saw her eyes open a narrow slit, and he pulled back the sheet, laying her baby in the crook of her arm. A long, languorous sigh of contentment escaped the lethargic mother. Then she closed her eyes and fell back into a deep sleep from which she would not waken for many days.

Emma had no sooner closed her eyes than the baby went into convulsions. Joseph snatched him up and raised the little body to heaven, calling on God to save his life. Isaac and Elizabeth stood in the doorway, weeping quietly. Joseph felt the baby stiffen, then relax, and he sobbed with the realization that this precious little life had gone from them.

No! No! Joseph's whole heart cried out to the God who governs all life, mortal and eternal. But there was no reprieve for him as there had been that ancient day when Abraham offered his son on the altar. Unlike Abraham, Joseph's son was taken. Hot tears coursed down the young father's cheeks, and he left the room so as not to waken Emma with his sobs.

He sat for a long time with the still, tiny form on his lap. When the anguish softened, he spoke woodenly, "We'll bury our son tomorrow."

Elizabeth looked out at the fingers of salmon clouds in the eastern sky. "It is tomorrow."

Isaac sat with his head in his hands. "Won't be able to have a Christian burial. The baby wasn't baptized," he said.

Joseph sat immobile. He couldn't believe his ears. Baptized! Not baptized? Where was there sin in this baby's short life to be absolved through baptism? He knew the doctrine of the day. Ministers taught their flock that infants who died without ceremonial sprinkling were damned and could never have a Christian burial or a hope of resurrection. Such doctrine infuriated him. This pure soul, damned? It was blasphemy!

His voice was hard and determined when he answered Isaac. "*I'll give* him a Christian burial. The child was perfectly innocent. If he isn't an heir of salvation, there is no hope for anyone else."

"You can't give him a Christian burial. You're not clergy." Isaac challenged him.

"I'm his *father!*"

Isaac stood up and walked to the door. "But you're not God. You can't absolve sins."

Joseph's response was authoritative. "What sins? This child had no sins and you know it. Our son has no need of your ministers!"

Isaac reacted immediately with rage. He took his wife by the arm, pulled her out the door, and commanded Sophia to leave also. The formidable father-in-law called out his anathema. "This is your punishment, Smith, for aspiring to be a prophet. Just pray that my daughter doesn't die too, or I'll see to *your* last rites."

Joseph sat by Emma's bedside as sunrise turned to mid-day. He sponged her face and neck. She did not respond. He kissed her forehead and whispered love words to her, but she didn't react. He tried to pray, but the heavens seemed closed. Nearby, his baby lay dead, wrapped in the soft wool blanket Emma had woven. He looked much like a little porcelain doll. Burning tears wet Joseph's face, and as quickly as he wiped them, they coursed down again. Sobs wracked his chest. Maybe Isaac was right — more right than he knew. Maybe God *was* punishing him. He had importuned the Lord after being clearly told that he should not let the manuscript go. He had tempted God. Now the manuscript was gone, the baby was gone, and Emma might be gone before nightfall. He cried out in his agony, "Oh God, all this I will bear! But I beg you, *don't take Emma!*"

Late that night, Joseph took the little body out to the shed, made a small coffin from scraps of wood, wrapped the child tightly in its blanket, kissed the cold forehead, and nailed the casket shut. Joseph felt hard and cold as stone. His heart had hurt so much that it seemed numb and unresponsive to the awful deed he had to do. He took up his shovel with one arm and carried the little coffin beneath his other. He walked up the road to the Hale family cemetery. The moon was so bright he could hardly see the stars. The night birds protested the intrusion into their territory as the sounds of shoveling began. It took only a little while to dig the tiny hole, but it took hours to actually commit his son to the earth.

Joseph knelt and wept over the little coffin. Dreams of a family were in that box. Such a beautiful baby, dark hair like Emma's, tapered fingers like his. Joseph's folks would be proud he had named him Alvin. He sat down beside the grave. He tried to ask God for comfort, but the heavens seemed closed to his pleadings. No amount of praying could assuage the grief that held Joseph captive. Each time he picked up the little box, he put it down again. What would Emma think when she woke and found no baby after all her agony? Oh Lord, if it were truly his fault . . . !

The moon was thinly covered with clouds, and the stars were lost in high wisps when Joseph finally placed the sealed casket into the cool earth. He stood over it, looking into the black hole he had dug. Then he plucked out several strands of hair and placed them on the little box.

"There," he said to his little son, "that's all I can give you until resurrection day." He lifted his arms to the dark sky and called aloud, "Oh God, hear my words, I pray! Take this child back to Thy holy bosom and crown him with glory and everlasting life, for he is sinless and covered by the atonement of Thine own sinless Son. Though I, thy servant may unworthy be, please bless this tiny babe and the mother who suffered to give him a few moments of life."

Still, there was no comforting reassurance from God. No warm sensation spoke of a heavenly blessing. So he began to softly sing, "Praise God from whom all blessings flow. Praise Him all creatures here below. Praise Him above ye heavenly hosts. Praise Father, Son, and Holy Ghost." His voice broke, tears welled up and coursed down his cheeks. Methodically, he filled the hole with dirt, and when it was done, he fell to the ground and gave himself up to wrenching despair.

Emma lay at the point of death for over a week. Joseph kept watch. Elizabeth came every day to check on her daughter. She had never seen her son-in-law so silent. He barely spoke except to thank her. Emma wasted away despite the nourishment they tried to spoon into her mouth. Some of it went down, some didn't. They sent for a doctor. He wanted to bleed her. Elizabeth snorted, "Bleed her?" The woman had bled half to death with the baby's birth. Emma's milk came in, and Elizabeth bound her daughter to inhibit its flow. Emma hardly roused no matter what they did. When, after two weeks Emma was no better, Joseph sank into the depths of darkness. His dreams were in ruins about him, and he had not heard from Martin Harris.

Emma woke slowly one afternoon, swimming toward consciousness as through a heavy sea. There was a mysterious weight on her chest. She felt as though she could hardly breathe. She raised her hand to touch it. She felt soft fine hair and warm skin. It was her husband's head. He had fallen asleep, kneeling beside her, his head on her breast. Oh, my love, she thought. My dearest, dearest love!

Her motion roused him, and his haggard face looked into hers. She was surprised, appalled. She had never seen Joseph like this. But he was just as worried about her. Her right eyelid drooped, and the eyeball had a fine film of blood covering it. The effort of childbirth had broken a vessel in the eye, and the strain permanently affected some muscles on the right side of her face. They responded little to her effort to smile and reassure him that she was all right.

"Joseph, let me have the baby now," she whispered weakly.

He put his forehead on her shoulder so she couldn't see his face. "Not yet, dearest. You must be stronger. Here, try a little of the broth your mother has made."

He spooned warm liquid into her mouth, gently wiping her lips. She swallowed with an effort, trying to obey so she could hold her baby. She stayed awake for only a few sips, then lapsed back into exhausted sleep. Joseph sat beside her, holding her limp hand, grateful that, at last, she seemed to be recovering.

Later that afternoon, Emma awakened again and asked for the child. Her color was better and her voice stronger. Joseph dodged the questions until he had fed her some biscuits and broth. She touched her tightly bound breasts, still hard with milk.

"Let me nurse him now," she pleaded.

Her husband's face dissolved into agony. Tears started to his eyes. "Oh Emma," he wept, "you can't. The babe is . . . he didn't . . . he was so beautiful — like you, he was dark-haired and beautiful. But he only lived a few hours."

Emma did not cry. She simply stared into Joseph's face.

"Did you hear me?" he asked, afraid she would faint again.

"Yes," she finally whispered. Then she turned her face to the wall and closed her eyes.

Joseph's cry was wrenched from his soul. "Emma! Don't! Please, my dearest. Please live for me. I can't lose you, too." He slipped his arms under her shoulders and knees and scooped her up in his arms, turning her toward him so she couldn't shut him out. He sat on the bed, holding her like that. Then he felt her wasted body begin to tremble and shake, and she uttered a deep, low sob, burying her face

211

against his neck. He rocked her for a long time until she cried herself to sleep in his arms. Carefully he lay back against the pillow, still cradling her against him, while he curled up around her back.

Her mother came that afternoon and was scandalized to find Joseph curled up around Emma in bed. But she was soon relieved as Emma awoke, stretched, then carefully sat up, leaning against her husband's shoulder. Elizabeth gave them both some soup and bread with milk.

"Does she know?" Elizabeth asked.

"Yes. I told her this morning." Joseph responded, his arm still possessively around Emma.

Emma looked up at her mother and tears slipped down her cheeks. Elizabeth sat beside them in a chair and patted Emma's hand. After a look at Joseph's haggard face, she reached out and patted his shoulder as well.

The next day, Emma was stronger yet. She recovered sufficiently to ask about the details of her baby's short life. Joseph hoped she would remember holding the child before it died, but Emma could remember nothing from that awful ordeal. At length, she thought of Martin Harris.

"Joseph, you'd better go find him," she said when she heard that Martin had not come back.

"I don't want to leave you. You mean more to me than the manuscript."

"Don't say that!"

"More than anything. More than the manuscript — more than the plates."

She could see that he meant it. His eyes were bleary from sleepless nights of pacing and agonizing these last two weeks.

"But you must go and get the manuscript. I'll be all right. Mother is here."

Reluctantly her husband packed a small knapsack with a few things to eat, his shaving cup and razor, and a change of clothes He left Emma in her mother's care, praying she would be safe until he could get back home. Elizabeth watched him walk off down the dusty river road and felt sorrier for him than anyone she knew.

It was at least a two-and-a-half day journey from Colesville to the Manchester-Palmyra area. This time Joseph traveled by coach, along with another male passenger. He looked so dejected that the stranger finally asked him where he was going. He replied that he had left his sick wife home, ill from the effects of childbirth, and that he was going to Palmyra to retrieve something of great value. The older man watched him quietly. His fellow passenger seemed to be a young man with a lot on his mind. Joseph rarely slept. He was deep in thought the whole way.

When the coach stopped at the Palmyra junction, the driver said he wasn't going that way. He was on his way to Buffalo and couldn't take the time. It was now night, dark as bootblack. Joseph had twenty miles to walk through a forest and over hills. He got out of the coach, and the stranger climbed down to join him.

"Are you going to Manchester, too?" Joseph asked in surprise.

"No, I have business farther on. But you can't walk alone through these woods as tired as you are. I'll walk with you awhile before I take the canal barge."

Joseph was too weary to argue. He accepted the man's assistance gratefully and began the long walk. By midnight, he was asleep on his feet. He stumbled once, then twice, and the stranger took his hand, put it on his shoulder and said, "I'll lead you. Keep your eyes closed if you want. I'll look out for both of us."

So on they went, mile after mile, until Joseph almost collapsed. His new-found friend stopped, ventured that they should rest, but Joseph was obsessed with walking on to his parents' home.

"No," he shook his head. "Let's go on. It's only another few miles. I can almost see it from here."

During those last miles Joseph's "good Samaritan" shook him every so often to keep him awake. They came up the grassy slope of the Smith home just at daylight. Lucy was already at work in her kitchen. She heard them on the steps and opened the door. Joseph all but fell into his mother's arms.

"Joseph!" she exclaimed. "Land alive! What's wrong with my son?"

"He is thoroughly worn out," the stranger exclaimed. "He has buried his baby, left his wife at death's door, and he says there is something here he must take back."

Lucy gave her son and friend some cracked wheat cereal which she had ready for breakfast. Joseph went upstairs to sleep, but not before thanking his departing companion and making a request of his mother. "Send for Martin and the manuscript." Then he collapsed into a deep sleep on the nearest vacant bed.

Samuel was selected to go to the Harris farm and summon Martin.

"Good morning!" Harris greeted him superficially. "You're out and about early."

"Joseph has come and asks that you bring the manuscript." Samuel studied the older man's face. He saw a shadow fall across his friendly countenance.

"Of course. Of course." Martin was a little less fervent than at first. "Come in, boy, and wait for me. I'll just be a moment, then we'll ride back together in the buggy."

Samuel sat uncomfortably in Lucy Harris's parlor. Martin went to the bureau where the priceless manuscript was kept. He recalled guiltily his promise to show it only to his immediate family and to return it to Joseph in two weeks. He had broken that promise. In fact, sharing it was so enjoyable, he had tried to forget the promise altogether. After a week of proudly displaying it to his family, a neighbor had knocked at the door asking to see the "curiosity" as well.

"The manuscript is not a curiosity piece," Martin refused haughtily.

"So! You haven't got it! I knew it was a hoax. Those golden plates of the Smith boy are all nonsense. Joe Smith has hornswoggled you. You've always treated him like a son, but he has played you for a fool. Anyone with plates of gold would be rich by now."

"You are ignorant, sir" Harris hotly rejoined. "I do have a manuscript, translated from ancient characters. Joseph dictated, and I wrote it all down with my own hand. Just wait, I'll show it to you."

He went to the bureau drawer, drew out the manuscript, and was thoroughly satisfied to watch his friend examine the work. That afternoon another friend came, and the scenario was repeated. Soon he was showing the manuscript to almost anyone who stopped by and asked to see it. He was a more important man than he had ever before been.

Now, with Samuel waiting in the parlor, he looked for the bureau key on the mantle. It was not there. He checked under the doily. No, not there either! A panicky feeling began to rise in Martin's chest. He hunted under the other doilies, in vases and behind pictures that adorned their fireplace mantle. The key was not to be found. All right then, he would pick the lock. He took a sharp file and went to work on the bureau. It was a weak little lock, but still he had splintered the wood around it by the time he worked it open. He drew out the little drawer, and it was empty! There was not a scrap of paper in it.

Martin could not believe his eyes. How could it be gone? Then he hollered long and loud, "Lu-u-u-cy!" His wife did not answer. She had gone an hour before to her cousin's home a few miles away. Frantically, Martin began to search through the whole house. Samuel quietly let himself out the back door. He couldn't watch the older man's desperate search. Martin looked in all of Lucy's favorite hiding places, searched every trunk. He looked under mattresses and, in desperation, sliced open pillow cases, flinging the contents across the beds. His promise to Joseph kept sounding in his ears.

"*This is our solemn covenant with the Lord.*"

"I promise, so help me God."

After hours of searching, a sob broke from the old farmer's throat. It was lost! The one hundred and sixteen pages of precious translation were gone! All Joseph's work, Emma's work, not to mention his own effort — all gone. This was Lucy's doing! She hated to admit she was wrong, that Joseph had actually translated something of value. She was determined that her husband not finance the project. She must have taken the manuscript. It was all her fault. Then the truth pierced his soul like a shaft from heaven. *He* was the one who had covenanted with God. He and Joseph had covenanted with God, and he had failed. *He* was the one who had broken their oath. There was no one else to blame. He had cared more for the opinions of man than for his covenant with God. Oh, miserable! He was the most miserable wretch of a man! How could he tell Joseph?

In abject despair, Martin hitched his horse to the buggy and slowly plodded toward Manchester. He rode with his head down, hardly holding onto the reins. When the buggy got to the narrow bridge crossing the canal, Martin glanced at the water. There were barges lined up. Business was booming. Voices called back and forth. But Martin saw only the water, cold, dark, deep. It was inviting. How could he face the Smiths? His heart was sick. His stomach had turned upside down, and bile rose to his throat. Days and months of work, gone, all because of his stupidity! He was unworthy of Joseph's trust, of God's favor. He could hardly bring himself to go on.

All the way to the Smith homestead, Martin rode in dread. He reined up his horse on the north side of the house, climbed down, secured the rig and started toward the front door. Then suddenly he stopped and climbed up on the top rail of the fence, took off his hat and put his face in it. How could he tell the awful truth? They would hate him for it — and they would be right to hate him. He was a liar and a coward, an oath breaker. If only the earth would open up and swallow him now, before he had to face them all. How could he frame the awful words that would bring their condemnation upon his head?

After a long time, when no answer was forthcoming, he let himself down and trudged with head bowed low to the back door.

"Good morning," Lucy greeted him.

Martin mumbled an answer. "Sit down," she directed. "We've been waiting breakfast for you."

He sat with the family, feeling like a traitor. Joseph finally roused himself and also came to the table. He sat down at the end. Martin was silent and downcast. Joseph watched his old friend with growing trepidation. All of a sudden, Martin cried out, "O, I have lost my soul! I have lost my soul!"

Joseph sprang to his feet. His voice was the voice of a condemned man. "Martin, have you lost that manuscript? Have you broken your oath and brought down condemnation upon us?"

"Yes, it is gone," replied Martin in agony, "and I know not where!"

Joseph clenched his hands and paced the floor, crying "Oh, Lord, my God! All is lost! All is lost! What shall I do? I have sinned! I tempted the Lord. I should have been satisfied with the first answer I received, for He told me not to let the manuscript out of my possession."

He wept and groaned, walking back and forth. The entire Smith family broke into lamentations with him. The women wept. The men groaned in despair. Martin felt as though he would rather commit himself to the cold, dark earth than to have brought such calamity on this family which he loved. He got down on his knees and begged their forgiveness. He appealed to each one, even little Lucy and Don Carlos. The youngest Smith children understood that a terrible loss had occurred, and they wept as their elders did.

Joseph was beyond comfort from his mother, his father, even Hyrum. He paced the floor, wringing his hands, sometimes pounding them against his temples. What could be done? Nothing, absolutely nothing! There was no going back, no making up weeks of grief, pain, and now this terrible loss. He had betrayed everything sacred. He had delivered the priceless translation into the hands of a foolish man, and a covenant was broken, not just between Martin and the Lord, but between Joseph and the Lord. Joseph saw the last few weeks clearly. He had refused to listen to the voice of God and, consequently, was facing the darkest days of his life. God had tried to teach him obedience, and he had failed. Now the inspiration was gone, the mantle of seership fallen away. He felt like Samson with his hair sheared off, weak and vulnerable, no longer a tool of heaven. He had tempted fate and lost everything — everything except Emma! Now, how could he return to her with such awful news? After enduring the news of her dead baby, and in a weakened condition, this catastrophe might kill her.

Against his family's protestations, with Martin's pathetic apologies called after him, Joseph left that very day to walk the long miles back to the coach stop. His sentence was to return like a beggar, empty-handed and under condemnation, to his Emma.

Chapter Nine

A Glorious Work

Rich fields of green stretched away from the road running between the Hale and Smith homes and through the quiet little village of Harmony. Two men worked side by side, waist deep in waving grain, sometimes almost hidden by rows of cornstalks reaching over their heads. They were an unlikely pair. One grizzled old veteran of the Revolutionary War, his face and arms tanned to a leathery brown like the hides of animals, and the other a young man, hair burnished almost blond in the intense Pennsylvania summer sun. His skin was golden brown as the pecans the women collected and stored in crockery. The two worked mostly in silence, the old man satisfied with the lessons of hard work, the young man listening for the lost whispers of the spirit.

Emma glanced frequently out the window of her parents' home, watching the two men she loved working the fertile fields together. It was something she had not dared to dream, Joseph and Isaac plowing together peacefully, with no animosity. It was an answer to her prayers.

When Joseph returned with the news that Martin had lost the manuscript, she saw a profound humility settle over her husband like a shroud. All vestiges of pride vanished. After the first few days of despair, punctuated by fervent pleas for forgiveness, he filled his time with the hard labor of farming. His attentions to her were more tender than ever before. In fact, in order to help her, he learned spinning, embroidery, and even cooking in the hours he was not working outside. At night, he read aloud from the Bible, while she sat rocking and pondering the deep hurt in his soul.

Alvin's toolbox was empty. The plates were missing along with the Urim and Thummim. Even if they had been there, the gift Joseph had to commune with the divine was gone. The light had gone from his face, and he smiled rarely, usually when he was trying to comfort his wife. When she was strong enough, he walked her to their baby's grave. She simply stood in silence. So weighed down was she by the terrible events they had endured that healing tears would not come, and sorrow bound her heart. Then he carried her home, afraid the exertion was too much for her still delicate state of health. He lay beside her at night, sweetly affectionate but not amorous. He said he felt unworthy of her love.

Unworthy! She shook her head. Joseph, unworthy? Like a child who had been disciplined, he now counted himself the most base of sinners. Emma tried to reassure him that a loving Father in Heaven forgives sinners. But Joseph was brokenhearted, for he had disappointed God and disappointed himself. He had come to expect more from himself. He had thought he understood obedience. He had truly considered himself God's chosen servant. Now he was doing penance.

Isaac Hale thought Joseph had finally come to his senses. He often saw him out working his field guiding the horse-drawn wooden plow with leather reins wrapped around his arms and broad shoulders. After several days watching the young man, he gave in to Elizabeth's urging and proposed a cooperative effort to his son-in-law. Joseph humbly accepted the offer. They would work together one day on Joseph's land and two days on Hale's larger property. Joseph would have the use of the horse and tools he needed. Young Isaac Ward and Reuben Hale, both strapping, strong young men, worked with him on their land and occasionally on Joseph's, but generally he worked late and alone. He liked it that way. His time alone was spent in deep reflection of lessons hard won. He went back over scenes of his youth, remembering little weaknesses and faults while growing up. He pondered on pride and how serving God could transform into arrogance. A man had to understand that he was nothing more than a tool in the hand of the Almighty. Joseph wiped the blade of the hoe and likened himself to it— a simple, plain, rudimentary tool, but one which could cultivate God's vineyard. He also compared himself to the scarred, wooden plow, toiling to break new ground. He pled from the depths of his heart to be cleansed of pride and to be worthy once more to work in the Lord's field.

It was hard for Joseph to keep dark thoughts away. He was depressed. He worked at appearing cheerful for Emma's sake, but once alone, the gloom would fall over him, for he had grown used to communication with the divine. No one knew of the waves of sorrow breaking over his repentant soul. No one knew how often salty tears fell on the garden soil, mingled with the sweat of labor and summer rains. Sunshine that usually lifted his spirits now found no opening to his heart. The adversary bedeviled him with thoughts of destruction and eternal damnation. Without the Holy Spirit, Joseph was far too susceptible to such torment. Emma eventually knew the depths he sank to in his lonely penitence. For now, he spared her what he could. Emma's life stream was slowly growing stronger, but Joseph was sinking.

Late that July, Joseph was asleep beside Emma, having gone to bed after a fervent prayer that God would forgive him his sins. His sleep was troubled. He tossed and turned restlessly until he awoke with a start. There was a presence in the room. Immediately he knew it was the Lord's messenger, Moroni. The familiar voice sounded in his ears:

"*. . . you should not have feared man more than God . . . Thou art Joseph, and thou wast chosen to do the work of the Lord . . . Repent of that which thou has done which is contrary to the commandment which I gave*

221

you, and thou are still chosen . . . " (excerpt Doctrine and Covenants, Section 3)

As the message was delivered, the room grew brighter with an unearthly incandescence Joseph had often witnessed before and feared he might never see again. An unbearable burden was lifted from his mind. Chastised, but forgiven! Still called to the work! Power surged through his body, head to toe — power over the dark, satanic gloom that had held him captive. Power from the knowledge of his special role in God's plan. He was chosen! He would falter no more. He would set his hand more firmly to the plow and never swerve again!

After the message was delivered, the angel withdrew, leaving a humble Joseph rejuvenated. He immediately left his sleeping wife and went upstairs to the writing desk. With trembling hand, he wrote the revelation delivered to him, not leaving out the reprimand, but recording even his own follies.

The long, languorous summer gave way to a pleasant, gentle fall. Joseph's humble attitude and hard work improved relations with the Hales. Isaac was hopeful that his son-in-law might become a farmer and provide for his daughter. There was no more talk of visions, angels, or translating golden plates. Why even his son, Reuben, had succumbed to the folly of writing down some so-called translations of Joseph's. Isaac was relieved it appeared to be over. The death of the baby and the protracted illness of Emma had put an end to such nonsense. Joseph had settled down at last. Isaac allowed himself a grudging respect for the young man. He might have more to him than first met the eye. He was an untiring worker, accepting his father-in-law's direction and never asking for anything. Now when the subject of Joe Smith came up with neighbors, Isaac defended him saying, "He'll make his mark in the world yet."

Emma was comforted to see Joseph regaining his natural, cheerful personality. One day he showed her the revelation he had written, and he told her about the visit by Moroni.

"Come up to the attic with me," he had coaxed her.

"Why? You said yourself, the plates were gone. There is nothing for us there."

He tugged at her arm. "Humor me. Just come upstairs."

The attic brought back memories. She looked around. It needed dusting. The blanket still hung as it had last June. She should wash it. The bed where Martin slept was still rumpled. Nothing had been touched since that fateful day when he had left with the manuscript and she went into labor. It wasn't a happy memory for her.

Noting the sadness of her expression, Joseph quickly opened the desk drawer. He handed her a piece of parchment, etched with his own faltering penmanship.

"Read it," he invited.

She read the words of chastisement and the promise. When she looked back up at his face, it was shining in the old familiar way. Then she understood. She had not had any doubt God would still use Joseph for his work. But he had. She saw the man her husband could become. She would always remind him of that and defend him from those who tried to diminish his special calling. She put her arms around her husband as if to shield him from a world that would assault his self-confidence. No one, nothing would harm him while she breathed.

No man ever felt more driven to provide for his wife. Through the harvest of 1828, Joseph worked long hard hours to lay in a winter's supply. It rubbed him wrong — as it did Emma — to rely on the charitable kindness of friends. He worked with Isaac and his sons to harvest the crops from their two farms. Joseph was such congenial company he finally won a grudging acceptance from his father-in-law. Reuben and Alva developed a genuine liking for him. Emma watched it all with satisfaction. She knew, however, her family never saw her husband at his best. They never saw him, as she did, endowed with the spiritual power that made him a prophet.

Joseph was never idle. He was always anxiously engaged with his day's work. When farm work was done and Emma sat rocking and mending, Joseph studied. He memorized Biblical scripture, analyzed passages, and debated issues with his wife. It bothered him that the Lord's church, as he had set it up, was nowhere to be found. Where were the apostles? Where were the ordinances, including baptism for the dead of which Paul wrote to the Corinthians? He found so many incongruities in the Bible that he told Emma it begged for revision. As he read aloud, he would often stop, look up and say, "This is wrong." Then he would explain how the passage should read in order to be in harmony with God's law.

One night, he told her about his conversation with her father about the burial of their baby. She put her sewing in her lap. Her whole attention riveted to her husband. She had heard the arguments for and against infant baptism, but this time it was not an academic exercise. She thought of the little soul who had struggled to be born. If he was born in sin, as the so-called "Christian ministers" said, then her love with Joseph was sinful. How could any marriage be righteous? Then why was marriage considered a sacrament of God? If it were sinful, how could mankind perpetuate the race and not offend heaven? It made no sense. Adam had not sinned in loving his wife; he had sinned by disobedience. If God had not wanted him to have posterity, He would not have given him Eve as a wife.

Emma was grateful to her husband for his courage and insight. Their son had been an innocent human being, and they were not about to be told any differently. The purest gift God ever gives us is our children. It was this kind of inspiration that set Joseph apart from all other men.

Truly he seemed set apart to a holy calling. His mind reached back to the teachings of ancient prophets. He studied their words, especially those of Isaiah. The lost manuscript had quoted Isaiah, and more than once he told her, "Emma, the golden plates contain scripture as important as Isaiah's words. I am eager to get back to the translation." She knew one day the angel would return the plates, and it would all begin anew. This time the work would not be stopped by any power under heaven. She also felt their future lives would never be quiet or serene again.

In late September, on the anniversary of Joseph's first visit from Moroni, the heavenly messenger came again. Joseph suspected that he might, so he waited upstairs on the little bed Martin had occupied. He spent most of that night in prayer. When the night was almost gone, and Joseph despaired of ever returning to favor with the Lord, his room began to grow light. In the midst of the brightness was Moroni. Joseph was taken aback. The angel's countenance was as terrible as thunder, and his voice unforgettable:

"*Thou wast chosen to do the work of the Lord, repent and thou art still chosen. Now let the work go forth!*"

With that, he returned the golden plates and departed. Joseph knew that heavenly angels would continue watching over him and the plates. To fail again was unthinkable. He placed the treasure back in their box, locked it, then went back down the steep staircase and into the bedroom.

Emma was not asleep. Something had awakened her. Something had disturbed her rest and quickened her body. She sensed that Joseph was entertaining spiritual guests. She waited for him to come to her.

Soon he descended the stairs and gathered her up in his arms. In a shaky voice he said, "There is good news, my love. The plates have been returned. I am to start translating again."

"That's wonderful!" she said, then practicality intervened. "But there is so much to do on the farm now to get ready for winter and father has just gotten used to counting on your help. I think it best not to speak of translating for now, not even to Reuben. I will write for you when I can."

"Everything in its season, Emma-rose. I am a more prudent man now."

The first of October, Joseph Sr. and Lucy Mack came to visit. They had worried about Joseph since the loss of the one hundred and sixteen pages and no less about Emma's condition since the death of the baby. They reported on the family back home. All were well. From his little spread nearby, Hyrum was managing the farm. Sophronia was happily married to William Stoddard, and Samuel had grown to be their right hand on the farm. Lucy chattered on pleasantly about family news until the last tidbit had been told.

She finally concluded by asking, "Don't you want to know about Martin?"

Joseph looked at Emma. Memories washed over him that still hurt. It was hard to think about it. Emma nodded silent encouragement.

"Yes, of course, mother. How is Martin?"

"Very humble and penitent."

"I understand." Joseph was still engaged in his own protracted repentance.

"He asked us to beg your forgiveness."

"He doesn't need my forgiveness. He needs the Lord's."

"And he is seeking it daily. I've never seen a man so brought down in my life. In fact, he looks so low I feel sorry for him."

"Martin must work out his own salvation before God, and I'm sure he will. This work is important, too important for any man to destroy. The Lord knows all things, and He knew this would happen. I am now trying harder than ever to understand His will and trust His guidance."

"Have you decided what to do? Will you re-translate?" his father asked.

"No. The Lord has told me not to. Like the Israelites of old and the lost words of God from Mt. Sinai, this part will be lost to the present world. I will go on to the next portion and translate from other plates. If I should re-do that work, corrupt men would change my original text and try to discredit me and the manuscript. There is much more to the ancient record than what Martin lost. God intendsthis work to come forth as another witness of Christ."

"When will you start on it?"

"I already have, sporadically. Emma helps when she can, and there are other duties . . .."

His father asked, "Joseph, how can I help? I want to be of assistance."

His son was touched. "I'll enquire as to what your calling should be. Father, your very presence is a strength to me."

The Smiths stayed a week. They visited the Hales and were pleased to see the cordial feelings that existed between their son and his in-laws. They knew it hadn't always been so. Emma's parents were pleasant and accommodating with them. Joseph had obviously mended fences where Isaac was concerned.

The day before they left to return home, Joseph placed his hands on his father's head and said, *"A marvelous work and a wonder is about to come forth . . . For behold the field is white already to harvest; and he that thrusteth in his sickle with his might bringeth salvation to his soul."* (Excerpt Doctrine and Covenants, Section 4)

With that blessing, Joseph Sr. felt renewed faith that his son would continue to fulfill his righteous calling. He and Lucy stood and embraced their son, then tearfully left him their blessing as they said goodbye. Joseph and Emma packed the wagon with their trunk, food enough for three days, and a few small gifts to take back for the family. They stood side by side and waved as the elder Smiths started for home.

Like the heavy atmosphere before a storm, Emma felt an ominous whirlwind gathering. Resting was over and real work would begin anew. She was grateful for the respite. It had allowed Joseph to gain maturity and understanding, while granting her time to recuperate from the ordeal of childbirth. As they walked back to their snug, warm cabin, she wondered what other ordeals awaited them.

One rainy day in March, a buggy was pulled up in the Smith yard. Splattered and dripping rain, Martin Harris knocked at their door. The sight of their old friend brought unexpected pleasure to the couple. Joseph welcomed Martin in with enthusiasm.

"Martin, it's good to see you. You're soaked. Come warm yourself. I'll get your trunk, and you can put on dry clothes."

Martin was grateful for Joseph's kindness and accepted his friend's hospitality with more soberness than ever before. When dinner was finished, Emma politely excused herself. Martin cleared his throat and hesitantly brought up his reason for coming.

"I know you wonder whatever happened to the manuscript."

"No. I am resigned to its loss."

"I still question my wife about it. It has been the source of much contention in my home."

Joseph nodded in understanding. Martin went on. "My family thinks I'm crazy, deluded. They fill me with doubt, so that sometimes I'm hard pressed to believe in my own sanity. I think back to those days I sat upstairs and listened to you translate. Was it all a dream?"

Joseph smiled. He knew exactly what Martin was going through. It was the trial of his faith. He was being tested above everyone else. God must have special interest in him.

"What do you think, Martin? Was it real? Was it a hoax?"

"I think it was real. I know it was real. I wrote most of the manuscript, didn't I? I surely didn't make up those words. I heard the rustle of the metal pages you translated. Joseph, I've known your character since you were a boy. I will testify before the whole world you are a true prophet, or I never drew breath."

Joseph was touched. "Thank you for that. There have been times when I've wondered . . . but God is merciful, my friend. The Almighty God is ready to recommence His great work. And for some reason, known only to Him, I have once again been called to assist. I believe you yet have a part in it too."

Martin almost burst into tears. He was so overwrought that he got up and walked about the room, his face was contorted strangely, and he blew his nose frequently. Finally, he stopped at the window, looked out over the river a few hundred feet away, and spoke with resolve, "Joseph, I think there must be other witnesses. The world will not receive this work any better than my wife has unless others see the record and testify that your story is true."

He could not even bring himself to turn and face the young prophet for fear he had offended him. Joseph crossed the room to his old friend and grasped his shoulder.

"Martin, you are an inspired man. There will be witnesses, perhaps several. When this work is published, there will be testimony enough for everyone. If you continue to humble yourself, you may yet be one of those special witnesses."

Then Joseph spoke with authority words of counsel which came powerfully to his mind. He told Martin to humble himself, keep the commandments, have faith, and to worry no more about the matter.

When he had finished, Joseph looked into his friend's eyes and concluded, "Thus saith the Lord." Martin's heart leapt for joy. In great amazement and relief, he turned and embraced Joseph. The two men thus renewed their lifelong friendship in an outpouring of happiness.

On April 5, a beautiful Sabbath morning, Joseph awoke with a great feeling of expectancy. Today he would have an important visitor. He lay quietly in bed and envisioned clearly a young gentleman walking toward him. The man was coming to help him with this translation. He was badly needed. Martin had returned to Palmyra, never again to enjoy the privilege of acting as scribe for the translation. Joseph had worked on it but little. He had been promised help and had been waiting as patiently as possible.

Before noon, Joseph looked out the attic window and saw the fulfillment of his morning vision. A man was nearing their home. He looked every inch a gentleman. Joseph put away the plates and hurried down the stairs to the door.

"Good morning," he greeted the visitor.

"Good day to you," the young man replied. "I am looking for Joseph Smith, Jr."

"And you have found him. I am the man. And I have found the man who is to be my new scribe."

Oliver Cowdery was astounded. After introducing himself, he replied, "I'd like to be. How did you know?"

Joseph was beaming. He shook Oliver's hand firmly. "Such things are often made known. Come in. Come in and I'll tell you about the work."

Cowdery was still amazed. What a singular experience. He was sure they had never met before. He would have remembered this tall, personable man. Why, just his eyes alone were unforgettable. Smith looked at him as though he knew his entire life's story. Oliver looked about anxiously. It was a small cabin, but comfortable enough. The floor was a beautiful maple, well-scrubbed, with a braided rug in the center. Everything in the parlor was neat and tidy. Some industrious woman's hand obviously cared for the place. In the corner a spinning wheel rested with fiber wrapped around it.

"You're not entirely unknown to me, Mr. Smith," Oliver said. "I have spent several months as a schoolteacher boarding with your parents. Your reputation there is remarkable."

Joseph laughed. "I'm sure it is. Whether good or ill I don't know."

"Sometimes both, depending on who was telling the story. In any case, the whole town thinks you're a wealthy man — some kind of Indian treasure, they say."

"And what do you think of their stories?"

"If the stories are true, you live prudently."

Now Joseph laughed heartily. "Yes, I do. 'Prudently' is a fine word. Frugally, simply! The truth is, I have a treasure all right, but it is a treasure from God, not the kind that makes one rich on earth. It is the sort that will make us rich in the eternities."

"I have some idea of what you might mean. I have learned something of it from your family. You certainly resemble your father and brothers, if I may say so. I think I would have known you anywhere. Your parents were understandably reluctant to talk much about your experiences. I'm afraid the citizens of Manchester and Palmyra have not been very kind since stories about you began to circulate. However, eventually your mother related the entire experience to me, including the tragic loss of your manuscript."

Joseph interjected eagerly, "So you decided to come and see if I needed a new scribe! God has sent you, Brother Cowdery! You are the very person I need. My wife is very occupied with her duties here at home and cannot help much. It puts too great a burden on her, and I am sensitive to her health. You are a welcome sight."

"Have you a place for me to sleep?"

"I have. You shall stay here with us. The bed upstairs is comfortable enough, and my wife is a wonderful cook. She'll fatten you up with her delicious donuts, bread and stew. It's a task, Oliver. I won't deceive you. It will be a lot of work, and you may grow weary before it's done. But it is a task worthy of your attention, and God will surely bless you. The Holy Spirit has told me about you, and I know you are worthy of great spiritual manifestations. You'll receive them, and more, as you assist in this great project."

Emma returned from her garden to find her husband more jubilant than she had seen him in a long time. The young man, whom he introduced as Oliver Cowdery, was courteous and well spoken. He had a rather wide, clear forehead and almost girlish eyes, with lashes so long she tried not to be envious. There was a look of intelligence about his face, and Emma particularly enjoyed his articulate conversation. They sat and talked until it was time for supper.

"It can be tedious work," Emma warned him. "But it is *glorious* work. You help my husband, and I'll do my best to make you as comfortable as possible. I can't provide the kind of assistance he needs, so I'll make sure you're both well fed while you do the Lord's work."

The next day, Oliver and Joseph walked and talked along the banks of the Susquehanna river. Joseph told his new friend about his experiences with the angel Moroni, of returning year after year to the hill Cumorah to view the golden plates, only to be disappointed each time.

"It was my schooling, Oliver. God can't use you as He desires until you have learned to be *absolutely obedient.* Many have faith and many have love, but few have the fierce self-discipline to be completely obedient. And full obedience to God's every command is the only way to eternal life. Do you see that?"

Cowdery nodded. Yes, he saw it. Obedience — over and over, the scriptures command obedience to God's law. He was coming to recognize in his new-found friend a greater degree of discipline than he had dreamed possible. Joseph not only sought to live the obvious commandments, but he sought out God's will in everything. He asked, he listened, and he walked in the spirit of daily revelation. Oliver's decision to stay and help Joseph with God's remarkable project was easily made. They began work the next day.

It was April 7, 1829. While the rest of the world awakened to mundane daily chores, slopping hogs, milking cows, plowing fields, Oliver Cowdery sat down at a little writing table in an upstairs attic, dipped his quill in the ink pot, and began to write the words that fell from a prophet's lips. It was a glorious experience, hearing an ancient tale full of prophecy and testifying of Jesus Christ on every page. Joseph's voice took on almost a hypnotic quality. It was measured and careful, but the words came to him like the flowing of a great river over a dam. Oliver felt a thrill pass through him, and he shivered with joy. From the silver light of the morning sunrise to the deep velvet hours of night when Emma had gone to bed alone, Joseph and Oliver worked on. By the power of God he deciphered the strange characters. Over time, they became familiar to the young seer. He often translated whole sentences, even paragraphs, without pausing, and Oliver had to hurry to keep up with him.

"Wait! Wait," Emma would hear occasionally, and she would smile as she sewed.

The presence of Moroni watching over the work was powerful. Joseph asked Oliver once or twice if he could sense their guardian, but his answer was no. His faith was strong, but he was not prepared yet to endure the glory of a heavenly being. His writing hand would sometimes cramp, his fingers drawing up rigidly. He would plead with Joseph to wait, and he would straighten his fingers, sometimes dipping them into warm water to loosen the muscles. Then they would resume the work. Joseph was under the same stress. His muscles became sore and stiff, translating for hours at a time. Several times each day the two men would get up, stretch, rub each other's strained neck and shoulder muscles, and hurry back to the story.

And what a story it was! The story of a whole civilization was revealed, the rise and fall of the tribe of Joseph of old. It told of their righteousness and their wickedness. It resounded with warning after warning from God and recorded the tragic consequences of their disobedience. There was a theme that resonated throughout the book. Disobey and be damned; obey and be exalted. So many questions dividing the Christian sects of modern day were resolved while translating the golden plates. Baptism was to be done by immersion. There was no sprinkling recorded in this holy writ. The Messiah was not a Jewish myth, nor Jesus Christ the wishful thinking of Christians. Christ was not just another prophet. The prophesied Savior was the veritable son of God, appearing in resurrected glory to the people of ancient America.

Wars and wickedness abounded in the tragic story. There were days when Joseph wept as he dictated the terrible tale of destruction stemming from evil men, their pride, their greed, their deceit. His heart mourned for them. Marching through his mind was a parade of their triumphs and their fall, and he wept for them.

More than once, when they paused from the work, Joseph mused aloud over the tragic story. "Is this the destiny of our people?

Will we, likewise, fall into utter destruction because of our wickedness? I fear for us, Oliver. I see this same evil devastating our land like
a flood."

Without Joseph's work, the early crops he had planted struggled.
The ground was frozen until March. He had put in some winter wheat
last fall, and peas as early as he could break the earth with a plow. By
late April and into May it was barely starting to grow. Emma had all
she could do to maintain the work of the house and her small vegeta-
ble garden. The fields of wheat lay unattended, left to grow if they
would grow, or fail if they would fail. Joseph's focus was entirely on the
work of translation. He had an unyielding sense of urgency now that
the gift had been restored to him. He often told Emma with exultation how much he was learning about the will of God from the pages
of the emerging book.

Isaac watched his son-in-law's fields go unattended and guessed
the reason. On the rare occasion he spoke to Joseph, he could see the
red eyes and pale features of a man secreted behind closed doors.
When Joseph Knight brought supplies to help the Smith household,
Isaac was furious.

"Why doesn't the man get out and work? He's shiftless, Elizabeth, just as I suspected all along. And who's that Cowdery man living
with them? Another religious dreamer, I suppose? I never thought my
daughter would accept charity. I raised her better than that. Why, I'd
starve first. Emma's a disappointment to me. After all I taught her, and
she ran away with a lazy beggar."

"Isaac!" Elizabeth reproved.

"Well, what else can you call him?"

"Our daughter calls him a prophet," she said, going quietly on
with her darning.

"A prophet!" Isaac snorted. "Poppycock! We have all we need of
God's word right here in our Bible," and he thumped the well-worn
old book. "If he thinks he can add to it, he is crazy. No one creates
scripture but God himself. Certainly not some uneducated plowboy.

Smith has a high opinion of himself."

"Well, he's not haughty. And a more attentive husband could not be found. I believe he loves Emma deeply."

"Hah! Then let him provide for her."

Emma and Isaac had a similar conversation when she took some early yellow flowers over to place on her baby's grave. Supplies were low in the Smith house. Samuel had come to stay with them a few days, and Emma was hard pressed to feed them all. Men had such appetites! Her garden had barely started to grow. Nothing was ready for picking yet. She was almost down to the bottom of her flour barrel. The pork was gone. It looked as though Joseph would have to stop translating and find some odd jobs to earn money for supplies. She hated to ask him to do it, but the situation was becoming serious. Perhaps Samuel . . . .

She stood looking down at the grave, lost in thought. When she heard the rustle of leaves close at hand, she looked up. A sense of dread came over her. She put it away. This was her father. She loved him dearly. Lately, however, his criticism of Joseph had put a wedge between them. She didn't want him to know how desperate circumstances were.

"You're looking a little peaked, Emma. Not expecting again are you?"

"No, Papa. Just a little tired, I guess. I thought I'd take a little walk and lay these flowers on the baby's grave."

"What's Joseph doing?"

"He's visiting with his brother, Samuel, and our friend Oliver. Samuel just arrived with news of Joseph's family in Manchester."

They stood together, father and daughter watching the lingering fingers of the sunset and listening to sounds of crickets growing louder and louder as twilight came on. Finally, Isaac could contain himself no longer.

"Emma, don't you get tired of doing all the work?"

She drew away. "Joseph works long and hard."

"I don't believe that. Most men are out in their fields cultivating and planting. You can't reap what you don't sow."

They had argued about Joseph before, but now she turned on her father angrily for the first time in her life. Her voice was testy and hard. "That's right, father. And Joseph is sewing the seeds of eternal life. I'm living with a prophet of God. By his efforts, countless souls will be saved. God has shown me that. You could be one of them. What will you reap in the hereafter? Unless you stop criticizing and fighting against my husband, you will reap damnation."

Isaac pulled back. He was astounded. His daughter had never spoken to him that way! And Joseph Smith was the cause. The man had turned his own daughter against him. Isaac's fury began to rise — not at the daughter he loved, but at the man who had stolen her.

"Joseph Smith will be in hell before I am! I would rather have seen you here in a grave than to marry him! You will live to regret the day you met him. I tell you, daughter, no good can come from him. You'll weep and mourn because of him. I can be a prophet too, you see! If he is so favored of God, why is his firstborn son lying here at our feet, without even a proper burial? Mark my words. It'll be a life of sorrow for you!"

Isaac Hale's voice had risen to a shout. Emma endured the onslaught with silent, unflinching dignity. When he had finished, she turned on her heel and walked away without another word. Isaac knew their relationship had changed forever.

The supplies Joseph Knight brought maintained them through the rest of the work of translation. The food was welcome, but the paper was even more valued. They were going through it at a great rate. Samuel Smith had come to try to understand for himself the work his brother was involved with. That his parents believed in it was not enough. He had to know for himself that this was the work of God. So he stayed awhile, working at odd jobs during the day to help provide some money for the little household. At night he listened to

Joseph's voice from the attic above, punctuated by protests from Oliver to pause a moment, or to exclaim over a particular passage. Sometimes they all held lengthy discussions about the story unfolding from the gold leaves. He heard his own name as given to a fiery, ancient American prophet, preaching repentance, testifying of Jesus the Christ.

The night Joseph dictated the appearance of the resurrected Christ to the ancient Americans, Oliver, Samuel and Emma all sat in rapt attention. Oliver stopped writing as Joseph's words mesmerized them.

"Behold, I am Jesus Christ the Son of God. I created the heavens and the earth, and all things that in them are. I was with the Father from the beginning. I am in the Father, and the Father in me; and in me hath the Father glorified his name. I came unto my own, and my own received me not. And the scriptures concerning my coming are fulfilled. And as many as have received me, to them have I given to become the sons of God; . . . I am the light and the life of the world. I am Alpha and Omega, the beginning and the end . . . And ye shall offer for a sacrifice unto me a broken heart and a contrite spirit. And whoso cometh unto me with a broken heart and a contrite spirit, him will I baptize with fire and with the Holy Ghost . . . I have laid down my life, and have taken it up again; therefore repent, and come unto me ye ends of the earth, and be saved." (Excerpt from the Book of Mormon, 3 Nephi, Chapter 9)

All four of them sat absolutely still, stunned by the power of the revealed words. Each of them had silent communion with the Savior, and each examined their own worthiness to "come unto Christ." If Samuel had any lingering doubts, this night he felt the power of God channeled through his brother. When he looked upon Joseph, he saw his countenance illuminated. Never had any of them heard more beautiful words testifying of Jesus Christ, words recorded almost eighteen hundred years ago and hidden in the depths of the earth to protect them. Now, by their meager efforts, this testimony of their Lord was about to burst forth upon the world and prepare the day He might come again! The realization of the magnitude of this work was so weighty, Joseph and Oliver simply sat staring at each other for a long time. Each man appealed silently to the Almighty, "Oh God, make me worthy."

One day in late May, Joseph was translating the words of Moroni, and his awareness of the angelic presence lent particular weight to each word. The southeast corner of the attic had become almost holy ground as the angelic presence permeated it. The rest of the room could be enveloped in late afternoon shadows, but that corner was always light. Finally, Joseph understood the great commission Moroni had received. He had been given guardianship on earth of the precious compilation his father, Mormon, had made from an abundance of other histories. Mormon had labored all his adult life, not only to keep the priceless writings of the kings and prophets, but to condense them into one record that could be saved, even if all others were lost. Besides that lifetime commission, he was also called to lead his own people to hopeless battle, time and time again — hopeless because of their wickedness, hopeless because, even in their extremities, they refused to turn to God. Yet Mormon loved them, as a father loves his wayward child. So in the face of their sure destruction, he continued to lead them until his death. When he turned his cherished record over to his son, Mormon charged him to guard it with his life. Moroni kept that trust with his earthly father, hiding the plates many times, working on them and adding his own words as often as he was able. At the end he challenged any who read the account:

"And when ye shall receive these things, I would exhort you that ye would ask God, the Eternal Father, in the name of Christ, if these things are not true; and if ye shall ask with a sincere heart, with real intent, hav-

ing faith in Christ, he will manifest the truth of it unto you, by the power of the Holy Ghost." (Excerpt from the Book of Mormon, Moroni Chapter 10)

During mid-May, Joseph had learned of baptism by water and by fire and wanted to understand. His desire turned to determination, and he took a breathing spell from dictating, and invited his scribe to go for a walk.

"Oliver. Let us put this aside for a time. Come with me. I want to go down to the river. We need to inquire about baptism. I have seen people baptized, many by immersion, but none by *fire*."

Oliver put the quill pen down slowly. "All right," he responded in a measured voice. He had seen Joseph pray before. Sometimes he had felt as though his bones would melt. Now, a feeling came over him he could not describe. He followed Joseph down the stairs and out into the yard. They walked over the spring grass, still small and stubby. The May sun was light upon their shoulders. All the world seemed to be singing — the birds, the river, the very leaves of the trees. Oliver thought he would remember to his dying day his awareness of every aspect of God's world as he walked beside the man he had come to revere as a prophet.

Joseph was serene. He was, by now, growing used to heavenly manifestations. He was going to inquire of God and was perfectly sure he would obtain an answer. But such an answer, even he could hardly anticipate.

The two men found a secluded place among the trees close to the water's edge. They knelt in the cool grass and began to pray. Joseph seemed full of energy, and when he prayed for understanding, he did so, not as a beggar, but with all the assurance of a son. After only a short time, the tiny hairs on the back of Oliver's neck suddenly stood up on end and a shiver ran down his spine. Immediately, a voice sounded in their ears. It penetrated to the marrow of their bones. A soothing voice, as melodious as a mountain stream, bade them be at peace. Then, the bright May sun paled as a greater light burst upon the two men kneeling.

At the center of the light was an angel, blazing in all the brilliance of his calling. The glorious force set them both back on their heels, and they were stricken with silence, staring into the awesome aura of a mighty angel from heaven. A flood of admiration and gratitude fell upon the two men as they experienced with wonder this manifestation of sublime glory that accompanies the angels of heaven. They would have been inclined to worship this being, but he proclaimed himself only a servant to the Almighty God. The angel placed his hands on their heads, and simultaneously Oliver and Joseph heard him speak.

"Upon you my fellow servants, in the name of Messiah, I confer the Priesthood of Aaron, which holds the keys of the ministering of angels, and of the gospel of repentance, and of baptism by immersion for the remission of sins, . . . " (Excerpt Doctrine and Covenants, Section 13)

He ordained them to the Holy Priesthood and commanded them to baptize each other in the clear river water. After they did so, with Joseph immersing Oliver first and then Oliver baptizing him, they stepped back into the little clearing. They were dripping water, their hair steaming, for as on the day of Pentecost, cloven tongues of fire accompanied the Holy Ghost which fell immediately upon them. It was the baptism of fire spoken of in the scriptures. It swept over them like a hot river, surging and consuming all boundaries. Pulsing as with the throb of a vast heartbeat, the two men knelt breathless at the water's edge.

The angel revealed that he was John the Baptist. He said he was acting under the direction of Peter, James and John who held the keys of the higher, or Melchizedek priesthood. He assured them there would come a day when they would be given those keys as well. The two men felt almost lifted off the ground as long as the angel remained and they were held in the grip of his celestial power. Then, as quickly as he came, the glorified servant of God left, wrapping, or so it seemed, his splendor around him like a cloak, and leaving them alone in their clump of trees.

Oliver immediately slumped over, limp as a wet rag. Joseph was used to the effulgence of the spirit. He could sustain it for hours at a time before feeling drained. But now, even he threw himself on the cool, damp grass and lay as in a stupor for a long time. When Joseph finally got enough strength to raise his head, he looked over at Oliver and said, "That was worth inquiring about."

One look at her husband told Emma that something special had happened. Neither man could bring himself to talk about it. Oliver was visibly shaken, uncharacteristically silent, and Joseph did not go back to dictating that day. It was a spiritually renewed and re-dedicated Joseph and Oliver who returned to their work on the morrow. Only sometime later were they able to describe to her the events of that day and of another, even more compelling experience in receiving the holy Melchizedek portion of the Lord's priesthood under the hands of the Savior's own disciples, Peter, James and John. Emma listened as the two men recounted these experiences, looking back and forth to each shining face. It was a glorious account, but she knew she could not share the news with her family. Such events of the spirit would never be accepted at the Hale farmhouse across the road.

On his way to Pennsylvania, Oliver had passed through Fayette, New York and stopped to visit his friend, David Whitmer. He had told David he was going to find out for himself if Joseph Smith was truly a prophet of God. During his stay with Joseph and Emma, Oliver had written Whitmer and told him he believed he had, indeed, found a modern day prophet. By June, rumors had saturated Harmony that Joseph was translating plates of gold, and he had so many curiosity seekers stopping regularly he could barely work. Since he would not show his manuscript, let alone the plates, most of the inquirers concluded it was a hoax. Inevitably, suspicion turned to animosity and some small mischief was done about the farm. Joseph's father-in-law didn't help matters. He would freely tell neighbors Joseph was a charlatan of the first water. Hostilities increased to the point that neither Oliver nor Joseph could get work nor buy their translating supplies.

When a letter came from David Whitmer suggesting the families in the Fayette area were interested in his work and favorably disposed, Joseph talked matters over with Emma and Oliver.

"If we went to Fayette we could finish our work in peace. We're almost done. I think with concentration we could finish it in a few weeks. Here we suffer constant interruption and our supplies are almost gone. Emma, I think you'd be better off without us here. The neighbors don't hate you, just me. What do you think? Should Oliver and I go to Fayette?"

Emma could hardly stand the thought of separation. Her first inclination was negative. "I don't think I could stand living without you."

"It wouldn't be for long. Just a few weeks really."

"Once you have the manuscript finished, then what?"

"Well, Martin has pledged to finance the publication."

"That means Palmyra."

He looked at her soberly. "That's right 'Palmyra.' There's a printing press there."

"Oh Joseph! What makes you think the persecution won't start all over again there?"

"Once the translation is finished, I won't have the plates. Moroni will take them back. There's no value in foolscap. People aren't after the manuscript. They are after the gold."

He hesitated before continuing. "Besides there is more to be feared here. There are men here plotting to kill me."

"Joseph, no! Do you think so? Who could it be?" Emma dreaded going back to the terror of mob violence.

Oliver spoke, "The Smiths have suffered no persecution since you left. I believe Joseph is right. When I was there I didn't sense violence, only ridicule."

The trio looked at each other. Ridicule! How could anyone ridicule this incredible gift from the Lord? So much ignorance! Emma could see Joseph wanted to go. His whole attention had turned to the manuscript. She understood, though it had lately begun to bother her that he had so little time for her. She had hoped she might carry his baby again soon. Even though the first pregnancy had turned to tragedy, it had brought them closer. Each month she hoped, but as yet, she was not expecting. Indeed, with so much company about, she wondered how she ever could. There was little privacy and precious little time. She had begun to yearn for a baby. Now her husband was proposing separation. Had he forgotten her in his obsession? Quick tears filled her eyes, and she turned away to hide them.

But Joseph had not forgotten her. He saw the movement and glistening in her eyes. "Come, Emma. I want to take a turn in the moonlight."

It was a full moon, so bright even the stars were dim. They hadn't taken a walk together for weeks. What with Oliver and Samuel always about, neighbors calling, the translation demanding attention, Joseph had been pulled in many directions. There was too much work, for her as well as her husband. She was getting tired. They meandered down by the river. With the spring thaw it had been full for several months. Now the riverbed had narrowed somewhat, and the flow slowed.

"You know you could go with us," he ventured.

"There's too much to do here. I can't just go off and let the garden go to ruin. Besides, my sister Elizabeth's delivery is close, and I promised to help with her baby."

Joseph knew her private longings. "You want another little one, don't you, Emma?"

"Yes, very much. But God does not seem inclined to send one."

"Perhaps we haven't done our part."

She looked up at her husband's face and saw that he was grinning. She loved his smile, sort of boyish. How long ago was it he persuaded her to marry him? Only two and a half years? So much had happened since then. She put her arms about his neck. Who was to see them kissing, here by the river in the moonlight? And how long would it be again before they had such privacy for their love?

"Oh, my Joseph, how I do love thee. Shakespeare was right, I'm afraid. 'We love that well which we must lose ere long.' I'm not strong. I'm weak where you are concerned. If anything should happen to you . . ."

"Now, what's gonna happen to me that has you worried?"

"Perhaps nothing. Maybe I'm being selfish, but I just feel safer when you are with me. Don't leave me, my love," she murmured against his cheek. But he stopped her protests with his kisses. He didn't really convince her — but he tried!

David Whitmer showed up at the Smith house in a week. Joseph had sent a letter to him and to his father, Peter, requesting help with the Lord's work and telling them of the threat to his life. David worried that he couldn't leave quickly. He had plowing to do and wheat to be sown. Peter told his son he had farm work to be done. David looked at his portion with a heavy heart. It would take a few days before he could get away and go to help his friend, Oliver, and the young prophet, Joseph.

After a full day's work he went to bed that night determined to get up and go to work even earlier the next morning. When he arose and went to his sister's adjoining home, he was astonished at what had been accomplished. Somehow three days work had been in one day. He never knew who had helped, but it left him free to go to Harmony. When David's wagon jolted down the road to the Smith spread, Joseph and Oliver were walking out to meet him. Joseph shook his hand and surprised Whitmer, telling him all that had happened to him on his three day journey. David Whitmer had never encountered such a man before. He was dumbfounded, but the young prophet just laughed and escorted him back to the farmhouse so they could load up their things.

Emma left before this. She had gone to her sister's home. Elizabeth Hale Wasson lived not far from Colesville. They had been close when Emma was younger. Now she went to visit, knowing her husband would be gone when she returned. The visit was far from satisfying. There was so little she could say about her life, for Isaac had poisoned the Wasson family with his accusations against Joseph. Emma felt her family would never accept her husband, so she left after just a few days to return to her empty house.

With Joseph gone, nothing was the same. She walked through the vacant house. The attic where he had worked was quiet. The chair where he had sat and read scriptures to her was still beside the hearth. His clothes were gone from the trunk. She tried to eat a light supper, but had no appetite. The first night alone in their house was so desperately lonely, not even reading her Bible helped. Her only consolation was that his life was not in danger, but the light had gone from her own life, and she knew she would not stay there long.

Mid-June was a pleasant time for a trip in an open wagon. The fields were green along the way. They smelled of pungent earth and crops growing. The forests were shady, and the streamlets cool. The three men talked of little else but the translation and the restoration of the keys of the priesthood. Oliver held nothing back from his friend David. Joseph found for the first time he did not have to prove himself. He had corroboration, one whose truthfulness was not questioned — at least by his friend. It was a great relief.

The Whitmer family was most hospitable. The home was small, almost too small for the eight children, Mother and Father Whitmer and Joseph and Oliver. Joseph wondered if he had been right to impose on this gracious family. He and Oliver were housed upstairs in one of the two bedrooms. Peter and Mary Whitmer slept downstairs in the main bedroom. The young men had a bed with a trundle underneath it. There was space enough for a small table for writing, an oil lamp, and not much more. The younger children were to sleep outside with bedrolls on canvas. Joseph tried to protest to Father Whitmer, but the children themselves refused to come back inside. They loved sleeping under the stars in the cool night air. They thought it much better than in the hot, stuffy upstairs. Privately Joseph agreed with them. He had only been separated from Emma for a few days, and he found himself missing her and their evening walks. He hoped she would follow him quickly.

Final work on the translating started the next day. The attic grew very hot. Joseph and Oliver immersed themselves in the work. Perspiration beaded their faces and was impatiently wiped away. Joseph's voice grew hoarse as he dictated all day, pressing to get it done. Now, toward the end of the work, he could dictate smoothly, rarely stopping. At times, when Oliver's hand and neck were cramped, David or his younger brother, John, took his place, and Joseph went right on.

The Whitmer family was fascinated by the strange tale Joseph was translating from the emerging *Book of Mormon*. Around the supper table, he retold the stories from the beginning, keeping them fascinated for hours. Oliver found admiration in the eyes of young Nancy Whitmer and often walked with her in the early evening, charming her with accounts of the amazing book. David and John brought their friends by, and Joseph found himself the center of an admiring group of converts. He retold his story many times of discovering the golden plates, visiting the hill every year, and finally obtaining them. Soon the question came up of creating his own church.

"I haven't any solid plans for that as yet," he confided. "My first concern is to get the manuscript published. My friend, Martin Harris, has investigated several print shops and concluded we should contract for five thousand copies with E.B. Grandin of Palmyra."

"You'll need people to help you sell it, Joseph." David Whitmer had become a valuable convert, eager to be of help to the young prophet.

At last, the years of ridicule seemed to be behind. Joseph was grateful for these new-found friends. A church! Yes, a church was needed, based on the principles he had learned from the sacred record. At night, as he lay awake in the small attic, he prayed for a clear vision of such a church. The work had already commenced, for here in Fayette he had friends with believing hearts. When the book was ready, he would begin a new church here — the Church of Christ restored to the earth.

He had a letter every week from Emma telling him of home and what she was doing. None of it seemed as important as having her near. The praise and admiration of new friends, the enjoyable social evenings, were all exciting, but fell flat without Emma by his side. He used his wife as a sounding board in every decision he made. He wrote her to close up the house and take their animals to her mother. Joseph wanted his wife by his side. A few days later, Emma arrived by stage from Harmony. It hadn't taken much convincing. She had missed him as much as he had longed for her.

"Praise God from whom all blessings flow; praise Him all creatures here below; praise Him above, ye heavenly hosts. Praise Father, Son and Holy Ghost!" The little group gathered in the Whitmer home held out the last note a moment, then the men's deep voices intoned "Ah . . . men."

"Lord God Almighty, look down on us your humble servants and bless the proceedings of this day with thy spirit in abundance!" Peter Whitmer, Sr. stood as the patriarch in his home and conducted morning services as usual. But this was not a usual day.

In the Whitmer home that morning, in addition to the Whitmer family, there were Oliver Cowdery, Joseph Jr. and Emma Smith, Joseph Sr. and Lucy Mack Smith, and Martin Harris. They all knew why Joseph had called this special prayer meeting. Martin sat looking down at his scarred, work-worn hands. He was almost trembling with anticipation and fear. The others watched Joseph expectantly. He was about to announce which men who would be privileged to look upon the golden plates and become special witnesses for the Lord.

The brilliant June sun fell across the shoulders of the young prophet as he knelt in their midst to petition the Lord. Emma noted with satisfaction that her husband looked every inch a prophet, from his fresh white shirt which she had pressed, to the new vest she had sewn, and his boots freshly oiled. She bowed her head obediently with the others but could not help watching Joseph as he bent his head in humble prayer. A ray of sun glinted red and gold on his shock of fair hair. Love and pride throbbed in her veins. Every day her husband seemed to grow in the certainty of his calling. Just when she thought he was immersed in his holy calling, he would throw himself on the ground and play games with the children. It was that change from prophet to boy which charmed her and his devoted followers.

This day, Joseph gave an impassioned prayer. His voice filled the room and spilled out from the windows. His spirit seemed to expand until it enclosed them all like a living force. He was seeking confirmation of God's choice of three witnesses. When he was done — and with the spirit still vibrating around them — he arose, walked to Harris and spoke to the old farmer.

"Martin, humble yourself before God and obtain forgiveness of your sins. If you do, it is the will of the Almighty that you look upon the plates . . ." he said as he turned slowly around and his penetrating blue eyes rested on two others, "Along with Oliver Cowdery and David Whitmer."

A shout escaped from David and his family. One of their own would see the fabulous golden plates. They jumped from their seats crowding around young Whitmer. Oliver and Joseph held each other by both forearms beaming into each others eyes. A penitent Martin fell to his knees in prayer. After a moment, Emma got up and went to

Martin. His eyes were streaming, and he was ineffectually trying to stop the tears with his handkerchief. Emma helped him to stand while Lucy patted him sympathetically on the back.

"Emma, I didn't expect this. I hardly dared to hope. After all I have done . . . my grievous sins . . . I couldn't even hope that God would forgive me — or that Joseph could trust me."

"It's all right, Mr. Harris. God is ever merciful, and Joseph holds no grudges. You have been his friend for many, many years."

"I'll try to humble myself to the very dust if that is what it takes."

"That is what it will take, all right," Joseph confirmed. "Let us go to the woods where the four of us can be alone." He turned to the others. "Wait for us here and pray. Pray that we may be successful, for I yearn to share this burden of responsibility."

Emma and Lucy stood together watching the four men stride off to the woods behind the Whitmer home.

The rest of the morning was spent in prayer. Finally the little prayer circle filtered out of the parlor. There was still work to be done on the farm. Mother Whitmer started bread, and Emma began a batch of donuts rising. Lucy sat spinning and chattering with all the family news. She hadn't seen her daughter-in-law for several months. The household gathered again about two o'clock. Still the men had not returned. After dinner, more prayers were offered and Peter started out to the barn. Emma went upstairs to write a letter to her parents. Lucy and Joseph, Sr. stayed in the parlor quietly talking.

The woods were usually cool and shady, but the day had become warm, and the men were a little sticky by the time they had crossed the fields and entered beneath the overhanging trees. A deep quiet prevailed. Beneath their feet, old decayed leaves emanated a warm, musty smell. They rustled as boots disturbed their slumber. Far overhead, diffused sunlight tangled in the branches of the pines and birds called back and forth. David led the way. He knew the woodlands behind his home. He had played there as a child. He had a favorite place. It was deep in the forest, and branches formed a natural cathedral ceiling. A large pine tree had fallen years before and had been stripped of its twigs by the squirrels. It was long enough that all four of the men could kneel beside it.

They knelt and began taking turns in calling upon their Father, the Creator of heaven and earth. Each one prayed in his turn, entreating God as a child pleads with a beloved parent. Joseph's voice shook as he petitioned the Lord for this great blessing for his friends. He knew it was all a part of God's great work for the sake of mankind. He pleaded with deity that this might be the longed-for day when the burden of testimony would be shared with others. Eventually their knees grew sore with pressure. When fervent prayer for several hours brought no results, the men sat on the log and looked at each other. Had Joseph calculated wrong? Perhaps this was not the right time. Were they doing something wrong? Maybe they didn't have faith enough.

Martin broke down in tears. "It is my fault. I am a sinful man. The Lord remembers I broke sacred promises to him. I am holding the rest of you back. I must leave or you will never have the desired results."

Joseph's sorrow for Martin welled up within him. He put his arm around him. "I believe you've been forgiven, or you wouldn't be here. Don't get discouraged. Spiritual experiences are not to be had merely for the asking. This will take mighty prayer."

"Still, I think I should withdraw. Let me find a place all my own, and I will continue to pray."

Joseph nodded, "All right. But I won't leave you alone for long. I'll come to you as soon as I know the time is right."

Sorrowfully, Martin got up, brushed the twigs and leaves from his pants and looking in all directions, picked a path through the trees and walked away. Oliver and David watched him go, pity on their faces. Joseph, however, knelt immediately. Instead of bowing his head, he turned his face to the heavens, and in a loud voice called the blessings of heaven down upon the two men who remained. Oliver had become somewhat accustomed to the authority with which his friend prayed, but David was astounded. He never knew a man might literally call down blessings with righteous power. He almost expected a clap of thunder. Instead, an amazing phenomena began to occur.

Their clearing became drenched with shimmering, diaphanous light. It was different from sunlight, different from firelight. It was far more glorious and pervasive. The trees and other surroundings seemed to fade from sight. An angel of God appeared in that light and laid the golden plates before their eyes as on a table. They saw the engravings upon those plates. What their eyes beheld was glorious beyond description.

A voice resounded through the little clearing. "Look well upon these plates. For you will be witnesses to all the nations of the world. These records have been translated by the gift and power of God. Of this you will testify as long as you live."

Joseph sat on the log while his two friends looked on in amazement at the golden plates. A great peace came over him. He breathed deeply as a man might who tried to clear his lungs of dust and cobwebs. He had prayed for this day to come, and it was none too soon.

The vision lasted for many minutes. Oliver and David sat entranced by the beautiful objects. When they had hoped to be the witnesses, they had little pictured how overpowering an experience it might be. Oliver thought he would be prepared for it, having sat for months transcribing Joseph's words. To him the golden plates were already a reality. But this! This shining manifestation of the record, accompanied by an angel of God was more than he had dreamed. It was, in fact, nothing like a dream. He had never been so acutely awake and aware at anytime in his life. His body was quickened from the top of his head to his boots. He felt more than alive, he felt magnified a hundred times beyond his natural state.

Oliver and David stepped forward and handled the plates, turning page after page of thin gold metal. David looked at Joseph with wonder that he could actually translate the strange markings engraved thereon.

After their complete and satisfying perusal of the objects on the table, the light began to falter, to thin, and as quickly as it came, the vision disappeared. The men sat in silence for awhile, each one trying to comprehend what he had seen and experienced. Joseph arose and took his leave, softly speaking of Martin. David and Oliver sat down on a log, too overcome to talk or to go back to the every day world. They had lived a few minutes in another realm, and all else seemed mundane.

Joseph found Martin after a short walk. Harris was sitting with his head in his hands, utterly dejected. Obviously he had not yet obtained his witness. The young prophet went to him and sat beside him. He put his arm over Martin's shoulders. The older man was almost like a father to him. Joseph wanted this glorious experience for him. He knew Martin was a good man and desirous of being of service. Over the years he had helped further the work, defending Joseph to critics, and generously contributed considerable money to help them. Joseph knew he hadn't been mistaken. The Lord actually did mean to allow Martin this honor. He was a man well respected in the community, and his testimony would bear weight.

"Martin, let's kneel."

"Will you pray for me, Joseph."

"I have been, and I will."

Joseph lifted up his voice and called for the heavens to re-open for his friend, that his testimony might go forth to all the world.

Again, the vision opened, and Martin fell back like a man stricken. He had never seen such a glorious light! An angel of God stood with golden plates before him, the very plates which Joseph had tried to describe to him. The brilliance was almost too much for Martin. He felt to shade his eyes, but he didn't want to miss a thing. His heart quickened and began to race. His hair seemed to stand straight up. He looked at his young friend, and Joseph's face was bathed in a white, almost incandescent light. He was perfectly tranquil.

Martin jumped up and cried out, "It is enough! Mine eyes have beheld! Mine eyes have beheld!"

Joseph stood as well, as the vision disappeared. They walked back to where Oliver and David sat quietly conversing. Martin was so elated he could scarcely contain himself. On the way back to the Whitmer home he fairly danced with excitement, skipping about like a young lamb and exclaiming ever so frequently, "Hosanna, hosanna! God is merciful. I have beheld with mine own eyes."

The four men walked into the house. Joseph Sr. and Lucy were still together downstairs. They looked up expectantly. Joseph crossed the room and threw himself down beside them. He was overjoyed that the experience was successfully complete.

"Father, Mother, it is done! The angel has shown the plates to these, my good friends, as witnesses. Now the world will have to believe, for there are others who have seen and know for themselves what I have said is true. I feel as though I'm no longer alone in the world. It is a tremendous burden off my soul."

Emma came down the stairs at the sound of her husband's voice. She paused at the bottom, and Joseph almost ran to her. Picking her up off her feet, he hugged her until she was breathless. She smiled at his excitement.

Peter Whitmer returned from the barn as his wife emerged from their downstairs bedroom. Then a direct question followed a lull.

"Am I to take it you were successful?" Emma teased Joseph.

He laughed out loud. Turning to his three friends, he asked, "Were we successful?"

With one voice jubilation broke out. "We were! We were!" Martin cried out in exhilaration, "Now there are three witnesses of the marvelous work and wonder! And we bear witness that Joseph *is, indeed, a prophet!*"

Chapter Ten

Coming Forth

It came to Joseph early one morning in mid-August, when he awoke at his parents home in Manchester. *The Book of Mormon* was finally going to press today! Oliver had been feverishly recopying the translation so they could take it a portion at a time to the Grandin printing office in Palmyra to be prepared for a press-run of five thousand books. They dared not let the original pages out of their hands. Joseph lay in bed imagining the title page as taken from the last leaf of the golden plates. Excitement kicked him out of bed and onto his feet. The time was here! He jerked on his trousers and pulled a shirt over his head. Scrubbing his fingers through his hair, he hollered at Oliver to awake and arise!

Oliver sat bolt upright in bed and rubbed his eyes. He had been dreaming of courting a bright-eyed girl in a field of flowers and wasn't sure he was ready to give it all up.

"This is it, Oliver! The printing begins today! What do you suppose people will think when our book is all published? Now they'll have to believe it, won't they?"

"No, they won't."

"Well, at least it will be proof that I wasn't just talking."

"Do you suppose folks will even care what it is?" Oliver wondered.

"They'll care when we preach the doctrine to them. I need to be thinking about how to promote the book and recover the investment."

"Well, it isn't even printed yet, and if we don't raise the money, it may never be finished."

"Be patient." Joseph admonished. "Martin pledged to mortgage his farm if need be."

Oliver sat up and pulled on his pants. It was Saturday. He needed a bath today for sure. "I know it. It's just that the copy is ready, and I'm anxious for the printing to begin."

"It'll be soon. I'm sure."

"Joseph, if some unscrupulous person got their hands on the manuscript, they could do us a lot of damage. I know that's why you had me recopy it, but there are other problems than that. We must get copyright to it, so some scoundrel can't steal it from us."

Joseph pondered this problem. "We'll send a guard with you each time you take a portion of it to the printing office. Porter Rockwell is itching to do something to help. He's tough on the outside, but a believer at heart, and we've been friends since our youth. I know he's to be trusted. He'll be tickled at having such an important position — guarding the writing. You have a point. We'd better secure the copyright as quickly as possible. Right now no one has secured rights to *The Book of Mormon.*"

Joseph had not originally intended to have the book published in Palmyra. The persecution of his family had been so intense that he had wanted no further involvement there. He had solicited a printer in Rochester, New York, but the gentleman had refused. Finally, he had gone to E.B. Grandin, the manager of the *Wayne Sentinel* in Palmyra. He owned the newspaper jointly with Mr. Pomeroy Tucker. They hesitated taking on the project. It was a rather large one. The book would be about six hundred pages long, and they still had a weekly newspaper to put out.

"How are we gonna get paid for this kind of work?" Pomeroy was a short round man with a perpetual worried frown. "This'll take most of a year. There's paper, printers' ink, not to mention labor. All that will cost us a lot of money up front. Then when it's done, how do we know we'll get paid?" The two owners sat behind a desk while Joseph, Hyrum, and Oliver stood before them.

"I guarantee you'll be paid. The Lord will see to that." Joseph assured them.

Grandin had a habit of tilting his head to the side and scratching behind his ear while he considered a problem. Then he tipped it the opposite way, as though to see both sides of an issue. Now he studied the young men before him. It sure was a gamble, and neither he nor Tucker was a gambler. He was a sober, hardworking printer and knew there was not much fat in the system. He could not afford to finance their project. He pursed his lips as he concentrated. Smith didn't have the funds; that was plain. On the other hand, folks had been hearing for years about this "golden bible." Word of it had spread over much of the state. There would be a lot of interest. It might be a valuable property.

He looked at Tucker. Pomeroy Tucker had never had any use for the Smiths. Rumors of golden treasure were mostly bunk to him. He didn't like controversy, particularly of the violent kind. These folks were just asking for trouble. He shook his head "no" when his partner looked his way. But Grandin was intrigued.

"Surely you can see my problem. This is not a bank, and we are not rich enough to finance you. Just how do you intend to pay for this?"

Hyrum spoke up. "You may not be rich, Mr. Grandin, but you're shrewd enough to recognize this is a manuscript that has already generated a great deal of excitement. We intend to spread out over the entire area and sell the book. You'll be paid out of the proceeds of the sales. My brother and I guarantee it."

Grandin and Tucker both cleared their throats. Tucker looked at the floor. Grandin looked at the men before him. "Sorry, gentlemen. That's not good enough. You could be right. The book may sell, or it may not. There's excitement, but there's also prejudice against it." He stood up to end the meeting.

Only then did Joseph go to his last resort. "Mr. Martin Harris has agreed to guarantee your fee."

Grandin was now on his feet. "Why didn't you say so before?"

"I wanted to see if you qualified for the Lord's blessing. What is your total price?"

"Three thousand dollars."

"Mr. Harris will visit you later today and add his signature to ours for a note to that amount." Joseph extended his hand. "Thank you for your time. Mr. Cowdery and Mr. Hyrum Smith will bring you segments of the manuscript in 'takes,' one page at a time. We expect all of it to be carefully guarded and kept confidential."

Grandin shook hands and, just for a moment, wished he had not forced young Smith to come up with all of the backing for the book. He had a flash of intuition that he should have part and parcel in this publication. Still, the deal was struck, and Smith could chance the potential controversy himself. He apparently already had.

Just a few days later, Martin pledged his farm, and they sent to Washington, D.C. to secure the copyright.

Every day, Oliver or Hyrum, under Porter Rockwell's careful watch, traveled to Palmyra, a mere two and a half miles away, entered Grandin's new brick printing office, and delivered another portion of the book to be meticulously typeset and printed. While Grandin himself set the tiny metal letters of type into the forms, another man prepared the ink, and blotted it onto the type. Then they inserted the paper, put the lid over the typeface, and pulled the roller over it all, "pressing" the paper onto the metal plates. There were sixteen pages set in each signature of type. The Grandin company pressed five thousand copies of the book in this manner, six hundred individual pages. It took a crew of workmen nine months to complete the publishing.

Once the work was underway, Joseph and Emma took the coach back to Harmony. They found everything much as they had left it.

Her mother had tended the little garden, picking the peas and beans, tomatoes and squash. They opened up the house and aired it out.

"It's good to be back in our own place," Emma remarked as she sat in her rocker.

"Perhaps we might be able to buy the farm outright from your father."

"How can we do that, Joseph? We have no money."

"I'm not altogether useless, you know. Now that the manuscript is done, I'll have time enough to work and earn the money."

"Where?"

Joseph had noticed Emma was increasingly impatient. He knew it bothered her to depend on the charity of friends. He wanted to stay around Palmyra to supervise the printing of the book. They could have stayed in his parent's home. With Sophronia married and gone, there was room for them as well as Oliver. But Emma was dead set against it. The memory of the persecution they had suffered there had not dimmed. She had also lived in Fayette with the Whitmers in their tiny home and felt that she was an imposition. So, knowing how hard it had been for Emma, Joseph decided it was high time he got back to work and provided for his wife.

"Mr. Knight and Mr. Stowell have both offered me work at their mills."

She seemed skeptical. "Work all day for them and work your own land all night? That sounds like a recipe for disaster."

He pulled her down onto his lap. Joseph loved Emma's smell. She always smelled of fresh cake. He nuzzled her ear and neck, pushing her hair back and kissing the nape of her hairline. "You've got a strong man for a husband — a little crazy sometimes, but strong. Don't worry, my Emma-rose, I'll become a respectable farmer yet."

Joseph was good for his word. He spent the next two months working all over the area, helping others bring in their crops. The land had pretty well lain fallow as he had been involved with the work of the Lord these last few months. They had been able to stock their root cellar with vegetables and fruit of all kinds, but wheat and corn — the staples — they had none. Joseph was often paid in kind and eventually accumulated quite a store of food, including meat, for the winter. The money he received they put away so he could one day go to his father-in-law and pay the two hundred dollars to buy the place.

Word came regularly from Palmyra that the printing was going very well, despite the efforts of the local citizenry to stop it. Some had even plotted to steal the manuscript in order to halt the printing. Joseph's family kept a twenty-four-hour watch over the manuscript. Lucy had put it in a trunk which she wedged under her bed, and she literally slept right on top of it every night. Even ministers of local churches tried to obtain it by deception, but she would never take it out to show them. Methodically Oliver, Hyrum, Samuel, and Porter carried the writings back and forth to Grandin's with diligent security.

Winter months in Pennsylvania were a welcome relief from the dawn to dark work of a farmer. When snow came, Joseph returned to thinking about the structure of a new church. It happened fairly naturally. He had, by now, learned to study a problem out in his mind before asking the Lord for clarification.

Christ's church should have apostles, prophets, the gift of tongues, healing and visions, as outlined in the *Book of Mormon* and in the *New Testament*. It should have elders, teachers, deacons, seventies. There must be no paid clergy, for that was priestcraft. Baptism would be done by immersion, and the priesthood of God would be passed on by ordination. Authority to act in God's name was a pre-eminent doctrine of His church. It was necessary to the law and order of God's kingdom. Nothing could be done without His authority. Even teaching His gospel must be done by those with authority and the Holy Ghost. The principles Joseph had learned from *The Book of Mormon* formed the basis of doctrine for a new church, and his mind was on fire with enthusiasm for work just unfolding.

If he had hoped persecution would cease with the testimony of the witnesses, he was wrong. Besides Oliver, David, and Martin, eight more men had seen the plates, though not the angel, and although they were all reputable and well known in the community, their testimonies were questioned. Even as the book was being printed, rumors abounded, neighbors challenged them openly on the "so-called" ancient manuscript. The reason was clear to Joseph. All the ministers were provided for by their congregations. Preaching was their livelihood. Each soul "saved" contributed to the comfort and ease of the minister's life. If a new religion should gain ground and parishioners become converted to Joseph's work, the ministers would lose their prosperous business. The Presbyterian minister, the Methodist minister, including uncle Nathaniel Lewis, had all to lose and nothing to gain if Joseph were successful. So sermons abounded from the pulpits castigating Joseph as a treasure seeker and glass-looker.

In January, Joseph Sr. made the long trip to Harmony to deliver bad news to his son.

"Joseph you must come. Abner Cole is printing all kinds of plagiarized and distorted material, pretending it has to do with *The Book of Mormon*. Hyrum found him, last Sunday afternoon, working feverishly over a page of type in Grandin's shop. When he asked Cole what he was up to, he told Hyrum to mind his own business. Well, it turned out *your* business was *his* business. He has lifted pages of the book from Grandin's printing and is printing part of it, mocking and ridiculing the book. He writes under the name of Obadiah Dogberry. He calls his rag *The Palmyra Reflector*. It's disgusting."

"What did Hyrum do?"

"What could he do? He forbade Cole to print that piece of filth. He swore and refused to desist. Hyrum told him we have secured copyright, and he is in danger of the law."

Joseph nodded his approval. "Exactly. Well, I'd best go back with you and confront the man. He always was a weasel. He was part of the mobs that violated our home more than once. It's jealousy, plain and simple."

With Emma's consent, even urging, Joseph returned in the buggy with his father. They spent the time discussing the foundation of a new church. Back in Harmony, Emma spent her time mending blankets and clothes, nailing up pieces of board the wind had torn off, and missing her husband.

Joseph met Cole in Grandin's print shop, as Hyrum had done.

"Hello, Mr. Cole," Joseph greeted him coolly. "You seem hard at work."

The older man squinted up at him. His pink, bald head shone in the lamp light as he bent to his work. "How do you do, Mr. Smith," Cole answered and kept on with his work.

Joseph picked up a previous copy of *The Palmyra Reflector* and looked it over. Hyrum was right. There were his actual words, interspersed with the most disrespectful kind of comments and badly composed satirical verse.

Joseph dropped his civil demeanor. "Mr. Cole, you know the copyright belongs to me and none else. You are forbidden to steal my material any longer."

Cole lost his temper and peeled off his coat. He had been preparing for this moment since his run-in with Hyrum the previous week. He smacked his fists together and roared at his young accuser, "Do you want to fight, sir? I'll fight you. I'll publish just exactly what I want to. Now if you want to fight, come on. I'm ready."

Joseph looked a full six inches down on the wry, feisty little man. The man was ridiculous and too foolish to realize it. He couldn't help a derisive smile, and that enraged Cole even more.

"Keep your coat on, Cole. I'm not going to fight you over this, with fists. I wouldn't want to be put into jail for assaulting you. But I will fight you before the courts over printing my copyrighted book. And I have the law on my side, as you very well know. You had best stop immediately."

Cole continued to try to get his opponent to throw the first punch. But Joseph knew his strategy — get him to fight, then claim

Joseph had attacked him. Just the difference in their ages would go against Joseph, and he knew it.

Cole must have known the truth of what Joseph said, for he stopped his weekly publications rather than face a copyright suit. But his influence prevailed in the community. He incited the citizens of the county to refuse to buy even a single copy when it was printed. He so upset Mr. Grandin that the printer refused to finish the job for fear he would not recoup his investment.

Joseph and Martin convinced Grandin to disregard the rabble rousers and go back to printing. It took all the rest of the money Martin could raise. He sold another parcel of land from his estate. But, at last, the job was done. In March of 1830, Joseph, Oliver, Hyrum, and David pushed open the door to Grandin's printing shop and picked up the first books, bound in soft, tan leather. *The Book of Mormon* was no longer a vision or a rumor. It was a real book, and it was for sale!

Tuesday morning, the sixth of April, 1830, dawned cool and clear in Fayette, N.Y. Emma awoke before first light. Joseph was still sleeping curled up around her, one arm thrown possessively over her. His breath tickled the hair by her ear. How can he sleep so soundly, she wondered? Today he will organize his church! But Joseph slept with the undisturbed rest of a babe. She slipped out from under his arm to stir the coals of the little stove and put one small stick on them, hoping to cut the still frosty air of early spring. She thought he was still asleep. His breathing was regular and deep.

Suddenly his arm shot out, and his hand captured her nightgown. He pulled her back down beside him with one decisive tug. Emma did not resist. The bed where he lay was warm as a brick oven. She could always depend on his feet to be warm no matter how cold hers were. When she was shivering, he radiated heat. And he did love to spend these early hours snuggled up in bed, while the rest of the household had not yet come to life. Her affectionate husband seemed to always find time for her. He thrived on her love, her approval. If she criticized, he was wounded all day long. If she complained, he was depressed. In many ways, he would always be working to overcome the accusation by her father that he was not worthy of her. Emma knew better, but it was a worry that goaded her husband to prove himself.

"Emma," he murmured. "Is it time to get up already?"

She was surprised. He was not normally a sleepy-head. "Not yet. I just put a stick of wood in the stove. Will you be lazy today of all days?"

"And just what day do you think it is?"

"It's the day you'll organize your church."

There was silence. She peered through the shadows. He was smiling. She knew he had not forgotten. He was teasing her as usual. Later, when daylight had roused the rest of the household, Emma rose again, put a small kettle of water on the stove top so they could bathe and Joseph could shave. That was a ritual she enjoyed watching — the lathering, the meticulous scraping, the wiping. She usually found a spot needing her attention, and she would wield the razor delicately, then kiss the spot after wiping it. This morning he hurried through the routine, and she quickly sponged off, then slipped her best Sunday dress over her head. He buttoned the long row up her back, and she turned to helped him with his cravat.

She patted his lapels. There! Now he looked just perfect, as befitting the head of a brand new church.

"Are you nervous?" she asked.

"No. Just anxious to get on with it. The Lord's church has been missing from the earth for eighteen hundred years."

"Well, you look every bit a prophet today!"

"Really? Do you think so?"

Emma regarded him critically. No more the awkward, earnest young boy she had married just three years ago; he was broader, more muscular. His face had taken on a more angular look, and his eyes showed more experience. He had seen much in these years. When he was serious, his face could seem a little haughty with those high cheek-bones, broad forehead, and chiseled lips. But when he smiled, which he frequently did, his face seemed wreathed in sunlight, and he became a boy again.

"Maintain your dignity," she advised and kissed him again, just for the pure pleasure.

Father Whitmer was not used to solemn occasions. He was a farmer, and there was work to be done this morning. He had been up early, to see to the animals and the plowing before devoting his day to Joseph's new church. He was used to losing a day's work on the Sabbath; that was the Lord's day and inviolate, but to lose another day, right in the middle of the week, was a sacrifice for the father of nine children. He was dressed in his Sunday suit by the time the group had gathered. His thick brown hair was neatly combed, and his red cheeks redder than usual as he looked with pride around the people crowded into his tiny home. His own sons were a vital part of this new gospel young Smith was preaching. David had actually seen the golden plates, and John had helped in the transcribing work. The rest of his family was also there, although the laws of the state required only six reputable men to legally organize a church.

Joseph's family was also there in force, even his newly married sister, Sophronia, with Calvin Stoddard. Neighbors had come. Some stood outside in the yard waiting to hear the young prophet speak. Among all there was a feeling that something of importance was about to happen, but mostly they were talking and gossiping about their families.

The meeting was opened by solemn prayer, followed by singing. Then each of the six men who were to sign as original members stood and spoke on the need for a new church. Their comments all rang with praises for *The Book of Mormon*. A vote was taken as to whether they would accept Joseph and Oliver as their teachers in the things of

God. It was unanimous in the affirmative. An affidavit was signed by each of the six men. Joseph stepped behind Oliver Cowdery, laid his hands on his friend's head and ordained him an "Elder" of the new church. Oliver rose while Joseph sat in his place, and Oliver likewise designated him a prophet, seer, and revelator.

The last ordinance of the meeting was the passing of the sacrament. They took bread, broke, blessed, and passed it. Then they blessed wine in the same manner and passed it. All was done in strict agreement with the ceremony recorded in *The Book of Mormon*. After that, the meeting came to life with rejoicing, praising God and bearing testimony.

Emma sat back and watched the proceedings with satisfaction and some foreboding. Now her husband was more of a threat than ever to the other churches around them. The other ministers would not take this lying down. Her uncle Nathaniel was one of them. Though he was careful around her, she knew he denounced her husband to all her neighbors. Emma feared what the next few weeks would bring, but she consoled herself with the thought that the furor would die out after a time.

"Your new church must have members," Joseph Sr. announced.

His son looked over the little congregation of friends. "Membership in God's church starts with baptism."

"I'm willing!" said his father.

"And I," Lucy declared.

A young man, short and stringy, with an innocent, round face, had stood quietly in the doorway watching the proceedings. Now he spoke up. "I want to be baptized, too." It was the prophet's friend and neighbor, Orin Porter Rockwell. "Port" had idolized Joseph since they were children. He would follow him the rest of his life.

"And I, a witness for *The Book of Mormon* should be baptized." Martin's voice was raised above the hallelujahs. He had not tired of testifying as often as he was able. There were those who had begun to avoid him on the street, knowing they would listen yet again to his rejoicing.

The whole group moved by wagon and buggy down to the banks of Seneca lake. Oliver was selected to be the one to perform the ordinance. He pulled off his coat and boots and waded down into the clear, cool water. Joseph Sr. did the same. With the simple repetition of the ordinance as it was written in *The Book of Mormon*, Oliver plunged him under the water. Joseph presided over the ceremony, standing with Emma at the water's edge, his heart too full with joy to contain it all. What a day it had been! His church officially organized, and now his parents baptized!

"Oh, my Lord, my God! I have lived to see my own father baptized!" Joseph exclaimed, with tears in his eyes. He knew how his father had resisted all the efforts of various ministers to join their congregations. Even when Lucy and several children had joined with the Presbyterians, Joseph Sr. had steadfastly refused. It wasn't that he was anti-social or irreligious. Far from it, he was a congenial neighbor and enjoyed the revival meetings. He had simply never found a church that taught the gospel as he understood it from the Bible. He had been skeptical of the men who deemed themselves shepherds over his neighbors. But he had believed in the inspiration of his own son since Joseph, at fourteen, had first told him of his vision of the Lord.

As the young prophet's father went down into the water, he declared, "At last I have found someone with authority to baptize me into God's kingdom."

Emma's baptism day was not so happy. Two months later, she and Joseph were in Colesville one Saturday visiting the Knights. A stream on Knight's acreage was dammed and a baptism scheduled for the next morning. The Knights were anxious to be in full fellowship with Christ's church, with its "restored" gospel of Jesus Christ.

Saturday night, Joseph stood in the center of the little parlor where he had so often been a guest and preached from *The Book of Mormon*. The Knight family had gathered, as well as Oliver Cowdery and young Emily Coburn, Sally Knight's pretty, younger sister. She listened to Joseph and Oliver with eyes shining.

Reverend Sherer appeared at the doorway and asked to speak to Emily. She went to the door reluctantly. He was her local minister. What was he doing here?

"Emily, dear, your father and I are concerned about your association with this apostate church of Joe Smith's. He is nothing but a glass looker, a treasure seeker! He has hoodwinked the Knights and will be their downfall yet. Your eternal salvation is my only concern."

Emily sweetly responded, "It is mine also, Reverend. I'm perfectly safe here with my sister."

"Your father has charged me with bringing you home. Your brother is outside in the wagon waiting for you. Gather up your things. We must leave immediately."

Emily peered into the darkness from the doorway. She didn't see the wagon, much less her brother. She ventured a few steps down the path, and the Reverend took her arm to lead her. She quickly saw there was no one in the wagon and turned back, her pretty eyes reproachful.

"Why, Reverend Sherer, my brother is not there."

Sally Knight had missed her sister and now came charging down the path.

"Emily! Emily, are you all right? Come in out of this night air right now." She took her sister's other arm and drew her back to the safety of the house.

"We'll see about this," the good reverend grumbled and withdrew to his waiting wagon.

When Oliver went to the stream to check the next morning, he found the dam broken and the stream too low for baptisms. He was very disappointed. Sunday was the perfect day for baptisms, and he had hoped to take Miss Emily down into the water. Disappointed, he walked back up to the Knights and informed Joseph.

"They can't stop the Lord's work," Joseph asserted. "We'll rest today on the Lord's day and repair the dam early tomorrow morning. By mid-day there should be enough water for the ordinance."

Before dawn, the Knights, along with Joseph and Oliver, went down to the stream and repaired the dam, making it even stronger than before. In the afternoon, the entire household took a walk down to the water for their baptism in the church of Christ.

Joseph officiated again, while Oliver waded into the water and held out his hand to the prophet's wife. With her eyes glued to her husband's, Emma gave her hand to Oliver and waded out. Her skirts were heavy and soggy with water. Her feet were chilled, and the stream tugged at her long dress. She stood facing her husband, her hands grasping Cowdery's forearm. Joseph beamed his approval. Then Oliver repeated the words of the ordinance, while she recorded in her life's memory the exultation on her husband's face. With a whoosh and a splash, Emma sank below the chilly surface of the little pool. Every particle of clothing went under. Every hair of her head was submerged. Her breath was stopped by the sharp cold, but somehow her body felt warm, tingling. Excitement ran through her, and she could feel herself smiling even while she was under the water.

Then, quickly, and with water streaming from the top of her head, it was over. Oliver raised her up and stood smiling before her. This was the same man who had baptized her husband in the Susquehanna river under the direction of John the Baptist. Joseph had wanted his wife to have the same experience he had. Now that desire was fulfilled. Emma beamed at Oliver. All of them burst out in pure laughter, and the little group on the bank of the pond began to clap and rejoice.

But the joy was short-lived. Before Emma could completely exit the waters of baptism, men emerged from the woods, calling taunts to

Joseph and Oliver, demanding the services halt immediately. Oliver calmly went on with the next baptism. Both Mother and Father Knight went into the water, the Stringhams, the Culvers.

A mob of about fifty neighborhood men continued to gather, and as their numbers increased, they escalated their threats and taunts. All too soon, the angry demonstration ended the baptismal service. Joseph urged his little band of new converts to walk back to the Knight's home. With every ounce of tact and patience he possessed, he tried to forestall the mob.

"Friends, there is nothing evil going on here! It's just a baptism."

One man shouted back, "We don't need your baptism! These people are already good church members. Why do you come here and tell us we are all wrong? You're an imposter, Smith! Nothing more than a carnival magician with a crystal ball."

Joseph groaned within. He had known that would haunt him forever. It had been useful in his youth to help him focus his mental forces. Now that he had grown older, with more and more direct communication with God, he rarely used it. Still, the charges would always remain and throw him into the category of a quack.

"Knight! Are you taking up with this so-called prophet?"

"I am a follower of Christ," Joseph Knight responded with dignity. "And I have just been baptized in His name. Can you say the same?"

"Joe Smith can't bring you salvation! You're all a bunch of sheep. Baa, baa. You'll follow him into hell!"

While Oliver urged the new converts back into the Knight's home, Joseph, along with Newel and Mr. Knight, continued to try to reason with the mob. Taunts turned into threats. Who had instigated it? What had these neighbors to gain by persecuting him and his church? He posed no real threat to their pocketbooks, and certainly he had done nothing immoral. Religion was a comfortable thing to them, and it was not comfortable to contemplate angels or new revelation. It required something from a man, a change of life, the commitment to live better. That was never comfortable.

Before any real violence could start, the men broke up, tired of shouting and receiving no bitter response. Their anger subsided like foam on the seashore. Joseph apologized to Father Knight for all the furor. The older man was worried.

"It's not over, Joseph. They'll follow you wherever you go."

Joseph shook his head in confusion. "I understood the persecution in Palmyra. They wanted riches, and the golden plates seemed to be a treasure. But here? Now? I don't understand why."

"Because if you are right, you make them all wrong."

Joseph stared into Father Knight's worn and weathered face, set now into deep lines of concern. Knight repeated his assessment. "You make them all wrong."

That evening was set for the confirming of the new members. Oliver had baptized; Joseph would confirm. The mob had reluctantly faded away and left them in uneasy peace. After supper they would begin laying on hands in confirmation. But Joseph's enemies had a different sort of "laying on of hands" in mind.

A sharp rap came on the door. Mother Knight opened it cautiously to find Constable Akins on her doorstep. He tipped his hat to Polly Knight, his neighbor and demanded to see Joe Smith, the Mormon Prophet. Joseph stepped quickly to her side. The constable was a man of angles. His shoulders were bony. His brow and jaw were lean and square. His nose jutted sharply from his face. But it was an honest face, even kind under different circumstances.

"Joe Smith, you are under arrest for the charge of being a 'disorderly person.'"

"I? I am accused of being disorderly? Constable, there is a mistake here. I have tried to carry out quiet, private baptisms. I haven't been disorderly. That charge should be made against Mr. Knight's neighbors!"

"Nevertheless, I have my duty. I am to bring you before Judge Joseph Chamberlain in Chenango County, and I will do it, sir, you may be sure."

"Constable, wouldn't you like to sit in on our little meeting here? We are about to confirm thirteen new members to the Lord's church."

"No sir. I have my duty, and I'll tell you the truth, young man. If I were you, I'd come quietly. Not a half mile from here there are thirty men lying in wait for you, when you leave this place. You'll be better off in my hands than in theirs, for there is no doubt they intend to do you harm."

Newel, Oliver, and Joseph Knight all crowded around their young prophet. Emma stood up at the end of the table. Her husband turned and looked at her. If he left, the violence would leave too. If he tried to take his wife home, she would be right in the middle of an angry mob. Her eyes implored him not to go. Joseph hated to disappoint her. He looked back at the constable. A plain man, in plain clothes, he seemed determined to do his duty.

"Don't worry, Smith. I am sworn to arrest you and also sworn to protect you. I intend to do both. Please come along peaceably."

Joseph reached for his hat and cloak. Emma went to him. In front of others she would never become emotional, but her actions betrayed her concern. She took his hat from him and carefully placed it on his head. She put his cloak about his shoulders, fastened it, and smoothed it over his chest. Emma's eyes were shiny with tears as she held fast his hand.

"Be careful. Go with God," she spoke softly.

"He's always with me. Don't fear. This is not the time for my enemies to prevail. There is too much work for me yet to do." Then his concern for her surfaced. "Emma, don't go home. There could be those who might look for me there, and I don't want you home alone. You could stay right here."

She shook her head. "No, we've been imposing on the Knights too long. I'll go to my sister Elizabeth in Windsor."

He agreed. It would be best. "I'll come to you there. Pray for me?"

"I will," she promised with all her heart.

"Constable, I'm ready."

Joseph wasn't quite as ready as he thought for the ordeal that followed. Only a mile or so away, the constable slowed for a bridge, and the road was suddenly swarming with men. They had been lying in wait for Joseph, just as Akins had warned. They seemed to think his prisoner was theirs.

"Git back! Git back, I say! This man is under arrest, and I am taking him to Judge Chamberlain for trial tomorrow."

"We'll give him a trial! Hand him over. I got his leg, boys! Pull him down from that horse."

Akins cracked his whip over the man's head. "Git back, I'm warning you."

"Akins, damn your hide, I pay your salary."

"You pay for a constable to keep the peace, and I aim to keep it. Now, go on. Go on home. Joe Smith'll git his trial, and you can have your say then."

He clucked to his horse and jerked on the reins of Joseph's mount. "Git up!" he snapped to his horse, and they trotted on, scattering men along the way. Joseph stayed overnight at a tavern in South Bainbridge, with the ever watchful constable. He spent almost three hours talking to the man, telling him about *The Book of Mormon*, and describing the ancient peoples and their religious beliefs. When Joseph lay down to sleep that night, Akins slept on the floor, with his feet against the door, his musket at his side.

At five minutes to ten the next morning, the constable and the prisoner started down the stairs and made their way through an excitable crowd to get to the Judge's chambers. Akins looked sideways at

Joseph. "You sure are a harmless feller to cause so much disturbance around here."

Joseph almost smiled back. "Aren't I though?"

"Mr. Seymour," Judge Chamberlain called loudly to the prosecutor while thumping his gavel. "Stop wasting the court's time and get on with the specific charges against this man."

"Yes, your honor." Prosecutor Seymour responded. He was a short, rotund man who smelled perpetually of stale bacon grease. "Joe Smith is accused of disturbing the peace on many occasions by preaching nonsense in the guise of religion. He has cheated people out of their property and is a glass-looker and a treasure seeker. In short, he is an undesirable element in our county, and we want him imprisoned."

The judge looked down over his pulpit, a scowl on his face. He had arisen that morning with three bunions instead of two on his aging feet, a boil on his buttocks, and an itch he couldn't scratch in public. All in all, it wasn't a good morning. Now these fools had gotten him to put on his robes and conduct this so-called trial on what sounded like trumped up charges. He fixed his steely eyes on the prisoner.

"Well, you don't *look* like the scoundrel the prosecution has described," he growled.

At that moment the door to his courtroom opened, and two men asked to approach the bench. Mr. John Davidson and John Reid had been sent by Joseph Knight Sr. to defend his young friend. Neither of them were lawyers, but they were both respected and intelligent land holders who knew the law. They lent an air of respectability to the proceedings and forced the prosecutors to substantiate their claims. Witness after witness was called who accused Joseph of stealing property. The only specific instance they could cite, however, was the case of Mr. Josiah Stowell's horse.

The prosecutor called him to the stand. "Mr. Stowell, is it true that Joe Smith there told you an angel said for him to 'appropriate' your horse, and he took it without paying you for it?"

"No," Stowell didn't hesitate. "I sold Joseph Smith my horse of my own free will. He gave me his note, which I hold as good as gold. The man worked for me for a year, and I never had a better farm hand. I've known him since he was a lad. He's an honest person. Not like some folks here, I might add." He glanced around the room, challenging every person with his gaze.

"You had Smith in your home. Weren't you afraid for your daughters?"

Stowell snorted in response. "Don't be a jackass! He's like my own son. The man is blameless, I tell you."

Judge Chamberlain gazing down on Joseph's clear countenance was inclined to agree. He yawned and shifted in his chair. "Go on," he instructed the prosecution, "if you've got more witnesses call them. So far you haven't proven anything."

The two Stowell girls were called separately and asked if Joseph had ever tried to be familiar with them. They both stoutly denied it. So the trial pressed on with the judge calling various people from the community, many of whom had never even met the accused, but came for the circus atmosphere of the trial. This dragged on until almost midnight. Meanwhile Joseph had had nothing to eat or drink the entire time.

"Your honor, this is a mockery," Mr. Reid finally charged. "I insist you make a ruling here. Absolutely none of these accusations have been proved. The man is obviously being harassed because of his religion, which, as you know, is a protected institution in America. This is reminiscent of the Salem witch trials a century ago. I thought we had come further than that in this country. He's hungry, he's thirsty, he's tired. And so am I. If it please your honor, I implore you to declare him not guilty and close this trial."

The judge looked at his watch, rubbed his bleary eyes and scratched himself discreetly. "I am in agreement with everything you have said, Mr. Reid. The prisoner can go free. Trial's over. I'm going home to bed."

Exultation on Joseph's part was followed by immediate frustration. He stepped out of the courtroom, exhausted and greatly desiring a bed himself, when another constable — considerably less gentle than Akins had been — roughly shoved Davidson and Reid aside and took Joseph into custody for another trial on charges of defrauding the public with regard to religious powers. Despite protests from everyone associated with Joseph, the constable took him on a fifteen mile ride in the dark of the night to Broome County for another trial the next morning.

They stopped at another tavern for the night. There Joseph became acquainted with the kind of treatment the Savior had endured. There was a mean spirit in the tavern. The men were obviously drunk and expecting him. They had stayed late, hoping for their turn at the so-called "Mormon prophet." Abuse began as soon as he stumbled into the tavern bound tightly by the constable.

"Ole Joe Smith ain't so holy now, boys! Look, he's thirsty. I'll give you something to wet your lips, Smith!" One drunkard shouted, then spit on Joseph's face and wiped his slobbering mouth on his shoulder.

"Never trust a glass-looking man. My pa tole me, any man says he talks with angels is a liar, cause there ain't no angels today."

"Not here anyway," Joseph murmured, looking around the room.

"What'd you say prophet-man? What you say about us?"

"I said, I can see you don't keep much company with angels."

A scrawny, dirty little man fell heavily against Joseph. Then he reached up and slapped the prisoner who stood helpless before his enemies.

"How's that?" the beggar belched as he leered at the crowd. "Where's his angels now?"

"Prophesy to us," the chant began. It soon was taken up around the tavern. "Prophesy to us, Mr. Preacher-man." He refused to answer and got kicks and cuffs for his silence. After a while — the hour being what it was — several drunks gave up the harassment and started out the door. They walked by the bound prisoner and alternately slapped and spit on him as they left. During all this, the constable occupied himself with a light supper and a cup of ale. When Joseph asked for something to eat and drink, the law man threw a couple of pieces of bread on the table and shoved a cup of water in his direction. Threatening instant death if Joseph tried to escape, the constable freed one of the prisoner's hands so he could eat the crusts provided him.

With just a few hours remaining before daybreak, the law man took his charge up to a room. He insisted on Joseph sleeping against the wall. He then lay down next to him and held on to Joseph's arm to prevent any possible escape. Despite his pinched arms and cramped position, Joseph fell into an exhausted sleep. He knew the worst was far from over.

The second trial was held in Colesville. This time, three justices presided in accordance with English law custom. The prosecutors were confident of success. They had sent runners out to round up witnesses against Joseph. Some of the witnesses came right from the tavern and were obviously drunk.

"Do you know of your own experience that Joseph Smith was able to cast out devils?"

"I do," the tipsy man informed the three justices solemnly.

"Did you ever see him cast out a devil?" Mr. Davidson asked.

"Not actually seen him, but I know he done it."

"How do you know?" Davidson persisted.

"Hector tole me. And he's my friend."

"And how does your friend know it?"

"He seen it."

"Really? And where did the event take place?"

"On that man's farm," the drunk pointed exultantly to Newel Knight.

"Call Mr. Newel Knight to the stand!"

The prosecution posed the first questions. Mr. Seymour was a determined Deist who believed in neither angels, devils nor prophets. He had a real problem with Joseph Smith.

"Did the prisoner, Joseph Smith, cast the devil out of you?"

"No, sir."

Seymour frowned. "Why, haven't you had the devil cast out of you?"

"Yes, sir."

"Tell us what he looked like."

"Mr. Seymour, do you understand spiritual things?" Newel innocently asked.

"No, unlike Smith over there, I don't pretend to such big things."

"Then it would be of no use for me to tell you what the devil looked like, because it was a spiritual sight, and according to your own statement, you do not understand things of the spirit."

The spectators guffawed. The lawyer stared angrily at the table, then dismissed the witness. He sent out for more witnesses. They swore to so many contradictory statements that even the three justices who wanted to convict Joseph couldn't find evidence enough to do it. Davidson and Reid proved so adept at Joseph's defense that the prosecution could make no headway even in a sympathetic court.

At last, it was two o'clock in the morning. Joseph had been sitting dejectedly for hours, too exhausted to participate much in his own defense. He was hungry and tired and thoroughly discouraged. Many of the people who had come to mock him in the courtroom he had once spoken to as friends on the streets of Colesville. In the year he had worked for Stowell and Knight, he had met most of the citizens of that town. Why turn on him like this? He looked around the courtroom. Only a few people remained. Newel Knight and Oliver Cowdery sat in one corner side by side. They were whispering. Cyrus McMaster sat by Seymour, the prosecutor. McMaster was another member of the Presbyterian church who had instigated the trial. His hatred was evident from the dark looks of derision he threw Joseph's way.

"Mr. Smith," the justices called to him. "Due to the late hour and lack of substantial evidence, we regretfully acquit you. It is apparent to us that, although these charges have not been proven against you, you are a disreputable person and a sore on our society. You have obviously hoodwinked a number of people. Well, we know the truth of it, even if it can't be proven here at this particular time. Time will prove to all concerned that you are a scoundrel of the worst kind. Leave this courtroom and never come back again, or we will find a way to punish you, you may count on it."

Seymour and McMaster were disappointed, though they nodded their heads to everything the justice said. Joseph stood beside the constable. The law man could see the prisoner was beaten down, but he had little sympathy for a man who caused trouble in the community. Still, he had a momentary twinge of conscience. The constable knew that when Joseph walked out of the courtroom, he would be met by a mob of at least three hundred men. They had been gathering all night. Now at two o'clock in the morning, they were drunk and bent on justice the old fashioned way.

"Thank you, your Honors," Joseph replied and turned in his weariness toward his friends.

"This way," the constable guided him. Oliver and Newel walked with them toward the front door. Seymour and McMasters were at the justice bench arguing with the three paid witnesses. The constable opened not the front door, but a side door, and led them to the back corner of the building.

"Out in front there's a few boys waiting to have a party with you, Smith — a tar and feather party. If I was you, I'd take off for the woods there."

The three friends stood listening to the noise of the crowd gathered in front of the building.

"You fellas had better go a different way," Joseph cautioned his friends. "If they catch you with me, it'll go hard on you."

"I'm staying with you," Oliver simply stated.

"Me too," said Newel.

Joseph looked into the eyes of these two loyal friends and shook his head. "Go to Emma, Newel, and tell her I'm all right. You can travel faster on the road than I can through the woods. Tell her I'll come as soon as possible. She's at her sister Elizabeth Wasson's over in Windsor, the last house by the bridge. Know where that is?"

"Yep. Be careful. God bless."

Joseph and Oliver caught a glimpse of torch fire around the front of the building and heard shouted threats. The woods looked much more inviting, though it was late May and still chilly in the dark of the night. Newel made his way to the coach house where his horse was stabled. Joseph and Oliver struck out through the shadows toward the woods. Once the lawyers and judge left the building, it was obvious to the mob that Smith had escaped. Immediately they guessed the truth. He must be hiding in the woods. Three hundred men dispersed to comb those woods. Exaggerated rumors and outright lies, circulated throughout the town by the very witnesses which the defense had discredited, had inflamed the citizens of Colesville until anger was at a fever pitch. Joseph and Oliver knew they were running for their lives. The fact that they ran, not to Harmony as the mob expected, but to Windsor, where Emma waited at the Wassons, was possibly the saving of their hides. Fifteen miles through the dark, through the roots, trees, vines that tangled their way, the two men ran crouched over much of the time, following the river which would lead them to safety — they hoped.

Emma waited at her sister's home. Elizabeth and her husband listened to her story of mob persecution, shaking their heads and sympathizing, but privately wondering what kind of a man could not get along with his neighbors. All the other churches lived peaceably side by side. Methodists, Presbyterians, Protestants, and even the more radical Baptists, managed to disagree on theology without undue rancor. However, Joseph Smith had stirred up a hornet's nest by preaching that they were all wrong, that only he and his church held authority from God. It wasn't a very popular position. Now they took his wife in with ambivalent sentiments. They certainly wanted to offer shelter to a family member. On the other hand, the Wassons were reluctant to expose themselves and children to such a demonstration of violence. Nonetheless, Elizabeth carefully avoided any mention of such concern to her sister.

She need not have avoided the subject. Emma was highly aware of the uncomfortable position in which she put the Wassons merely by her presence. Not that the violence was directed at her, but she knew Joseph would come to her there if he could. If it were known, it could lead the mob right to her sister's front door. For a few days she maintained a positive outlook with the Wasson family, but prayed continuously for Joseph's acquittal and for the violence to stop. It was a touchy subject, one that she and her sister diplomatically agreed not to discuss. Instead, their conversation centered around family matters.

Emma sometimes looked at herself in the mirror and wondered that such a quiet, peace-loving person as herself had married a man who seemed destined to stir up violent feelings in the people who knew him. If she had not known — absolutely known — that he acted under direction from heaven, she would not have been able to tolerate the conflict which constantly surrounded Joseph. But she had seen him as he translated under the spirit's influence. She had seen him acting as a spokesman for his God. She had witnessed the humility with which he recorded heavenly reproof for his own transgressions. No other spiritual leader recorded God's reprimand for his own sins. Joseph did not hold himself up as infallible, to be worshiped by his converts. He was a humble man, unlearned, until the spirit of revelation rested upon him. Then, as Emma had so often witnessed, he became almost a luminescent white, and his voice took on authority and power. When the moment passed and the spirit left him, he would sit down heavily, as though drained. She had come to call it in her own mind, the transformation. It was this process, as she watched it happen over and over again, that convinced her Joseph was no ordinary plowboy. He was an imperfect human being through whom God had chosen to work. Because of this conviction, Emma would endure the humility of poverty and the threat of violence. Because of this, she would defend her husband to any and all critics, even her own family, and she would accept his word as God's word.

She watched the road from her bedroom window until late into the night. When Joseph hadn't come by the second day, her prayers became more fervent. She determined to pray until she had some word that he was all right. Mr. Wasson rode into town and came back with the news Joseph had been acquitted in South Bainbridge, but had immediately been arrested a second time and taken to Colesville. He had no word on the trial there. Emma resumed her watch.

It was a little after three o'clock in the morning when Newel stopped his horse outside the Wasson home. He saw a small flickering lamp in a back bedroom. As he peered in the window, he could see Emma resting in the rocking chair, her head uncomfortably pressed against the high back. He tapped on the window, and she awoke with a start. At first she drew back in fear, then seeing Newel's friendly face, quickly arose and opened the back door. He paused long enough to tell her Joseph had been acquitted again and was heading for the Wasson place. Relief was short lived for she realized Joseph was on foot, making his way through the woods. She thanked Newel, and he left on the twenty-mile ride home. She sat up all that night, keeping the lamp lit inside and a torch flaming outside as a beacon for her husband.

Just as the day was breaking, Joseph and Oliver emerged from the woods near the bridge by the Wasson home. They were both dirty, scratched, and spent. Joseph had not eaten a meal for two days. Oliver had twisted an ankle in the woods, and Joseph carried him the rest of the way. Emma, dozing in the chair, heard a heavy thud against the door and cautiously looked through a small side window. On the doorstep, her husband and Oliver had thrown themselves down, too weary to knock and wait. With a cry, she opened the door and helped Joseph to his feet. Oliver limped to the table and sat.

"Have they nearly killed you?" she asked.

"No. They wanted to, but we escaped into the woods. It's the fifteen mile run through the woods that nearly killed us." Joseph sat opposite Oliver, his head resting on his folded arms.

"Will they follow you here?"

"No. I believe they gave up the chase hours ago. The whisky wore off, and they have chores to do. But I think we should leave your sister's as soon as possible. I don't want to put them in danger."

"After you've eaten and rested, we'll have James take us back to Harmony. Here, I've kept the soup stock warm all night." Emma set before them a crock of soup and yesterday's biscuits. Joseph tried to restrain himself from gulping the food. Before either of them could finish the meal, they laid their heads down on their folded arms and dozed off. Elizabeth came downstairs and saw the two disheveled men at her table. She looked at her sister questioningly, and Emma made their apologies, then helped her husband to their bedroom. Oliver simply wrapped up in his cloak and lay down before the parlor fireplace.

"Is your husband hurt?" Elizabeth asked.

"No. Just tired and hungry. He's had nothing to eat but bread crusts and water for two days. When he has slept a few hours, we'll go back home. Can James drive us?"

"I think so. I do hope your husband will be safe in Harmony. Of course, living so near father, you should be safe enough."

Emma didn't answer. She knew there was some truth in it, but she also knew Isaac could not be counted on to protect Joseph. Last night, his sympathies would have been with the mob.

"Joseph, if you go back to Colesville, you'll be lynched. Just let the feelings die down a little. I know you want to do the confirmations yourself. But it isn't wise. Remember your own words, 'wisdom in all things.' Well, there is no wisdom in putting yourself in danger."

"Why shouldn't I practice my religion as I see fit? Do I not live in the United States of America? And doesn't the constitution grant me freedom of religion? I promised the Culvers and the Stringhams I would do their confirmations. I intend to keep my promise."

"You're just being stubborn. You know I'm right."

"I know I won't be beaten by a bunch of ignorant men with a yen to whip me."

"So it's a matter of pride?"

"Maybe," Joseph conceded. "But it's also commitment to the work I began. If I let them whip me now, at the start of the church, the work will die in its tracks. How would it look for me to hide out like a coward?"

"You'll be putting us all in danger. If that crowd gets violent again, it could spill over here, at the Culvers and Stringhams. The Knights have already had wagons turned over, plunged into the pond, crops destroyed. All I'm asking is for you to wait a little. I'm tired of running off to Fayette, or South Bainbridge."

Her voice was pleading and strained. Joseph sighed. Actually, he knew she was right. He had already tried to go to Colesville, but was run off the road by three men who seemed to be guarding it. The people of Colesville were determined his church should gain no footing there. Joseph was determined it would. Right now, however, reason dictated that he remain secluded and let the furor die.

"Maybe I'll send Oliver. He's apparently not as easily recognized as I am. Ideally, one of us should do the baptism and one the confirmation, but he has authority to do both, if necessary. I'll stay home and tend to other matters."

She came to him and put her arms about his shoulders, her cheek against his. He sat back in the chair knowing she was right, and hating it. He could give in on this issue. She had so faithfully followed him up to now, and he didn't blame her for being tired of it all. Both of them were feeling a little like prey for the hunters.

Oliver was to leave the next night, stay over with the Stringhams, and ride back the next day. Joseph had to admit he relished the prospect of having a night of privacy with Emma. He thought about just the two of them watching the river roll by.

Emma had just fixed their dinner, and the three of them sat down to eat. Joseph bowed his head to say grace, and something else began to flood his mind. He said a hasty thanks for the food, and then turned to Oliver.

"Get your quill and paper. I have more to say." He turned to Emma who sat perfectly still, her hands in her lap. Her eyes were fixed on his face, but he seemed to see beyond her. He pushed back his chair and went to stand behind Emma as she sat at the table. His voice was sharp with urgency.

"Emma, there is a blessing for you. I feel it flowing through my mind.

"A revelation I give unto you concerning my will; and if thou art faithful and walk in the paths of virtue before me, I will preserve thy life, and thou shalt receive an inheritance in Zion. Behold, thy sins are forgiven thee, and thou art an elect lady, whom I have called . . . Murmur not because of the things which thou hast not seen, for they are withheld from thee and from the world, which is wisdom in me in a time to come. And

the office of thy calling shall be for a comfort unto my servant, Joseph Smith, Jun., thy husband, in his afflictions, with consoling words, in the spirit of meekness. And thou shalt go with him at the time of his going, and be unto him for a scribe, while there is no one to be a scribe for him, that I may send my servant, Oliver Cowdery, whithersoever I will.

And thou shalt be ordained under his hand to expound scriptures, and to exhort the church, according as it shall be given thee by my Spirit. For he shall lay his hands upon thee, and thou shalt receive the Holy Ghost, and thy time shall be given to writing, and to learning much. . . .

And it shall be given thee, also, to make a selection of sacred hymns, . . . For my soul delighteth in the song of the heart . . . Wherefore, lift up thy heart and rejoice, and cleave unto the covenants which thou hast made. . . . Keep my commandments continually, and a crown of righteousness thou shalt receive . . . Amen." (Excerpt Doctrine and Covenants, Section 25)

Emma felt a stream of warmth descending from her head, down her neck, spreading down her back and making her tingle. Joseph finished speaking and stood silently, his hand on her head. She relished the warm sensations, afraid to move and end the moment. Finally, she turned to look up at him. His face was flushed pink and his eyes were moist. Oliver left the room as quietly as he could.

"Oh, Joseph, I'm sorry."

"You have nothing to be sorry for."

"Yes, I do. I get so demanding sometimes. I think I know best. I need to trust you more, to trust that you're acting under God's direction. Forgive me?"

"Of course. Sometimes you're right, and this was one of those times. It is better for Oliver to go than for me. Besides, we'll have some precious time to ourselves. Will you go walking with me beside the river?"

"What did it mean, that I should make a collection of hymns?"

"Who could do it better? You're experienced with church hymns. Collect the best, the songs that tell what we teach, and we'll see they are published. A new hymnal by Emma Hale Smith — it's exactly what the church needs."

"Maybe I can do it. I think I could make a contribution."

He nuzzled her hair and neck. "Your greatest contribution is loving me."

Her eyes twinkled. "Now, was that the Lord or you talking when the revelation said I should be 'a comfort unto my servant Joseph?' I'm thinking that sounded a lot like a husband."

"You mind being a comfort?"

"No, not really. I can enjoy that assignment — except when you're being pigheaded."

"Me? Not me."

"Yes, even the prophet of the . . . ." Her words were drowned in his kiss. But the revelation Oliver wrote down would be Emma's comfort in the times of trouble to come.

Chapter Eleven

Unity in All Things

mma stood at the door of her parents' home, the home she had known since childhood. Here she had played, prayed, and watched her brothers and sisters marry. Here she had been happy. She had at times felt a little guilty in knowing she was the favored child. Now as she studied the cozy little kitchen and dining area, she could see back through the years as if through a filmy window. There she was at nine, sitting before the fireplace, hugging her knees and warming her little toes. She seemed to hear her mother call her, and when she arose from the fireplace, she turned into a young woman with a long, full skirt and a simple daisy stuck into her curls. She thought she could see herself sitting in a chair close to Isaac's, reading the Bible with him. *Oh, Papa*, she thought, *where are you now? My Papa who kissed me and gave me pony rides? I miss you. More than you'll ever know.*

Quick tears came to her eyes, with memories so poignant she clutched her handkerchief to her heart to stop the pain. Isaac would not even look at her. He sat with his head down, whittling wood. Elizabeth put down her dishtowel and went to her daughter.

"The house is clean and locked," Emma said woodenly. "Joseph has the wagon packed and ready to go. Guess we'll be leaving soon."

Isaac went on whittling. Elizabeth looked into her daughter's face with concern.

"How are you feeling? You look a little peaked."

"I'm fine, mother. Just a little tired, that's all."

"Sure that's all? Not expecting again, are you?"

"I don't think so. I haven't been sick."

"Well, you rest as soon as you get to Fayette. And you don't have to kill yourself getting there. Take the trip slow and easy."

"I'll be fine. Really, I will. I'll have two days of just riding along in the wagon while Joseph does all the work."

Her father cleared his throat loudly and raised his eyebrow.

"You staying with the same folks?" Elizabeth asked.

"The Whitmers? Yes, we'll be there a few weeks until we get a place of our own. I'll let you know. Maybe you could come see us next winter while things are slow here, or I might come back to visit." This was a harder parting than Emma had thought it would be.

Now her father spoke without looking up. "If you go, you go. You left us once before, ran off with him. I sent your brother to bring you back. You left us to go with him to Fayette and finish that book, but I gave you back the house when you wanted to return. I've been embarrassed in front of my neighbors and friends by a son-in-law accused of cheating, stealing, and defrauding, not to mention glass-looking and treasure-seeking. You fell right in with him translating some 'golden plates.' Now he has produced a book he claims to have gotten from God and goes about trying to sell it."

Isaac had turned full face to challenge his favorite daughter. He stood up, towering over her and Elizabeth. "Emma, if you leave again, that's it. I'll close up the house or rent it to someone else. I've had enough. I've had enough of the shenanigans of your husband and your blind devotion to him. His pretense to religion doesn't work with me. His so-called revelations don't ring true to a man who reveres the prophets of old. I've read the Bible. I attend to my weekly devotionals. That's more than you can say for him."

Emma responded quietly, hoping to keep her father calm. "Papa, Joseph is a good man. He holds devotional not once a week but every day. You taught me the Christian life, and you taught me well. Don't you think I could tell if my husband were an imposter? Don't you think I would see if he were cheating people? Don't you think I could tell if he were merely pretending revelations, or pretending to translate? Believe me, I wrote for him. I saw him at work. I felt the presence of angels. I even touched the metal plates when they were covered with just a cloth. I dusted around them. I have seen Joseph humbly appeal to God for wisdom and for help, and I have seen him speak under the influence of the Holy Spirit. I am fully satisfied he is a mouthpiece for God."

Isaac heard his daughter through with an expression of incredulity. "Emma, I just don't believe Joseph Smith is a prophet!"

"Well, I do!"

Their eyes had locked and now held. Both were stubborn in their way. Isaac might be more verbose and commanding, but Emma was intractable in her mind set.

His voice was low and sad. "Then, you might as well go. You have chosen him over your family."

She tried once more. She reached out to put her arms around him. "Papa! Papa, I'll come back. I promise. I'll come back this winter."

He shoved his way past her and to the bottom of the stairs. "Don't. I won't allow you to hurt us like this again." His anger had him in a tearing grip. His voice rose until it filled the little room, assaulting his wife and daughter. "Go on! Leave my house! You're no longer a Hale. You're no longer my daughter. I would rather have buried you in that cemetery there. If you leave with Joseph Smith, don't you *ever* come back! And you mark my words, no good will come of your life with that man!"

His blazing eyes and condemnation struck Emma like a physical blow. She staggered backward, her shoulder striking the doorpost. "No, Papa. . . , " she cried.

"Yes!" he roared.

"Mama!" Emma appealed.

"Out! Out of my house! Out of my life!"

Elizabeth tried to calm her husband. "Isaac! Not this way. Don't make her leave like this."

"Quiet! I will have quiet in my home! Say goodbye to your daughter, woman, and shut the door!"

Emma stumbled outside. Elizabeth followed, closing the door behind them, trying fruitlessly to comfort her daughter with her embrace. Over Emma's shoulder she could see Joseph tying down the rocking chair on the back of the wagon. Elizabeth Hale couldn't understand why it should have come to such an impasse. Smith was not a bad boy. Anyone could see that, just by looking at his face. She didn't believe — at least she didn't want to believe — the rumors and charges. Besides, Emma couldn't love a bad man. Couldn't Isaac see that?

Emma's tears wet the collar of her mother's dress. Elizabeth tried to wipe the tears from her daughter's face, but her own cheeks were just as wet.

"Oh, Mother! Mother! What can I do?"

Elizabeth could hardly speak. Indeed, there was nothing to say. She knew her husband. She knew he meant every word.

"Nothing to do, Emma, but what you have to do."

"Mother, I don't want to leave you." Emma looked into her mother's face. Every wrinkle now was streaming water. Every line in the dear old face was etched in Emma's memory. All the years — all the years were running out now like sand from a broken hourglass, and there was no going back. There was no changing her heart or her decision to marry a marked man. God had commanded her to follow, and she could do nothing else. Oh, but leaving like this was so hard, so hard!

"My girl," her mother managed to say brokenly.

"I love you, Mama!"

"I know. I love you too. God be with you." Elizabeth broke down and pulled her apron up to cover her face while she wept uncontrollably.

"Talk to Papa." Emma pleaded.

"Won't do any good. He's set. It's been coming a long time."

"And it's my fault. I know it is. I should never have eloped. Tell him I'll always love him."

"I'll . . . tell him," Elizabeth promised.

They kissed on both cheeks, and Emma turned to go. But Elizabeth wasn't ready. She put her hand on her daughter's shoulder, and they fell into each other's arms again weeping. When Emma finally gathered her courage and pulled away to go, a low groaning started in Elizabeth's chest. All the way to the wagon, with every step she took, Emma heard her mother's deep sobbing groans. Joseph held out his arms to her, and she fell upon them like a beggar, her eyes pleading with him to make it all better. But he couldn't. As he embraced his wife, holding her while she wept piteously, he knew that there was nothing he could say or do to make her heartache better. After several minutes, he helped Emma up onto the wagon seat, climbed up after her, heaved a sigh of resignation, and clucked to the horse. They started with a lurch and a roll, and with the creak of the departing wagon, Elizabeth sat on the doorstep with her apron over her face and gave herself up to heartbreak.

Upstairs, Isaac stood by the window, but he couldn't see a thing. His eyes were shut to the agonizing scene below, yet tears ran unheeded down his cheeks. His grizzly forearm was pressed against his mouth, so no one heard the sobs that racked the old man. But his arm bore deep, purple marks of his teeth for weeks.

Emma did not look back.

"You'd best be getting some rest," Lucy said, observing her daughter-in-law who was pale and hollow-eyed.

"I had a good rest last night, Mother Smith."

"For how long? You didn't go to bed until after I did, and I know that was midnight. You were up cooking before the birds."

"Well, there's a lot to do to get the missionaries ready to go. I think I will finish Samuel's frock coat today."

Emma was determined that no one should feel sorry for her. She could pull her own share of the load. After all, Mother Whitmer had not complained when, month after month, she shared her tiny home with strangers and new converts to the church. Joseph and Emma had stayed there for two weeks this time before moving into a tiny cottage in Waterloo. They were right down the road from Lucy and Joseph, Sr.

All the women of the church were hard at work making clothes for the missionaries who were to leave after the September 1830 Conference. Samuel, Joseph Sr., Oliver and Peter Whitmer were to go out to teach the Indian people their *Book of Mormon* heritage. There was great excitement over it in the little church. This was the remnant people of Israel who were to be gathered the last time before the great and dreadful day of the Lord.

The summer had been hectic, first moving, then looking for a new home — for Emma was determined not to impose any longer on the Whitmers — and dealing with Hiram Page's philosophy that every man should have his own seerstone and his own revelations. Joseph had once taught his closest followers that every man was entitled to revelations of his own, but he had not meant those revelations to be for the church as a whole. Revelation for one's own stewardship and responsibility was appropriate and desirable, but Hiram, and even Oliver, had been writing their own revelations for the church, many of which conflicted with Joseph's.

Joseph had been meeting with the two men well into the night, trying to reason with his friends.

"Oliver, is the Lord not a God of order?"

"Yes, of course, He is."

"Have you ever seen a dog try to obey two masters? One whistles here and the other whistles over there and the poor dog runs in circles. That's not what we want for the church."

"Joseph, I feel the spirit so strongly. My heart is on fire with the memory of my ordination to the priesthood. I feel as though I want to live and breathe and walk in the spirit daily. You can't tell me my revelations are wrong."

"I'm simply telling you they are not for the church as a whole. I know God puts thoughts in your head. I know He wants to work through you, Oliver. You are a chosen servant, chosen to help bring about new scripture in our modern day, chosen to be ordained by the very angels of heaven. No one knows your virtue more than I. But God cannot have every man running after his own whims and visions, drawing the members first one way then another. Why, some of the things you wrote don't agree at all with Hiram Page's revelations. And many of the things Hiram wrote completely disagree with what God revealed to me. Our God is not the author of confusion. Can't you see the problems you're creating?"

Oliver's usually tender expression was obstinate. "I know I was under inspiration when I wrote. You are not the only one who speaks to God."

Joseph was silent under his friend's rebuke. He knew the church was balanced precariously. He had moved to Fayette at just the right time. The sixty members in Fayette, Palmyra, and Waterloo had enjoyed a close feeling of unity until the last month when Hiram Page and Oliver had begun using seerstones of their own and recording revelations, which they circulated among the members. If the new church were to survive, there must be unity of purpose, unity of understanding, and clear lines of authority. It was a dilemma. Oliver was the "second Elder" of the church. His polish and command of the language gave him stature in the eyes of many of the other members, who tended to be less educated. They admired Oliver. *He* admired Oliver. He had taken Oliver to his heart like a bosom friend. They had suffered together and exulted together. *The Book of Mormon* would likely not be finished by now if Oliver had not stepped in and acted as his scribe. Joseph owed a tremendous debt to Oliver Cowdery, and he was acutely conscious of it. How could he reason with his friend without ill feelings?

The effort went on for weeks. Joseph called in Hiram Page as well and begged him to set aside the revelations which he was circulating. For the good of the church, the leaders must be united, and doctrine must be declared by one person only. Hiram disagreed.

One day, after an exasperating session with both Hiram and Oliver, Joseph left the Whitmer home discouraged. He had been praying constantly about the schism that was widening in the struggling church. He wanted to be open-minded. He had read Hiram's "revelations," and a spirit of darkness fell over him. Why, this was nothing more than a flowery rehash of Methodist doctrines. If this dissension prevailed, the church would be torn apart before it had a real chance to live and breathe.

Emma asked him, "Where is this coming from? Any revelations given to Hiram and Oliver would agree in substance with yours, if they were all coming from the same source."

He nodded in agreement. "Exactly! That's my point — and my fear. I know where my revelations come from. It hasn't changed since I was a boy. If theirs are coming from somewhere else, I have to conclude it's from the adversary. But how can I say that to Oliver and Hiram? They'll be offended, Emma. They might even leave, and that would tear the church apart."

He had no sooner stabled his horse than he was met by two men who had traveled far to see him. They looked like brothers, though one was large and burly, and one was more slender with sensitive eyes and a humble expression. The taller man approached Joseph with his hand outstretched.

"You are surely Joseph, the prophet! You must be. I am Parley Pratt, and this is my brother, Orson. We have just come from Palmyra. We read *The Book of Mormon* and found what we've been looking for." He looked triumphantly at his brother for a moment, then announced, "We desire to be baptized."

Orson Pratt nodded in agreement and shook Joseph's hand. Joseph looked from brother to brother and instantly knew their spirits. Other problems left his mind as he saw two men of faith before him, each bearing testimony of *The Book of Mormon*. Just as important as that, they both knew by the spirit that he was a prophet. Resolve strengthened within him. He was the chosen mouthpiece for God, and no one could convince him to give up the reins of the church.

"Brothers Pratt, you are welcome, most decidedly welcome. I've been waiting for you to come. Your enthusiasm is needed here. We have our church conference next week. You'll stay with me until then. I want to hear about your conversion."

Emma came in from feeding chickens to find the three men engrossed in a story of faith and conversion. She greeted the brothers, then went on with her work of preparing supper.

Parley was the more effusive of the brothers and happily told of his quest for truth. He had had a prosperous farm in Cleveland, Ohio and went, one evening, to hear a Campbellite minister by the name of Sidney Rigdon speak on salvation.

"Well, sir, he is a mighty fine spokesman for the Lord, that Mr. Rigdon. And I was convinced — so convinced he was right I sold my farm and struck out for Kirtland, Ohio where his parish is located. My wife, Thankful, wanted us to go to New York to visit relatives. On the way, I heard about this 'golden bible,' and curiosity got the better of me. I read that book and knew it was scripture from the moment I laid eyes on it. What a fascinating work! What a testimony of the saving power of Jesus Christ! I couldn't put it down. I tell you, Mr. Smith, the spirit of God bore witness to my soul that this was His work. I sent my wife on to her family, and I went to Palmyra and Manchester. You know, some folks just don't *like* you in that community!"

Joseph smiled. "You're right. On the other hand, some folks do. You must have talked to at least a few of those."

"I talked to *your scribe*, Mr. Martin Harris. He bears a strong witness for the book."

Emma looked up from her work, a slight smile on her lips. Her eyes caught Joseph's for a moment. "Your scribe!" she thought. Martin would forever take pride in that, even though all he had written was lost, and he had cost Joseph dearly. Then again, he had also *paid* dearly, financially as well as spiritually in repenting.

"And you, Mr. Pratt?" Joseph addressed the younger brother. Orson was about twenty years old, fine dark hair, dark eyes and the ample shoulders of a farmer. He was also highly educated, with a brilliant mind for math and physics. His broad forehead seemed to evidence that.

"I could find no flaw with the book. When my brother presented it to me and asked me to read it, I was reluctant. But I read it. I must tell you I tried, really tried, to find a flaw in it — at first, that is. After a few chapters, I forgot about trying to discredit it and simply allowed the pure doctrine of God to flow into my mind. I've read extensively, the works of the great theologians, the apostles, the works of the great military leaders. I've never read anything to compare to this book. Either you are a highly educated, widely-traveled man of the world, or you are a prophet of God, who has produced a book that will revolutionize religious thinking."

"What do you think?" Joseph asked.

Orson didn't hesitate. "I believe the latter."

"You're right, Mr. Pratt, I'm not an educated man. I don't pretend to be a brilliant thinker or writer. I only write what God dictates."

Later that evening, Joseph confided in Emma. "The Pratt brothers came at the best time possible. I have argued with Oliver and Hiram so long I started to doubt my own ability to lead. I know it sounds arrogant to say I'm the only one who can receive revelation for the church. These men who have contributed so much to the work naturally want to use their authority too. But, Emma, it brings so much confusion. If God wants to remove me and choose another prophet, He'll do so, but He won't start working through other men and undermine my leadership. Someone has to be the head. Parley and Orson have renewed my belief in myself as that someone."

Emma was sitting up in bed watching her husband. Her eyes were blazing. "Joseph, don't you ever doubt your calling! I don't care if Oliver did do the physical writing and oversee the publication. He could never do what you did. He only wrote the words you translated. I never, at any time, heard of God calling him to receive the golden plates, or the angel tutoring him. He and Hiram may covet your position. In their zeal, they may aspire to take your place, but they can't do it! God could have chosen either of them. Just because Oliver is more educated than you doesn't make him a prophet. Joseph, don't you realize God chose you for your humble, uneducated background? He wanted someone who was like an unwritten book, a clean page, open to His teaching, not the world's teaching. That way, no one could ever say you made up *The Book of Mormon*. A learned man might be accused of that. So, don't be shaken by Hiram's and Oliver's arguments. You know who you are, and I know who you are! I'll bet, if you put it to a vote, the rest of the members also know who truly speaks for God. Just ask them!"

"I'm afraid it's coming to that. Next week, I'll have to put it before the membership. I have to ask for a vote of confidence or things will get out of hand. What if some want to believe Hiram?"

She shook her head. "They won't. They all know Hiram Page and Oliver Cowdery. But *you*, they have seen under the spirit, and that is their proof. When you raise your hand to heaven, and the spirit settles over you, you are almost as bright as an angel yourself. Come here! Sit beside me here on the bed."

She wanted to touch her husband, to let her sure confidence in him flow between them. "The people who are closest to us know us best — our mothers and fathers, brothers, sisters, wives, and husbands. Every one closest to you knows your heart and knows your calling. When you call for that vote of confidence, your wife will be the first to stand up for you."

He put his arms around her and kissed the top of her head. "You are my rock, Emma. You've always believed in me, even though you know exactly how flawed I am."

"Why shouldn't you be allowed some faults? The rest of us are. But God has to work through mere mortals just like you. You're just a man — until the spirit touches you."

That was the way the rest of the church saw it too. On September 26, 1830, the second conference of the church was held at the Whitmer's home. The Pratt brothers were there, newly baptized and waiting to be confirmed. The debate over Hiram's revelations raged through the new congregation for hours. At length, Joseph stood before the little church and appealed to the members.

"Because of the spirit of confusion which has come over us, I feel prompted to call for a sustaining vote. You have all seen or heard Hiram's revelations and Oliver's. You have all read *The Book of Mormon* and other revelations which I have given. Our Lord will choose one head of this church and one only. I will not attempt to lead you if conflict reins. You must choose. Either I am a prophet, and you are willing to hold with the spirit of revelation which is in *me*, or you will give ear to every wind of doctrine taught by other men in this church."

A ripple of anxiety ran through the congregation. They were seated out in the open air, on benches under the trees. Joseph stood before them in his best suit of clothes. Oliver and Hiram sat behind him at the front of the crowd. The Whitmers were gathered, along with their in-laws. The Smiths sat together. The Pratts and Martin sat together. The members looked at one another, considering the problem. Every man there was an independent thinker. They wouldn't have left established churches to join with this little band of believers if they weren't. That was the main issue. If every man could decide doctrine for himself because he felt inspired, they would be little more than another Protestant sect with each minister interpreting scriptures independently. In order to follow a living prophet, they *had* to have enough confidence in his divine calling to submit their wills to his.

Joseph gave them time to consider this. He looked from face to face, from eye to eye, and as he did so, he seemed to grow in stature and assurance. Finally, he called for the vote.

"Let every member who feels he can accept Joseph Smith, Jr. as prophet, seer and revelator, and the only mouthpiece for God and heaven, raise his right arm to the square and sustain him in his calling as such."

The Smith family voted as a block, each hand going up immediately. The Pratt brothers also voted at once. Then, as more and more hands went up, Emma suddenly stood, towering above the rest of the seated congregation. Her hand was upraised, like a beacon of faith in her husband. Every eye went to her, and she stood unperturbed, perfectly cool and collected, with the determined look of a Viking maiden etched on her fine features. The reaction was instantaneous. The others began standing until every member was on his feet. Joseph turned and looked behind him to see Oliver's and Hiram's vote, and he felt a rush of joy when he saw them both standing with arms upraised in full support of him as their prophet. Hiram Page stepped forward, put one hand on Joseph's arm and shook hands vigorously. He turned to the congregation.

"Brothers and sisters, I too support Joseph as the prophet, seer and revelator, and the only mouthpiece for God in the church. If I have caused dissension and confusion, I humbly beg your pardon. Perhaps I have been overly zealous in my desire to serve and to lead out in proclaiming God's word. Satan can pervert even righteous desires, if we are not careful. Joseph, forgive me."

"With my whole heart," said Joseph.

Oliver came forward, also, and embraced his friend and spiritual head. "I, too, need your forgiveness. If anyone knows your calling as a prophet and seer, I do. Obedience is a principle I must work on."

Joseph turned back to his little flock of supporters. They had remained standing, all of them watching with satisfaction the unity of the three men. A spirit of rejoicing came over Joseph, and he looked with pride on his wife who so publicly declared her faith in him.

Oliver asked for the opportunity to speak to the church, and Joseph sat beside Hiram. With more humility than Joseph had ever seen from Oliver, he paid tribute to Joseph's inspiration from God.

"Brothers and sisters, a few days ago in company with others, I witnessed the divine calling of Brother Joseph yet again. The spirit of revelation rested on him, and he spoke to us so many great and marvelous principles that have never before been revealed. Brother Page and I have been misled if we have thought we have half so much to offer you as the pure word of God that comes through Joseph.

"Now, friends, I have come to realize the persuasive power of the devil in tempting us into disobedience. How easy it is to become proud in our abilities and to unwittingly subvert the will of the Lord. Had not Joseph labored with us, reasoning and praying and loving us, we might even now be in danger of spiritual death, having split away from our prophet, seer, and revelator.

"I want to bear witness of the bold doctrines Joseph has revealed from God. Brothers and sisters, we have a prophet indeed, and we will find salvation in following every word he declares from on high."

For the rest of the three-day conference, Joseph spent his time instructing the missionaries called to go to the American Indians and carry *The Book of Mormon*. Oliver, Parley, Ziba Peterson and Peter Whitmer, Jr., were called to the work. He instructed them in doctrine and in political considerations. The Indians were being gathered and marched onto reservations. President Andrew Jackson had signed legislation to move them west of the Mississippi. Even peaceable tribes were rounded up and forced to march hundreds of miles, dying along the way of starvation and disease. The United States government enforced strict regulations on teaching and mingling with the tribes.

While the men were becoming steeped in the message they were to carry to the lost tribes of Israel, the women continued their feverish preparations for the missionaries' needs. The men would be gone for months, during the dead of winter. They needed warm clothing, boots, dried meat and other food, blankets, socks. Emma and Lucy headed up that work. Emma worked with such fervor that it eventually took its toll on her, and she fell ill in mid-October.

She protested Joseph's attentions, saying it was just a feeling of tiredness, but she sank lower and lower until she gave up all pretense and went to bed. No matter how much rest she got, she never seemed to feel better. A few hours of work, just to keep the basic chores done, and she was right down in bed again.

"Bring me some hand stitching," Emma begged Lucy.

"I should say not. If you're down, I know you're sick. Just rest, Emma."

"How can I rest when there is so much to be done? You carry just as heavy a load as I do. Now, I can certainly sew while I lie here. I'm not that sick."

"I've never seen a woman in my life who could endure fatigue and hardship with your courage and zeal, Emma. You are uncommonly patient in the face of trial. Even when you're sick, you don't complain. Sometimes I pray to be like you, but I don't suppose I am. I raise my voice to complain as well as praise, if I feel the need. Now then, how do you feel exactly?" Lucy looked her over from head to foot. "No fever that I can tell. Headache?"

"Yes," Emma replied.

"Stomach ache?"

"Well, a little sickish feeling in the pit."

"Let me look at your eyes. Kind of dull. None of your usual spunk and sparkle. Are you having a touch of the vapors?"

"Why, yes. Quite often, in fact. And nothing tastes good."

"Hmm. Well, you might be sick. On the other hand, you might be expecting."

Emma didn't know whether to be elated or scared. "I was wondering about that."

"Could be." Lucy sat back in the rocker, satisfied with her diagnosis.

Memories came back to Emma that she had buried. The pain, the wrenching pain of childbirth — could she endure that again? Of course she could. It was time to try again. They had lost their first son. Maybe God would send them another.

"How did you do it, Mother Smith? All your children. Eleven is so many. I'm not sure I could endure eleven births."

Lucy laughed. "Well, you don't have to do it all at once. The good Lord usually sends them a few years apart. Besides, the first one is the hardest. Your next one will be easier."

"Do you think so?"

"I do. Your body is more used to it. The baby has easier passage."

"I lost a lot of blood last time. That worries me."

"No two births are the same. What happened last time has no bearing on what will be this time. Just you and Joseph remember that. It takes a lot of suffering to bring children into this world, but it's worth it." Lucy smiled in reflection. "Especially when you get children as good as mine. And you will. I'm sure of it. You will."

Emma stayed in bed another few days and watched what she ate, noting the queasy feeling within. When another two weeks had passed and she had not bled in her monthly cycle, she knew the truth. She *was* expecting. The initial feeling of dread changed to a cautious excitement. Another chance to bear children — it was a blessing from God! At least, she was not infertile as some women she had pitied.

Joseph was even more concerned than she was. His remembrance of that terrible night, a dead baby in his arms and a wife lying nearly lifeless, made it hard to rejoice. Experience was a hard teacher, and the anticipation of youth was replaced with the realization of the dangers. Certainly he wanted children. He hoped for sons, as all men did, but he wasn't anxious to risk his wife. He could only pray for her well-being. And he did just that. For the next eight months, he prayed Emma's life would be spared and the child would live.

In December, Joseph met a man who would change the course of their lives and the course of the church. One cold mid-day while Joseph and Emma were in father Smith's home, Joseph was preaching to an assortment of farmers, wives, departing missionaries, and even a barge captain, when he heard stamping and horses whinnying outside. Joseph stepped over to open the front door. A middle-aged man, rather robust, with a high forehead, deep-set, impressive eyes and a florid face, was knocking snow off his boots and rapping on the door. Behind him, still tying up the horse and securing the carriage, was a smaller man, neat and well-dressed.

"Brother Joseph! Allow me to introduce myself. I am Sidney Rigdon, the newest member of your church, unless someone else is as crazy as I am to break ice off the pond and be baptized. This is Edward Partridge, my friend, and also a new convert. Both of us have fallen victim to the brilliance of *The Book of Mormon*."

Joseph invited the men into the tiny parlor. Emma looked them over. Prosperous, she thought, . . . both of them obviously prosperous, and several years older than my husband. The missionaries have been doing their work. That was true. So far, most of the converts had been farmers around Manchester, Fayette, or Colesville. Sidney, however, had been proselyted by Parley Pratt and Oliver Cowdery in Kirtland, Ohio, while on their way to teach the Indians. He told a vivid story of their work.

"They spoke to my congregation in Ohio. Their testimonies of you and your work were very impressive. But the book was most convincing. I could hardly eat or sleep as I read it. The spirit of the Lord worked on me through that book, until I knew I couldn't deny its holy origins. Then, of course, I had to meet the seer who translated it. You know, Brother Smith, people say the prophets are dead, that there are none today. Yet *you* seem to be alive and kicking." Rigdon's sonorous voice was fascinating, and his bushy eyebrows raised and lowered, regularly punctuating almost every phrase.

Joseph laughed with his guests. "Probably more in need of *being* kicked, if the truth were known." Then he became serious. "Brethren, God is working daily to reveal His eternal truth. Sometimes I feel I can scarcely receive fast enough all that God has in store for us. I'm busy day and night organizing the priesthood offices of the church, studying the scriptures and receiving answers to my questions. It's highly gratifying to find men like yourselves who recognize the value of the book and are anxious to contribute to the Lord's work. You're welcome here, and just in time to join with us in praise and prayer to the Lord."

Edward Partridge spoke up. "Mr. Smith, in all honesty I must tell you, I am a believer in your work, but not yet baptized. I wanted to meet you first. We have been to Manchester and inquired of you around the area. The reports from your neighbors were very favorable for you and your family up until the time you discovered the plates of gold. At that point, I must tell you, your reputation suffered." He looked at Rigdon, then back to Joseph. "We believe, however, it is possible that greed and jealousy influenced their complaints. Brother Sidney, here, has been my religious counselor for some time. He heads a zealous congregation in Kirtland, and there are many of us who consider *him* inspired. However," Edward's sweet tenor voice slowed, and his words became measured, "since reading your book, he defers to you in spiritual things. I could not be sure until I knew the Lord's spirit truly rests with you." He paused, his brown eyes gazing squarely into Joseph's. "Now, I'm ready to be baptized."

Joseph had turned his attention to the gentle, unassuming Edward, and the Spirit revealed the nature of this man to him. He felt the quiet strength of Edward Partridge who recognized the spirit of God working through a young, inexperienced modern day prophet.

"I understand, and, Brother Partridge, God will bless you for seeking that confirmation. I promise you in the name of the Lord that He will fill your whole soul with a witness of the truth, a witness so strong you will never be able to deny this work or the spirit of revelation it rests on. You will yet become a mighty force in the Lord's work, a pattern of piety for all men."

Sidney asked many questions of Joseph pertaining to points of theological doctrine. Joseph continued to address his explanations to all present, until one by one, they began to take their leave. There was dinner and then chores to attend. The two men from Kirtland accompanied Joseph and Emma to their home, which was a convenient walk down the road from the elder Smiths.

Emma listened silently to the men's conversation as she prepared dinner. Rigdon was a very powerful speaker. He used excellent logic, and he knew the scriptures backward and forward. He could be overpowering at times. Emma need not have been protective of her husband. It became apparent as the night wore on that Joseph could hold his own in a theological discussion with the Campbellite minister. Finally, she said goodnight and retired, leaving the three men to talk on into the night.

The next morning, Edward Partridge wanted to be baptized, even if it meant clearing the snow and breaking the ice. Sidney had decided to ask Joseph for the privilege of working with him on his revision of the Old Testament, since Oliver was away on a mission. Joseph inquired of the Lord, and to Sidney's joy, received a revelation for him.

"I have looked upon thee and thy works. I have heard thy prayers, and prepared thee for a greater work. Thou art blessed, for thou shalt do

great things. Behold thou wast sent forth, even as John, to prepare the way before me, . . . And a commandment I give unto thee — that thou shalt write for him; and the scriptures shall be given, even as they are in mine own bosom, to the salvation of mine own elect: . . . " (Excerpt Doctrine and Covenants, Section 35)

Rigdon sat staring at Joseph in amazement when the revelation was finished. Emma had taken it down as her husband spoke the words in measured, even tones. She had seen Joseph under the spirit so often she knew when the revelation was coming on, but it was all quite new to Sidney, and he was astounded. He looked from Joseph to Edward Partidge and over to Emma as if to question, "Did you see what I saw?" Emma was quietly smiling. Edward was in deep contemplation. Sidney felt as if lightning had energized him. He was up. He was down. He paced the floor, large hooded eyes glued to the younger man. He shook his head, trying to understand what he had just seen and felt. For all his self assurance and understanding of the Bible, he had never before experienced the power of God flowing through an individual. To think Joseph could just ask the Lord and receive such revelation for him!

"Brother Joseph, I want you to come with me to Kirtland. I have a great congregation there, already living righteously, waiting and wanting God's word. Your missionaries have preached to them, and many are inclined to believe. When I return and tell them all I saw and experienced here, they will want you to come personally. You have sixty members here. You can more than triple that in one visit to Kirtland. I tell you, they are primed and waiting."

"I'd like to go, but not until spring. My wife is expecting and has been very sick. We lost our first child, and I feel as though I should stay with her." Joseph responded to Sidney's enthusiasm, but watched Emma's face to catch her signals.

"Then bring her! I beg your pardon, Mrs. Smith. I don't mean to be so bold in directing your life. It's just that, if you want the church to grow, here is the perfect opportunity. In one effort, the church will leap forward." He turned back to Joseph. "We have a community of Christians who have covenanted with each other to have all things in common. Just think, the spirit of greed has been banished! Have you ever considered that economic order for the church?"

Joseph was on his feet, like a hound upon the scent. "I have. In fact, I have been waiting for the right time to propose that very thing to the members of the church here in Fayette and Colesville. It's the most Christian way of life there is. What can be more Christ-like than to dedicate your means to the church for the good of all? We spend too much time worrying about getting and spending. God has never meant for one man to live in comfort and riches, while another lives in poverty. Of course, all must work. There will be no free ride for the lazy and the improvident. Consecration of our lives and our means is the most pleasing in the Lord's sight.

"Sidney, I'll go with you to Kirtland. In fact, we'll all move to Kirtland and invite the rest of the church, here and in Colesville, to move there as well."

Emma looked up from carding wool. Her husband was on fire with that familiar glow. She, however, felt a tremendous foreboding. Would the members here want to give up their farms, their homes, their lands? What would they have in Kirtland? They would just be starting all over. Would they agree to share all they had with total strangers? She doubted it. Joseph might have a harder job on his hands than he realized. Religion was one thing; money was another. If he were really serious, this could precipitate an even larger schism than the one he staved off in September.

Joseph called a conference of the church for January 2, 1831 and declared a new revelation, calling for the church to move to Kirtland. He spoke of the richness of the land there, the appointment of men to administer to the poor and needy and govern the affairs of the church. He promised them riches, if they sought for them — the riches of eternity — and advised them to beware of pride and to repent of their sins. Finally, he ended by saying, *"Be ye clean that bear the vessels of the Lord. Even so, Amen."*

As Emma anticipated, the revelation was not enthusiastically received, particularly by the Whitmers. David was quite prosperous and comfortably engaged in the Lord's work. There would be sacrifice ahead. He saw that clearly, though he couldn't get Joseph to accept it. Joseph was completely caught up in his vision of the Kirtland he wanted to establish, and Sidney Rigdon, almost as much a visionary as Joseph himself, had become his closest confidant.

Chapter Twelve

Land of Milk and Honey

lipping, slipping, tipping — then a face full of snow. Snow in her mouth, in her nose, down her collar when the sleigh carrying Joseph and Emma, Sidney and Edward to the promised land — otherwise known as Kirtland, Ohio — skidded off the icy, rutted road and unceremoniously dumped the couple into the field of snow. For a moment Emma was face down in the soft snow with Joseph beside her and their two friends in a tangled heap behind them.

"Emma! Are you hurt? Are you hurt? Have I killed you with this move? We shouldn't have come. I shouldn't have made you move in the dead of winter. You should be at home, safe and sound in front of the fireplace. Emma, please tell me you're not hurt."

"I'm not hurt," she obliged him quietly.

They looked at each other for a moment, he agitated and she composed. They were both covered with snow from stem to stern. She had a large, white, round spot on her cloak where her stomach protruded slightly. She was kneeling, and he was squatting like an Indian, his head totally white, clumps of snow clinging to his eyebrows and nose. Emma burst out laughing.

"You're really all right?"

"Yes," she hiccupped in the middle of a laugh. "I'm simply grateful for the fresh snowfall last night. Otherwise I might have had an icy landing."

Sidney and Edward struggled to stand and ended up sitting on the trunks which had likewise been upended in the snow. Ezra Thayre and Newel Knight had ridden ahead and were well out of sight around the bend when the accident happened. Their horse stood looking back at them and the sleigh which had tipped when it hit converging ruts. Luckily the sleigh was undamaged, though it lay on its side with runners in the air, but all their carefully packed belongings had to be reloaded, redistributed, and retied. Too many heavy items concentrated on the right side had contributed to the accident.

"Well, that was a ride!" Sidney exclaimed.

Edward Partridge was concerned for Emma. "Mrs. Smith, are you sure you or the baby haven't been harmed?"

She looked back at him and Sidney and laughed anew. They were dusted in white and looked like two very cumbersome snowmen. "So far the baby isn't complaining, Mr. Partridge, so neither shall I — at least unless I get really cold. I've lost the hot bricks somewhere in the snow. Maybe we can find them by looking for puddles of water."

Joseph helped her to her feet, turned her round and brushed her off as best he could. Then she did the same for him. Sidney and Edward straightened the sleigh and started carrying parcels to it. But their horse had other ideas. Freed of his burden, he began to amble along the snow-packed road. Sidney called out, "Whoa! Whoa!" in his most commanding voice. Dopper's ears twitched, his tail flicked, but he continued at a comfortable pace. Sidney broke out into a run to catch up the reins, but the horse increased his pace. Soon they were a hundred feet away. Joseph turned from Emma in time to see Sidney chasing the horse and sleigh. Now he laughed. Sidney's exasperated words wafted back to them.

"You rascal! Whoa, whoa I say. I'll sell you for glue, you four-footed jackass. Whoa, I say!"

Joseph whistled one long and one short blast as he had heard Newel do, and old Dopper obediently stopped and dropped his head as if in mortification. Sidney quickly caught up, jerked the reins and brought the horse's head up stiffly. Then he attempted to make the animal back up to the pile of trunks and goods, but Dopper would not budge.

"Sidney, he knows me. I'll do it," Joseph called out. Emma was still trying to contain her laughter. Sidney was stomping through the snow, pounding one fist into his other palm. This was obviously not a humorous matter to Rigdon. Edward Partridge trudged over to her side.

"It's a good thing for old Dopper that you are with us, ma'am. He might have been called worse than a jackass if no lady were present."

Emma feigned surprise. "Surely not, Mr. Partridge. I'm sure a minister's language is beyond reproach."

He shook his head doubtfully. "We all need the gift of forgiveness for some weakness. Dumb animals can certainly be exasperating, and as it appears, not always as dumb as they seem."

She laughed again. She liked this man. He was thoughtful and constant. Now she gratefully accepted his arm to guide her back to the trunks. Once seated atop their linen trunk, she rubbed her stomach with a light caressing motion. The baby had started to move sharply, probably in response to the jolt. Her voluminous cloak hid any personal movements and kept in her body heat, so that even in the February chill she was still warm. While Joseph patiently coaxed the horse back to the accident site, the other men collected the parcels. Soon the sleigh was repacked, and Emma was comfortably seated on the back bench. If only she still had bricks for her feet, she wouldn't be sorry for the little adventure. As it was, all four travelers were ready for the warmth of the hearth at the inn when they stopped for the second night.

The sleigh glided into Kirtland over rolling hills, past snowy fields that yielded abundant supplies of food in the summer and winter. Thick forests told the tale of just how much sweat and muscle it had taken to clear the land for planting. When the early settlers had come to Ohio, the trees were so thick the sky above could hardly be seen. In order for the sunlight to penetrate and nourish crops, the forest had to be beaten back. It was well worth the effort, for just as Rigdon had promised, the soil was so black and loamy that a man had to do little more than stick a twig in the ground and the plant would grow. The beauty of the countryside, farms, rivers, and occasionally deer and darting rabbits occupied Emma's interest as they traveled. Towering trees were encrusted with sparkling snow, and rolling hills alternated with forests and meadows thickly blanketed in white. For all the cold, travel in the winter was smoother and more comfortable than over the rutted roads of summer. With fur blankets and fresh, warm bricks, the travelers in the sleigh were fairly comfortable. Emma, however, suffered with back pains and began to wish for the journey to end, just to get relief from continually sitting on the hard bench.

They stopped first at Mr. Gilbert's place where there might be suitable rooms for Joseph and Emma, but they were at the top of very steep stairs and were constantly filled with smoke from the chimney. One look at his wife told Joseph she was at the end of her considerable endurance. They went on to Newel K. Whitney's mercantile store, just down the hill toward the Morley settlement.

The Whitney-Gilbert store was the center of social life in Kirtland. It was chock-full of all the goods that came by barge down the canal and the lake. There a man could buy a new stock for his rifle, gunpowder, scythe, knife, flax, wool, sugar, flour, horehound candy, molasses, and cloves for a toothache. If he wanted to please his lady, he could purchase gingham, lavender oil, vanilla, and even ready-made bonnets from New York. Best of all, he could stand in front of the oversized potbellied stove, warm his hands, warm his backside and swap news with a half dozen travelers from Missouri to Vermont.

Whitney had a good supply of tobacco and plenty of coal. Winter was the time for socializing. Crops were in, and snow made laggards of them all. This day there were only a few customers, with chairs pulled up to the stove, trading stories and puffing on pipes.

Joseph handed Emma down from the sleigh. Sidney and Edward had gone on ahead to open the door for the prophet and his lady. Newel K. Whitney saw them at the doorway and came out from behind the counter. Just as he reached the door, Joseph strode up on the small porch, stretched out his hand, and greeted a man he had never before met.

"Newel K. Whitney, thou art the man. I'm Joseph Smith, the Mormon prophet. You prayed me here, and we've come all the way from Fayette, New York. I am pleased to meet you."

Whitney's round, pleasant face lighted up. His naturally high voice soared with enthusiasm. "The Mormon prophet! I'm pleased to meet you, sir. Mr. Rigdon and Mr. Partridge told me they were going to discover for themselves if a New York farmer really had translated golden plates in order to write *The Book of Mormon*. And you're the one, eh? Well, I'm delighted, simply delighted. Sidney, what's your conclusion then?"

Rigdon looked on Joseph with the pride of a parent. "Isn't it obvious?"

Whitney slapped him on the shoulder in congratulations. "So, you pulled off quite a feat. Not only met the prophet, but brought him back to the rest of us. If anyone could do it, you could. Oops, I beg your pardon, ma'am. I almost missed this lovely lady in all the hurrah of the moment. This would be Mrs. Smith, I'll venture."

"Yes, Mr. Whitney, my wife, Emma Hale Smith, from Harmony, Pennsylvania."

Emma accepted a more decorous handshake. Newel turned aside, reached inside the partially open door and drew out beside him a slight woman with light brown hair. "And this is my wife, Elizabeth Ann Whitney. She really runs the store. I just sit around and jaw with

315

the men. She buys the goods. She keeps the books. And she keeps me on the straight and narrow path."

Joseph reached out for Elizabeth's hand, taking it warmly between both of his. A blush of modest pink lit her cheeks, and she stuttered a reply. Emma had seen just such a response from many women to her husband's personal way of greeting them. Poor Elizabeth Ann was so genuinely unnerved at meeting the young prophet that Emma could hold nothing against her. She too reached out and took Mrs. Whitney's hand.

"Elizabeth? It's so very nice to make your acquaintance. What an accomplished woman you must be. Your husband speaks so highly of you," Emma complimented her.

Mrs. Whitney concentrated her attention on the dark, gracious woman before her. It was safer than looking directly at the handsome young man at her side.

"Won't you come in? I can make you quite comfortable inside. I have a small parlor away from the men and their pipes."

"Yes," Newel remembered his manners. "Come in, come in! We're all standing out here in the cold. Mrs. Whitney, is there some tea for our guests? Chase away some of the chill of the sleigh ride. Isaac Morley, meet Joseph Smith, the Mormon prophet!" He turned to Joseph and Emma. "They'll be my guests for a few days — won't you?"

Pleasure lit Joseph's face. "Happily. I think my wife will agree to that. We've been traveling for three days, been dumped out of the sleigh once, and slept in smelly taverns two nights."

Elizabeth clucked her sympathy. She took Emma by the arm and guided her to a door at the far end of the room. Emma left Joseph greeting the circle of men that surrounded the stove, already engrossed in his story of his new church. Elizabeth took her to a small, but comfortable little room equipped with rocking chair and padded seat, a foot stool, a basin for washing after the long trip, a beautiful lamp, fragrant candles burning, and a small sideboard which held apples, fresh bread, cheese, and a flagon of water. Her hostess took her cloak and laid it aside.

"Oh, my dear Mrs. Smith, have you made this journey and you in a delicate condition? My gracious! Sit here, do. Let me serve you a bite to eat."

When Emma started to protest, Elizabeth would have none of it. "But you must! At least a bite of apple and cheese. It has been such a cold winter. I can't imagine that you're not frozen after that long journey. Was it terrible?"

Emma could not resist her friendship. "Not really. I have to admit the bench got hard. My baby protested more than I did, though. The worst part was having to listen to the men's talk for three days running. I'll admit I've been dying for some quiet time by the fireplace with a little needlework in my hands."

Elizabeth served her guest and pulled over another chair to sit beside her. "It must be such an honor to be married to a prophet."

Emma sipped her cup of warm chamomile tea and chuckled. Elizabeth's bright eyes reflected her naivete. "Yes, sometimes."

"Sometimes?"

"Um hmm. And sometimes it is pure terror."

Elizabeth's eyebrows shot up. "Terror?"

"Well, when God tries to do a little good, Satan goes on the warpath. We've been through persecutions enough over *The Book of Mormon* and the starting of the church. Joseph is hoping that here in Kirtland the people will be more accepting of new ideas. Mr. Rigdon says there are already over a hundred converts to the church here. I can hardly imagine living without the daily fear of Joseph being bullied, chased, imprisoned, prosecuted, and threatened with murder. I'm looking forward to settling here in Kirtland."

Elizabeth impulsively took her hand. "And we're so glad you're here! I hope you'll be happy as we have been. I'm sure you'll be honored as royalty. Why, you almost *look* like royalty. Mr. Smith is so tall and . . . well. . . handsome, and you — well, you're simply the most beautiful woman . . . ." She had blurted out her true feelings and halted abruptly, embarrassed by her own impetuousness.

Emma smiled with good humor and gratitude. "Elizabeth Ann Whitney, you are a welcome friend for a woman who has been friendless too long. I feel right at home here already. I left my mother and father. We left Joseph's family. I should be feeling cut off from everything and everyone, but it must have been the right time. For instead of trepidation, I feel free for the first time in a very long time."

"And I feel free, for you and your husband are surely the answer to our prayer. Not long ago, Newel and I were praying to be shown the way to the Lord's true church. We wanted so much to have His Holy Spirit and knew that none of the churches we had been attending offered that to us. One night, it seemed that an actual cloud enveloped our house and our minds. Not a dark cloud, you understand. More perhaps, like the cloud that led the children of Israel by day. There was no doubt it was a spiritual manifestation, for both of us heard an audible voice in the cloud tell us to prepare to receive the word of the Lord, for it was coming. That Mr. Smith should know Newel on sight is just added witness that he is the prophet Mr. Rigdon says he is."

Emma listened to yet another testimonial of her husband's power. It only served to reinforce the many others. She knew how Joseph had known Newel. Of course, both Sidney and Edward had told them about many members of the small town of Kirtland, but Joseph had actually seen Newel Whitney in vision while they were yet hundreds of miles away. He had seen him kneeling in prayer, just as Elizabeth Ann described. It was one thing that contributed to his decision to move to Kirtland.

The two new friends sat rocking and talking until Elizabeth suddenly realized Emma was drooping and insisted that she lie down and rest. Emma didn't protest at all. The baby had been cramped as she sat for three days, holding onto Joseph to keep her balance in the unsteady sleigh. It would feel good to lie on her side and let the bed support the baby. She lay down to rest, quickly falling into a deep, welcome sleep with the sweet scent of candles burning.

Joseph and his lady stayed with the Whitneys two weeks. While Isaac Morley prepared a home for them on his own property, Emma rested and regained her strength. Joseph spent his time talking about the new economic order of all things in common.

"Believe me, Newel, I have just as much appreciation for comfort and worldly goods as any other man. I like a fine horse and carriage. I admire your wife's beautiful dinnerware. Isaac Morley's farm is grand. Do I wish to possess such things? Yes, of course I do. But at the same time, can I see my brother barely scratching out a living while his children go hungry? No. I'm afraid my enjoyment of those worldly goods would go sour if I were blessed while my friends and brothers were in want. I'm convinced the Lord has given us this earth to divide equally, not to grasp and hoard its riches for ourselves. Let us all grow rich together. With the right system and the Lord's help, I'm sure it will be possible."

Newel shook his head. "I don't know, Joseph. Isaac Morley is truly a saint. He has built a hundred homes on land that he simply donates. But how long can that go on? After all, he has to keep enough land to farm. You can't give away everything you have."

"That's exactly what Christ asked of the rich young man. Will you do as he did and turn away sorrowing?"

Whitney heaved a sigh. "I don't know. The folks on Morley's settlement have been trying communal living for over a year, and it isn't working so well. There's bickering and quarreling over the most trivial things. I'm not sure I want to get involved with it. I have a partner, too. He'll have his say in it. How can you carry on business in that kind of society?"

"You simply make your excess available to the church for equal distribution."

"Well, I confess, I don't understand it yet, nor who might keep the order running smoothly. There are bound to be slackers as well as workers. How are you gonna withhold flour and sugar from a family because the father has been fishing instead of working the fields? It could be sticky."

"Yes, it could be. It will take a saint to manage it all."

"You're the only one people will submit to. You'll have to be the head."

Joseph shook his head. "No. I have other things to do. The Lord isn't finished with me yet. He will call someone when it is time."

The next week, in a gathering with twelve of his closest followers, Joseph received a revelation outlining a complete pattern of the United Order. For many, it was their first time to see him under the influence of the Spirit. Sidney acted as scribe. The others sat in a circle, and Joseph stood in the middle. He had been presenting his views on the pros and cons of communal living. There had been discussion and some dissention. Then he called on Sidney to pray for more light. Sidney had no sooner finished praying than a light seemed to fall upon Joseph. His face brightened, even his hair seemed illuminated, and he began speaking again, this time not with the urging and reasoning he had previously used. This time he raised his arm to heaven, and just as though he were a lightning rod, words of power fell in measured precision from his lips.

"And behold, thou wilt remember the poor, and consecrate of thy properties for their support that which thou hast to impart unto them, with a covenant and a deed which cannot be broken. And inasmuch as ye impart of your substance unto the poor, ye will do it unto me; and they shall be laid before the bishop of my church and his counselors . . . every man shall be made accountable unto me, a steward over his own property, or that which he has received by consecration, as much as is sufficient for himself and family.

"Thou shalt not be idle; for he that is idle shall not eat the bread nor wear the garments of the laborer." (Excerpt Doctrine and Covenants, Section 42)

Joseph went on, well beyond the consecration of all things. He laid out the procedure for the church to judge transgressions. It was to be done by the elders of the church, with at least two witnesses called. Personal offenses were to be settled between the two individuals, quietly and privately if at all possible.

The revelation pertained mostly to the organization of the church. It was concise, clear and extremely fair. The men who sat in that meeting left the Whitney store convinced that they had seen a miracle — a man through whom God spoke. It was that, and that alone, which convinced those men to put aside their natural pride of ownership and consecrate their homes, farms, and money to the Church of Christ, as the church was called in 1831.

Edward Partridge was called as bishop to oversee the consecration of all property and the deeds of stewardship to every man. Women were called in along with their husbands and asked for their pledges to uphold the new order. It was made clear that this was not a whim. This was a covenant with God, which covenant would bring them blessings in heaven and on earth. All excess that was earned, farmed or traded would be turned over to Partridge to be equally divided according to the needs of the members. It turned out to be the only way the members of the church could assimilate the numbers of converts that flooded the Kirtland area, for they came by the hundreds in the next few years. Many of them came with nothing more than faith in the young Mormon prophet and their own hardworking two hands. Whitney's and Gilbert's mercantile store became the clearing place for traded services and goods.

This was an honor to which Edward did not aspire. He often felt as though he bore the weight of the world on his shoulders, but the confidence Joseph had in him was almost reward enough. Little had he suspected when he was baptized on that cold winter's day that he was getting into very deep water indeed.

The little log house which had been hastily erected for Joseph and Emma on the Morley farm was drafty and damp. The fireplace did not draw well, and smoke frequently filled the small parlor. Emma was constantly wiping the smoky dust from her dry sink, the dishes, the chairs, the door. At first, she thought she and Joseph might have privacy again, but that was a beggar's dream. If she thought he had been busy in Fayette and Harmony, it was a vacation compared to their life in Kirtland. Her little parlor was constantly packed with elders asking for clarification on doctrine, and Joseph firmly outlined the Lord's word. He placed greatest emphasis on his revision of the Bible. He made no pretension of translation from Greek or Hebrew. He went through the Holy Scriptures asking for clarification and inspiration. Sidney usually acted as his scribe, and as long as the work went on, Emma carried on the work of the house and the farm with her customary patience and grace. There were usually more mouths to feed than she had supplies. Emma's considerable skill as a cook was tested. She found herself applying to Bishop Partridge's storehouse as often as any of the new converts flooding in. Edward set up a daily draw with the Whitneys, given the continual drain on Joseph and Emma's finances. To complicate matters even more, Joseph had an open-door heart and an open-door home. Anyone who lacked a place to stay had only to mention it to the Smiths, and they were invited to stay with them. Their own bed was often given to strangers, while Joseph rolled up in a blanket and slept on the floor, and Emma tried to sleep in her rocking chair by the fire.

In March, Lucy Mack Smith and many of her family arrived from Fayette along with other Colesville saints. It was a joyous reunion, with Lucy in her glory reciting all the adventures they had had along the way. Her husband had traveled to Kirtland six months earlier to prepare a place for her. Her bright eyes sparkled as she rehearsed the journey by barge, the follies of some of the travelers, the flirtatious younger women, the mothers who appealed to her for help in controlling their children, and the breaking up of the ice so their boat could navigate the canal. She was not hesitant to declare herself the unabashed leader of the little group. She had organized morning and evening prayer, the singing of hymns and lodging for the women and children when the boat was stopped by the ice floes. How grateful she was at arriving on the shores of Fairport to find Samuel and Joseph there to meet her with a carriage to take her to her husband, Joseph. She found occasion for a good six months to tell the story and remind the Colesville saints — who eventually all made their way to Kirtland — of the foibles of that trip.

Early crocuses had just begun to poke yellow heads from the soil in April. After a day of light rain, Emma was out of the house early the next morning to plant her garden. All sign of frost was over. Even the nights were milder now, though the house stayed damp and chill. She scuffed her shoe in the black earth, outlining the rows of beans, cabbage, turnips, corn, peas, and tomatoes. She had to get them in before the baby came — or the "babies," as Lucy had predicted. Emma unconsciously rubbed her back. She *was* carrying this pregnancy low and seemed much larger than she had been with their first child. Could she really be expecting twins? Lucy seemed dead set on it. Well, twins might make up for the son they had left behind in Harmony. She shielded her eyes against the bright morning sun as she looked off in the direction where she imagined Pennsylvania to be. Would her mother visit the grave sometimes? She had a sudden vision of the little grave on the rise above the river, the yellow wildflowers sprouting in the springtime warmth. A sharp pain seemed to strike at her heart when she remembered the joy with which she and Joseph had anticipated that child, and then the terrible days and nights of illness and despair. Her memories were dim recollections of fading in and out of consciousness and seeing Joseph sitting beside her bed, his face haggard and his eyes hollow.

Emma impatiently waved her hand as if to wipe away the disturbing memories. She had no time nor inclination to dwell on that painful time. She was a pragmatist. As painful as it had been, it was over. This was a better time, a better place. Here Joseph was revered instead of hunted, and she was respected as his companion. Soon there would be another baby, perhaps even a son. They both liked the Biblical name, Thadius. If it were a girl, she favored Louisa. It had such a modern sound. Yet it was soft, rolling sweetly off the tongue. Louisa, a baby girl. She gave in to dreams of a bright little thing with blue eyes and fair hair like her father. Then, with determination, Emma pulled herself back to the moment, looked critically at the garden space, and estimated how many rows she would need and how likely it was that she could plant them all today.

Already her back was hurting, and every so often, she felt a cramping low in her belly. So, she grasped her hoe, pulled it easily across the damp earth, and in no time had a dozen rows neatly laid out. Then she went back and began sprinkling the precious seeds and covering them lightly with the dirt. After a few rows, her husband strode out to her little plot of land, reached around his very pregnant wife and commandeered the hoe.

"I told you I would do this," he chided gently.

She responded with a short laugh. "Hah! And just when exactly did you think you would have time, between your work on the revision and meeting with Edward on division of lots, and preaching to the boatload of saints that just came in from Buffalo? You haven't time to get this planted."

"Yes, I do. I'll make time. I'll plant it at midnight, if necessary."

She wrested the hoe away from him and poked him with it. "Go on with you," she chided her husband. "You'll soon have a crowd tromping through my garden, ruining my rows and tromping on my seeds."

"Emma, you are near term. You should be resting."

"Phooey. I've been resting. It's harder than working. The baby will come when it's good and ready, and a little hoeing isn't going to bring it faster. If I thought it would, I'd have been out here weeks ago."

Joseph followed her down the row, kissed the back of her neck and wrapped his arms around her. He rubbed her belly, and she glanced quickly around.

"Joseph! You know we can be seen from Sister Murphy's house!"

"Um hm. And won't she be jealous, seeing how much your husband loves you?"

"Yes, and won't she be surprised at seeing her prophet so uncouth in public?"

"Come on inside, my Emma-rose, and let your husband do that later," he murmured in her ear.

Joseph hadn't called her that in a long time. It brought a twinge of longing for the first, magical days of their love. His tenderness had left her breathless. Lately he had been so preoccupied with the continuing need for organization and missionaries that the little private time they had was unfulfilling. She loved to see him finally taking his rightful place at the head of a church based on his work of translation and his calling as a seer and revelator. He was a natural leader. His love of the people was so obvious that they flocked to him. He seemed to thrive on the challenges that the growing church brought. Every convert who wanted to meet the prophet was welcome in his home. That she was married to a unique man was obvious to Emma. That he loved her was her delight.

She reached up and patted his cheek. At that moment, she felt a gush of fluid down her thigh. Her eyebrows went up and a startled cry escaped her.

"What is it?" Joseph pulled back.

"I think the baby must be coming. There's . . . there's . . . uh, fluid," she finished delicately.

He threw down the hoe. Drawing her under his left arm, he started purposefully toward the house.

"Now, don't leave that hoe there overnight, Joseph. It'll rust in the dirt and dew. And get those last few rows covered over with dirt, or the birds will get my seeds."

"Yes, ma'am."

"And if you have time, we really should get the last few rows planted today as well. If you can do that, we'll have peas and beans by July."

"Yes, ma'am."

"In this pocket of my apron there are some flower seeds. I wanted to plant some marigolds and hollyhocks by the front door. They can wait another day or two, but not much longer."

"Yes, ma'am."

"Oh, stop that. You're trying to be funny, and I don't feel so funny right now."

He looked sharply at her pinched face. Emma wasn't looking her best lately. Back in February and March she had had good color in her face. Her cheeks were pink and her eyes bright. She had, in fact, looked wonderful, as though she were blossoming. No one would accuse her of that now. The last few weeks had taken their toll. She had not slept well. Her appetite had fallen off, and she had begun losing her breakfast again. Guilt swept over him. He had been too busy to be concerned about her. He had simply gotten used to Emma handling every problem of the household. She was so competent, too competent, probably. Now the old fear came galloping back. She had almost died with the first baby. Was she frightened? He hadn't even asked her. Was she haunted by the dark memories of the first experience as he was?

"Emma, dearest, I have a very good feeling about this birth. Last time you suffered a great deal, but that is behind you. This will be much less painful. You won't get sick again. Elizabeth Morley, Jerusha and Mother are all just waiting for the word. I'll go get Elizabeth as soon as I get you settled."

She knew he was trying to comfort her. She appreciated it, but when the cramping, searing pain hit her, she forgot everything except the babe inside. With Joseph's help, she struggled up the steep steps. Next to their bedroom was a little nook where she often bedded

326

guests. Thankfully, the last couple had moved in with other friends just two days ago. She had fixed up the bed for birthing, knowing it would be soon. Now she eased onto the straw mattress. She shivered in the chill of the morning. Joseph saw it and tucked a blanket over her.

"Will you be all right until Elizabeth can get over here?"

"Of course."

"I'll go right now. It'll be just a few minutes."

He knelt beside the bed. A deep line furrowed his brow. He brushed back her dark hair and kissed her forehead. Her eyes had a glazed look. He could see she was trying to smile to reassure him, but it was no good. Quickly he jumped up and started down the stairs.

"Hurry," she urged him as he went.

Elizabeth Morley grabbed her bag of medicinal herbs and bandages. She was the oldest of Isaac's daughters, large, rawboned, with a face too much like her father's to appeal to any man. But she was a wizard with herbs. She attended every birth, and consequently considered herself the auntie of almost every child born in Kirtland. She was in Joseph's carriage within minutes after he came hurrying into her kitchen. He didn't have to tell her the news. One look at his face and she knew Emma was in labor. They drove quickly to Joseph's home on the edge of the settlement. He handed her out of the carriage and jumped back in, turned the horse, and headed toward the small house up on the new section where his family had built homes.

Emma felt as though she were on fast rapids headed for a waterfall. She wished at the height of her pains that she could stop this pell-mell rush, go back a few days, and start this all over, slowly with more control. But every wrenching cramp pushed her closer and closer to the climax when she would go with the flood over the rocky falls, for good or for ill. She tried to push away the foreboding feeling of impending disaster. It was just the bad memories of the last birth. Still, she felt a struggling within that was unfamiliar and unsettling.

When Lucy came bustling up the stairs, followed by her sister-in-law, Jerusha, who was also expecting, Emma felt for the first time that she could let go and trust someone else to manage everything for her. Lucy would see that all was prepared. It was a relief to turn all the preparations and concern over to her.

"Mother Smith, I think you were right. I think there may be twins coming," Emma forced out between clenched teeth.

"Elizabeth, Jerusha, get two sets of gowns and blankets ready!" Lucy grasped the reins immediately. "Is the water warm?"

Elizabeth was reluctant to turn over the birthing to Sister Smith. To preside at the birthing of the prophet's children was a feather in her cap. Still, Lucy firmly took charge. So Elizabeth took up her vigil at Emma's side, rubbing her back and the contracting muscles of her abdomen. Jerusha quietly went about laying out the sheets and baby things they would soon need. After two hours of increasing pain, Emma began to moan. She was perspiring now, and Elizabeth wiped her brow every few minutes. All at once, Elizabeth gave a cry, and Lucy came rushing to the foot of the bed. Emma had grasped Elizabeth's hand, gave a hard jerk when the pain had hit her, and brought Elizabeth right into bed with her. Elizabeth was stretched out alongside Emma, and one prolonged moaning cry brought a tiny head pushing its way into life.

"Quick!" Lucy cried. "Get me my twine and snipper. This one will be here in a wink! He's not waiting any longer!"

Jerusha thrust the medicine bag toward her mother-in-law and put a flannel blanket in Lucy's lap just in time to catch the tiny infant that slipped from his mother's womb with the next push. Yes, it was a boy! Emma could hear Lucy's triumphant affirmation. But Emma knew she wasn't done. Just as she had suspected, there was still a very full feeling, and another small head was moving toward birth.

"Hold back," Lucy all but shouted at her.

"I can't," she gasped.

"You'd better. I've got to get this one breathing."

Lucy was working on the little babe in her lap. He hadn't cried as yet, and she was cleaning his mouth and nose with warm water.

Then she spatted his bottom, and he let out a sharp little cry. She quickly tied off his umbilical cord and handed him to Jerusha. Emma was shaking from the effort of holding back. She had been breathing so hard and fast that she felt lightheaded, and Lucy had to yell to make Emma hear her.

"All right. You can push. Go ahead."

Emma was bearing down, but the baby proved stubborn. Every pain that washed over her seemed as though it would bring the child, but each time it receded and the baby retracted. After another half hour, she was worn out with the torment. She was too tired to work through the pain. Then, as suddenly as the first child, the second baby slipped out of the womb, and with a shudder and a cry, Emma pushed it into the experienced hands of its grandmother.

"Ah," Lucy let out a long sigh of relief. "A girl! Emma, you've got a little girl and a little boy. It's a blessing from God."

Emma had fallen back onto the pillow, nearly collapsed. "I want my little boy," she croaked weakly. Jerusha had wrapped him in a soft blanket and now laid him in the crook of Emma's arm. Emma ducked her head and kissed the soft, pink skin of her son's head. Elizabeth pushed on her stomach, kneading it. Jerusha sponged off the baby girl, while Lucy cleaned up the exhausted mother.

Spent as she was, Emma would not close her eyes. As soon as she saw Jerusha had the little girl cleaned and wrapped, she held up her hand and pleaded, "Let me hold her, too."

Thus Joseph found them, when his mother called him up the stairs. Emma lay in pleased exhaustion with a baby in the crook of each arm. She had made it past the falls. Now she could rest. He found her smiling.

"We have a son and a daughter," she looked into his eyes for the approval she knew would be there.

Approval, almost adoration, had brought quick tears to her husband's eyes. Children at last! It had not been the ordeal the last birth was. Emma was awake and smiling. Joseph's heart expanded until he thought it would burst with happiness.

"Let me hold my son."

Gingerly he cradled the tiny infant in his big hands. Yes, the child was tiny, smaller than baby Alvin had been. This babe could almost fit in his hand, fingertip to wrist. Joseph carefully unwrapped the little bundle. All the fingers and toes were there. The limbs were all formed perfectly. The only thing that caused concern was the large, spreading, deep blue bruise on the top of the baby's head. Joseph wrapped him back up and held his son against his cheek. He listened to the shallow breathing. He put his finger next to the baby's hand, but the little boy didn't grasp it like a healthy strong child would. He just lay weakly in his father's palm. Joseph whispered to him and stroked his cheek. The tiny eyes opened, rolled around and closed again.

Joseph's stomach turned over. His heart sank. He tried to keep his face from showing his alarm. He walked over to Lucy who was washing up in the other, larger bedroom.

"Mother, the boy seems awfully weak."

"Course he's weak. He's just been born. He's tired. It's a lot of work, for the baby and the mother."

"No, Mother, I mean, weaker than he should. Look."

Lucy turned and saw Joseph trying to rouse the child. The baby hardly opened his eyes. He was mostly unresponsive. His pink color had turned to a mottled blue and purple. The bruise on his skull was growing larger and darker.

Lucy turned stricken eyes up to her son. "Joseph, take him back to Emma. Maybe being next to his mother will give him strength to live."

"Then, I'm right?"

"Yes, you're right. This baby is too weak. He may have bleeding on the brain."

Joseph turned back to the small bedroom, where Emma lay with the other twin. She lay with the baby's cheek resting lightly against her lips. That way she could breathe in the scent of her little daughter. She could feel the softness of the baby's skin against her lips. She was perfectly blissful.

"Emma, darling, put this baby on your chest, next to your heart."

"All right. Just lay him there. He's warm. It's so much better to have them here in my arms than inside. Just think, Joseph, we have a real family now, a boy and a girl. Do you like Louisa? I mean the name, Louisa?"

"Yes, darling. I like the name. What do you like for a boy's name?"

Joseph's face betrayed his concern. The joy had gone out of his eyes, the excitement was replaced with sadness. Why? What was wrong?

"Joseph? What is it?"

"Nothing. Nothing, I hope. He's just a little small — a little weak. He needs to be here next to you."

Emma looked at her tiny son. Yes, he was small, and listless. He wasn't crying like a healthy child would be. A cry of terror escaped her. She struggled to sit up in bed. She gave the little girl to Joseph and hugged the boy child to her breast. A long sob rose in her throat. She rocked the baby and kissed him. She put his little nose and mouth next to her cheek, so she could feel him breathe. Only a faint wisp of breath fanned her cheek.

She whispered to him, "Live, son, little Thadius. Live for me, your mother. Cry, little boy, fight for life. I'll help you; just try! Please try. Try for me."

The three women who had been with her through the ordeal stood in the doorway watching the scene with somberness. Jerusha's hand was resting on her own blossoming abdomen. Lucy was twisting her apron slowly, and Elizabeth Morley had buried her face in her hands.

"Joseph," Emma appealed to her husband, "is he going to die?" Joseph didn't answer. Her voice came fiercely. "Don't *let* him! Joseph, don't *let* him! Ask God for his life! We've already lost one son. Isn't that enough. Why should God want both our sons?"

Her voice rose with anger. "*Joseph! Do* something! Bless him. Bless our son! I want this baby to live. Take him right now, while he is still breathing, and ask God for his life! God will answer *your* prayer. Here, take him! Hurry, hurry."

Emma had turned frantic with worry. She grabbed the little girl from her husband's arms and thrust the boy toward him. Joseph's heart had sunk to his toes. Carefully he took his son in his hands. Every nerve in his body cried out as though warped with pain. He wanted to bless the boy! He wanted a son! What was this desolate feeling that no blessing would save his short life? Joseph's empty eyes wandered around the room. The late afternoon sun was slanting shadows across Emma as she clutched the other twin to her breast. The place smelled of warm, sudsy water and pungent candles. He tried to begin. He opened his mouth, but no words would come. Emma called out to him again, and he knew he had to say something. Teardrops spilled onto the soft baby blanket. He lifted the little eyelid and saw the infant's eyes rolled back in his head.

"Oh God, help us, we pray thee! Help us. Help us!" His voice was a sob.

"Plead with God, Joseph! Hurry! Bless him to live!"

"I can't," he said, brokenly. "It doesn't seem to be God's will. I can only bless him to die in peace."

Emma cried. Joseph came and sat on the floor beside her, the little son in the crook of his arm, while she held the little girl in hers. They held each other, crying. After a time, Emma looked down at her little daughter, and her weakening sobs turned to a sharp cry of terror.

"Oh no! Joseph, *no!* Our little girl isn't breathing either. I haven't even been watching her. I was so worried about the boy! Mother Smith! The baby isn't breathing! Hurry, hurry!"

Lucy and Elizabeth rushed to the bedside. Lucy took the infant, turned her upside down and smacked the bare bottom. She waited in vain for the cry of outrage from the child. She put her mouth over the tiny nose and mouth of the baby girl, and she blew shallow breaths in and out, in and out, hoping the child would respond and begin the rhythm on her own. But there was no response. The little heart was still beating, although irregularly, but the baby didn't take a breath. Lucy checked the eyes. They were rolled back in the head. She pressed on the tiny chest, but nothing worked.

Emma had her little boy clutched against her cheek, whispering over and over, "No, no, no!"

Joseph stood helplessly beside his mother and daughter. The little girl was going fast. Her skin was a pasty, whitish-blue, and her little hands jerked occasionally. Elizabeth plunged her into the bucket of warm water, but even that did not rouse her. Elizabeth looked up at Lucy and shook her head. Lucy held her granddaughter while the baby drew one last, deep shuddering breath and died.

Elizabeth went to Emma to comfort her, while Joseph and Lucy stood together weeping over the tiny body. Jerusha couldn't bear the scene any longer. She made her way carefully down the steep stairs and let herself out the front door. She simply had to get away from the terrible scene. Both hands now were pressed against her rounding belly and tears streamed unheeded down her face. A carriage was starting down the hill toward the Smith home. Friends of Joseph's were coming to celebrate. They had heard Emma was giving birth and wanted to congratulate Joseph. When they reached Jerusha, she turned them back. No celebration here. Death can strike even God's chosen.

Emma would not speak to Joseph. He thought she was angry with him, and she was. She was angry — angry at him for not crying to God and demanding that they live. He was God's chosen prophet.

She had seen him bless other people, and they got better. Why not her babies? She was angry at herself for not having healthy, happy babies like other women did. How could Joseph love a useless woman who couldn't successfully give him children. The way he loved children, he would surely come to disdain her. Furthermore, she was angry at God for teasing her this way with three babies, born alive, just long enough to give them hope for a future, then snatching them away. How could He be so cruel? Were they not worthy to be parents? How many more times could she go through this only to see her children die in her arms? It would turn her into a bitter, sour old woman. Already she felt an icy finger of resentment that seemed to stifle all the words of protest and grief that wanted to burst from her. A prophet's wife could not curse God, even when He took the fruit of her womb. She was expected to meekly bow her head and say, "Thy will be done." Those words strangled within her. So she said nothing. She simply sat in bed, staring out the window, waiting for the hurt to subside.

Four days later, Joseph came upstairs and asked her to get dressed. He had a man he wanted her to meet. She turned blank eyes toward him.

"Brother Murdock is here to meet you, Emma. He has a special request. Here is your dress. Put it on and come downstairs."

She shook her head and turned back to the wall.

"Yes, Emma. If you won't do it yourself, I'll help you."

He pulled a loose dress over her head and fastened the hooks in the back. He brushed her hair, tied it back with a ribbon, and helped her out of bed. With his arm around her, he started for the stairs.

"Take a deep breath. When we get to the bottom of the stairs, I want you to smile and shake the man's hand. He has something to propose to us."

She didn't answer, just looked at him vacantly, but she obediently made her way down the stairs. Brother John Murdock stood by the hearth, turning his hat over repeatedly in his hands. He looked hollow-eyed as though he hadn't slept in days. His beard was scruffy and his nose was red. He looked almost as miserable as she felt. Emma stood a little straighter, smoothed her hair, and held out her hand. Her own voice sounded scratchy to her when she greeted him.

"Brother Murdock. I'm pleased to meet you. My husband says you have a request of me."

"Yes, ma'am," he began. "I'll come right to the point. You see, I have lost my wife. She . . . she . . . died . . . in childbirth. I have three little children already to care for, and now I have twin babies — a little boy and a girl — to care for. She . . . well . . . the labor was too long. She just wasn't strong enough. She'd been feeling poorly before the babies came, and she just sort of faded away there at the last. She was the best thing that ever happened to me, now she's gone."

John Murdock broke down. He couldn't speak for several minutes for wiping his eyes and blowing his nose. "Anyway, I don't quite know what to do with these little ones. I've been trying to care for them, but I'm no good at that. Then, the other young 'uns, they take a lot of my time, too. They're only two, three and five themselves. Up at Whitney's store, I heard you and Brother Joseph have lost twins, like mine. Well, anyway, Joseph and I got to talking. He said you might be willing to help. . . I know it's a lot to ask, but I need help, and maybe it would help you, too. I know it's hard to lose children. Well, it's also hard to lose a wife."

Emma stood stock still, staring at the grieving man before her. His words sounded like gibberish to her. Her twin babies were gone, and he wanted her to play mother to his babies. That was too cruel. How could he ask such a thing? Did he think she could just pick up any baby and care for it, then hand it back to him as though it was a thing, a doll, for playing with? A spot of pink appeared in her cheeks. It was hot anger. And to think her husband had actually thought she could stand such an arrangement! Her voice was icy when she answered.

"Brother Murdock, while I appreciate your position, I hardly think I could bring myself to care for your children and then hand them back to you one day, as though I had no womanly feelings for them."

Murdock sat down on a chair and bowed his head over his hands. Finally he asked, "Sister Emma, I'm asking if you would please adopt them."

Emma swayed. Joseph steadied her and led her to a chair. "Adopt?" she whispered. "Would you give your children up for adoption?"

"Certainly not happily. But the babies badly need a mother. Mrs. Smith, I have prayed about this these last few days, and I feel in my heart that God has sent me here. He knows you need children, and my babies need a mother. Couldn't be no better parents than you and Brother Joseph."

Emma felt as though she could hardly breathe. For days she had had one prayer in her heart, that God would give her back her babies. Of course, she knew it was crazy. Her children were dead — all dead. Was she an unfit mother? By revelation, He had called her an "elect lady." Well, how could she be elect and still unworthy of motherhood? Would she ever have children that lived? How could she give Joseph posterity, children to gladden his heart and to carry on his name, when they were all so sickly they died? All those questions raced around in her brain, but over-riding all was the constant plea, "O God, give me back my babies." Now, he was doing just that. Hope dawned at last.

"Brother Murdock," she began gently. "If you give your children to us to adopt, it would be best they never know. It could cause problems. It would be an honor to be a mother to your babies, but no one must ever know."

"I know that, ma'am. I've thought about it a lot. I loved my wife . . . still do. And I've got three other children to raise. I can't handle any more. . . I ask you, please, adopt my little twins, and take them to your heart, just as though they were your own. Just pretend, if you can, that God gave your babies back to you."

With that phrase, Emma broke down. Her natural reserve and poise disintegrated, and she put her face in her hands and sobbed. Joseph was alarmed. Had he pushed too hard? He had thought this would be good for his wife. She had been so bitter, so preoccupied with her tragedy that he had thought this might be a way for her to forget her hurt and be comforted. Murdock looked up at him, the same question in his eyes. The men waited for Emma to get a hold on her emotions. When she did, she simply said, "Where are the babies now?"

"My sister, Florence, has them outside in the carriage."

The three of them walked outside, and Emma reached into the carriage for one little bundle while Joseph reached for the other. She looked down into the fat pink face of the baby girl. She was a beautiful baby, just nine days old. She had dark hair like Emma's, with bright eyes that squinted against the midday sun. A tiny mouth was opening and closing like a little bird, and a gurgling cry of hunger pierced Emma's heart. Almost as though on cue, Emma felt a tingling sensation and milk came surging into her breast. She turned away from Mr. Murdock. The joy was too intense to let a stranger see. Her joy at his expense — it would be too thoughtless. She called her thanks back over her shoulder.

"Brother Murdock, I . . . I . . . God bless you! You know I'll take the best possible care of these sweet little ones. Joseph, give me half an hour with our little girl, and then bring our son to me for nursing."

She escaped with her precious bundle into the house where she could rock and nurse and hold the baby to her heart. She was a mother at last!

"Purchase the land from Ezra Thayre and Leman Copley. It will be the perfect place for the Colesville saints to settle. They've been flooding in here for a month, living in tents, crowding in with the saints already settled here. They want to stay together, so let's give

337

them that opportunity. Brother Ezra will consecrate his land and so will Leman. Give them a fair price for it and lay out lots for the immigrants." Sidney Rigdon spoke in full support of Joseph's plan.

Joseph had called a high council meeting. Bishop Partidge was also in attendance. The incoming immigrants had become a considerable problem. The hospitality of the Kirtland saints was being tested to its limits. Not only were the Colesville saints in need of provisions and housing, but other converts of the very zealous missionaries out preaching the gospel in other parts of New England were moving to Kirtland to be near the prophet and the headquarters of the church. They came with little more than the clothes on their backs and a few seeds for planting. Some of them walked, carrying their children, expecting a Zion where everything would be provided. With two new babies in his house, there wasn't the room Joseph and Emma once had for accommodating pilgrims, and every other member of the church was experiencing the same drain. Where only a few months ago there had been two hundred people in Kirtland, the number was fast approaching five hundred, and most of them destitute. Joseph worried for fear Kirtland was becoming a city of beggars.

"Joseph, there is one other matter of business." Newel had been sitting quietly through most of the discussion. He had other things on his mind. "Last night Sister Thorne came to me about a meeting she had attended, thinking to hear good church doctrine taught and ended up witnessing the most hair-raising spectacle. It seems Sister Hubble has her own method of revelation. She has been holding what amounts to little more than seances, purporting to see spirits, departed loved ones. She gives revelations in a loud voice, her face contorted, and speaks words from strange tongues. She claims to be a prophetess, and she is leading some poor fools away from the true gospel of Christ."

"Really?" Joseph considered the problem. "Let's pay a little visit to Sister Hubble's meeting the next time it happens. I'd like to hear her revelations."

"It might not be pleasant," Newel warned.

Joseph laughed. "Oh, I rather disagree. I think it will be entertaining enough for anyone."

"Well then, the next one is set for Friday night in her barn down by the road that leads to Thompson."

Joseph looked around the group of men who formed the bedrock of the church. They were good men. They were sensible, hardworking, and they knew their scriptures. At every meeting he taught them from *The Book of Mormon*. The book was its own witness. If he could get a man to study it, that man would usually become entirely converted and well-educated in the commandments of God without much additional preaching. Joseph loved to read aloud with his friends the lessons from Alma, Nephi, and Moroni. He thought back to the lonely days when he felt the entire burden of carrying on God's work. Now he had good men to share the load, and his role had become that of an administrator and teacher. It felt good.

Friday night in the twilight shadows, Joseph, Sidney and Newel Knight tied up their horses and walked across the field to the little barn behind the Hubble home. It was already filled with neighbors, many of them members, some of them not. Lantern light streamed out around the edges of the door left slightly ajar. They could hear shouts, laughter, and some singing. Newel's face reflected his wariness. Sidney's had a determined set. Joseph was smiling from ear to ear.

"We'll just take a seat in the back corner, brethren. Keep your hat low over your faces. Say nothing. Just watch. We'll soon see what kind of a spirit is revealing things to Sister Hubble."

"I can guess from here," Sidney scowled.

"Me too, but I want to see it all."

The singing grew louder. Shouts of "Glory! Glory hallelujah! Glory hallelujah." rang out of the little barn. "Touch me Sister Hubble! Heal my leg, lame these many weeks! Glory, sister, glory! What is God's message for us tonight? Teach us, Sister."

Joseph led the way into the crowds at the back. He sat down low on a protruding log. Even from that position he could see through and over most of the crowd. Newel stood in shadows on his left, and Sidney put his broad back into the corner, also obscured by shadows and a few jittery women. The females of the group soon began jumping, then dancing, swaying to and fro. Their normal reserve peeled away like an onion skin as a wild spirit rampaged through the crowd. At the front, a man shouted out unintelligible gibberish and presently his whole body seemed out of joint. He twisted his limbs like a hemp rope, and Sister Hubble pointed a pudgy finger at him. She stood on a crate at the front of the barn. She wore a red bandana around her hair and had it tied in the back. Round eyes and round eyebrows were set in a florid face with two double chins celebrating her prosperity. Her ample bosom heaved with excitement. Her hands were raised over her head as though calling on some god for power. From time to time, she would point to a person, and he would immediately begin to shout gibberish or throw himself on the floor in contortions.

"See, my friends! Our brother is speaking in tongues, just as the Bible promises. He is so full of glory, he can't stand on his feet. You can have his happiness! It's free to all. You needn't be in want, my friends. God has an abundance to give you. Just come forward, and I will give you his blessing. Mary! Mary Hargrove, do you want the gift of tongues? I can give them to you right now. Come forward, Mary!"

A slim young woman came hesitantly toward Sister Hubble. The "prophetess" called out again. "Do you know how I knew you desired the gift? I knew it through the power of my God. Don't be afraid, Mary. Come here, right by my side, and I'll give you that same power."

The girl stopped in front of the portly Hubble, and just as she pointed to Mary, the girl crumpled into a heap on the floor, sobbing and crying, "No, no. I don't want the power. Please, please, no."

"I want the power!" Joseph stood up in the back of the room. His voice rose above the din. Suddenly the singing and swaying ceased. Sister Hubble still stood on her crate, and her eye caught Joseph's. One man lay still contorted at her feet, moaning in pain.

Joseph walked forward, and the crowd fell away from his path. He recognized many of the people as new converts to the church. Some of them had been in his home. Pity for them flooded his heart. They were babes in the gospel, infants in the knowledge of the ways of the Lord. Oliver looked at Sidney. They silently agreed to stand by the door and keep it clear.

"Sister Hubble, where does your power come from? I know my God. He is a God of order, reason, love as gentle as the dew from heaven. Why is it that He has never twisted me into a piece of hemp like this man?" Joseph's voice was carefully modulated. He seemed to invite discussion. The Hubble woman slowly lowered her arms, then abruptly pointed a finger at Joseph.

"You are not the only one who can receive revelations. God has given me this power."

Pity fled. Righteous indignation rushed in. Joseph's voice was as penetrating as his eyes. "Old Scratch has given you this power! You are under the influence of the devil, and you have brought it on your followers. 'Get thee behind me, Satan.' This man on the floor in contortions is possessed of an evil spirit. Mrs. Perkins there, who has been shouting in tongues, is possessed by an evil spirit. God speaks in tongues also. His are the tongues of angels and eternal judgment."

He turned in all directions speaking to the crowd which had now gone silent from a sense of shame. His eyes seemed to seek each person out. His face began to shine with a brilliant, white light, and he turned back to the woman on the crate. Her face was now contorted with hatred and anger. Joseph's voice which had been so quietly controlled, roared his condemnation.

"You are an imposter and a servant of Satan, Abigail Hubble." Now Joseph pointed a finger at her. "God has sent me to Kirtland to speak His almighty word. In the name of His holy Son, Jesus Christ, I command all evil spirits to leave this place. I have been sent to prepare this people for the great and dreadful day of the Lord when Jesus Christ himself will reign, and all who harken to the voice of Satan will be destroyed! Repent of your iniquity, or be destroyed. You cannot be of God and worship Satan. God will not be mocked!"

Abigail Hubble tried to speak. Her mouth was dry. Her tongue cleaved to the top of her palate and her vocal cords were raspy. Only dry rattling issued from her. Young Mary at her feet was sobbing.

Joseph bent down and raised her up, placed his hand upon her head and quietly said, "Mary, go your way and sin no more. God has instructed me this night to seal you up against the power of the destroyer."

Then he knelt and put both hands on the head of the man on the floor who still seemed bent into knots. He commanded the evil spirit to leave, and within minutes the farmer opened his eyes, looked into Joseph's, and began to weep.

Sidney, standing by the door, raised his voice. "Go on home now, friends. There is nothing for you here. Satan has been banished by a true prophet. Go home now and, henceforth, seek to hear the word of God preached in purity within the Church of Christ."

The crowd filed past Sidney and Newel. They were silent, ashamed. Some felt as though they had come back from a trance and wondered why they had been so deceived by Abigail Hubble. Joseph finally turned to her. His voice was quiet now, but firm.

"Sister Hubble, you have been deceived, but of your own choosing. Lay aside your peepstone and pretend not to the mysteries of the kingdom. The power of God is for no one's individual advantage. His power is for the purpose of serving others, not taking glory unto ourselves. This you have not understood. Repent and seek God in His restored church, or your soul will be lost. Humble yourself and confess your sin, and you will be forgiven."

From the front of the barn came a distinct snort of disapproval. Sidney's inclination was to condemn and excommunicate her on the spot. With his own congregations he had brooked no rebellion. Newel was not surprised at Joseph's approach. He had seen his friend stern with errant members one minute, but kind and loving the next. He smiled at Rigdon and privately rejoiced that Joseph, not Sidney, was the prophet.

In May, Parley Pratt came back. He had been eight months in the western wilderness known as Missouri, preaching *The Book of Mormon* to the Indians. Parley was an able preacher. He was fiery and colorful. He learned to speak in the simple terms that his Lamanite brethren could understand. He saw them oppressed and humbled by the injustices of the United States government. He had good success and gave many of them hope they had lost under duress. He told them the great white God of whom they spoke in legend was, in fact, the Lord Jesus Christ, whom their white Christian brothers worship. He read the great sermons in Third Nephi from *The Book of Mormon* which came from the teachings of Christ to their ancestors in this very land. The elders of the tribes, listened politely, sitting in their circles around the fire, puffing on their pipes. They nodded at the wisdom of the scriptures, but when it came to absolute conversion, they held back. They had had too much abuse at the hands of their "Christian" brothers to believe the white man's God would extend much help to them.

Parley spent his first night in Joseph's and Emma's home and regaled them long into the night with vivid stories of the western Indians, their customs and beliefs. With colorful words he painted the beauty of the prairie, awash in yellow, purple and pink flowers. He was anxious to give his report to the council the next day, and he was equally anxious that the church move as a body to the western frontier. He had a letter from Oliver to Joseph explaining how the United States military would not allow them to preach to the Indians as they would have liked. There were regulations against much interaction of trade or teaching with them. They had spent most of their time in

Jackson County, Missouri seeking those who would listen. Oliver reported a spirit of interest and open minds in that area.

Joseph knew that Kirtland was not the permanent settling place of the saints. It was far too worldly and too convenient. God had always pulled his chosen people from out of the world and sent them into the wilderness, thereby setting them apart and giving them a theocratic form of government. In Kirtland, they were subject to the worldly influence of barge traffic, the standards of established religions, the approval or disapproval of the local press, and the economy of the general country. God meant to keep His people apart. That had been in Joseph's mind for some time, but he had not had a clear vision as to where Zion would be. The saints in Colesville were waiting for a revelation as to Zion's permanent establishment. After moving this far from Pennsylvania, they did not want to put down roots and then have to move again. So the homes they built were rough and hastily constructed. They were little more than squatters, waiting for their call to go to Zion.

At the council meeting the next day, Parley spoke while Newel and Joseph Knight listened with particular interest.

"Joseph, maybe it is the promised place. Inquire of the Lord. Our Colesville brethren are anxious to establish a real home."

"So, you're not tired of traveling yet," Joseph smiled. "Let me pray about it. Conference is only a week away. Perhaps we will have some direction by then."

Parley had the gift of gab, and in the next week had so many people excited about the prospect of moving to Missouri that they all considered it the promised land. Conference started on June 3, 1831. Quorum priesthood meetings were dominated by rumors of Missouri. Parley related in a general meeting the adventures he and Oliver had had as missionaries among the Lamanites. Joseph spoke on doctrines of the kingdom, repentance, forgiveness, charity, and consecration. He called for periodic fasting and donation of the food to the Bishop's Storehouse. They set aside the first Thursday of every month for fasting, and he promised it would be a spiritual day, and the saints would benefit much by their sacrifice. Finally, on June seventh, the longed-for revelation came.

Emma sat in the congregation beside Elizabeth Ann Whitney, holding her twins and listening with concern to the revelation as it fell from her husband's lips.

"I, the Lord, will make known unto you what I will that ye shall do from this time until the next conference, which shall be held in Missouri, upon the land which I will consecrate unto my people, which are a remnant of Jacob and those who are heirs according to the covenant.

"Wherefore, verily I say unto you, let my servants Joseph Smith, Jun., and Sidney Rigdon take their journey as soon as preparations can be made to leave their homes, and journey to the land of Missouri." (Excerpt Doctrine and Covenants, Section 52)

He went on to call away most of the strong leadership of Kirtland. Lyman Wight, John Murdock, Newel Knight, Isaac Morley, Hyrum and Samuel Smith, David Whitmer and Harvey Whitlock, Levi and Solomon Hancock — all were to go, preaching along the way. Emma looked around. Scarcely a family was unaffected. The women would have to do for themselves. Their men would all be gone. She shifted little Joseph Murdock Smith, put him into Elizabeth Ann's capable hands, and then took up Julia who was fussing from the warmth of the day.

Well, if their men would help get the crops planted, the women could manage while they were gone. Emma found herself infected with the same excitement as the rest of the congregation. Zion! A permanent place for the saints. It evoked visions of peace and prosperity, of industry and spiritual heights, a place to receive the Savior when He came again to the world. Still, even in the flush of exhilaration, Emma held some reservations. With due respect to Joseph and his revelation — Missouri, of all places?

Now it was Emma's turn to see her husband go on the Lord's errand. She supposed that she had been spoiled. Since they had been married four years ago, Joseph had taken only short excursions. Now she was comfortably situated in their little home in the Morley settlement. She had her babies. Now the Lord was calling him to go west to prepare the land of Zion and organize the church there. She could hardly complain. Parley's wife had not seen him in almost a year, and there were many others like him. So, Emma steeled herself against the day that Joseph would leave her.

That day came all too soon. She packed up a small knapsack of food to see him on his way. She put in a satchel a change of clothing and underwear, several copies of *The Book of Mormon*, and foolscap for writing along the way. Joseph was in high spirits. His love for Emma and the two little ones was keen, but his enthusiasm for "the Lord's errand" was even keener. At times he would stop and pick up the babies and kiss them, or turn to Emma, break in the middle of a sentence and kiss her, but she could tell the prospect of seeing the country, especially with such an important mission, filled him with anticipation. This expedition would make an experienced traveler of him. He would come back a more experienced man, not the boy prophet he had been in Palmyra, New York. What he had lacked in worldly education, his spiritual tutelage had supplied. Soon, he would have both. She had already seen him grow and expand his capabilities as the unchallenged leader of a burgeoning township. He became more confident and competent every day. His opinions were stronger, his vision clearer, and his enthusiasm for the future of his church knew no bounds.

Finally, the moment arrived. Emma stood in the doorway, a baby in each arm. The hot July sun danced with red highlights in her dark hair. Joseph kissed her goodbye and started to leave. Halfway to the carriage where Martin and Sidney waited, he turned and hurried back to embrace her once more.

"You'll be all right?"

"Of course. You know the Lord will provide for us." She smiled a little wryly and said, "And if not, Mother Lucy will."

"Stay close to Mother. She does have a way of making things happen."

"I'll be fine. We'll miss you. Take care. Don't stay out in the hot sun too long."

"Don't worry. We'll go by water as much as possible, and I suppose there are stages even in Missouri."

"Just be careful. I can part with you for a little while, just promise to come back to me."

He kissed her forehead. "I promise."

"Joseph, will we move to Missouri? I mean, the whole church?"

"Possibly. The revelation said it is consecrated to the Lord's people."

"They say it's wild."

"It's the frontier, Emma. But God is in the wilderness just as much as He is in Ohio. Sometimes you find Him best when there are no other distractions."

"Good luck. I mustn't keep you. The others are waiting. I'll miss you, Joseph. Write to me."

"I will."

He squeezed her hand, then bounded quickly to the carriage, jumped in with a greeting to Martin and Sidney, and by the time the carriage was turned and on its way, he was in spirited conversation with his friends. Emma watched until the buggy was out of sight. Her heart was sinking. Two months, possibly more — it was a long time to be hungry, for Joseph was the only one who fed her soul.

Chapter Thirteen

The Quest for Zion

My Dear Wife,

I arrived in Independence last week with Brothers Martin Harris, Edward Partridge, and William Phelps, having traveled the last two hundred and fifty miles on foot. The forepart of our journey was most enjoyable. I have never seen such beautiful sights as a ride down the Mississippi river affords. Green forests and prosperous settlements were everywhere. The most ambitious of the settlements is St. Louis, Missouri. It is all mud, squalor, people, animals, noise, and industry. I feel to warn people against congregating into the cities of Babylon. They are not favorable to the spirit of the Lord. Still, it was interesting to walk about and observe the bustling commerce on all sides.

As we could not afford a stage to take us to Independence, we concluded to walk and trust the Lord to help us find food and lodging. We were not disappointed. Although the weather was hot and muggy — it being more than a hundred degrees many days, and that combined with mosquitos, flies, and a variety of insects we have not known in the east — nevertheless, we encountered many good people who shared with us their bread and board. We have slept in all kinds of circumstances, in barns, under trees, and once or twice, on decent beds.

Missouri is all Parley proclaimed it to be. In addition to colorful prairies with a carpet of flowers, there are great varieties of trees including black walnut, cherry, oak, and hickory. We have shot wild turkey for dinner more than once and been grateful for it. We also see flocks of wild geese and ducks. Once we awoke in the middle of the night to a roar that sounded like a great waterfall. As the ground was shaking, we wondered if it might be an earthquake, but lo, to our amazement, a small herd of buffalo passed within a few yards of us, pounding the ground with their hooves, and stirring up a great quantity of dust. What do you think of that, my affectionate Emma? Your husband has become a frontiersman, in addition to all his other accomplishments.

Despite my disappointment in the settlement at Independence — for it is very rough and the people generally uneducated, speaking with a strong dialect, and living in crude cabins which seem to want badly the gentling hand of a good woman — the Lord has designated this place "Zion." We have been commanded to purchase land here for the building of a temple. Sidney consecrated this area for the gathering of the saints, and we have laid the logs for the first house. Brother Gilbert is to establish a store for the saints. Bro. Phelps and Oliver will start a printing office to publish the revelations. I am writing to Newel to instruct the Colesville saints to settle in Zion as soon as possible. Edward will remain here as the new bishop and head of the church. I have never trusted a man more than Edward Partridge. His wisdom is great; his heart is true, and his patience is legendary.

Well, dearest Emma, the mail is about to leave, so I close with hope that my children will remember me. Kiss them both for me. I pray our loving Father in Heaven will watch over my beloved family while I am away on his errand, and this letter finds you well and happy.

Always your loving husband, Joseph

Emma put the letter on the table where she could see it each time she passed by in her daily work. Missouri! She was just getting comfortable here in Kirtland. Most of the Smiths had settled with the Colesville saints out in Thompson, but Hyrum stopped by almost every day to inquire after the babies. Sometimes Jerusha came with him, sometimes young Lucy. Emma did not lack for company. In Joseph's absence she took in two families who had arrived more or less destitute on her doorstep to meet the prophet. They were surprised to find the head of their church no better off than themselves, but true to Christian custom, she took them in and shared her food with them. One family was very grateful and helped all they could by chopping wood, milking, gardening, carding, weaving, and doing the other chores about the place. They stayed until the first body of saints started for Missouri in July. The other family was so disappointed at not finding Joseph that they ate up most of his provisions, slept in his bed, and left for greener pastures with not so much as a farewell. Emma came in from making soap one day, and they had packed up and gone. She breathed a sigh of relief.

In the latter part of June, she said a sad farewell to her old friends, the Knights. In response to Joseph's invitation to gather in "Zion," they packed up their few belongings and boarded a barge at Fairport. They headed first to St. Louis before journeying on to Independence. Emma thought Polly didn't look very well as she sat in the wagon. Her color was not good, and her eyes were sad and tired.

"Mother Knight, do take care. I worry about your health. Are you sure you are well enough to make this journey? You could stay here with me and go later."

"Oh, no, my dear. Joseph has had a vision of Zion in Missouri. You'll all come there to see us soon enough, I believe. Why, just consider, I'm going to make a place ready for you. I have faith the Lord will get me there, just as he brought me here. I feel a good deal better than I did when leaving Colesville. When I left my beautiful home there, I thought my heart would break. I could scarcely see the boundaries of our farm for the tears flooding my eyes. I left my broom in the corner and logs on the hearth for those that bought our place. But leaving here is no trouble at all. I believe Mr. Copley is the only one who resents our leaving." She leaned toward Emma and whispered, "Notwithstanding we left his house and land in far better condition than when he leased us that drafty old cabin."

Emma kissed Polly's cheek and gave her a handkerchief to take on her way. She put a letter into Joseph Knight's weathered hand along with five dollars.

"Give the letter to Joseph. Use the money as you will. Take care of Polly, Father Knight. She's not strong."

"I know. But she's faithful."

"And she'll be blessed. I'm sure."

"Goodby, Emma. May God bless you. Come to Zion as quickly as you can, for we're to build a house of the Lord there."

"We are all in God's hands. Goodbye, goodbye."

She waved until they were out of sight, wiped her tears, and ducked back into the cabin to feed her beautiful twins.

In August, Joseph came home. Only Sidney accompanied him. Martin, Oliver, Edward, and William Phelps had all stayed in Missouri to help settle the immigrant saints who had already started coming. Lydia Partridge had a letter from her husband instructing her to sell their Kirtland home and bring the children. He was very concerned about laying such a burden on her, but there was nothing else to be done. He was the church authority in Independence, and he was already very busy in helping the saints purchase land and build homes. In addition, he helped established the United Order in Missouri as he had in Kirtland. Lydia would have to manage with the help of the brethren in Ohio, which she did as well as she could. Her younger children were just recovering from the measles, and her oldest was very sick with a fever and lung congestion. Joseph and Hyrum laid hands on him for a healing blessing, and the boy recovered the next day. Still, Lydia felt the heavy burden of managing her husband's affairs and frequently called on Joseph for consultation and legal help. At last, she was ready to go and made final rounds at the Morley settlement, saying her goodbyes to her long-time friends. She traveled in a company of a hundred other saints bound for Zion. She left on the steamer from Fairport, waving her handkerchief, clutching her children and weeping.

Joseph and Emma had peace for one night. Just lying in each other's arms, dozing, talking, dreaming, and getting up to feed the babies was like honey nectar. Emma thought she would never get enough of it.

"This, right now, is the happiest time of our lives, Emma. At least, it is mine. To be able to play with our babies, watch them being loved by the most beautiful wife in the world. Ah, Emma, this must be heaven."

She laughed at him. "You'll always be a romantic, Joseph."

"Why? Because I love my wife?"

"No, because you love everything, everybody. You have the great gift of loving the gift of life. You enjoy whatever you are doing at the moment. You see the beauty of life when others see the hardships. I think that is why our people love you so. You give them the vision of a better world. And it is not just a 'better world to come,' for you live daily in that better world. You carry it within you."

"Now who's being a 'romantic?'"

"I'm just the helmsman on our ship of life. You don't give two hoots for the steadiness of the vessel. You rock the boat every chance you get, and I'm back here bailing like mad."

"Are you suggesting I get all the fun, and you get all the work?"

She leaned over their son's head and kissed him with a long, lingering savor. "I'd never say that."

He chuckled. "No, you wouldn't. You're not a complainer, Emma, but I guess you think it sometimes."

"Just sometimes, when you're off gallivanting with your friends, doing God's errands. I am mostly content to just stay home with our children."

Peace for Joseph was fleeting as moonbeams. The next day he was plunged into the problems of Kirtland, problems that were exploding. With the stream of converts bulging the boundaries of the township, the older residents were growing alarmed. Soon they would be outnumbered two to one by the Mormons. The public offices would be claimed by the newcomers, and their town would not be their own. The angry citizens began to band together and refused to sell grain, food, or lumber to the saints. That put even a greater burden on those who took in the immigrants. The temperament of the town was changing. Where once Joseph and Emma had felt secure and safe, threats on his life were surfacing. More than once, prayer meetings held under the trees were broken up by threatening mobs.

"Go back where you came from. We don't want you here. You come in and take our land. You squat three and four families on a lot. You've made our town into a beggar's camp. Go back home! You too, Joe Smith! Take your followers and go back to New York, or on to your precious Zion!"

Joseph could understand the feelings of the Kirtland residents. They were right in many respects. He was trying to alleviate the problem by settling the saints in smaller communities around Kirtland, but the converts were coming faster than houses could be built or provisions gathered. He called Newel Whitney as the new bishop of Kirtland. It was an honor Newel wasn't sure he wanted. After much prayer, he received an answer from the Lord, "Thy strength is in me," and he shouldered the load.

With the responsibility for the immigrants lifted from his shoulders, Joseph went back to work on an inspired revision of the Bible. It was slow going for he sought enlightenment on every verse and clarification of gospel doctrine. Revelation was an ongoing daily experience for him as well as Sidney who worked with him and acted as scribe.

"I had a visit from Deacon Ruggles the other day, and he asked for light on several Bible subjects. He asked why we are so anxious to proselytize people away from his church," Joseph reported to Sidney with amusement.

"And what did you tell him?" Sidney expected an offhanded comment from Joseph's look. He was surprised at the seriousness of the answer.

"I told him what we espouse: faith, repentance, and baptism for every soul on the earth. It is the passport into the kingdom where God lives. I told him that with proper authority they lead to the reception of the Holy Ghost."

"Did he like that answer?" Sidney's bushy eyebrows almost met his hairline.

"I guess he did. He said he wanted the Holy Ghost, for surely it is the comforter spoken of by Christ." Joseph rubbed his forehead. "I invited him to come into the true Church of Christ, and he would receive his desire."

"And?"

"Like the 'rich young man' of Jesus' day, he went away sorrowing. Deacon Ruggles has a comfortable life, supported amply by his congregation." Joseph wasn't smiling now. He was contemplating the sorry situation of a man who would seek comfort rather than truth. "Ah well, perhaps he'll come around yet. The spirit will work on him, I'm sure."

"Joseph, we stopped last time in John. Our Lord said, 'I will not leave you comfortless.' What should we understand by this?"

Sidney had a fresh quantity of ink and a new quill pen. This time with Joseph was meat to his hungry soul, for his spirit thirsted for revelations from the Lord. He watched the younger man expectantly. He knew exactly what to expect, since he had seen Joseph under the spirit before. As the young prophet began speaking, his face became the clear, transparent white that clearly characterized his channel to heaven.

"There are two Comforters of which the scriptures speak. The first is the gift of the Holy Ghost. It was given on the day of Pentecost, and we receive that after faith, repentance, and baptism. This Comforter has the effect of pure intelligence. It is more powerful in expanding the mind, enlightening the understanding and the intellect when it falls on a man who is the literal seed of Abraham, than one who is a Gentile, though it may not have half as much visible effect on the body.

"The Second Comforter also spoken of is a subject of great interest. After a person has faith in Christ, repents, and is baptized for the remission of sins, and receives the gift of the Holy Ghost — or the First Comforter — then if he continues to live righteously, it may then be his privilege to receive the other Comforter, which the Lord has promised the saints.

"Now, what is this other Comforter? It is no more nor less than the Lord Jesus Christ Himself. The visions of the heavens will be opened unto him, and the Lord will teach him face to face. He may have a perfect knowledge of the mysteries of the Kingdom of God."

Joseph tore his gaze from the glazed window and turned to his friend. "Do you understand, Sidney? This is the state the ancient saints arrived at when they had such glorious visions. The scriptures once told these things plainly, as I tell you now. Most men don't want to know because of the responsibility it places on them. Do you want that Comforter, my friend?" His voice was low, pleading for the right answer.

Sidney had been recording every word. His paper told the tale of his excitement. The writing was shaky, almost erratic. The normally fastidious Rigdon had spilled droplets of ink on the foolscap, and he had it on his fingers.

"I want what you have. I want that communion with my Savior."

"Do you want it more than food, more than drink? Do you hunger and thirst?"

"Yes."

"Do you want it more than life itself, Sidney?"

The man did not flinch. "Yes, more than life."

Joseph leaned forward, his forehead almost touching Rigdon's over the ink-stained paper. "Don't forget, 'Thou sayst.' There will come a day you will be required to live by those words. You will suffer for Jesus' sake, for His word's sake. Don't forget what 'Thou sayst.' If you truly want it, you shall have it, for Jesus Christ himself has promised it."

Sidney felt a thrill race down his spine, whether from joy or fear he couldn't say. When Joseph spoke this way with that peculiar light round about him, he spoke with the authority of God. When Emma came in some time later, she saw her husband still happily expounding scriptures and Sidney sweating and writing all with trembling hand.

Joseph spent one fair September morning chopping wood with his brothers, Hyrum and William. They were laying in fuel for the winter. It was a perfect autumn day, with the red blaze maple in full glory and the oaks shouting their last golden hurrah. The afternoon was spent studying the New Testament, and in the evening, a meeting was scheduled at the Smith home. There were a dozen people crowded into Emma's small parlor, when a man named Ezra Booth brought Mr. and Mrs. John Johnson from Hiram, Ohio, some thirty miles south. They had come to experience the phenomenon of Joseph the Mormon prophet. They had heard both good and bad reports and wanted to know the truth for themselves.

"You don't look like the skunk people say you are," Johnson got right to the point. He was a hard handed farmer, square as a granite block and direct as a Cherokee arrow. He wasn't really sure he wanted to be here tonight in the man's home. After all, this so-called "prophet" was probably an imposter and enemy to God.

"Looks can be deceiving." Joseph returned his frank stare with good humor.

"I find I can usually tell a man's nature by the look in his eye."

"Rightly so, Mr. Johnson. Shakespeare says it is the window to the soul. But how do you *judge* a man's soul?"

The answer was immediate. "You judge on honesty, integrity, and if he confesses Jesus as the Christ."

"Suppose he professes Christ and still cheats his neighbor?"

"He's no friend of Christ in that case."

"So you believe in works, not grace?" Joseph probed.

"I believe in God's grace. A man is only saved by the good will of Christ."

"Can he lie, cheat, steal, and still be saved by Christ's good pleasure?"

"Jesus Christ is the author of our salvation. No man ever worked out his own salvation. It's impossible. We're all sinners."

Joseph could see the farmer was adamant in his position. He put his hand on Johnson's shoulder to forge a bridge between them. Then he agreed with the man and set him at ease.

"You are absolutely right, sir. We are all sinners. It is our nature, and we rely completely on the mercy of the Lord Jesus for *salvation*. We certainly agree on that, but if you would know God, you must get beyond salvation to exaltation! Even the dirtiest, most cowardly liar and cheat will be resurrected, but not necessarily *exalted* to live in the presence of God. If this season on earth is to test us to see if we will keep God's commandments, would a just God reward every soul the same regardless of the good or the evil they may have committed? A universal single reward would make a mockery of heavenly justice and convince us God had no genuine concern as to whether we live the commandments or not. In short, Brother Johnson, Christ is the author of salvation for our souls, and it is freely given to all men through His atonement. We are the authors of our own exaltation as we live obedient to every word proceeding from the mouth of God. He will offer us this exaltation and all else when we are willing and able to walk the same path of sacrifice and obedience His Only Begotten Son walked."

Mr. Johnson took his wife's arm, and they settled into chairs near the hearth. "Let's hear about your golden Bible, young man."

Emma smiled at little Julia, eight months old, who was waving her arms as she played on her mother's lap. Little Joseph was on Mrs. Morley's lap, and he was busily cramming his fist into his mouth and crowing. Emma knew what was coming. Johnson had just prescribed his own conversion, for when Joseph told his life's story, there was hardly anyone who could resist the truth of it.

Joseph began describing his early confusion about which church to join and quickly moved to his encounter with the Angel Moroni and the golden plates. He held up a copy of *The Book of Mormon* as evidence of his story. After reading several passages from it, he offered the copy to Johnson. The farmer took the book and commenced his perusal.

Ezra Booth spoke up. "Well, here is Mrs. Johnson with a lame arm. Of course, a prophet would know that. Can you invoke the power of God to heal her?"

Sidney stood and began lecturing on the healing grace of Jesus Christ, reporting several instances of healing he had witnessed. Another guest contested the long range benefit of so-called faith healings. A few moments later, Joseph, staring straight at Mrs. Johnson, arose from his chair and walked across the room. Heated conversation went on about him as to the effectiveness of healing on demand. Joseph took hold of Mrs. Johnson's afflicted arm. The knuckles of her hand were enlarged and bulbous, the fingers were twisted, and the arm as useless as a rag. She looked up curiously into his eyes.

He spoke softly to her, but his words quieted the whole company. "Woman, in the name of the Lord Jesus Christ, I command thee to be whole." He touched her hand and lifeless arm, holding her gaze captive, then quite suddenly lowered her hand to her lap and left the room.

There was astounded silence. Even Sidney didn't know what to say. Finally a woman spoke up.

"What a presumptuous act. Next he'll be saying he can forgive sins."

Mrs. Johnson looked around the room as if dazed and immediately lifted her lame arm, raising it high above her head, and shaking it in pure amazement. Joy was bursting from her. She stood on her feet and called out clearly, "Presumptuous or not, my arm is healed! There is no pain. I haven't lifted this arm over my head in three years. Now it is healed, I tell you, and that young man did it. John, that man is a prophet, and you know it. We both felt it from the minute he spoke to us. Quit being stubborn."

Emma had seen her husband heal people before. He usually laid his hands on their heads and pronounced a blessing. This time he had healed Mrs. Johnson with just touch of his hand and a direct command. Had he become that confident of his authority? How could so much favor from the Lord fail to protect him from his enemies? He might be loved and revered by the converts who arrived daily, but there were growing threats and insults by angry Kirtland residents who would love to run Joseph Smith out of town on a rail.

By now, Emma had become nervous and protective of her husband. She wasn't sleeping well at night. She heard every little sound. At first, she was sensitive to sounds from the twins, but of late, other sounds kept her from sleeping. If the cow bell clanked too violently, she got up to investigate. If Isaac Morley's dogs bayed during the night, Emma was up. Joseph slept soundly always. At times, she became exasperated with herself and with him. How on earth could he sleep when his life had been threatened? He needed a bodyguard. She decided to ask Joseph to secure one for protection. Maybe she could then get some sleep.

The Johnsons were baptized the next week in the Chagrin river, Mrs. Johnson's arm remained healed. A week later, Johnson came with Sidney again to the Smith home and proposed to Joseph, for his protection and seclusion that he and Emma move to Hiram to the Johnson farm. Sidney urged that idea, saying they could work there in peace and quiet revising the Bible, since Sidney would occupy a small cabin across the road and down a bit from the Johnsons. Joseph's enemies might be appeased to have him out of their immediate area, and every new convert coming to Kirtland would not have the option of interrupting the inspired revision of God's word.

Joseph and Emma discussed it that afternoon. It was tempting. Emma was nearly worn out with the effort of running her household, caring for the twins and providing for a continual stream of guests. Then too, winter was coming, and their little house was cold and drafty. Emma had to be very careful the children didn't catch the croup in their chilly cabin. The Johnsons had a large, comfortable farmhouse. Almost all their children were grown up and into homes of their own. There was plenty of room for the Smiths. The prospect of being able to work without interruption was most appealing. Progress had been slow lately. Finally, all things considered, they decided to go.

Phoebe Rigdon became good friends with Emma and with Elsa Johnson after the move. Hiram was a small settlement several miles southeast of Kirtland, built on gently rolling hills. Phoebe's cabin was only a hundred yards down the road from the Johnson farmhouse. When her household work was done, she would walk to the dusty road and sit with the ladies carding or mending or weaving. She was a soft-spoken, gentle woman. Her hair had gone prematurely gray, and she wore it tucked back into a white, linen cap. Only her husband knew it was long and thick and wavy. It had been her pride in her youth.

The babies kept them all amused. It was a wonder to Emma how it took three grown women and young, sixteen-year-old Miranda Johnson, to take care of two little babies. But it was a delightful time for her. The company of other women and the respite from constant work more than compensated for their lack of privacy.

The Johnsons slept upstairs, while Emma, Joseph, and the twins had the guest bedroom off the parlor downstairs. It was warm during cold winter days and very convenient to the kitchen. Mrs. Johnson discovered Emma's skill with raised bread donuts. They became a favorite treat on chilly winter nights after Joseph and Sidney rested from their work on the Bible.

October, November, December passed away in relative peace. The revision was slow, but fascinating work. Sidney was a great help to Joseph, being very well versed in the Bible. They would read aloud the passages and pause to consider and discuss. Many times Sidney would give his interpretation as to the meaning, but whenever Joseph spoke with authority, Sidney yielded to his interpretation. It was tempting for Sidney to desire the same powers of revelation Joseph had. While they were together, there were many times he felt caught up in the heavenly influence working through Joseph, and at times Sidney tried to dictate revelations as Joseph did. Biblical verbiage rolled off him naturally, but his "revelations" fell short of Joseph's. Emma had witnessed many other men desire to assume Joseph's privilege of revelation and seership, including Oliver, but all had failed. Oh yes, there were personal visions and inspiration that came to them, but revelatory doctrine for the new church was sent only through the Lord's prophet.

Late one snowy evening, when Sidney had reluctantly put down his pen and started for home, Joseph lingered by the flickering fire pondering Old Testament events which they had been studying. His mind was restless, puzzling over the society and history of the ancient prophets. There was much he did not understand and that always sat ill with him. God seemed to be strict and exacting. Joseph had learned from those Biblical scriptures to fear God, but far preferred the New Testament profile of a loving, forgiving Lord. He seemed to see in the licking flames in the fireplace the image of Moses agonizing over the children of Israel worshipping the golden calf. Joseph was given to understand that the Ten Commandments were actually a weakened version of the fullness of the gospel that God first desired to reveal. The whole Christian world, down to the present time, was basing salvation on that lesser law. Joseph's soul seemed to be bursting with the knowledge that God was revealing the fullness of His everlasting gospel to him.

As he reflected, many impressions flooded his mind. One troubled him. He tried to dismiss it as unimportant, but something kept bringing it back to his attention. The great Patriarchs had many wives. He had always known that, yet had never questioned why. Now he seemed consumed by questions. Joseph opened the Bible and reread Genesis, then he read of David in Second Samuel and Solomon in First Kings. All of these great men had many wives, and yet the Lord condemned the practice in *The Book of Mormon*. He opened a well-thumbed copy of the book and turned to Jacob. Here was a prophet who had witnessed his people turning the old practice into wickedness. Whereas in the Bible, Abraham, Jacob, and Moses had practiced plural marriage upon commandment of the Lord, others had turned it into a lascivious practice and were chastised.

Then the Spirit whispered to Joseph, "This ancient principle will be restored *for the building up of My Kingdom* in this, the dispensation of the fullness of times."

Joseph sat bolt upright in his chair. His heart seemed to skip a beat, then it began to race, and he began to tremble. Along with that unmistakable witness came the realization that he would have to teach this restored principle to his people. Though the fire still burned cozily in the hearth, Joseph felt a chill grip his chest and spread until he was shivering and shaking to his toes.

He left the little parlor and went into the bedroom where Emma lay curled around baby Julia. He stood over them, looking down on a picture of serenity.

"No," he whispered.

Once again the dreaded impression flooded over him. "Yes," came the voice in his head.

"Why?" Joseph asked silently.

"There cannot be a restoration without testing my people."

"I am afraid we will fail the test. At least, I know the people are not ready for it now." The heavens were silent. "Maybe one distant day . . . ."

His own words to Oliver came thundering back to him. "Many have faith and many have love, but few have the fierce self-discipline to be completely obedient. And full obedience to God's every command is the only way to eternal life."

Then, still shivering, he lay down with his wife and daughter, curled up against her back, and gave himself over to despair, for he knew that if this ancient principle had to be restored, it would sorely test many souls.

Joseph kept the incident to himself while he and Sidney went on examining the Bible and asking for clarification when the scriptures were unclear. On February 16, 1832, in the presence of a dozen brethren, Sidney sat beside Joseph when a vision of the resurrection of the dead enveloped them both. They saw holy angels worshipping at the throne of the Father. They saw the fall of Lucifer as he was cast out of heaven. They saw three degrees of glory where sanctified souls would be consigned. Most important of all, they saw that, contrary to the Christian teachings of their day, the next world consisted of much more than simply heaven and hell. In fact, the emphasis was on rewarding good on all levels, and punishment was a lesser, though necessary, factor.

They sat on chairs in full view of the other men who recorded exactly what took place. Philo Dibble felt the power and saw the glory that surrounded the two seers. Joseph and Sidney both were surrounded by a brilliant radiance, their bodies having taken on a white luster. Joseph would say, "What do I see?" and proceed to give an account of it. Sidney would respond, "I see the same." Sidney would then relate what he was seeing in vision, and Joseph would confirm, "I see the same."

In measured tones, following this vision of the eternities, Joseph dictated the words which circumscribed his whole life's work.

"And now, after the many testimonies which have been given of him, this is the testimony last of all, which we give: that he lives! For we saw him, even on the right hand of God; and we heard the voice bearing record that he is the Only Begotten of the Father, that by him and through him, and of him, the worlds are and were created, and the inhabitants thereof are begotten sons and daughters unto God . . . ." (Excerpt from Doctrine and Covenants, Section 76)

The heavens had truly been opened! In years to come, this experience would simply be referred to as "The Vision." When it was over, and the spirit subsided, Joseph sat quietly but upright. Sidney nearly crumpled. He was clearly exhausted by the experience.

"'Pears Brother Rigdon is considerably affected," Philo observed. "I've never heard such beautiful language and perfectly clear doctrine."

Joseph reached out to his friend, Sidney, and squeezed his shoulder. "Brother Sidney just isn't as used to it as I am. But we take no credit for this revelation. We are merely men, subject to common weakness and flaws just as you are. The sublime beauty of the language, the description of the rewards of the faithful and heirs of salvation, is not of ourselves. It came from God."

That he spoke the truth was evident to everyone in the room. They had at various times heard him speak under the power of the spirit. It was that spirit which persuaded them to sell homes, leave family, give up the pleasant things of the world, and contribute every cent they had to the building up of the kingdom. It was their witness of Joseph's prophetic calling that saw them through persecution in Kirtland and throughout the rest of their lives. They would go hungry for Joseph, walk a thousand miles, preach and be cursed, and actually lay down their lives for the man. To be in the presence of a living prophet of God was a spiritual event most of them never forgot nor denied.

Persecution was their fate as well as Joseph's. It came also to the Johnson home. Not surprisingly, it was centered around money and worldly possessions. Oh, there was some disagreement over revealed doctrines which conflicted with the popular thinking of the day. Philosophical differences, however, don't move men to anger the way money does. Olmstead, Eli, and John Johnson Jr. were concerned. They watched their parents begin to fall under the influence of Joe Smith. When their mother was healed, they had all joined the church in the flush of wonder over the miracle. It wasn't long before the man intruded into their family home. Their father was a large landholder. This property was their inheritance, and when they overheard a discussion between their father and Joseph concerning the Johnson's large parcel of land in Kirtland being donated as a temple site, they drew the line.

Olmstead privately cornered Joseph and told him the property belonged to his family, not to the church. He would oppose any transfer of property no matter how holy the purpose.

"Guess I made myself clear to Mr. Joe "Prophet" Smith. If he knows what is good for him, he'll go begging somewhere else for land for his temple." Olmstead bragged to his two other brothers, John Jr. and Eli.

"Luke and Lyman don't even seem to care that Smith is stealing our parents blind," Eli said bitterly.

"Aw, they have joined this 'united order,' where they sacrifice everything and get a pittance back. Nobody will ever persuade me to turn over everything I own while my own family goes hungry. It's crazy, purely crazy." Olmstead had observed as much as he cared to of the saints living arrangements in Kirtland.

The town had swelled to twice its size and was still growing. Its "milk and honey" had been sipped away, and the cup was empty. Still, the demand grew. The impoverishment of Kirtland came to rankle the residents of the whole country, and though Joseph and Emma had hoped to escape it by moving to Hiram, bitterness followed them wherever he went. It was a mercurial life, living one moment in the sublime and the next in the grip of hell.

One evening when dinner was over, Joseph sat with Martin, Sidney, Orson Hyde — who was a neighbor — Luke and Lyman Johnson, and their father, John. Martin had just returned from Missouri and spent the morning helping the Johnsons work with the animals, pitch hay, clean the barn, and groom the beautiful horses John Johnson loved. The afternoon hours held study of the Biblical patriarchs, and some questions were raised. Joseph waited until the women had served up the hot cider and were busy in the kitchen to question his closest friends on the subject which now tortured him.

Joseph opened the discussion, getting right to the point. "Abraham had two wives we know of - Sarah, then Keturah, when he was over one hundred and thirty-seven years old. Beyond them, he had concubines. Genesis says so. Jacob had two wives and two concubines. Then, of course, there was the multitude of wives of David and Solomon. Brother Sidney and I have been pondering this practice. Can we call this a heathen practice when our patriarchs lived it?"

Sidney contributed. "It was the common practice — and still is — of the tribal communities of the Middle East. It is not considered a sin. It may be a decisive factor in sending missionaries to those countries eventually. Our people would not know how to deal with such a practice."

Martin put his cup down on the hearth, raised a shaggy eyebrow and studied Joseph. "What do you think of it? You're the prophet."

That meant everything to Joseph. This old friend who had known him as a mere boy was declaring his conviction that Joseph was spokesman for God.

"Martin, you're a wonder! You still remember wiping my nose and giving me a ride in the back of your wagon, and here you are with full confidence in me."

Martin flushed a delicate pink. "Well, we all know you're a prophet. So tell us what you think about having plural wives."

"The men must have had the sanction of God, or they would have been evil men, unworthy of a prophetic calling. Obviously, there have been times men have been commanded to do things that seem wrong. In particular, I think of Nephi under strict commandment of God to slay Laban for the brass plates. I would have been pretty reluctant. I've never killed a man in my life, and hope I never have to. I imagine young Nephi felt the same way. Then too, the Ten Commandments forbid killing. What a difficult problem. It is obvious that, at times, God sanctioned having plural wives."

Father Johnson spoke in his slow deliberate way. "But Jacob in the Book of Mormon condemns it. I just reread that part last Sunday."

Joseph nodded. He had struggled with that too, but the spirit had made it clear. "The key here is obedience to God's commandments. When God commands it, it is right. When He forbids it, it is wrong! Killing is wrong in most instances. However, if the Lord commands it, His is the voice we listen to, for He knows the end from the beginning and what is needful at the moment. Obedience is the consummate commandment, for without it man cannot please God. I don't see any reason why a righteous man might not have more than one wife. I think the abuse of the principle by lustful, greedy men would be repugnant to the Lord. I wouldn't want to deny membership in the Lord's church to . . . say . . . a righteous Turkish man because he had more than one wife."

The men were all silent, staring into the fire, trying to envision the stir that would be made in the church from a man bringing three to ten wives into their modest, straightlaced Christian community. Martin was certain of his wife's reaction. She would probably take her broom and beat the Turk over the head. Sidney thought of Phoebe's gentle, serving nature, but he knew she had her limits. No such man would be welcome in her home, and no plural wife would have the benefit of her friendship. John Johnson pictured Elsa throwing her apron over her head at the sight of such a man and his harem. Joseph imagined Emma, her back straight, her lips pursed, her brown eyes hard. Women didn't have equal rights, even though the constitution promised equality under the law. They could not own property. They could not vote. They could not hold public office. They had cherished customs, however, that made their secondary position and their grueling workload bearable. One of those customs was the honor accorded them by husband and society. A woman's honor was to be fought and died for, if necessary. She was respected for her purity and her tenderness. Motherhood was held up as a position of veneration. The title of wife and mother was the highest title to which most of them aspired. To share her husband with other women would diminish that highly esteemed role and make her little more than chattel.

Finally Sidney spoke. "I think Almighty God has ways we do not understand. Let us hope He recognizes the delicate feelings of our women and never puts us in that position. I'm afraid all hell would break loose in this church if *any* man brought with him a harem of wives."

"I'm afraid you are right," Joseph agreed reluctantly. "But this is the dispensation of the fullness of times. A restoration of *all* things might include some ancient practices which suit us very ill in our day. Is God a changeable god? And under what circumstances does He permit many wives in one time and forbid it in another?"

The men looked at one another. Most of them shook their heads. It was a bucket of worms with which they did not want to fish.

That conversation added fuel to Olmstead Johnson's fire. When he overheard Luke and Lyman discussing it, he assumed the worst. His outrage was immediate, and he quickly leapt to the conclusion his sister Mirinda, who was still living at home, was in danger of being compromised.

"Don't be a jackass, Olmstead," Lyman spoke disdainfully. "Men can discuss the Bible without being as Cain, or Solomon, or Judas."

"Yes, but I wouldn't put anything past Joe Smith."

"Just shut up," Luke was ready to fight. "I've heard that man speak with God's authority. So have you. I've seen him heal others besides our mother. You have too. You're just jealous, jealous and greedy. It begins and ends with the question of the property Father wants to donate to the church. That is all you are really concerned over."

"I care about the blindness of my family. Joe Smith will take every cent we've got and leave us destitute and deserted."

"Joseph Smith can have every cent I've got, any time he wants it," Lyman said defiantly.

Olmstead repeated that conversation with a few changes to everyone he met the next few weeks. When he talked to Simonds Rider, he found a real cohort in crime. Simonds had been a convert a few months back, but when Joseph misspelled his name in a revelation, Simonds decided he was a fallen prophet. A spirit of rebellion possessed him, and he was eager to exaggerate Olmstead's reports. Simonds was a would-be preacher, and now he preached anti-Mormon sermons. But worse damage would be done by another disaffected elder.

Ezra Booth, a former minister, had a tendency to preach his own doctrine instead of principles revealed through Joseph Smith. Soon he was forbidden to preach. That, combined with disappointment in all he had found in Missouri, turned him against the church. He began to write articles for the newspaper, articles attacking the young prophet and labeling him a despot among his own people. More than that, Booth asserted, Smith was tampering with the Holy Bible. After six months of highly inflammatory writing, Ezra had a substantial following ready to believe the worst about Joseph. Booth was the flame that set the county afire.

"Joseph, the children are sick. These measles are bad. I'm hoping we won't spread it to the Johnson family. They have high temperatures too. Will you sleep beside little Joseph tonight on the trundle bed? I'll take care of Julia. I know I'm overwrought. I can't help it. After losing three babies, I couldn't stand it if anything happened to these."

"I know. Adoption is a wonderful thing. We love them as our own."

Emma paused in her preparations for bed and pondered her husband's growing proclivity for philosophical things. When they had first married, she had been far ahead of him in general education and Christian doctrine. Now he had leapfrogged far past her. Of course, she thought, he has had the advantage of time and the tutelage of angels. Still, she wouldn't change a thing. She loved doing exactly what she was doing, caring for their children. As they were now almost a year old, there were fewer demands on her. Miranda Johnson adored children too, and she helped with one or the other twin constantly. Emma was content to glean the distilled truths Joseph had received, as they lay together in the quiet of the night, and he shared the many things on his mind.

There were times lately, as he had been completely submersed in his study of the Bible with Sidney and receiving individual revelations for every brother who asked for direction, that she had felt left out. Where once he had come to her with every worry and every triumph, now he went to Sidney. She was grateful for the influence Rigdon had exerted in their behalf. Certainly he had added respectability to the infant church. Still, she resented sharing her husband, even with him. She was glad each evening when Sidney would pull on his great over-coat and walk back down the road to his own house. Her moments by the dying firelight with Joseph were cherished. It was impossible to be critical of a man who reassured her daily of his love. Every little accomplishment the children made he turned into a compliment to her motherhood. She tried to tell herself she could not be everything to Joseph — a wife, a mother, a scribe — though that was precisely what she wanted. When such thoughts ran through her mind, she would laugh at herself and remind herself she had her mission and he had his.

Emma was uneasy tonight. Perhaps it was because the children had been so sick. She had worried as she saw them grow more and more listless, whimpering or crying aloud with the vexatious measles. Their chests and limbs were bespeckled with red dots. Both had raging fevers. She cuddled Julia against the curve of her body. Joseph worked with little Joseph to keep him in bed. The boy kept trying to climb off the trundle bed, all the while crying piteously.

"I'm afraid we're keeping the whole house awake. Elsa hears every little noise. Simonds Rider was around here today, looking for a biscuit and some milk and asking about you."

"Was he now? What did he want?"

"Wanted to know if you were here or in town."

"Why would I be in town? It's thirty miles."

"Sometimes you go with Father Johnson to town. It's not such a surprising question."

"Well, he didn't seek me out. Sidney and I were just upstairs going over Isaiah. I don't trust Simonds. He's a bit of a bully and very loud in criticism of things he doesn't understand — which is most everything. Now, son, come on, stay under the covers with me. The floor is too cold. We can't have you getting consumption as well as the measles. Now, just lie still, here with Papa."

Emma was visibly worried. "If we can just get them through the night and tomorrow, the measles should all have broken out by then, and they'll start to mend. Joseph, have you ever had the measles?"

"Yep, when I was a boy in Palmyra. Have you?"

"Yes. I must have been about four years old. I don't remember much about it except mother saying later we all got the measles and just about died from them."

They were both silent, thinking of those consequences. Death came so often, in so many disguises, and there was so little they could do about it. The night wore on. The babies fussed themselves to sleep, and Emma and Joseph fell into exhausted slumber too. It was about midnight when Emma roused slightly to the sound of tapping on the window. She listened for a moment, then decided she was mistaken and fell back to sleep. Within minutes, the front door burst open and then the door to their bedroom. Emma screamed. The babies cried. Joseph awakened to a dozen rough hands grasping him by his nightshirt, pinning his kicking legs and binding his flailing arms. Before he was quite awake, he was in the clutches of angry, vindictive men who smelled of liquor and cursed him with every vile name they knew. He tried to jerk free. It was no use. They carried him bodily out of the house, three men on each leg. One whiskied, bearded attacker looking for a hold, grasped him by the hair of the head and whooped with glee when clumps came out in his greedy hands.

"Murder!" Emma screamed. "Murder! Help! O God, help us. Murder!"

Joseph heard her screams and protests as the sharp night air hit him. He managed to kick one of the assailants in the face. The man came up swearing and spurting blood from his nose.

"Damn ye," he cursed. "I'll fix ye!" He seized Joseph by the throat and began to choke him. Joseph saw more and more men gather round the little group that had hold of him. Torches gave off a pungent smell and lit the angry faces with a ghoulish light. They carried him to a cornfield behind the farmhouse. From the corner of his eye he saw Sidney lying stretched out on the cold, damp ground. He was perfectly still. Joseph thought he was dead.

"Sidney!" he called out, but his friend did not answer. In despair, he implored, "Have mercy and at least spare our lives!"

A shout went up. "Mercy! He wants mercy. Call on your God for help, we'll show you no mercy! You are a dead man, Smith. You've been warned. Now your time has come."

One man came carrying a plank. Joseph supposed it was his deathbed.

"Tear off his nightshirt," came the cry. "Simonds, where's the tar bucket."

"Ain't ya gonna kill him?" The voices sounded disappointed.

The ringleaders gathered for counsel. Joseph was still held immobile off the ground, with men holding all four limbs and his head.

He plead once more, "Brethren, I've done you no harm. Spare my life!"

"Ain't he some kind of a 'prophet?' Smith wants us to spare his miserable life! Ain't that a pretty plea? Why don't he save his own life?"

Joseph heard a sharp, nasal voice like Rider's demand, "Eli, where's that tar bucket?"

"Don't know where he left it," another man responded. "He ain't here now."

"I know!" came the gleeful shout. "Bucket's here! Here 'tis! And don't it smell purty? Hey, Smith, you had yer dinner yet? How about a mouthful of this?"

With that, they tried to shove a ladle of hot tar into his mouth. Joseph began to thrash anew with all his might. Every muscle in his body was as taut as a spring. He clenched his teeth, twisted his head to and fro until they gripped his hair and chin and wrenched his head to one side. They beat the ladle against his teeth until his lips were scalded with the tar and his tooth was chipped. Meanwhile, he felt his clothing rip, and his naked skin was exposed to the frosty air. Still, he struggled like a tiger.

All at once, sharp fingernails raked his chest and legs, digging at the flesh. A fiendish cackle rang out over all the other voices. "Hah, hah! That's the way the Holy Ghost falls on folks! It ain't such a holy experience after all, is it? Hey you, pretty preacher boy, how your women gonna like you now?"

At the same time, hot searing tar streamed down on Joseph's chest and belly. A wrenching cry tore from his throat. Then hot tar burned his face. He closed his eyes tightly to keep them clear. It covered his nostrils, and he couldn't open his mouth for fear of the ladle. He was suffocating!

"Come on, boys! We got him where we want him. Do your worst! Where's the knife?"

"We ain't gonna kill him, I said. I ain't gonna be guilty of murder."

"Don't mean to kill him. Got something better in mind. Doc! Where's the doc? Got your scalpel, doc? Let's fix him so's there won't never be no more little Smiths!"

Joseph was stripped naked and stretched and bound on the wooden plank. He was helpless before them. The so-called "Doc" stepped up to his nude body, covered only with smouldering, stinking tar. The crowd fell silent in contemplation of the terrible deed about to be performed. Joseph tried to open one sticky eyelid. Through a mere slit he saw the awful sight of a florid, pudgy man above him, the torchlight glimmering obliquely from the blade of his sharp knife. A strangled cry of pain and horror escaped Joseph, and he lost consciousness.

In what seemed but a moment to Joseph, but was, in reality, almost half an hour, the crowd of men dispersed. Some thought they had killed him and slunk off toward home. Several, including Simonds Rider tramped the road back to his barn, where he passed the bottle and rejoiced that Smith was dead. The doctor put away his knife and refused to perform the dastardly deed. He mounted his horse and rode away in disgust.

When Joseph drifted back into consciousness, he discovered that the ropes which had bound him were not tied very tightly, without his attackers jerking them. He worked at loosing them. His body felt as though it were on fire. The tar had eaten into his raw flesh and blistered it. His scalp was screaming from raw spots of torn out hair.

He pulled the sticky tar away from his nose and lips as well as he could, then staggered to his feet. Off in the distance, he could make out two dim lights. He started toward them. As he neared the house, he could hear crying within. He recognized the cries of the twins and then Emma's voice, lower and softer. The door was locked and bolted. He reached up and pounded twice on the door, falling backward when the door was opened a crack.

"Emma," he croaked, "it's me."

Emma took one look at the ghoulish figure before her. Can this be my husband? she wondered, as she fainted dead away. Miranda and Elsa Johnson were right behind her. They were bending over Emma when Joseph called from outside.

"Throw me a blanket, for the love of decency. They have stripped me naked."

Elsa ran to get a blanket, then threw it out the door. Joseph covered his tortured body, and crawled back to the house. Emma recovered her senses quickly, opened the door, and grasped her husband's black, sticky hand, pulling him indoors. In an agonized voice, she called for lard and camphorated cotton. Joseph lay on an old tanned hide on the kitchen table while his friends, the Johnsons, the Hydes and his wife, scraped the sticky, smelly stuff from his trembling flesh. Some scraped, some scrubbed and everyone prayed. Tears trickled down Emma's face throughout the ordeal.

"Oh, Joseph," she whispered over and over.

It was daylight before they had cleansed his body. When the friends had left with a prayer for his well-being, Emma put Joseph to bed, and he slept fitfully with his raw, scarified body still smelling strongly of camphor.

Joseph awoke groaning in pain. His arm was wet. Still in the throes of exhausted sleep, he thought it was blood. He kept trying to wipe it away. Emma might be frightened of the blood. But each time he wiped the warm wet spot, another drop wet his arm again. He struggled out of sleep and was finally aware it was not blood he was feeling, but his wife's teardrops seeping out even as she slumbered beside him.

Still later, they both arose. Joseph bathed painfully in fresh, clear water, then insisted on putting on his Sunday clothes and preaching as usual to the crowd already gathering. Word had flashed through the little community of Hiram, and almost every citizen was standing in John Johnson's bower. Speculation was rampant. Rumor had it Joseph was maimed beyond recognition. He was crippled for life. He had been cut to ribbons. Tar had destroyed his vocal cords, he would never preach again. Such rumors Joseph wanted to put to rest. So, hurting or not, sick or not, with his hair still black from the residual tar, he put on his best coat and went out to greet his neighbors. Many of them had never been to hear him preach, the prejudice was so great. Many of them believed every lie Ezra Booth and Simonds Rider had published. But every one of them gave credit that day to Smith's courage and determination. He preached on forgiveness and baptized three people that afternoon.

Sidney was not so fortunate. Along with the tarring, they had dragged him by the heels along the rough road and lacerated his skull. He was bedridden for several days and suffered hallucinations for a long time afterward. Yet, Sidney and Joseph had been spared.

There was only one true martyr from that night, and it was neither of the men. Little eleven-month-old Joseph Murdock Smith died three days later from the exposure to cold night air. Emma was disconsolate. She could not be comforted, not by Joseph, nor any of the women who so tenderly tried. Only little Julia's care kept her from returning to the morbid state she had been in after the death of her other children. Continued rumors reached them of more threats on Joseph's life from dissatisfied members of the mob. The thirst for blood was unabated. Joseph and the Johnsons lived in fear of yet another break-in. Their baby son was buried quickly and quietly not far from the Johnson home. Martin dug the grave and Joseph prayerfully consecrated it in God's name. Emma held the little body wrapped in a blanket until she was forced to give it up to the small box. During the prayer, she trembled from the effort of containing her grief, but as soon as it was over, she fell back into Joseph's arms, while Martin and Philo Dibble buried the little casket. They stomped the dirt down and replaced sod, endeavoring to make it as obscure as possible.

That night Joseph broke the news to her that he had to leave.

"It's for your safety as much as my own. What can I do, Emma? I can't stay here any more. You are all in danger, just being near me. Do you understand that? I put the Johnsons in jeopardy and have caused a rift in their family. I know too much about who was responsible for that tarring. It wasn't just Simonds Rider. I'm quite sure both Olmstead and Eli Johnson were involved. I haven't told John. That would be too unkind. Kirtland is still unsafe for me, too. Ezra Booth has turned the whole country against me, writing as a disaffected member of the church. He considers me a despot and the whole plan of the United Order just an effort to steal the property of all my converts. Sidney, Newel, and Peter Whitmer all want to go to Missouri. The saints there have had a struggle, and I promised them I would be back to oversee the church organization."

He talked on and on, justifying to her his leaving. She set her lips and looked at her little Julia asleep in her arms.

"Do you understand what I'm saying?" he asked solicitously.

"Yes."

"Do you understand you and Julia are in danger as long as I'm here?"

"Yes.

"Well then, can you not wish me farewell and God's speed?"

"No!"

"Emma, for the love of heaven, you must realize it is best that I go!"

"Then go!"

"What more can I say to reconcile you to this?"

"Nothing! We married for better or for worse, and when the worst comes, you leave. What do you propose I do? Stay here, knowing full well the Johnson boys hate us and wish us out of their lives? Shall I stay with your parents? They hardly have a bed to sleep on themselves! Our cabin on Morley's farm has been let to two other families. Would you go and leave me, with our third son so recently dead?"

"Newel suggests you stay at his home. There is more than enough room for you and Julia. You've stayed with Elizabeth Ann before. I know you like each other, and you'll be comfortable."

"You know how I hate to be an imposition on people. Elizabeth has not invited me, whatever Newel might tell *you*."

Joseph went to Emma and knelt beside her rocking chair. "You know I wouldn't leave you unless it were absolutely necessary."

She was unmoved. Then he told her about the doctor who had taken pity on him at the last minute during the tarring and refused to perform the operation. She stared at him in horror during this recital. When he had finished, she shuddered and threw her arms around her husband. Her heart had been broken so thoroughly, she wondered if it would ever be whole again, and now when she needed him most, her husband was leaving again. She could face anything with Joseph. Without him she was simply desolate. But this new information was the final straw. She knew it would be selfish to try to hold him here. He was not just hers. As much as she loved him and relied on his radiant spirit, he was not hers. He belonged to the Lord.

Joseph left two days later for Missouri with his friends, after arranging for Emma to be driven to Kirtland to stay with Elizabeth Ann Whitney.

"Elizabeth Ann is too ill to receive you. I am her Aunt Sarah. Who might you be?"

The question came from a tiny wrinkled face which looked like a dried-up apple. Bright, suspicious eyes peered out at the woman with a little child in her arms.

"I'm a friend — Emma Smith. Mr. Whitney has gone with my husband to Missouri and left instructions I am to stay here with his wife for a season. Will you inform Elizabeth Ann I am here?"

"Well, I don't see how Mr. Whitney expects her to entertain guests. She is ill, and in any case, all the beds in the house are in use. I, myself, have to sleep in a trundle in a tiny nook in the attic. I'm afraid there simply would not be room for you and your child. You'll simply have to find lodging elsewhere."

Emma's dull eyes looked beyond Aunt Sarah to the comfortable parlor within. "Please just tell her I am here." Her voice was tired and defeated.

The old aunt closed the door, went to Elizabeth Ann and told her there was a woman wanting shelter. Elizabeth fretted. What should she do? She was duty bound to provide shelter for the immigrants, but Aunt Sarah was a finicky woman.

"If she stays, I cannot, for there is not enough room for all of us. Make up your mind, Elizabeth. Will you put your old Auntie out for a strange woman?"

"No, of course not. Ask her if she hasn't relatives in town she might stay with."

Sarah nodded and returned to the front door.

"Haven't you relatives, young woman? Your first duty is to give them opportunity to take you in. Elizabeth is much too unwell to have any more guests."

Emma looked at Julia who was squirming in her arms. She straightened the little girl's bonnet and blinked back her own tears. No, she would not cry. Not all the sorrow in the world would make her cry in front of this dried-up, old prune of a woman. She would sleep under a tree before occupying the same house.

"Thank you for your kindness," Emma said as she turned back to the wagon where Levi Hancock waited.

"What's wrong?" he asked.

"There is no room at the inn," Emma responded dryly.

"Shall I take you home to my family?"

"No. No, I have imposed on you more than I ever should have just in asking you to drive us so far. Take me down the road to the Cahoon place. Brother and Sister Cahoon are old friends of mine. Perhaps they have room for us."

They arrived at supper time. Reynolds opened the door and immediately stepped forward to put his arm around Emma and help her in.

"See here, Thirza, Sister Smith has come! Emma, are you all right? What are you doing in Kirtland? I thought Joseph was on his way to Missouri."

"He is. He left this morning with Newel Whitney and others. Newel sent me to town to stay with Elizabeth Ann. I just went to her home and found out she is ill and under the care of a maiden aunt who is determined there is no room for me. I know you are crowded here, but would you have a little corner for me and Julia for a few nights. Then I'll find another place."

"Emma, you can stay as long as you like," Thirza consoled her. She quickly set another place at the supper table, while her twelve-year-old daughter took Julia from Emma's arms. Reynolds went out to invite Levi Hancock inside also, but Levi was anxious to return to his own family. The men unloaded Emma's few belongings, and Levi went his way.

Emma collapsed on a small trundle bed which she shared with her active toddler. The baby woke with every footstep on the stairs. When morning came, Emma was just as tired as when she went to bed. She plodded through the next few days, not even trying to be cheerful, just barely surviving each joyless day. When word reached her in-laws, the Smiths, who had settled with the Colesville saints at Thompson just east of Kirtland, that Emma was alone and relying on the kindness of friends, Hyrum came to find her and take her home.

Riding in the wagon with Hyrum, Emma's heartache was opened afresh, for her brother-in-law related his own sad story of the loss of his little bright-eyed, three-year-old daughter, Mary.

"Not Mary!" Emma cried.

"I'm afraid so. We hardly realized she was sick. It all happened so fast. One day she was skipping about the place, when a fever came on . . . . Then . . .," and his voice broke. Hyrum's brow furrowed and his face contorted in an effort to hold back tears. Doggedly he went on, "Then, just days ago, she took a turn for the worse, cried incessantly with stomach pains, and by evening, she drew up into a tiny ball and closed her eyes. She was gone!"

His voice was hoarse, and he wiped at the tears rolling down his cheeks. Emma wept with him, remembrance of little Joseph's death still fresh in her heart. They rode in silence the rest of the way, mourning for the sweet innocence so often taken from their midst. Hyrum's manner reminded Emma of her husband, but he was not Joseph. The past few weeks had been, perhaps, the worst of her life. Her thoughts had gone back more than once to her father's words, "No good will ever come of it." It had been a curse, and it had surely marked her life with Joseph.

Mother Smith was her usual cheerful self and tried her best to raise Emma's spirits. Hyrum's little cabin was too crowded for Emma, and she knew it. Despite their generosity, she could not stay there long. Emma prayed for a solution to her problems and for strength to endure for Julia's sake. There was another incentive to carry on despite her sorrow. She was expecting again. She had not told Joseph. She hadn't been sure at the time, and the tarring had taken precedence over all else, but now there was no question. Emma was overly tired, but this time she had a healthy appetite. Lucy saw to it she ate plenty.

"Finish those turnips. And the milk too. It'll make for a healthy baby."

Emma prayed for that daily. The devastation of having lost four babies never left her. Now she was plagued with terrible thoughts of bearing another child, only to have it die in her arms. Emma meekly obeyed her mother-in-law's orders about her health, resting when directed, eating even when she wasn't hungry. She was protective of her body as never before. A pervasive feeling of vulnerability influenced how she moved and sat, carefully as though she were protecting herself. Emma's worst dream was of a faceless child floating like bubbles on a stream, and she would wake panting, pulling her little Julia closer to her, stroking her hair for a time before being able to go back to sleep.

Julia was a dark-haired little thing, with shiny ringlets and large dark eyes. She could have been Emma's own, blood daughter, and no one in Kirtland ever referred to her as anything else. No mention was ever made of the adoption, even by John Murdock. He visited the Smith home occasionally, and as a friend, would bounce Julia on his knee. If he ever regretted giving his children up to Joseph and Emma, he never showed it. Emma could not have endured it if he had. All the love she wanted to pour out on her other children now centered on Julia. She fairly doted on every step the little girl took and every small syllable she mouthed. Emma coaxed her first efforts and taught her to say, "Papa." Joseph would be so pleased when he came home.

The Smith home was so crowded that she soon sought another arrangement. Frederick G. Williams and Rebecca offered a place with them. Williams was a physician, better educated than most country doctors, and owned a comfortable farm just outside Kirtland township. Rebecca was a large, good-natured woman who seemed to have no trouble bearing or rearing children. She managed them and a large farm with a cheerful, even jolly, hand. She had been disowned by her father when she joined the Mormons, just as Emma had been. So, in that they had common ground. Emma decided to accept their offer, and Hyrum drove her and Julia out to the Williams' farm. It was a much better arrangement. She had a bed. Little Julia had a bed. The hustle and bustle of the farm was good for Emma, and Rebecca took such an optimistic view of everything that Emma's spirit yearned to respond.

Emma received a letter from Joseph, written at the same time Newel wrote his wife. Apparently Joseph thought she was living with Elizabeth Ann, and when he didn't get a return letter when Newel did, he thought Emma didn't care to write. The letter he wrote back was crushing to Emma, who still smarted after being turned away like a beggar from the Whitney home. When she received Joseph's accusing letter, however, all the life seemed to drain out of her.

Dear Wife,
Sister Whitney wrote a letter to her husband which was very cheering, and being very unwell at that time, I was filled with much anxiety. It would have been very consoling to me to have received a few lines from you. But as you did not take the trouble, I will try to be contented with my lot, knowing God is my friend. In Him I shall find comfort. I have given my life into His hands. I am prepared to go at His call. I desire to be with Christ. I count not my life dear to me, only to do His will.

It was a dagger that went straight to the heart of a lonely, depressed wife. Emma sat down that very day and wrote a long letter back to her husband, hiding from him her difficult circumstances and reassuring him of her love and esteem. Still, Emma pondered his letter at length, agonizing over what her husband must be thinking of her. Joseph's esteem was everything to Emma. Like the many followers that felt their spirits lifted by him, she too had come to rely on his radiance. During his absence she contemplated life without him. She dared not let herself dwell on it. Oh Joseph, she thought, I know the kingdom of God is your first responsibility, but surely I have been of comfort to you. If you count your own life not so dear, know that I count it so. Come home, my beloved, come home and find solace in my arms. Our parting was strained, but surely you know I have always loved you, and always shall.

As his absence stretched into two months, Emma grew more and more despondent, covering her feelings only with a thin veil. She passed her time by making her husband new pants and shirt. Only when those were finished did she begin weaving a blanket for the new baby. She also rehearsed Julia in calling out "Papa" for the time when he would arrive.

Emma was in the yard hanging out clothes on a line to dry in the June sunlight when she heard voices. A breeze blew a strand of dark hair across her eyes. Impatiently she swept it away, only to have it fly again in the way of her clear vision. But she didn't need to see. Voices came wafting on the afternoon breeze. She heard his voice, and her whole spirit leapt. She set down her basket of clothes and grabbed Julia's hand.

"Come on, darling. Papa's home! Remember, say 'Papa, papa.' It will make him so happy."

Emma stumbled over the uneven ground, tugging Julia along, almost running to get to the farmhouse. The wind kept whipping her hair around, and she kept brushing it back. Then she stopped. There by the well stood Joseph, watching her run. Was he smiling? Was he happy to see her? No. He wasn't smiling; he was crying! In seconds he swooped toward them like a young eagle and swept them both up in his arms, kissing each one fervently. Julia was screaming her protest instead of calling "Papa." Emma and Joseph laughed and set the little girl down and turned to the important matter of making up.

Chapter Fourteen

Divinely Daring

Joseph paused, gazing at the front of the Whitney store for just a moment. It was a blustery November day. Home had never looked so good, for he had spent the last two months in New York. It had been a distinctly different experience from his trip to Independence, Missouri, but just as necessary. Still, the affairs of the Kingdom did not always blend well with family needs. He looked up. From the upstairs he heard a baby's cry. It was a lusty wail. He dashed inside, bounding up steep steps two at a time, and burst into the northwest bedroom of his wife and newborn child.

"Emma! Emma! I'm here! I'm home! Have we a new baby? Oh Emma, it's a son, and he's fat and healthy! Listen to him cry. He's beautiful and he's strong!" Joseph was so excited that he took the baby from the midwife before she had a chance to wash him off. The boy was squalling vigorously, protesting the trauma of birth. He was still covered with a white film. His little bottom was blotchy from the spat administered just moments before. His facial features were plump, pink, and a little distorted from a long, hard birth, but he was beautiful to his father and obviously healthy.

"You've done it this time, Emma. This is a perfect child."

Emma looked up at her husband. His face was aglow with happiness and the chilling ride from Fairport on a November day. He had just come in a carriage from the dock, having cut short his trip to New York in an attempt to be home for the birth of his child. His cheeks were flushed, his hair windblown, and he carried with him the refreshing smell of autumn. He was robust and vibrant, exuding enthusiasm for life. His wife was exhausted.

It had been a very hard labor for Emma. She had started her pains the previous morning and labored more than twenty-four hours. Rebecca Williams and Elizabeth Morley had attended her, with Frederick checking on her progress every few hours. Now, after hours of pain, her lower back felt as though it were broken, and she was completely drained.

But the birth was successful. She could hear the baby still protesting loudly, even while Joseph proudly displayed their son to the two friends cleaning up the birthing bed. She heard her husband laughing and talking to the boy. She heard it all as through a fog. Then Joseph was beside her, kneeling to kiss her cheek and her perspiring forehead. Tears of simple fatigue slipped from the corners of her eyes.

She whispered, "You're here. Oh Joseph, I've prayed you here."

"I know. I saw you in a dream. I came as soon as Newel could finish purchasing the goods. We left the same day we signed for the merchandise. I was so afraid I wouldn't make it in time. Emma, dearest, what a wonderful thing you have done. Three times you have gone through this terrible pain. This time we have a living child. I have a feeling this boy will live long and be a great blessing to us all the years of our lives."

He gave the baby to Rebecca and remained beside his wife. He could see she was spent. She scarcely moved a finger or turned her head at his voice.

"Emma, can you hear me?"

"Yes," was her weak reply.

"Do you know I love you? I see your sacrifices for me and for God's work. I do not take for granted all you have suffered for our sakes. You are the foundation of my life, though God is the tower, and

I call down a blessing from heaven for you to regain your health and energy quickly. This time we have a vigorous little boy who will delight our hearts. I'm so happy for you, for us."

Emma's hand was enveloped by Joseph's larger one, and she was content to lie quietly, gaining strength from him. When Rebecca had washed the wailing infant and wrapped him in a soft blanket, his protests weakened. Then she brought him to Emma and laid him on her breast. His cheek was soft against her skin, and she smiled for the first time at seeing his bright eyes, peering out from the blanket.

"He looks like you," she said.

"Oh no! He's far too beautiful to look like me. He is your spitting image."

Rebecca spoke up. "Well, if you ask me, he looks just like the little piggy my Susan bought from Luke Johnson. Same little pushed up nose and greedy mouth."

Joseph laughed. "Looks like me, huh?"

"You said it. I didn't!" Rebecca laughed and went back to her business.

The little Smith family now lived upstairs over the Whitney store. Newel's full time was devoted to his work as bishop, directing the business of the storehouse, and managing the settlement and relocation of the converts arriving every day. He didn't have time to also run his mercantile business. So Joseph, feeling that the church members still needed a general store, decided to go into business himself. Newel had all the experience and contacts in ordering goods. Since those contacts were primarily in New York, the two men had gone in October to make the arrangements.

It had been an eye-opening experience for the young prophet. He frequently wrote to Emma the feelings of his heart. "The thoughts of home, of Emma and Julia rush upon my mind like a flood, and I wish for a moment to be with them. My breast is filled with all the feelings and tenderness of a parent and a husband, and could I be with you, I would tell you many things."

He spent most days walking about New York, while Newel was negotiating with suppliers. At night, he would return to his hotel room to meditate and think of home and family. He shared many impressions with Emma through his letters. She had waited eagerly for them. They were her only link to him for that month, and as her pregnancy had worn on, she had longed for his vitality and affection.

On October thirteen, Joseph wrote his impression of the crowded metropolis of New York. "I have been walking through the most splendid part of the city. . . . The buildings are great and wonderful to the astonishing of every beholder. The language of my heart is like this: can the great God of all the earth, maker of all things magnificent and splendid, be displeased with man for all these great inventions sought out by them? My answer is no. It cannot be, seeing these works are calculated to make men comfortable, wise, and happy. Therefore, not for the works can the Lord be displeased. Only against man is the anger of the Lord kindled, because they give Him not the glory. Therefore, their iniquities shall be visited upon their heads, and their works shall be burned up with unquenchable fire."

He continued on to say that iniquity was imprinted on nearly every face he saw, and only their fine dress made them appear beautiful. Contemplating all this, he had called up memories of his truly beautiful wife, the clear, pleasant expression of her face. The night before he had gone away, they sat together before the fire, their daughter on Emma's lap, the little girl asleep while dark ringlets fell in damp disarray against her temples. It was a tender picture in Joseph's mind and far more precious than all the worldly display around him.

He also became more aware of the national events unfolding. Everywhere he and Newel went, discussions about the tariffs were heated. South Carolina was threatening to secede if attempts were made to enforce the federal tariffs of 1828 and 1832. John C. Calhoun was arguing for sovereignty of the states if they decided a federal regulation was unconstitutional. South Carolina had so decided and rejected the tariffs. Joseph's focus had been on spiritual matters for so long, he had paid little attention to national events. With time on his hands in the hot-bed of political affairs, he looked about him and saw the tumultuous condition of his country's affairs.

"Will South Carolina secede?" was the question of the day. Joseph received his own answer shortly after arriving back home in Kirtland. On Christmas day of 1832, with his son just a month old, and Emma newly recovered from childbirth, Joseph recorded the impending conflict as a scourge upon his country and correctly predict that it would begin in South Carolina.

The major base for Kirtland's economy was the continual influx of new converts. Three of those converts came to Kirtland on November 8, 1832, just two days after the birth of young Joseph Smith III. Emma was still exhausted with the effort of childbirth and recuperating at home under the no-nonsense eye of her dear friend, Rebecca Williams. Meanwhile, Joseph was in the nearby woods working with his brothers cutting trees and hauling logs. Three men ventured out to meet him. Brigham Young, of Mendon, New York had read a copy of the *Book of Mormon* left at the home of his brother-in-law, John P. Greene. He was at first fascinated, then converted, and once convinced of its truth, went straightway to Canada and presented it to his older brother, Joseph Young, who was a Methodist minister on assignment there. The same book was read by the Young brothers and then given to their cousin, Heber C. Kimball. All three men were amazed that God would bring forth new scripture and raise up a prophet in their day.

The prophet wiped a sweaty, grimy hand on his trousers and extended it to first Brigham, then the other two men. "How do you do. I'm happy to meet you brethren. Where have you come from?"

"Lately from Canada," Brigham replied. "I, however, have been living in Mendon, New York. Your brother, Samuel, left a *Book of Mormon* in our area. Many of our family have read it. Mr. Smith, I can tell you I have never read anything with the exception of the Holy Bible that so clearly teaches the word of God. If God sent this book through you, you must be a prophet."

At five feet eight inches, Brigham was half a head shorter than Joseph, but he was rock solid. Joseph looked into his hazel eyes and knew he had a faithful friend. The men stood for a moment talking, then Joseph started to turn back to his work, but true to character, invited them to his home for more conversation.

"You'll be needing lodging, brethren. Stay with me. I live here in town over the general store. My wife just recently gave birth to our son, but if you can wait for me to finish up here, you'll be more than welcome in our home."

Emma was not even up and about yet and totally dependent on Rebecca and Elizabeth Ann Whitney to help her care for Julia and her home. The birth had taken much away from her natural energy. More than anything else she craved time alone with her husband. She lay in their bedroom in the northwest corner of the second floor. It was roomy and bright, but she was restless, waiting for Joseph. The baby fussed for his feeding. Emma snuggled him into bed with her and with satisfaction noted her milk was coming in. He seemed more satisfied with every feeding. Once he latched on and was nursing vigorously, she closed her eyes in pleasure over this feisty baby boy. Sometimes when he slept longer than usual, she would go and peer at him in his cradle to make sure he was still alive and breathing. Life was perfect at that moment. She had her husband back, they had their privacy, and they had a healthy son. She sighed with contentment and drifted off to a light sleep.

A short while later, hearty voices broke into her tranquility. Emma heard her husband in the store downstairs saying, "There's so much needed here in Kirtland, a printing office, a schoolhouse, a mill. We can't keep up with the needs of the saints, and I am faced with sending our best men on missions with nothing but a few books in their knapsacks and a blessing on their heads. Still, it has been success-ful. You're here, aren't you?"

Who was he talking to? Then she heard Joseph's footsteps on the stairs. But wait, there were others! It sounded like a herd of buffalo to her. The conversation didn't stop. Deep voices asked questions, and Joseph was going on about relations in town between members and non-members. She heard Rebecca protesting the intrusion, and Joseph thanking her for her concerns and inviting friends upstairs anyway. There was shuffling and scraping at the top of the stairs, then footsteps going in the direction of the parlor. Joseph opened her door and came in.

"Are you rested, Emma? How is our baby? Still sleeping a lot?"

"Joseph, have you brought home company?" The expression in her voice was incredulous.

"I have. Three brethren from New York and Canada came into the woods to meet me today. They are newly arrived with no place to stay, so I invited them here."

She started to protest, but he hurried on. "I've already thought about where to put them. You don't need to fret. I'll help them. You won't have to do anything. I insist you stay down and rest."

"Joseph!"

He looked at her in surprise. "What's wrong?"

"What's wrong? This is! This is all wrong. You've been gone for a month, our son is only two days old. You've been cutting wood yesterday and today. I thought we might have just a little time together. Could you not have found another place for them to stay until I am properly able to care for guests?"

He was disappointed. Emma rarely chastised him. Perhaps he had been thoughtless. His countenance fell, and he looked so dejected Emma softened her tone.

"It's just that I want to be as hospitable as you are, but I can't right now. Months from now will I hear secondhand that three men came to my home, and I was too lazy to get out of bed and care for their needs?"

"No, dear, of course not! They know the circumstances. They all have families of their own and understand these things."

Emma was dejected. She had looked forward to the evening with Joseph and the children. Now it was stolen from her. She couldn't have felt more the sense of being robbed if a thief had broken in and taken her things. He always seemed to need other people around, but she needed some peace and quiet. Emma could bear heavy burdens as long as her inner soul could find peace somewhere. For her that peace was in the love of her husband.

"How long will they stay?" she asked woodenly.

"I'm not sure. Probably just a few days. You'll like each of them very much, Emma. Once you have rested and are on your feet again, you'll see what fine fellows they are. Brigham is a rock. I have already seen he'll be a staunch supporter, and the other two as well."

Emma closed her eyes, shutting out her husband's cheery, healthy glow. "Never mind about me," she acquiesced and waved him away from her bedside. "Go see to your guests. I'll sleep awhile. Rebecca has stew in the pot and warm biscuits in the oven."

He bent to kiss her cheek, but she turned over, so he kissed his son instead. "I won't be up late," he promised and slipped out the door.

Joseph was wrong. She didn't like Brigham at all. She could hear him in the parlor talking incessantly. He was a fervent admirer of Joseph's accomplishments. He could talk faster and longer than her husband, and his opinions were fervently stated. He did, however, listen closely to Joseph's rehearsal of the church's history up to the present date. Then he started in on his observations of Kirtland. She dozed off while Joseph was explaining the gifts of the spirit. She woke again, with a start, when the sounds of singing came from the other room. The walls were thin, and she thought for a moment the men were right at the foot of her bed. The baby woke and started to cry.

Then she started to cry, too, and prayed fervently for the strangers to go away, leaving her in peace with her newborn baby and her too sociable husband.

Weeks later when she finally regained enough energy to maintain her house again, Emma found she actually did like Heber Kimball very much. He was an unassuming man, willing to be taught, thoughtful of her and her situation. He had a slight problem with stuttering when he was agitated and consequently underestimated his great personal qualities. His warm, brown eyes twinkled with good humor, and he played with little Julia while Emma tended the new baby. That won her heart immediately. I hope his wife is as pleasant, Emma thought. We might be excellent friends if she is.

Emma had many admirers but few friends. Rebecca was closest to her heart. Elizabeth Ann was another. When she had learned of her aunt's treatment of Emma, she was mortified. Her husband had offered Emma shelter precisely because he knew his wife loved her as a sister and would be glad to share her home. Aunt Sarah had known nothing of the arrangement and never told Elizabeth the name of the homeless woman she had sent away. When Newel returned with Joseph, Elizabeth Ann was simply horrified to learn it had been Emma. She could not do enough to make it up to her. Emma tried to assuage her embarrassment and made it a point to ask her advice over all matters pertaining to the store.

Joseph's general store proved to be a tremendous blessing for the saints — and a tremendous burden for the Smiths and the Whitneys. As she regained her strength, Emma became not only the mother of an infant and a toddler, but a shopkeeper as well. Joseph was an easy touch. Members came to the store in serious want, and he could refuse no one. They had precious little money, and most people wanted goods on credit. Little by little the store goods were "loaned" out, and Joseph had no money to purchase replacements. The Whitneys still had the larger stake in it, with Newel's good name on the line with his suppliers.

Emma finally persuaded Joseph to let her run the store while he did other things. The other things he did consisted of opening a sawmill and a tannery. Unfortunately, despite the many warnings from his wife and friend, Newel, he operated them the same way. The members considered him a generous, first rate fellow. They loved him and were as devoted to him as he was to them. But they still didn't have money to pay their debts.

The people of Kirtland regarded Emma with considerable awe. To be married to the prophet was a great honor. She looked and acted regal, and it inspired respect in all who met her. Beyond that, it was Emma who sacrificed to satisfy the needs of the people. Joseph would welcome them to their home, but in short order, he would be involved in other things, correspondence, petitions, plans for building, or Bible revisions. Emma would be the one who went to her own larder and filled a basket of food for the needy families. She gave away blankets, newly woven, and socks just knitted. Her tireless efforts on their behalf were legendary, and the whole town rejoiced when little Joseph III was born healthy.

"Brother Williams, Brother Rigdon, the Lord has called us to come before Him in mighty prayer, and He will show us a new temple to be built. Not just in Missouri, but here too, in Kirtland. The church is moving forward, brethren. The saints in Zion need a temple, and the church in Ohio is just as much in need. It will be a house of prayer, a house of fasting, a house of faith, a house of learning, a house of glory, a house of order, a house of God."

It was December, 1832, and Joseph had been thinking of a temple for months. It seemed an impossible task, considering the poverty of the saints. He had been fasting for days about it. Emma would wake at five o'clock to find her husband already awake, pondering and praying. This morning he was up before she, lighting the little stove in their room.

"What is so on your mind that you are already up and about?"

"Just a thought which has been recurring for weeks."

"A thought?"

"Well, a plan."

"What is this plan?"

He paced the floor for several minutes, barefooted and in his nightshirt. Finally, he stopped and looked at his wife.

"Would you think me crazy if I told you we are supposed to build a temple here in Kirtland?"

She stared at him through the darkened room. "How?"

"How?"

"Yes, how? We can hardly keep up with building simple homes for all the converts. We can't cut enough trees, or make enough bricks. People are living on top of one another, and your empty store can attest to the fact that none of them have money. How will we build a temple? Out of what?"

"We'll build it on faith, Emma! We have a brickyard. The Israelites made bricks for the Egyptians with less means than we have. The wood we can cut and finish for benches, pulpits and doors. The church can't meet forever out in the bowery, Emma, under the open sky. And we are too many to meet in any home, no matter how large. I need to be able to speak to all the members, not just a few in one place and a few in another. It takes all my time going from one small meeting to another just to keep the people spiritually fed. This temple will serve many purposes, as well as being a house that the Lord Himself can visit."

Common sense told Emma such a task was herculean, but when Joseph conceived a plan he would not be reasoned out of it. Faith was his forte and vision his tool. He was divinely daring, while others were earthbound. No task was beyond his means when he was working for the Lord.

"Take it to the people," was her advice.

"I will. But before that, I'll take it to the Lord. He'll show me what to do."

"Then it will get done." She considered it a matter of fact, for she had implicit faith in Joseph's inspiration.

Thus he called in his two new counselors in the presidency of the High Priesthood. Sidney Rigdon and Frederick Williams spent the day with Joseph in fasting and prayer. The result was more than they had expected. The three men were on their knees in prayer when all three of them saw in vision a building as though at a distance. After several minutes, the building seemed to come right over them so as to afford a perfect view of the inside as well as the outside. The inner court was sixty-five feet long and fifty-five feet wide and one hundred and ten feet to the dome. They saw two floors with two pulpits, one at each end of the main floor, and row after row of benches. The outside of the building glistened as though a million jewels shone from its mortar. It was more beautiful by far than anything they had previously imagined.

When the vision receded, Sidney and Frederick were weak from the experience. Joseph was excited.

"Some have thought we should build with wood. I knew the Lord had something better in mind for us. You don't erect a log house for the temple of God. We must set our sights higher, brethren. Nothing is too good for our God."

If Sidney and Frederick wondered about the means to accomplish such a fantastic building, they didn't voice objections. The vision was altogether convincing. They had all three seen the same thing. They knew what had to be done. But where to start?

Joseph continued, "We need someone with building experience — an architect, a stone mason. I have heard of such a man in Canada, Mr. Artemus Millet, a recent convert. We must bring him to Kirtland. He has considerable resources and is just the man who can build the Lord's temple the way we have seen it.

"The next thing to do is to call capable supervisors to help him. I have Levi Hancock and Truman Angell in mind. Also, Brigham says he will stay and work on the temple, even if he never gets a morsel of bread for doing so."

Levi Hancock responded to Joseph's invitation to meet at his home. He brought with him his niece, Fanny Alger. Joseph had mentioned that Emma was having a hard time caring for their two little children and accommodating the constant visitors graciously. When people came to visit with him, to consult, to study, to complain, or even to help, as Sidney and Frederick did, she had to provide food. She rarely cooked for fewer than a dozen men, and in wet weather she constantly swept and mopped the floor as snow and mud were tromped in. Besides being hostess, Emma ran the general store as well. She was clearly stretched too thin. And she was thin. She was ramrod straight and thinner now than when Joseph had first married her. A permanent frown line had appeared in her brow, giving evidence to the burdens she carried.

Levi's niece, Fanny, was a gentle young woman who loved children. She was looking for work. Her parents had a large family, and when they all joined the church, Fanny went to stay with Levi's family to relieve the cramped conditions in her parents' home. Having her now stay with the Smiths seemed to Levi like a perfect solution to Sister Emma's problems.

"Joseph, this is my niece, Fanny Alger." Levi introduced them. "I've been thinking she might be of help to Emma, and she needs a place of her own to stay."

Joseph shook hands. She was almost timid, hardly daring to look at him.

"Fanny, I'm pleased to meet you. Is that arrangement agreeable to you?"

Now she lifted her eyes to his, and her lips formed a silent "yes." She had light brown hair and large hazel eyes. She was a very simple young woman, yet there was something special about her. Joseph sensed it immediately.

He also sensed she would be more comfortable with Emma. "Well then, Miss Alger, we should consult my wife." Then he turned away from the girl and called upstairs to his wife. "Emma, oh Emma, dear! Come down. Levi is here. He has brought someone to meet you."

He could hear her starting down the stairs. "Won't you sit? When did you join the church, Miss Alger?"

She took off her bonnet and sat primly. Her voice was clear as a tinkling bell. "Almost two years ago. My parents and siblings all joined. Our home here in Kirtland is so small I've been living with Uncle Levi's family. I'm perfectly willing to do any kind of work to earn my keep. I just want to be in Kirtland with the saints."

Joseph studied the young woman and thought her very sensible and sweet. Emma appeared at the bottom of the stairs carrying the baby. She approached her guests and held out a hand to Levi, then to Fanny. She was introduced.

"Welcome, Fanny. You come from a stalwart family. Your Uncle Levi is my husband's most trusted friend."

"Sister Smith," Hancock began, "knowing how pressed you are to keep up with the store, the visitors, the cooking, cleaning, children. . . well, all that is required of you as the prophet's wife . . . I . . . or we wondered if you might have need of a young woman to help with all those chores. Fanny, here, has left her parents' home, and she needs a place to stay. She's been staying with us, but my wife thought she might be a godsend to you."

Emma regarded Fanny pleasantly. She was probably capable enough, but did she want someone permanently living with them? She had precious little time alone with Joseph as it was. On the other hand, having another woman around to tend the children and take over some of the chores might give her more time with her husband.

"We do have a little spare room, but it is frequently taken up by visitors. You might have to be content with sleeping on a cot in an upstairs nook. How would that suit you?"

Sunshine broke over Fanny's clear countenance. She had felt like a burden to her uncle. If she could be of help here — to the prophet! and his wife! — it would be the answer to her prayers. Surely, in time, she would get over the feeling of awe in his presence.

"I would be so grateful, Sister Emma! I love children! And I would be honored to be a part of your family."

Emma looked at Joseph. He sat in the corner watching the whole exchange with a sober expression.

"What do you think?" she asked.

"It is up to you, my dear. If you need the help and don't mind adding someone to our little family circle, I am agreeable."

"Oh, I believe I can make a little room." Emma had brightened considerably, just anticipating a little help with her chores.

Joseph stood and motioned to Levi. "Let's go up to the parlor. I have a special calling for you. I want you to assist Artemus Millet. He is coming here from Canada to take charge of building a house of the Lord which we shall soon erect."

After the men left the room, Emma took the baby to Fanny. "Here, you should meet little Joseph. Julia is just as dear, and sleeps a little more than her brother."

A chill ran through Emma, and she shivered. It was a cold January. Her blood was thinner than it used to be. As Fanny took the baby, Emma thought, Oh to be so young and fresh again. She's probably never cold or tired. Am I doing right? Will I be sorry for this decision? But she shook off the doubts and allowed herself the pleasure of the young woman's company.

They talked for some time while the men were upstairs. Fanny readily told the story of her conversion. It started with the copy of *The*

Book of Mormon her uncle had loaned them. Then, the more she heard stories of the Prophet Joseph, and the gathering of the saints, the greater her desire had grown to be a part of it all. After their family settled in Kirtland, she decided to strike out on her own, confident the Lord would bless her for her faith and testimony.

Emma smiled. "And He will, my dear. God always blesses us when we do what is right. Fanny, have your uncle help you gather up your things and plan on moving in here tomorrow. I'll make room for you upstairs. I'm sure we'll become great friends."

Emma slept fitfully that night. Perhaps it was the barren limbs of the tree outside scratching the window that kept her awake half the night. Joseph slept deeply beside her with an arm often thrown over her possessively. She awoke several times, listening for the children's cries. But no, though they made little sucking or gurgling sounds, they both slept peacefully. Well before dawn, she fell asleep at last and dreamed a strange and disturbing dream.

She heard hounds in her sleep, baying and panting, and she saw men dashing through a forest following the lead of the dogs. She seemed to stand concealed in the shadows of a tree and was undetected as the hunting party went storming past her. She was dimly aware that somewhere in the tangle of the woods, Joseph ran before the dogs. Then, to her horror, the hounds changed to wolves. Joseph came to stop at a dark, wide river, and she could see him pause before the black waves, then turn to face the onrushing wolves.

Emma tried to call out to him, but he could not hear her. She tried to run to him, but seemed rooted to the spot. Then, like ghostly shadows, women appeared, moving through the trees. They glided toward Joseph, leading the deadly hunting party right to him, and then surrounded him, even while the wolves leapt and nipped at his feet and hands.

"Run, Joseph, run," Emma called to her husband. In her dream she saw him on his knees with the wolves attacking. The phantom women swayed and wailed but did nothing to drive the animals away.

Joseph cried and reached out to her, pleading for help. But, though her heart was wrenched with pain, she couldn't go to him. She stood immobile and watched him slowly sink beneath the onslaught of the wolves.

In her sleep, as in her dream, she wept, and her pillow was damp and cool beneath her cheek. Still she slept, as though captive to the fearsome vision. Hatred for the women rose and filled Emma's whole being. They turned vacant eyes in her direction, while Joseph lay dead at their feet. Emma shook off the inertia that bound her and drove herself toward her husband's body. The ghostly women faded back. She was about to clasp his lifeless form in her arms when an angel appeared, separating them with a drawn sword. Sunlight gleamed from it so brightly she had to shield her eyes.

He advanced until he overshadowed her, and she shrank back. She knew the mighty sword would fall upon her own head.

"Slay the wolves that have killed my husband!" she begged.

"Thou art the one," he censured.

"No," she whimpered.

"You have brought him to this end," the angel indicted her.

"No," she wept anew.

The ghostly women chanted, "Thou, thou, thou hast done this thing."

Emma awoke with a start, the terrible chant still ringing in her head, and her heart filled with absolute dread. Joseph still slept peacefully at her side, and she sat up in bed studying the strong profile of the face she loved so well. I would never, never bring him to such an end, she thought, soothing her frayed nerves. But the sense of dread remained, with the puzzle of wolves and the shadowy women.

Later that January, Joseph began the School of the Prophets. He hired a man to enclose a room upstairs directly over the kitchen below. The room was small, only eleven by fourteen feet in size, but it was his

403

delight. He could get away from the activities of the house and study there and meditate. When it was ready, he dedicated and consecrated the room to the Lord.

From that time, the School of the Prophets commenced. Only men who were specially invited were allowed to come. Attendance was preceded by fasting. At the end of the study time, they broke their fast by partaking of the sacrament. During that winter, Joseph made much use of their time in preparation for missions and for leadership. Besides spiritual instruction they learned grammar, penmanship, arithmetic, and geography. He had felt the lack of education in the past and wanted his people to be learned. Ignorance was not of God. Brigham Young was especially anxious to be a part of this school, as he was completely uneducated and could not even spell his own name. He was an apt pupil, too. The favorite lesson time came when Joseph spoke to the school about faith and knowledge. It was a subject that fascinated him. He believed the scripture, "If any man lack wisdom, let him ask of God." It guided his life. It was the moving force behind all his revelations. Man should strive to understand as much as humanly possible. If faith could move mountains, as the scriptures said it could, he wanted to know how, and its relationship to knowledge. So he spent much time in reasoning and contemplation. All he discovered he shared with his brethren and compiled his thoughts into seven lectures on faith.

Emma's home was the very center of the church, the school, and the daily needs of the people. There was almost constant traffic through her home. She was accustomed to this by now. One thing, however, to which she could not accustom herself was the obnoxious mess made by men gathered for hours in the small room above her kitchen. Although engaged in weighty spiritual discussions, the men had habits revolting to Emma.

"Is that a tobacco streak on my wall? Look, Fanny, up towards the ceiling. It is! It is! Brown streaks, and I bet I know where they are coming from. Someone can't hit the spittoon! I've cleaned up around the spittoon as often as I can stand it. Joseph simply must do something about it."

Fanny looked up and shook her head in disgust. "I'm sure you're right. They just don't realize how awful the tobacco habit is."

"Well, if Joseph can't convince them, I can. I'll give them each a bucket of water, some lye soap and put them to cleaning up after themselves. I don't intend to do it anymore."

Fanny started to say, "I could . . ."

Emma interrupted shortly, "No, you can't. The men must learn some manners."

Fanny had been a great help and Emma was quite pleased with her decision to take the girl in. The children loved her already, and so did Emma. It was quite impossible not to, for she was sweet and accommodating and always ready to help. She studiously avoided being with Joseph alone and never flirted with him as some of the giddy women in town did. Emma was as fond of her as she had been of her own sister. She felt herself regaining strength as Fanny took over many of the chores. Emma even had time to sew a new dress. It was a task she enjoyed. Her needlework was a source of pride. Her stitches were perfectly even and small. With more time to sew, she worked on shirts and pants for the missionary effort, and wove heavy woolen cloaks for them to take. It was often their only cover as they slept in barns and under the stars.

Later that day Emma confronted her husband. "Joseph, we have three spittoons in that room and still the men make a mess. It looks and smells like a pigsty. Now, just look." She took him by the arm and ushered him into the kitchen. "My new kitchen! And look at this brown dribble on the wall! It's revolting! Would you like me to talk to the men, or will you?"

She was eye to eye with him and unflinching. She would do it. He decided his friends would rather hear it from him than her. They all admired her. They trusted and loved her for all she did. Still, a reproof from her could be stinging.

"I'll do it."

"When exactly?"

"Tomorrow."

"Today!"

"Yes, dear, today!" Then a thought hit him. "Emma, I think there may be a greater principle here than tobacco juice on your wall. I need some time to ask the Lord."

She raised an eyebrow. "Hmm. Well, soon, or I will talk to them."

"You won't have to."

The next day he gave the brethren counsel "adapted to the capacity of the weak and the weakest of all saints, who are or can be called saints." He knew it wouldn't be popular, but he was also certain it was God's counsel.

"In consequence of evils and designs which do and will exist in the hearts of conspiring men in the last days, I have warned you, and forewarn you, by giving unto you this word of wisdom by revelation — That inasmuch as any man drinketh wine or strong drink among you, behold it is not good, neither meet in the sight of your Father . . . Strong drinks are not for the belly but for the washing of your bodies." (Excerpt Doctrine and Covenants, Section 89)

The men looked at Joseph. What was wrong with wine? They used it for the sacrament, for goodness sake. Even Jesus drank wine. Was this Joseph, or the Lord, speaking? Joseph went on:

"Tobacco is not for the body, neither for the belly, and is not good for man, but is an herb for bruises and all sick cattle, to be used with judgement and skill."

They looked at each other. He couldn't be serious. All the saints used tobacco, at least the men did. It was one of their little pleasures in life, and the custom went back to their ancestors.

"But Joseph!" Martin began.

"It's from the Lord," the prophet said firmly.

"But Joseph!" Sidney exclaimed.

"It's from the Lord!"

"Well, is He sure?" Martin asked after a moment of silence.

Joseph was stern. "It is a sure 'word of wisdom.' Any one of you think you are wiser than the Lord?"

"Jesus drank wine," Williams pointed out.

"He didn't get drunk."

"No, but He drank it."

"The Lord said there are evil designs in the hearts of men in the last days. Those designs will be the complete undoing of many of the saints. This word of wisdom will set our people apart and keep their bodies pure."

The room dissolved into a babble of voices. "I don't like it and the saints won't like it."

"You can't expect a man to give up all pleasures in this life."

"Is it a commandment? Do we really have to live it?"

"Go back to the Lord. Ask again."

"No. I did that once. He taught me that perfect obedience is necessary for exaltation. Do you brethren want to be exalted? You have to live by every word proceeding out of the mouth of God. If you want to go where God is, you have to be clean every whit. Just look at you! Martin, your beard is a mess from tobacco. Sidney, I've seen you take more than just the sacramental wine. Can you picture walking and talking with the Savior like that?"

There was embarrassed silence. Finally Hyrum warned, "This will be harder for our people than the law of consecration."

Joseph nodded in agreement. "But this is nothing, Hyrum." The commandment of the restoration of ancient principles seemed to blaze through his mind. "There is so much more the Lord has to teach us. We are still babies in the doctrines of the kingdom. He can't reveal it all at once, so He is teaching us little by little, line upon line, precept upon precept. We must learn to live it all as quickly as we can so He can teach us more. There are revelations to come which will really test your faith and commitment. Those who wash out over this 'word of wisdom' would never stand the trials to come."

After a moment, Hyrum asked, "Did Emma have anything to do with this?"

The prophet just laughed.

Joseph stood at the bottom of the stairs looking up. Fanny was coming down. She stepped carefully since the steps were so steep. He turned back and busied himself by the hearth. He knew — had known for weeks — that God had a reason for sending her here, and that reason filled him with dread.

"Fanny, are you happy here?" he asked somberly as she descended the last stair.

"Yes. Yes, sir," she answered politely.

"Have you thought of marriage? You are old enough you know. Many girls your age are already mothers."

She nodded. "I have thought of it."

"And what kind of a man would you marry?"

"He would need to be just like you."

"Why?"

"I want a man of God, like you. One who will love me as you love Sister Emma. One who will love our children and make a happy home."

"Have you anyone in mind?" he asked gravely.

She shook her curls. "No. I am content here with your family."

He still poked at the fire. "Maybe you need to marry and start one of your own."

She started and drew back quickly. "Please, no! I haven't any marriage prospects. I feel I belong here. I'm working hard. Sister Emma needs me — and likes me — and so do the babies."

"I'm sure they do. We all do."

"Then what more should I do?"

He turned away. "Nothing, Fanny. Don't change a thing."

Joseph walked out into the spring morning and started up the hill to the temple site. He had marked it out just a few weeks before. He had meant to get started on it, but had spent much of his time lately between the School of the Prophets and the civil courts. He had been summoned almost a dozen times to answer frivolous charges — stealing, rabble rousing, drunkenness. None of them was substantiated. Even the accusers knew they were false. The judge in Amherst was growing weary of seeing Joseph in his courtroom. At his last courtroom appearance, charges had been dismissed after ten minutes. Still, it took his whole day to travel, appear, and answer any kind of formal charges. He was very frustrated. The temple needed to be started, and he was wasting his time and the Lord's in Judge Hascom's court.

Sidney had arrived before Joseph and was pacing off the perimeters of the temple.

"How do you see the layout, Joseph?"

The young prophet took a stick and drew in the dirt a blueprint of the outside wall, then another diagram of the inside configuration. "Like this."

Sidney studied it. "Yes, that is what I remember also."

Joseph mused, "Remember how it glistened?"

"I remember. We need to get started. It's spring. The weather is warming up. The temple will help unify the people."

"I know." Joseph rubbed his forehead. "My mind has just been all a muddle lately. I haven't even been able to work on the revision of the Bible."

"I know. I've been wondering . . . ."

Joseph had to talk to someone. "Sidney, have you thought any more about Abraham and plural marriage?"

Rigdon looked at him strangely, his bushy eyebrows knitted together. "No, not much. It was just a practice of ancient people."

"Why do you suppose the Lord countenanced it?"

"Expedience, probably. They were always on the move. Their families were their kingdoms. There was no limit to land, so they could have as many children as they wanted and still have room enough for all. The children grew up and helped protect them from other tribes."

"Is that all? Do you think it was just practical? The Lord always has a spiritual reason for things."

"You see the spiritual side of every question, Joseph. Some things are just practical."

"No, Sidney. To God everything, *everything* is spiritual. Even the temporal is spiritual."

"So what is the spiritual reason for the practice?"

"I don't fully understand yet. But what I do understand scares me."

Sidney looked at him in surprise. "It scares you?"

"Yes. It is strong meat, and I fear the saints will not be able to choke it down."

"What are you thinking, Joseph?"

Worry lines had begun to deepen around the young prophet's eyes. "Sidney, I think . . . I really think . . . we may have to live the principle some day."

Rigdon was astounded. He didn't answer. The thought was overwhelming.

"I think it all has to do with our eternal natures. Our spirits come from God and are capable of expanding, effulgent love. Not just for our wives and children and a few good friends. Our very natures are permeated with love. If I let my spirit soar, it would encompass the whole earth and wrap it in love. I could seal you and your family to me for eternity. I could seal up all the saints to be my family, my kingdom for all eternity! Love, Sidney, is the moving, breathing, living force of the universe! Do you see how paltry it is to confine ourselves to loving just one or two beings? God doesn't. He loves us all. He loves every soul that lives or has lived on this earth, because, just because they are His. They are His family, His entire purpose for being God. He has no other purpose than to love us and teach us and help us to become as He is, a God possessed of all intelligence and all power and all love!

"What are we learning here? Are we learning to limit ourselves in those capacities? If we do, then when, when are we to learn those Godlike qualities? It's here and now. This is when we learn. This is when we develop our spiritual natures. And no one sees it like I do. I feel sometimes like I'm dragging a mountain behind me. My soul wants to soar, to meet God on His own plane, to put off the shackles of the earth and simply rise up to meet Him. I can't teach the saints fast enough, deep enough. Their minds are dark. They don't understand me. They don't understand God's concepts. There's so much more, Sidney. Do you understand? Do you?"

Rigdon was touched as he watched Joseph struggling to express a soul longing for heaven. He was humbled, and he hardly knew what to answer. He thought he had loved God all his life, but he had never gone where Joseph went. His spirit was earthbound and Joseph's was soaring.

Joseph sat down despondently on a rock. "The day will come when I must reveal everything God has taught me, though my people apostatize and leave me, though my enemies kill me and my wife desert me. Yes, I'm afraid! The time is getting close, and I don't know how to teach this principle of the restoration to the saints. It will have to be carefully done, selectively done. And then, how do I make sure it is practiced in righteousness, by me as well as everyone else? I don't know all the answers. I'm not even sure I'm equal to it."

What Joseph was really talking about was still unclear in Sidney's mind. It had to do with the Abrahamic covenant — but what? He was silent. He wasn't sure he wanted to know. This was one time he couldn't counsel the prophet of God.

Joseph knew this. He looked up bleakly at his friend, then arose and turned away, sorrowing. For some time he walked the streets of

Kirtland, feeling as though he could die and be glad of it. Finally, he came to a group of children playing in the road. He stopped to watch and one of them ran to him. He swung the little girl up on his shoulder and grabbed a little boy into his arms. He thought his heart would burst with love. This is heaven, he thought, this innocence and faith. He stayed to play hoops with them for awhile, until his heart felt comforted and he had gained enough strength to go on.

Joseph rehearsed the whole thing to his brother in the woods the next day. Hyrum sat stone still through the whole recital. He had never seen Joseph in such a miserable state. Hyrum was solemn. What it meant for Joseph was appalling. Then he considered what it meant for himself. He shook his head.

"I don't think I could ever live it, Joseph."

"Hyrum, the Lord says that I have to teach it to the whole church! The whole church! That's you too, and Samuel, and father, and . . . God help me, Emma!"

"I don't know, Joseph. Every man will have to receive revelation himself for this. You can't condemn those who don't believe."

"Condemn you! I can't condemn anyone. I have yet to take the first step myself. I have a young woman in my home the Spirit has repeatedly told me to take to wife. And I can't do it! I can't bring myself to suggest such a thing to her, much less to tell Emma. Hyrum, what am I to do?"

His brother shook his head. "Heaven only knows. Emma is a strong woman. She's stayed with you through thick and thin, and she loves you above anything on this earth. She'll take it hard."

"I know. I know! I have to rely on the Lord to convince her. That is the only way she'll accept it — that any of the saints will." Joseph pounded his forehead with his fists. "Hyrum, I would die before I would do this to Emma, but the angel of the Lord has commanded me. There is no way out. *No way.* I am the most miserable of all men."

Hyrum silently agreed. He didn't envy his brother the enormity of the task, nor could he envision himself living this principle.

Joseph perceived his doubts. "In order to believe this, the saints will have to know beyond a shadow of a doubt I am a prophet, acting under direct command from the Lord."

"I know that," Hyrum consoled him, "And Emma knows it."

"Yes, I think she does." Joseph stared at the ground. "But she still may not consent."

"What will happen if she doesn't?"

"The same thing that will happen to anyone else — if they will not receive God's law, they will not receive God's blessing. That goes for Emma, too. Oh, I fear for her, maybe more than I fear for myself. I know what I must do, and though I dread it, I will do it. But Emma? I don't know, Hyrum. I don't know if she will ever, ever consent, and I could lose her eternally."

Hyrum got up to leave. He felt as if he shared the weight of the world with his brother. "This is a hard law, Joseph. If Emma doesn't kill you, Mother will!"

"Yes, I know," Joseph agreed glumly. Then he sighed, "But it is only so because of the customs of our day. If we lived when Jacob did, or David and Solomon, we would think nothing of it. God knows that. The law is no different. Perhaps it falls to us to have the courage to show mankind God's law doesn't change until He changes it."

"Go tell that to Emma."

Joseph fell silent and hardly noticed when his brother arose to walk to his horse. What it would portend for the church Hyrum could not imagine. He went home to his sweet Jerusha and took her on his lap, rocking there with her for a long time. He didn't tell her a thing.

Something was afoot. Emma didn't know exactly what, but she knew her husband. He had been acting strangely for weeks. Last night she had slept restlessly and awakened several times. Joseph had not been beside her. This morning he had left early, without a bite to eat, and had been gone all day. There had been none of the usual play with the children, nor scripture reading, nor prayer together. At supper, he was uncharacteristically quiet, even subdued. Normally, if he had a problem on his mind, he came to her for consultation. She valued that, for she knew that many husbands did not trust their wive's opinion. But then, she had *always* been his trusted counselor. That relationship had forged the bond between them which carried them through persecutions and enabled her to leave father and mother, following Joseph into poverty. Poverty could be endured for the Lord's work. She was not sorry for her choice.

After supper, Joseph went out again. He didn't come back until Fanny and the babies were in bed. Emma turned away half a dozen men who came to the door wanting to see him. She waited up for her husband. She knew he would eventually return to her. She was a patient woman. So, she sat downstairs darning until the door opened about ten o'clock.

"You're home late," she said quietly.

His countenance was still somber. "I have much on my mind."

"So I presume. Do you want to talk about it?"

"I scarcely know how."

He took a chair across from her and sat down heavily. She still rocked and darned serenely, glancing at him quizzically from time to time. He drew a deep breath and plunged in.

"The Lord has revealed something to me which I am reluctant to obey."

"Joseph! Reluctant?"

"Yes, reluctant. It is a very hard thing."

"But if it is from the Lord . . . ?" He could see she disapproved.

"It is. No doubt of it! I have known it for some time and refused to think of it, much less obey."

"Have you had direct revelation and still not obeyed?" Emma replied incredulously.

"Yes," he admitted miserably.

"What are you so reluctant about? When God speaks, you have always obeyed. To do otherwise puts the whole church in danger. This could explain the current persecutions and not having the means to start on the temple."

"I know. I know! I just can't bring myself to do it, much less to require it of the whole church. If you think living the United Order has been difficult, or the Word of Wisdom, you have no idea how hard this will be."

She put down her darning, tucked it away, and turned her undivided attention to her distressed husband. "All right," she said with determination, "tell me."

He hung his head, shaking it slightly. "O Emma, how can I? You will hate me for it. The saints will hate me for it."

"What on earth are you talking about?" She ventured a wild guess. "Can you be thinking of destroying the church after so much effort to build it."

He heaved a deep sigh. His head in his hands, he groaned, "This law could be the means of my destruction."

Now Emma was truly concerned. "I don't believe it! I simply don't. God would not destroy His prophet nor His restored church. It is too vital to the preparation of the earth for His Second Coming. He will build the people up to be able to receive Him when He comes. This church will never be destroyed as long as it lives by God's law — as long as we have a prophet to reveal it to us. Now tell me what it is you cannot bring yourself to obey!" She pinned him with her gaze. Her dark brown eyes were direct and determined, and Joseph felt like a small boy being disciplined.

He sat silent for several minutes. Emma did not budge nor speak. She simply waited. At last, he rose and went to the mantle where his Bible lay. He took it down and opened it to the Old Testament. Painfully, he turned to his wife, his puritan Emma.

"You know the Old Testament. Is it from God?"

"Of course," she answered without hesitation.

"Was Abraham God's chosen prophet?"

"Yes, of course."

"Were Isaac and Jacob?"

"Certainly. Why are you asking this? It's elementary."

"What about David and Solomon, were they righteous kings?"

"For the most part. Certainly they were loved by the Lord." She was confused. "Are you testing my knowledge, Joseph?"

"No." He laid the scriptures in her lap. "Read this aloud, Emma." It was Genesis, chapter sixteen.

She began. "Now Sarai, Abram's wife bare him no children: and she had a handmaid . . ."

Emma read on through verse three, ". . . and gave her to her husband Abram to be his wife."

She looked up. "How far shall I read?"

"That's enough. Now turn to chapter twenty-nine, verse twenty-three."

She did so.

"Read it aloud," he said woodenly. "I'll tell you when to stop."

Emma read from the scriptures the story of Jacob and Leah and Rachel, through chapter thirty, verse four, ". . . And she gave him Bilhah, her handmaid, to wife: and Jacob went in unto her."

"That's enough. Now turn to Second Samuel, chapter two, verse two."

She turned the pages slowly. A feeling of dread began to creep over her. "So David went up thither, and his two wives also . . ."

"And chapter five, verse thirteen." Now his voice was hard as a rock.

Again Emma turned the pages slowly. The house seemed tomb-silent. The verses seemed to swim before her eyes. She found the verse with difficulty and read it slowly, "And David took him more concubines and wives out of Jerusalem, after he was come from Hebron: and there were yet sons and daughters born to David."

The dream came back to her and with it new terror and agony. She looked up at her husband with an expression of dread. He pitied her as he might a lamb bleeding upon the altar.

"Do you want to read more?" he asked gently.

"No!" Her voice was a cry. "I know about Solomon." Her heart had dropped. The room was spinning, and her ears were ringing. Her voice sounded hollow and far away. "What about the *Book of Mormon?* It forbids this practice."

"I know." Joseph ran his fingers through his hair, his face appearing shadowed and ghastly in the firelight. "I know that well. I remember translating it. I also remember asking the Lord about it at the time. It was my first premonition concerning this doctrine. It seemed so simple then. The old kings had been wrong. But what about the patriarchs? If it was an evil practice, were they evil? I could understand where King David and Solomon might be wrong, but the prophets? Why would God bless them as his prophets and patriarchs if they were living in sin?"

"What was your answer?"

"The Spirit told me it was a righteous principle. The patriarchs were not behaving wickedly. But it is a principle to be practiced only at God's command, and righteously practiced. The Lord can command or banish the practice at will, but He has commanded it now. I don't know why, but He told me it is necessary for the restoration of all things." Her husband raised his right hand high above his head. "That is the truth, so help me God!"

There was silence. Emma stared at him as though stricken. The meaning of her dream flooded her mind. She could not speak. There were simply no words. The expression in her eyes begged him that it not be so. Then an awful thought wrung a cry from her.

"It's the children, then! You think I have failed you by giving you babies that died! Is it that? Is it my failure that has brought this on us?" The color had drained from her face, and horror was a perfect mask.

Joseph fell on his knees at her side. "No, Emma, no!" Tears spilled over onto his cheeks as he tried to take her in his arms.

She shrugged him off and backed away. "Yes! That's it! I cannot give you healthy children that you want, so you fall back on this . . . this . . . barbaric principle!"

"No! Emma, believe me, it's not true! I adore you and the children, especially those that died. You are not to be blamed in any way."

Still she stared at him with panic in her eyes. "Then you find me lacking. I am inadequate for you." Emma's heart seemed to stop, and she could not catch a breath.

"*No!*" Joseph begged her to listen and believe him. "No, darling. I have never found you lacking *in any way*. There is no other woman in this world I could ever love as I do you. You are my heart. I beg you to listen. This is not a principle I have dreamed up. God explained it to me. He really has, and the answer is not meant to hurt us, but to prepare us for eventual exaltation. Love is not divided, nor divisible. It is a growing, expanding, all encompassing thing."

But Emma was not listening. She sat as though in shock, staring into the flickering shadows. Her dream had come back to her most vividly — the sight of Joseph dead under the slobbering fangs of the wolves, the phantom women who led them to him, and the terrible threat from the Lord, "If you will not abide my commandments, you shall be destroyed." But she could not bring herself to accept all that it meant.

He put his head in her lap and began to sob. "Now you see why I've been so reluctant."

"Yes," she whispered. "Oh, yes."

"Tell me what to do," he pleaded.

"I'm not that clever. How can I argue with the Lord?"

"That is precisely my predicament. How indeed, how can I? And how can I teach this to the saints? I can't even teach it to my wife. The whole countryside is up in arms against us over the law of consecration. Can you imagine what a wildfire the practice of plural marriage will light, here in the midst of civilized society? The fathers of old had no shocked Methodist ministers to contend with. We have to live in a Christian world which will never countenance the practice of many wives, even if it is all over the Bible."

Still stunned, she stared into his face, just inches from her own. Almost in a trance, she noted for the millionth time the curve of his lips, his high cheek bones, his brilliant blue eyes. It was the face that had captured her heart almost eight years ago. It still bore the same pure look of honesty and integrity. A little older, a little wiser, but it was far more appealing to her now than when he was an inexperienced youth of nineteen. She put her hand on his cheek. Time seemed to stand still.

She whispered, "Oh, Joseph, no." She shook her head gently, sorrowing. "No. Please say 'No'."

He held her gaze, understanding her shock and pain. Hating his answer, he said, "Yes. I'm afraid God has said, 'yes.'"

She sat stone still for another few minutes staring off into space. Then she stood up abruptly, deliberately banishing the dream and the threat. Her words were clipped and bitter, "And you will take another wife?"

"I must."

"Never!"

"Soon."

"No!"

He sat right down on the floor. He held his weary head in his hands. He knew the onslaught would come.

Emma's voice was scathing. "God cannot require this of us. It's cruel! It's evil! It's wrong! I don't care if the old patriarchs did practice it. It was convenient for their times. It is not for ours. How can He possibly think we could live this way, here in modern times, with good, modest Christian people. We have to live by the rules of our society! People will cast us out. They will shun us as the Quakers shun law-breakers. There will be no trade, no money to build with or live on. They'll never allow it. And our own people, what about them? Joseph, can you imagine these good women allowing such a thing? It will break their hearts. They will feel like chattel, less than the dirt beneath their man's feet. To share their husbands — to send them to another bed! *No! No!* If you try to teach this to the saints, they will apostatize and the church will be destroyed."

"Exactly, Emma. That is exactly what I fear. Do you think I haven't wrestled with this? Do you think I don't know the consequences? I foresee them all too well. It is miserable to be a seer sometimes. I see the future all too clearly, and it will be beyond hard."

"Why does God want us to do this?" Her voice had risen to an unnatural pitch. She had become frantic, pacing the small parlor like an animal.

"I truly do not know," he answered wearily. "The angel would only say it is wisdom in the Lord. He said the principle will try the saints, but it is necessary for the church to grow."

"But the church *is growing* by leaps and bounds."

"Yes, and many are dedicated. But some will fall away as soon as they are really tested. This can be that test — a test to see if we are determined to obey at all costs."

"Are you?" She stopped and stood over him, looking down.

"Of course," he said, looking up into her eyes. "There is no other way for me. I am in a terrible position. Some men might choose to ignore God's law and live as other men live. For me, to ignore it means I would be cut off as a prophet and the head of His church. The mantle would pass to someone else."

"Who? Who could take your place?"

He answered miserably, "I don't know. Maybe Oliver, maybe David. I'm sure the Lord can raise up anyone He chooses as a prophet."

"They wouldn't have the strength to teach this either."

"I know," he said in frustration. "I *know*, Emma! It is a predicament with no solution — at least, no good solution. It'll be the death of me, I'm afraid."

The baying of the wolves sounded far away in her mind, but she ignored them. She had calmed to a stony determination. "You haven't begun to practice it yet?" Her tone was a warning.

"No."

Relief kindled in her eyes. "I don't think I can stand it, Joseph. I haven't the grace, nor the strength to live this principle." Her voice broke again, and her hand flew up to her mouth to stifle a sob.

"All right, then," he said with resignation. "Shall I go back to the Lord and refuse? I will, you know." He rose up before her on his knees, and grasped her by the waist. His voice was hoarse. "Emma, I will if you want me to."

She stared down at him. She loved this man more than life and family. She knew him as a man, and she knew him as a prophet. Before Joseph, she had never dreamed the Almighty God would speak again to human beings on this earth. She thought of times she had seen him transfigured before her when the spirit of revelation touched him. Could she see him fall from that great height? Could she see him stripped of his spiritual powers?

She whispered the question, "Will He really cast you off?"

"Yes. He really will. And choose another. And leave me utterly alone and defenseless before the world. My life will not be worth the dirt beneath your feet. My enemies will pull me down and kill me before a year is over."

Emma couldn't move. Just as in the dream, she stood rooted to the spot. The room seemed transformed into shadowy woods. She saw Joseph as though from a distance, and he was on his knees before the wolves. Her mind had stopped working, the gears ground to a halt.

"So, tell me what to do," he begged his wife.

Like a statue, she stood silent. He waited, but she did not move. He had thought she would cry or scream, but she did nothing, said nothing. Emma, his beloved, affectionate, enduring Emma, had become a sculptured ice queen, with an insidious crack through the heart.

After a time, she looked at him with glazed eyes. She seemed as one blind, trying with all her might to see but unable to penetrate the darkness. She looked at him, but he knew she didn't see him. When she finally spoke, it was a desolate, bitter whisper. "Do what you must, but I don't want to know."

She pushed his hands from her skirt and turned away, leaving him alone on the floor by the dying fire.

Late into the night Joseph still lay inert before the cold hearthstone. He was desolate. He had lost all. With this one attempt to teach his wife the commandment of God, he felt he had lost all, for he had lost her trust. *O God*, he prayed silently, can I not go back and become as any other man, just a follower, not a prophet? Wouldst Thou require me to sacrifice even my wife, my Emma? But no answer came to soothe his tortured mind. He had broken the heart of the truest, most affectionate companion in the world, she who had sacrificed everything and everyone else she loved for him.

He was so lost in hopeless reverie that he did not hear her bare feet on the steps. He didn't realize she had come back to him, until he felt the soft brush of her hair against his neck and smelled the scent of roses which clung to her nightgown. It was like cool water to a parched soul. Joseph turned over, looked up into her eyes, and suddenly his eyes were like a fountain, spilling over and wetting them both. Emma raised him from his cold hard bed on the wooden floor, enfolded him in her arms, and cradled his head against her heart.

He sobbed and she sobbed. He crushed her against him like a desperate man, and she clung to him. Yes, her heart was broken. Yes, he had done the damage. But still she loved him . . . and would forever.

"You came back," he whispered brokenly. "Why?"

"Because . . . because . . . I love you. I will *always* love you. You are my *prophet* husband."

"Then you do believe me?"

"I have always believed you and believed *in* you. My struggle is not with you; it is with myself and my God."

To Be Continued

(Look for Volume Two which continues the story with the completion of the Kirtland temple, the trip to Far West, the horror of Liberty Jail, the building of Nauvoo, the persecution of the saints and of the church, Emma's finest moment, and Joseph's ultimate sacrifice retold in a way you have never read before.)

References

Anderson, Karl Ricks. *Joseph Smith's Kirtland*. Salt Lake City, UT: Deseret Book Co., 1989.

Barron, Howard H. *Orson Hyde, Missionary, Apostle, Colonizer*. Bountiful, UT: Horizon Publishers, 1977.

Bushman, Richard L. *Joseph Smith and the Beginnings of Mormonism*. Urbana and Chicago IL: University of Illinois Press, 1984.

Cannon, George Q. *Life of Joseph Smith the Prophet*. Salt Lake City, UT: Deseret Book Co., 1964

Doctrine and Covenants of the Church of Jesus Christ of Latter-day Saints. Salt Lake City, UT: The Church of Jesus Christ of Latter-day Saints, 1981.

Crowther, Duane S. *The Life of Joseph Smith*. Bountiful, UT: Horizon Publishers, 1989.

Evans, John Henry. *Joseph Smith An American Prophet*. New York, NY: The MacMillan Co., 1943.

Faulring, Scott H. *An American Prophet's Record, The Diaries and Journals of Joseph Smith*. Salt Lake City, UT: Signature Books, 1989.

Gentry, Leland H. *A History of the Latter-day Saints in Northern Missouri from 1836 to 1839*. Provo, UT: BYU Seminaries and Institutes of Religion, 1965.

Hill, Donna. *Joseph Smith: The First Mormon*. New York, NY: Doubleday & Co., 1977.

History of the Church of Jesus Christ of Latter-day Saints. Period I, History of Joseph Smith by Himself. 6 Volumes, Introduction and notes by B.H. Roberts, Salt Lake City, UT: Deseret Book Co., 1964

Jones, Gracia N. *Emma's Glory and Sacrifice, A Testimony*. Utah: Homestead Publishers and Dist., 1987.

Porter, Larry C. *A Study of the Origins of the Church of Jesus Christ of Latter-day Saints in the States of New York and Pennsylvania*. Provo, UT: Joseph Fielding Smith Institute for Latter-day Saint History and BYU Studies, 2000.

Proctor, Scot Facer and Maurine Jensen. *The Revised and Enchanced History of Joseph Smith by His Mother, Lucy Mack Smith*. Salt Lake City, UT: Bookcraft, Inc., 1996.

Smith, Joseph Fielding. *Teachings of the Prophet Joseph Smith*. Salt Lake City, UT: Deseret Book Co., 1964.

Youngreen, Buddy. *Reflections of Emma: Joseph Smith's Wife*. Provo, UT: Maasai, Inc., 2001.